12 ANIMAL LAND

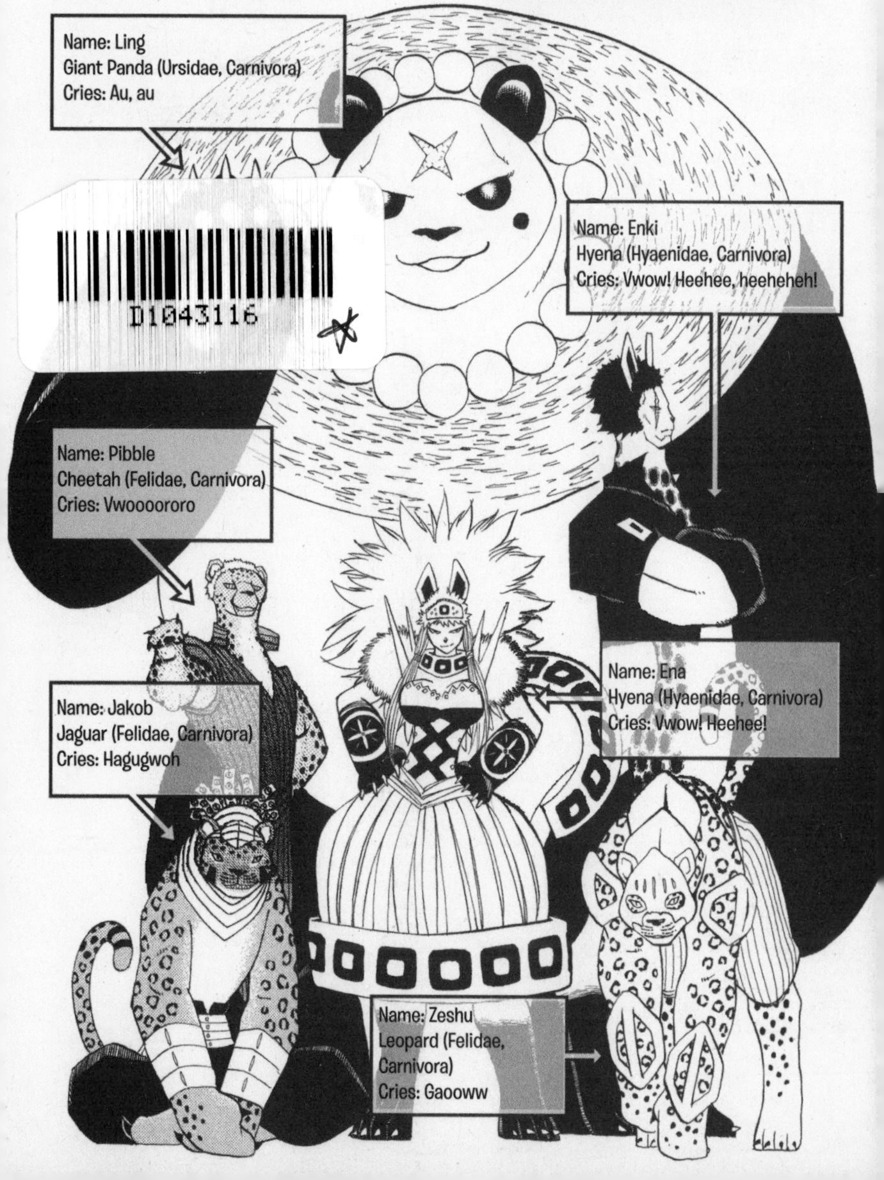
Name: Ling
Giant Panda (Ursidae, Carnivora)
Cries: Au, au
Name: Enki
Hyena (Hyaenidae, Carnivora)
Cries: Vwow! Heehee, heeheheh!
Name: Pibble
Cheetah (Felidae, Carnivora)
Cries: Vwoooororo
Name: Ena
Hyena (Hyaenidae, Carnivora)
Cries: Vwow! Heehee!
Name: Jakob
Jaguar (Felidae, Carnivora)
Cries: Hagugwoh
Name: Zeshu
Leopard (Felidae, Carnivora)
Cries: Gaooww

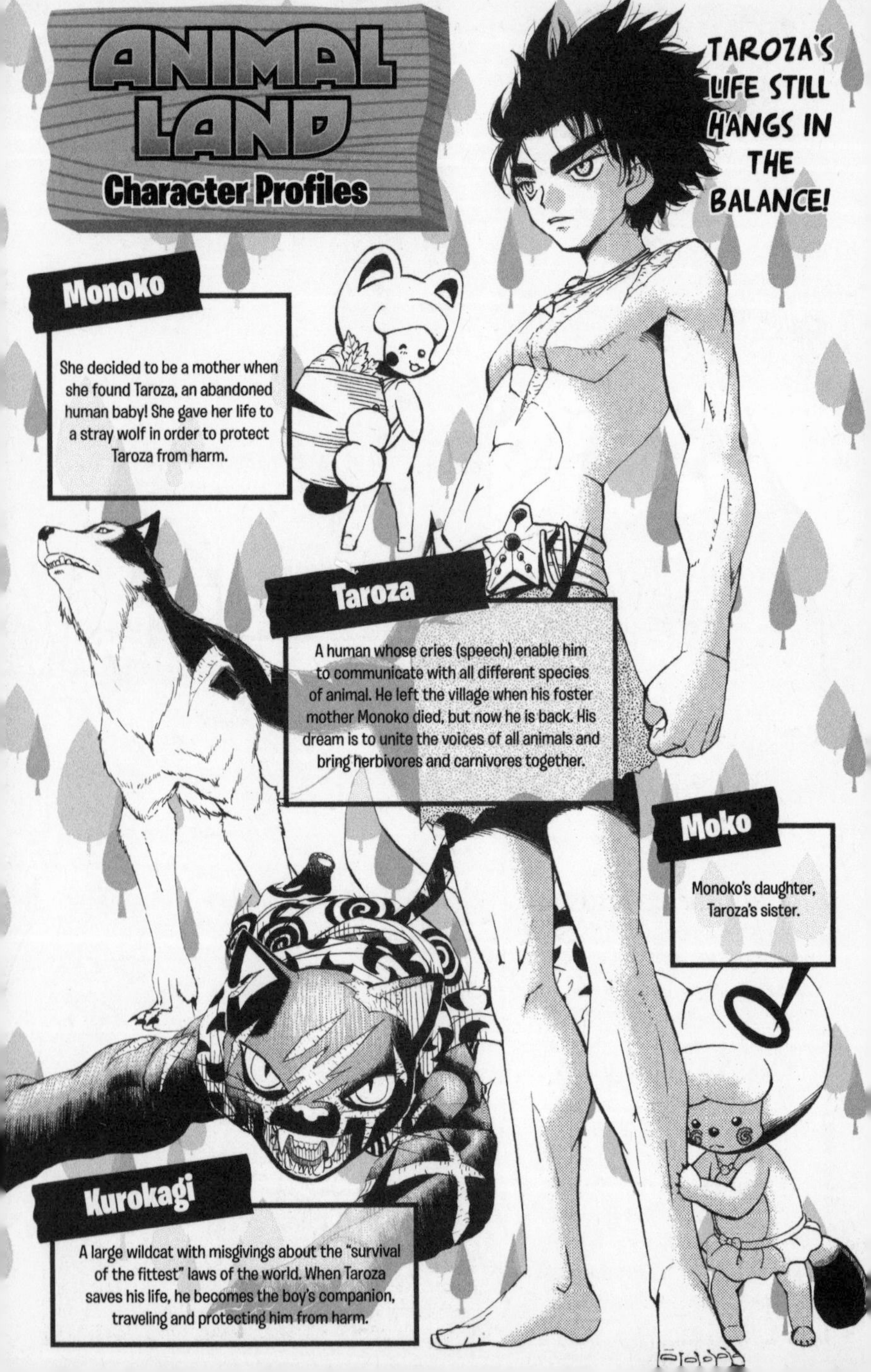

ANIMAL LAND

Character Profiles

TAROZA'S LIFE STILL HANGS IN THE BALANCE!

Monoko

She decided to be a mother when she found Taroza, an abandoned human baby! She gave her life to a stray wolf in order to protect Taroza from harm.

Taroza

A human whose cries (speech) enable him to communicate with all different species of animal. He left the village when his foster mother Monoko died, but now he is back. His dream is to unite the voices of all animals and bring herbivores and carnivores together.

Moko

Monoko's daughter, Taroza's sister.

Kurokagi

A large wildcat with misgivings about the "survival of the fittest" laws of the world. When Taroza saves his life, he becomes the boy's companion, traveling and protecting him from harm.

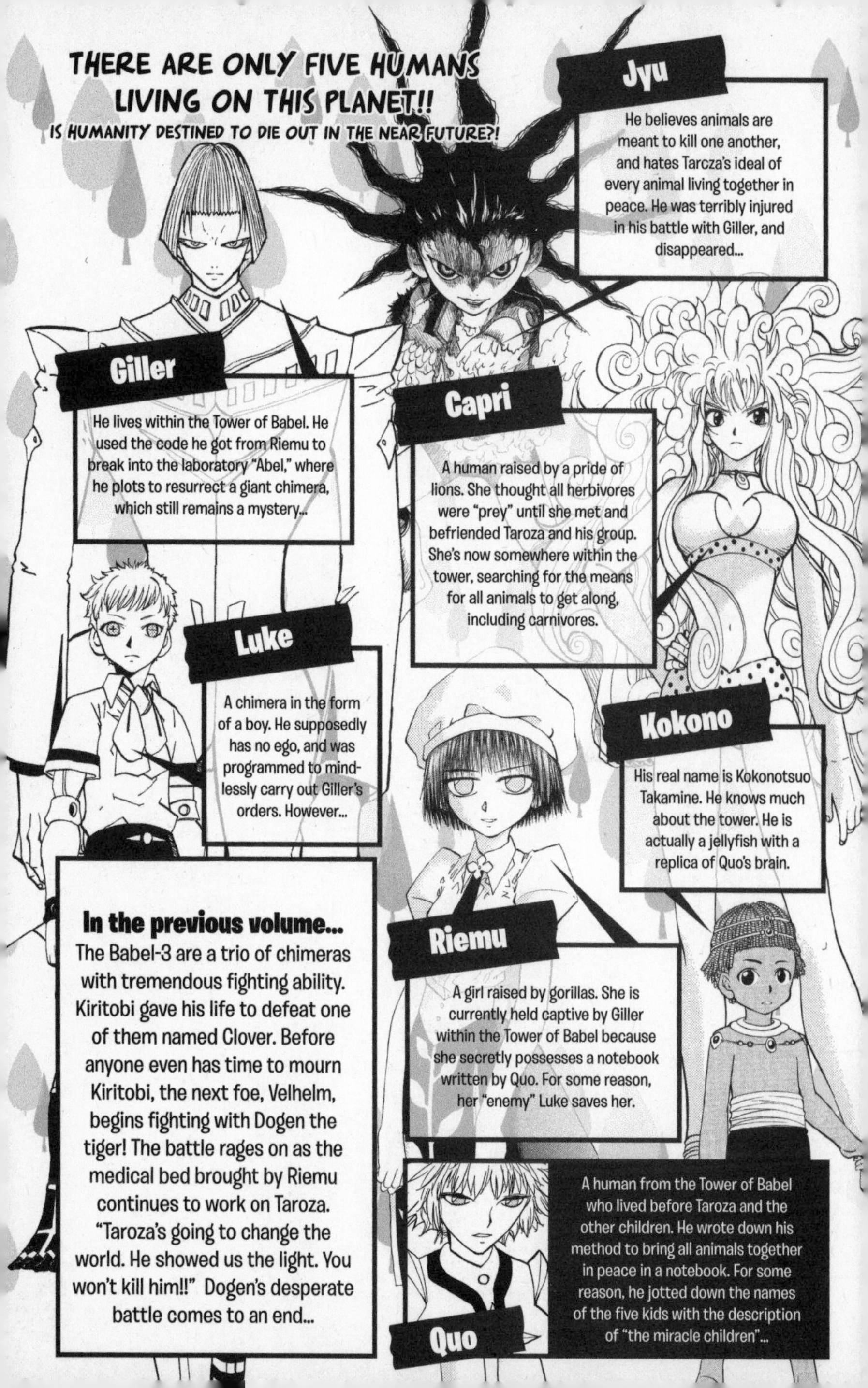
THERE ARE ONLY FIVE HUMANS LIVING ON THIS PLANET!!
IS HUMANITY DESTINED TO DIE OUT IN THE NEAR FUTURE?!
Jyu
He believes animals are meant to kill one another, and hates Tarcza's ideal of every animal living together in peace. He was terribly injured in his battle with Giller, and disappeared...
Giller
He lives within the Tower of Babel. He used the code he got from Riemu to break into the laboratory "Abel," where he plots to resurrect a giant chimera, which still remains a mystery...
Capri
A human raised by a pride of lions. She thought all herbivores were "prey" until she met and befriended Taroza and his group. She's now somewhere within the tower, searching for the means for all animals to get along, including carnivores.
Luke
A chimera in the form of a boy. He supposedly has no ego, and was programmed to mindlessly carry out Giller's orders. However...
Kokono
His real name is Kokonotsuo Takamine. He knows much about the tower. He is actually a jellyfish with a replica of Quo's brain.
Riemu
A girl raised by gorillas. She is currently held captive by Giller within the Tower of Babel because she secretly possesses a notebook written by Quo. For some reason, her "enemy" Luke saves her.
In the previous volume...
The Babel-3 are a trio of chimeras with tremendous fighting ability. Kiritobi gave his life to defeat one of them named Clover. Before anyone even has time to mourn Kiritobi, the next foe, Velhelm, begins fighting with Dogen the tiger! The battle rages on as the medical bed brought by Riemu continues to work on Taroza. "Taroza's going to change the world. He showed us the light. You won't kill him!!" Dogen's desperate battle comes to an end...
Quo
A human from the Tower of Babel who lived before Taroza and the other children. He wrote down his method to bring all animals together in peace in a notebook. For some reason, he jotted down the names of the five kids with the description of "the miracle children"...

CONTENTS

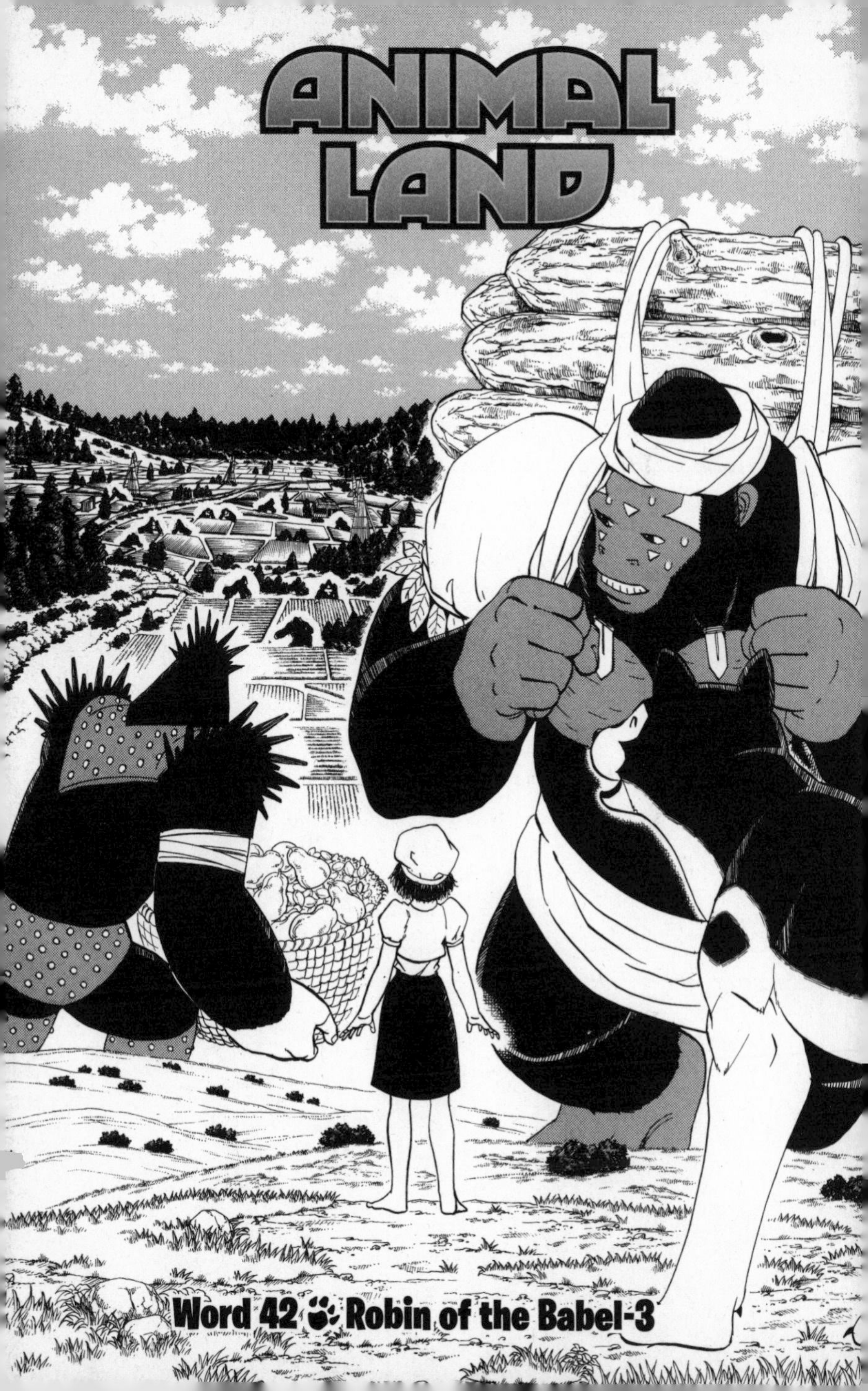
ANIMAL LAND
Word 42 Robin of the Babel-3

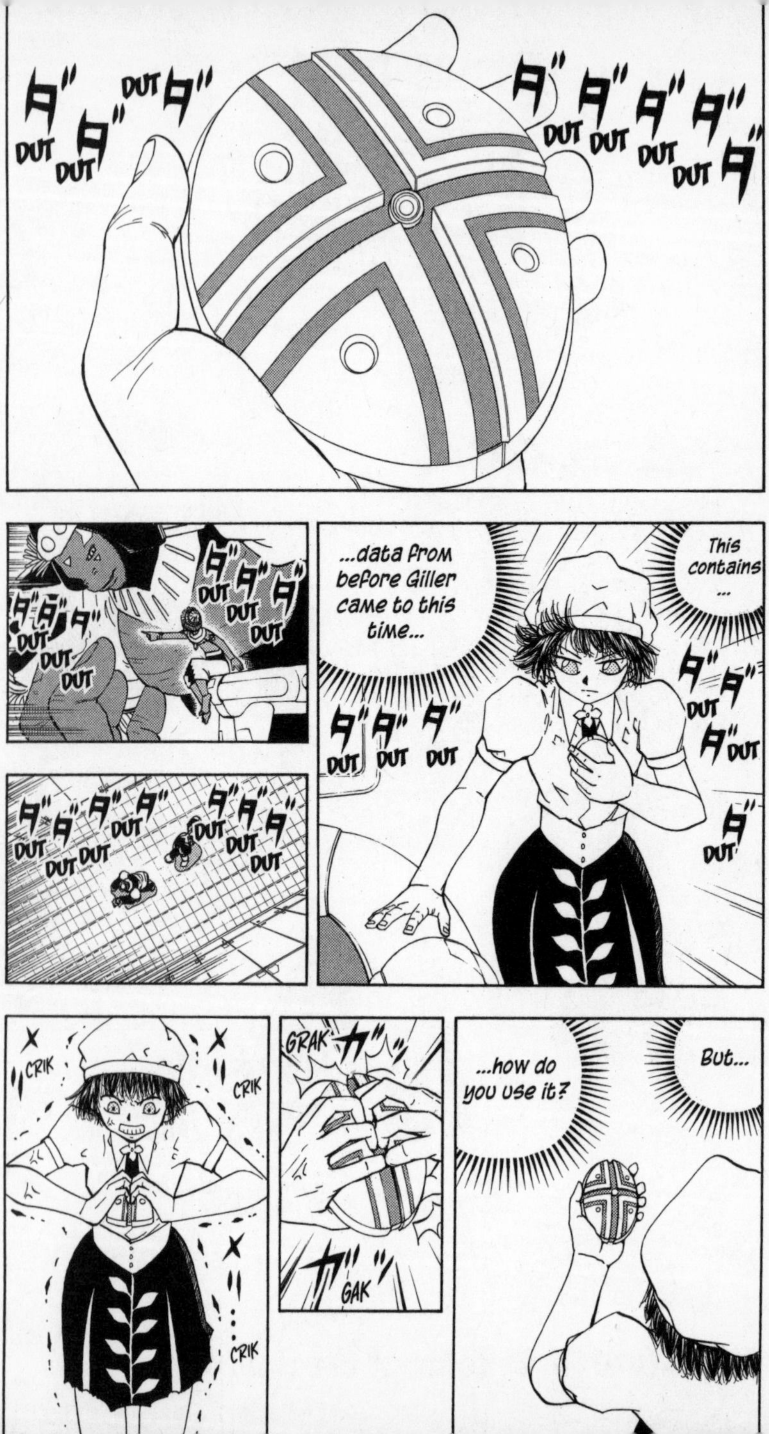
ダ DUT ダ DUT ダ DUT ダ DUT ダ DUT
ダ DUT ダ DUT ダ DUT ダ DUT
This contains...
...data from before Giller came to this time...
ダ DUT ダ DUT ダ DUT
ダ DUT ダ DUT ダ DUT ダ DUT
ダ DUT ダ DUT ダ DUT
ダ DUT ダ DUT ダ DUT
ダ DUT ダ DUT ダ DUT ダ DUT ダ DUT ダ DUT ダ DUT
But...
...how do you use it?
ガ GRAK
ガ GAK
CRIK
CRIK
CRIK

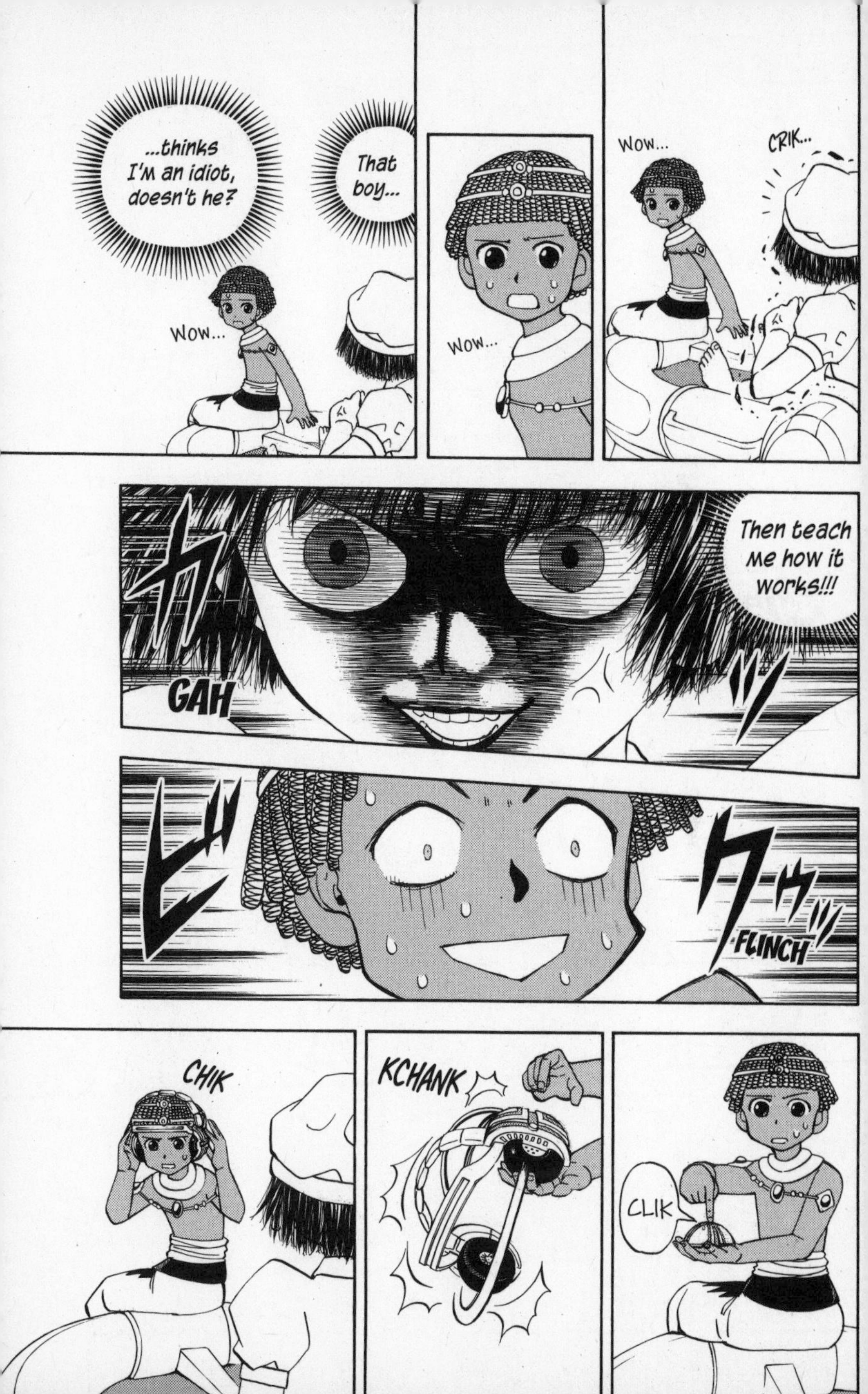
CRIK...
WOW...
WOW...
That boy...
...thinks I'm an idiot, doesn't he?
WOW...
Then teach me how it works!!!
GAH
FLINCH
CLIK
KCHANK
CHIK

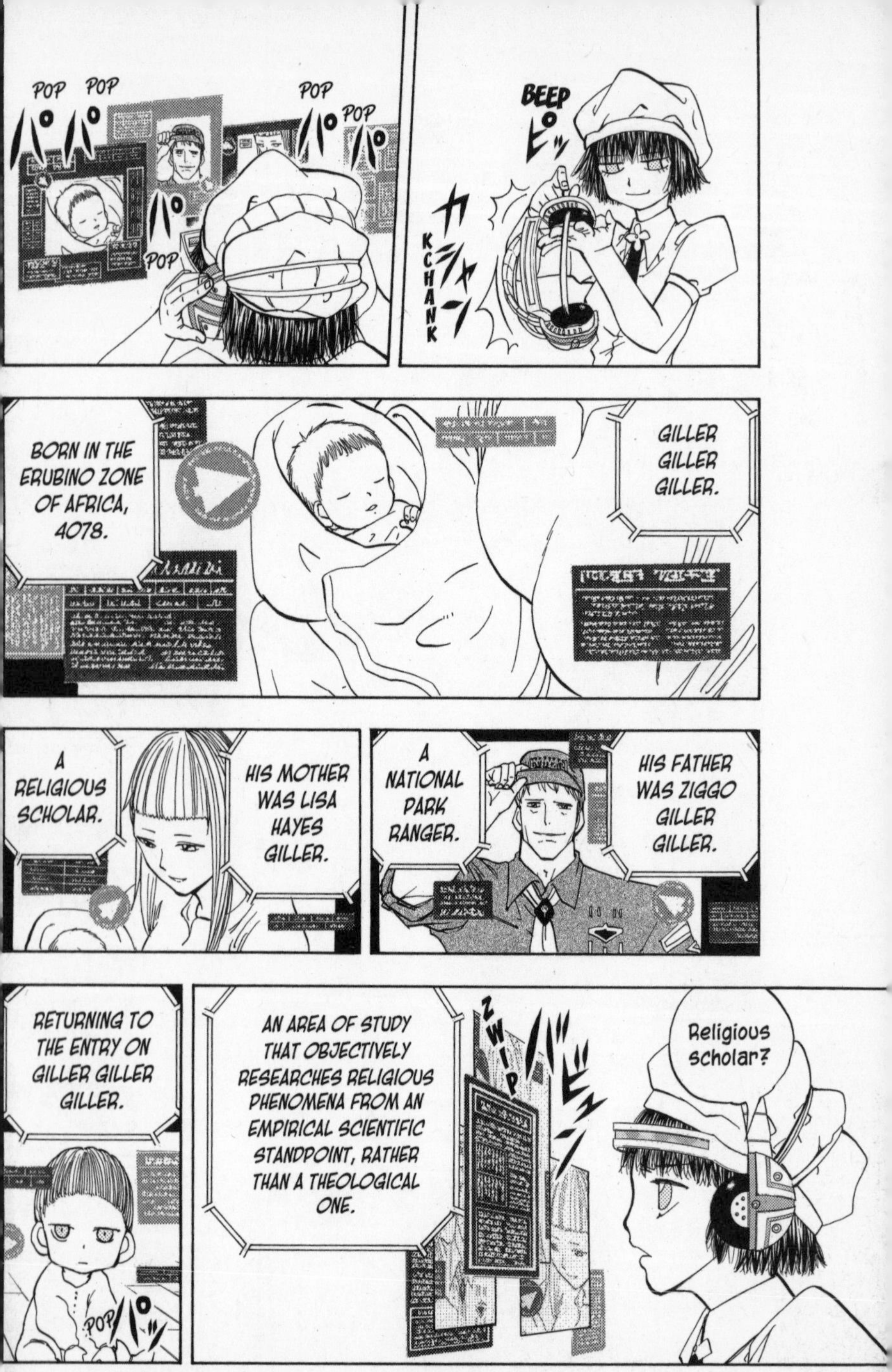
BEEP
ピッ
KCHANK
カシャーン
POP
POP
POP
POP
POP
GILLER GILLER GILLER.
BORN IN THE ERUBINO ZONE OF AFRICA, 4078.
HIS FATHER WAS ZIGGO GILLER GILLER.
A NATIONAL PARK RANGER.
HIS MOTHER WAS LISA HAYES GILLER.
A RELIGIOUS SCHOLAR.
Religious scholar?
ZWIP
AN AREA OF STUDY THAT OBJECTIVELY RESEARCHES RELIGIOUS PHENOMENA FROM AN EMPIRICAL SCIENTIFIC STANDPOINT, RATHER THAN A THEOLOGICAL ONE.
RETURNING TO THE ENTRY ON GILLER GILLER GILLER.
POP

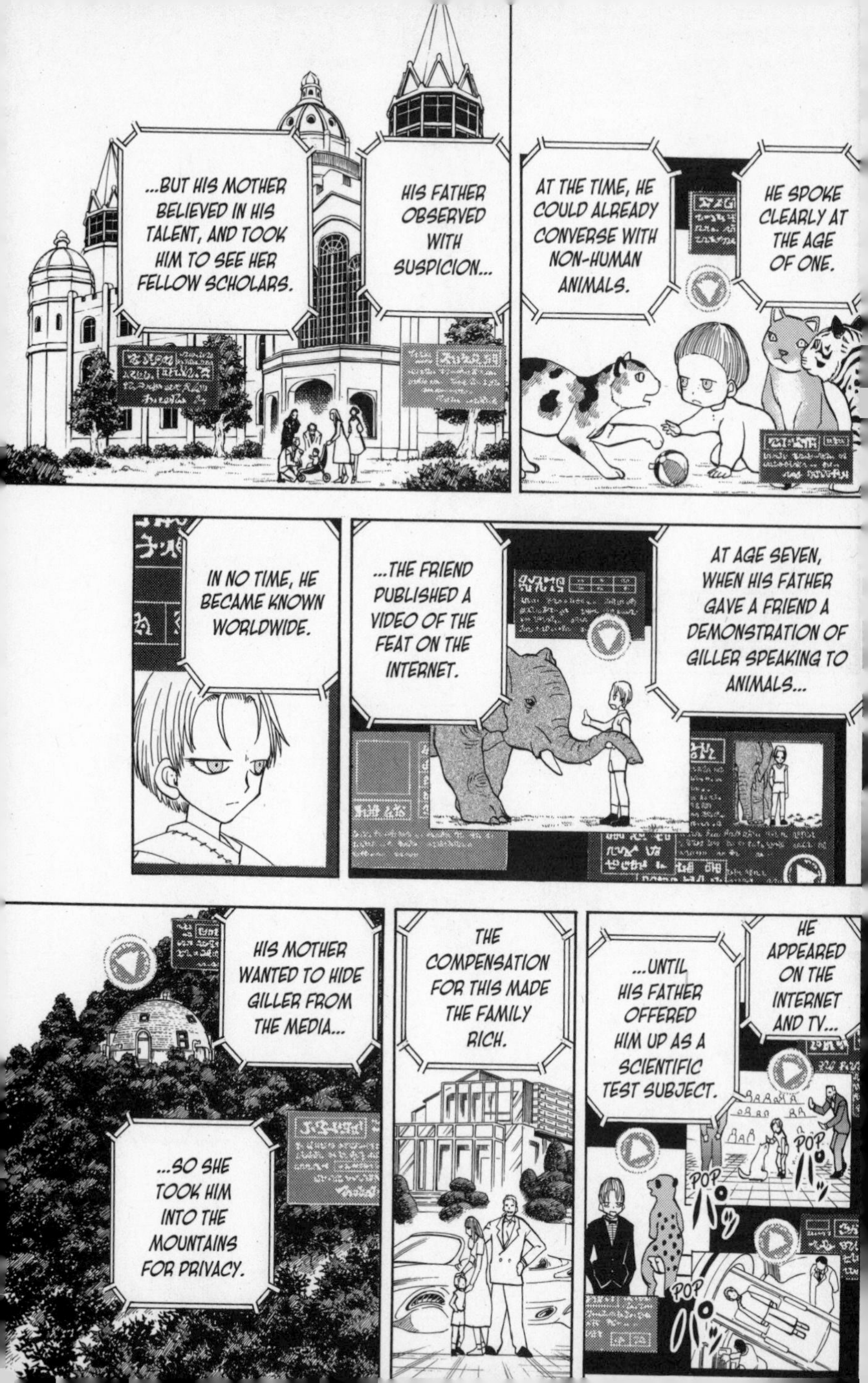
HE SPOKE CLEARLY AT THE AGE OF ONE.
AT THE TIME, HE COULD ALREADY CONVERSE WITH NON-HUMAN ANIMALS.
HIS FATHER OBSERVED WITH SUSPICION...
...BUT HIS MOTHER BELIEVED IN HIS TALENT, AND TOOK HIM TO SEE HER FELLOW SCHOLARS.
AT AGE SEVEN, WHEN HIS FATHER GAVE A FRIEND A DEMONSTRATION OF GILLER SPEAKING TO ANIMALS...
...THE FRIEND PUBLISHED A VIDEO OF THE FEAT ON THE INTERNET.
IN NO TIME, HE BECAME KNOWN WORLDWIDE.
HE APPEARED ON THE INTERNET AND TV...
...UNTIL HIS FATHER OFFERED HIM UP AS A SCIENTIFIC TEST SUBJECT.
POP
POP
POP
THE COMPENSATION FOR THIS MADE THE FAMILY RICH.
HIS MOTHER WANTED TO HIDE GILLER FROM THE MEDIA...
...SO SHE TOOK HIM INTO THE MOUNTAINS FOR PRIVACY.

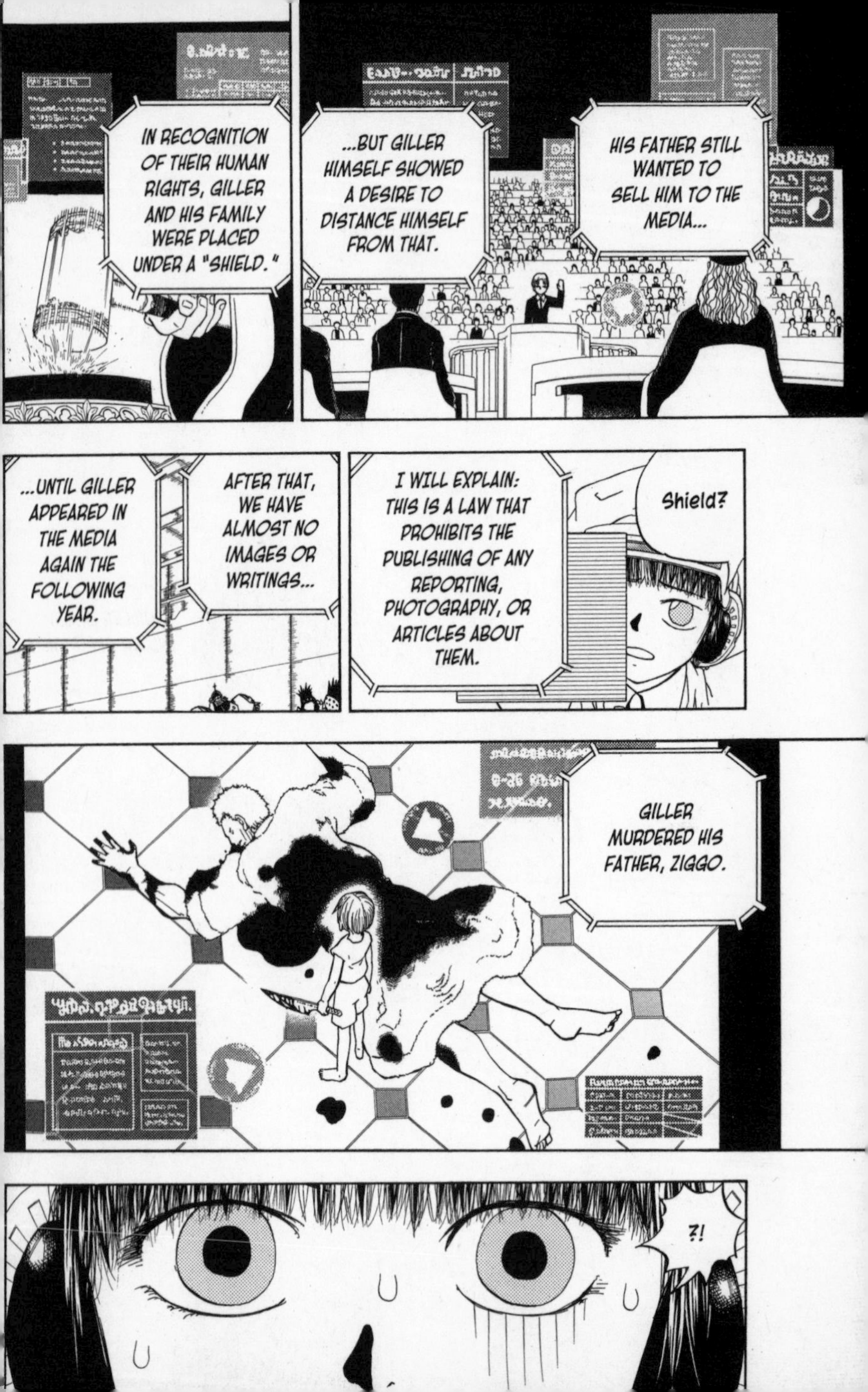
HIS FATHER STILL WANTED TO SELL HIM TO THE MEDIA...
...BUT GILLER HIMSELF SHOWED A DESIRE TO DISTANCE HIMSELF FROM THAT.
IN RECOGNITION OF THEIR HUMAN RIGHTS, GILLER AND HIS FAMILY WERE PLACED UNDER A "SHIELD."
Shield?
I WILL EXPLAIN: THIS IS A LAW THAT PROHIBITS THE PUBLISHING OF ANY REPORTING, PHOTOGRAPHY, OR ARTICLES ABOUT THEM.
AFTER THAT, WE HAVE ALMOST NO IMAGES OR WRITINGS...
...UNTIL GILLER APPEARED IN THE MEDIA AGAIN THE FOLLOWING YEAR.
GILLER MURDERED HIS FATHER, ZIGGO.
?!

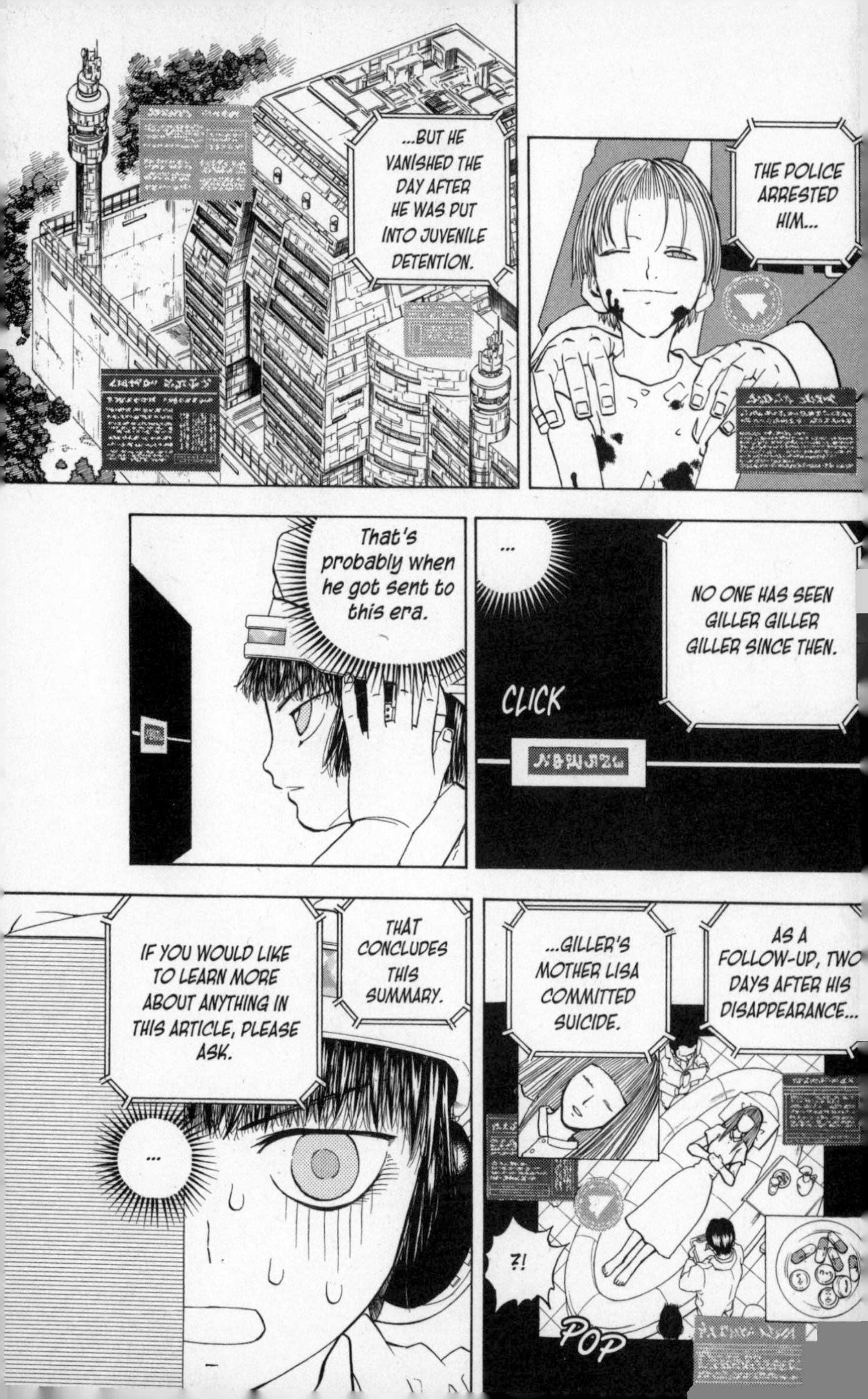
THE POLICE ARRESTED HIM...
...BUT HE VANISHED THE DAY AFTER HE WAS PUT INTO JUVENILE DETENTION.
NO ONE HAS SEEN GILLER GILLER GILLER SINCE THEN.
...
CLICK
That's probably when he got sent to this era.
AS A FOLLOW-UP, TWO DAYS AFTER HIS DISAPPEARANCE...
...GILLER'S MOTHER LISA COMMITTED SUICIDE.
?!
POP
THAT CONCLUDES THIS SUMMARY.
IF YOU WOULD LIKE TO LEARN MORE ABOUT ANYTHING IN THIS ARTICLE, PLEASE ASK.
...

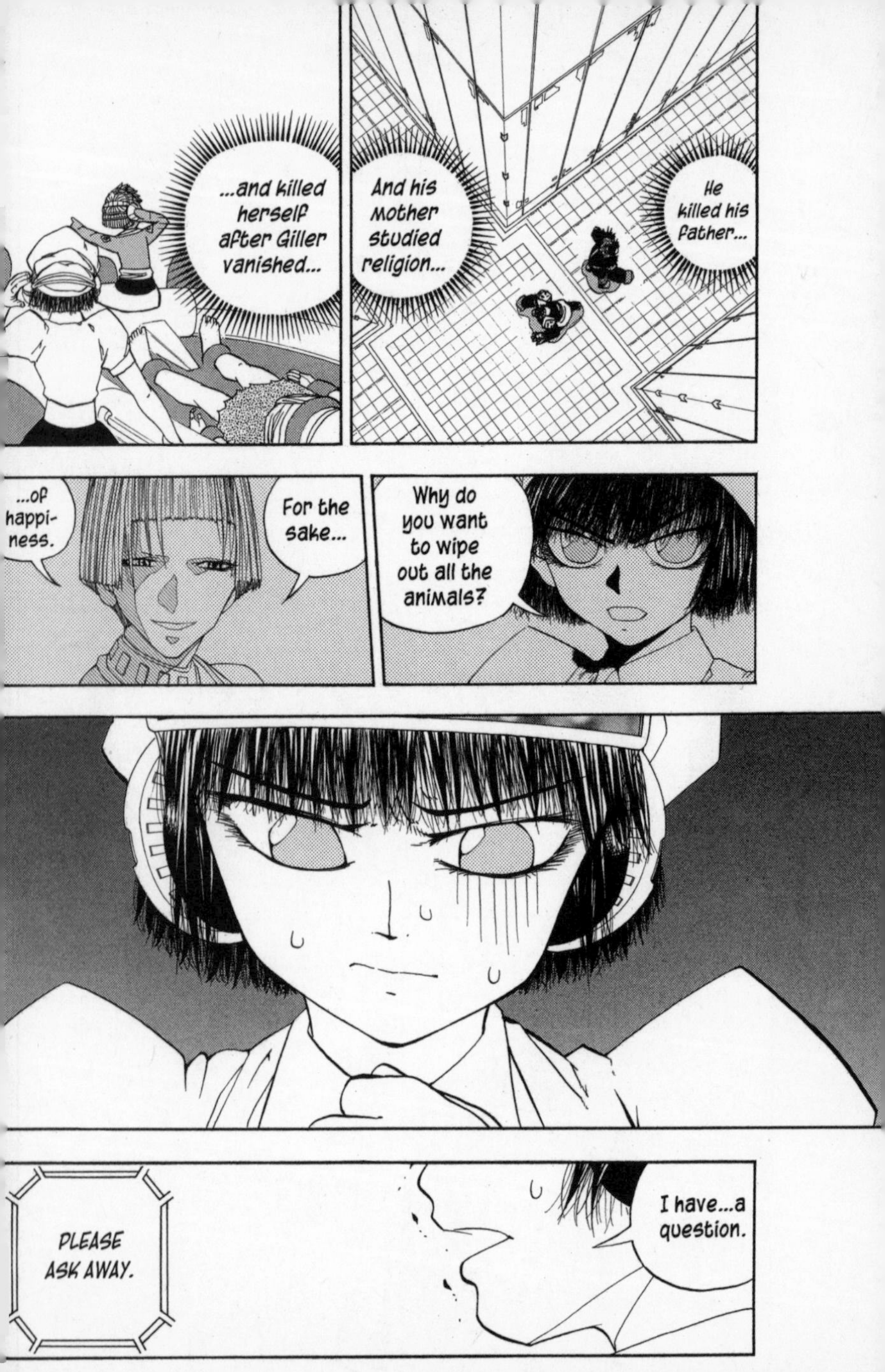

He killed his father...
And his mother studied religion...
...and killed herself after Giller vanished...
Why do you want to wipe out all the animals?
For the sake...
...of happiness.
I have...a question.
PLEASE ASK AWAY.

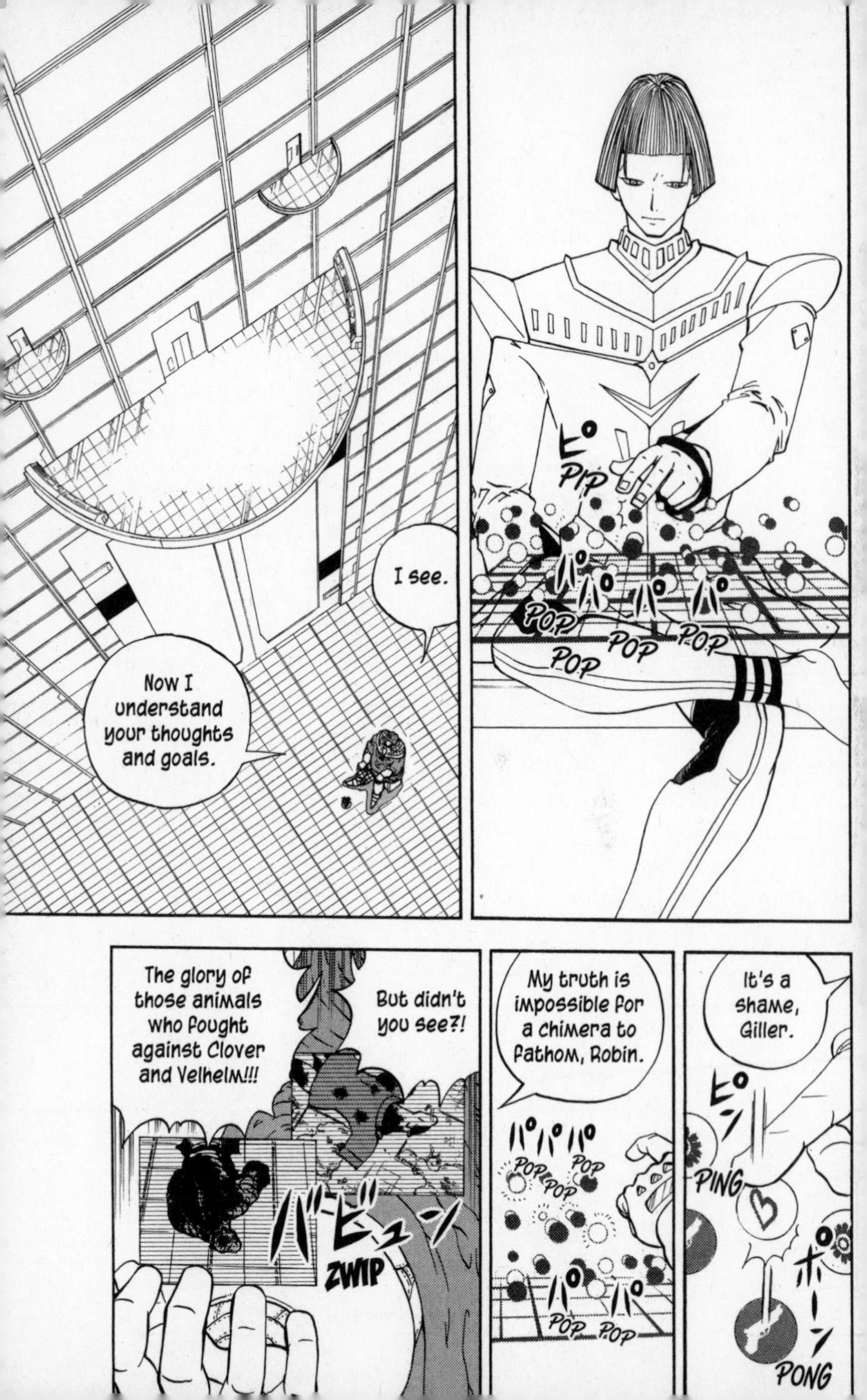
PIP
POP
POP
POP
POP
I see.
Now I understand your thoughts and goals.
It's a shame, Giller.
PING
PONG
My truth is impossible for a chimera to fathom, Robin.
POP
POP
POP
POP
POP
But didn't you see?!
The glory of those animals who fought against Clover and Velhelm!!!
ZWIP

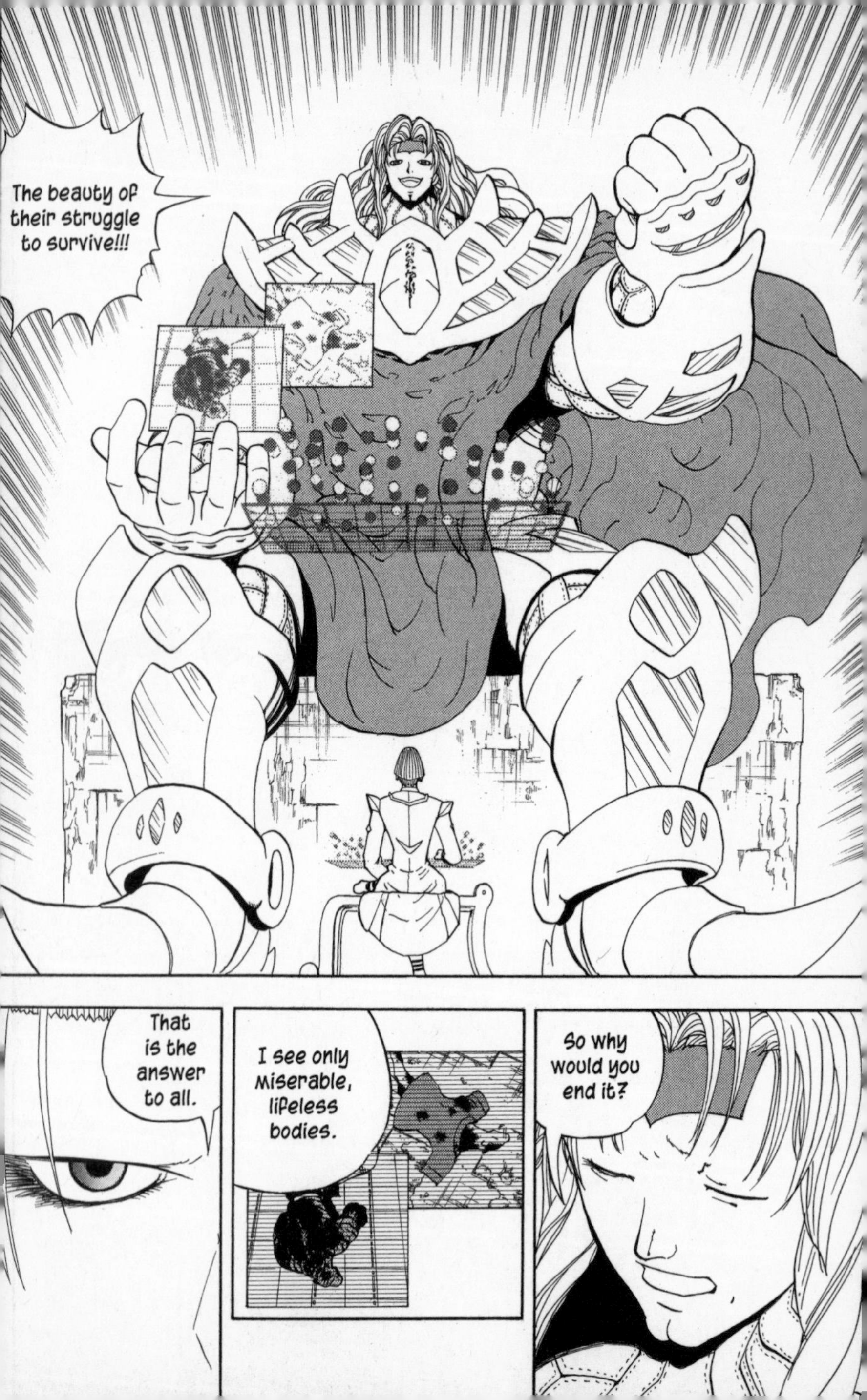
The beauty of their struggle to survive!!!
So why would you end it?
I see only miserable, lifeless bodies.
That is the answer to all.

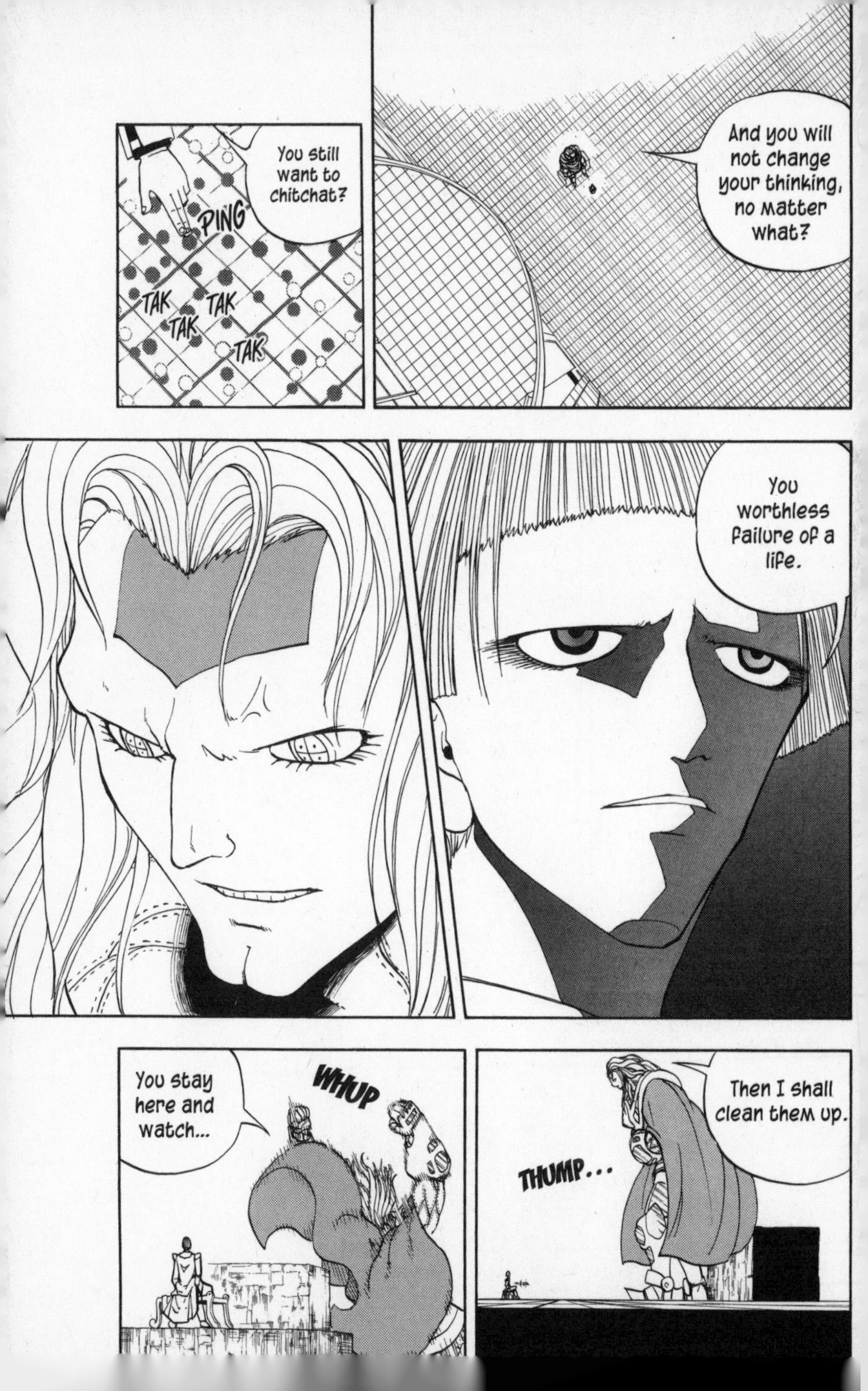
And you will not change your thinking, no matter what?
You still want to chitchat?
PING
TAK
TAK
TAK
TAK
You worthless failure of a life.
Then I shall clean them up.
THUMP...
You stay here and watch...
WHUP

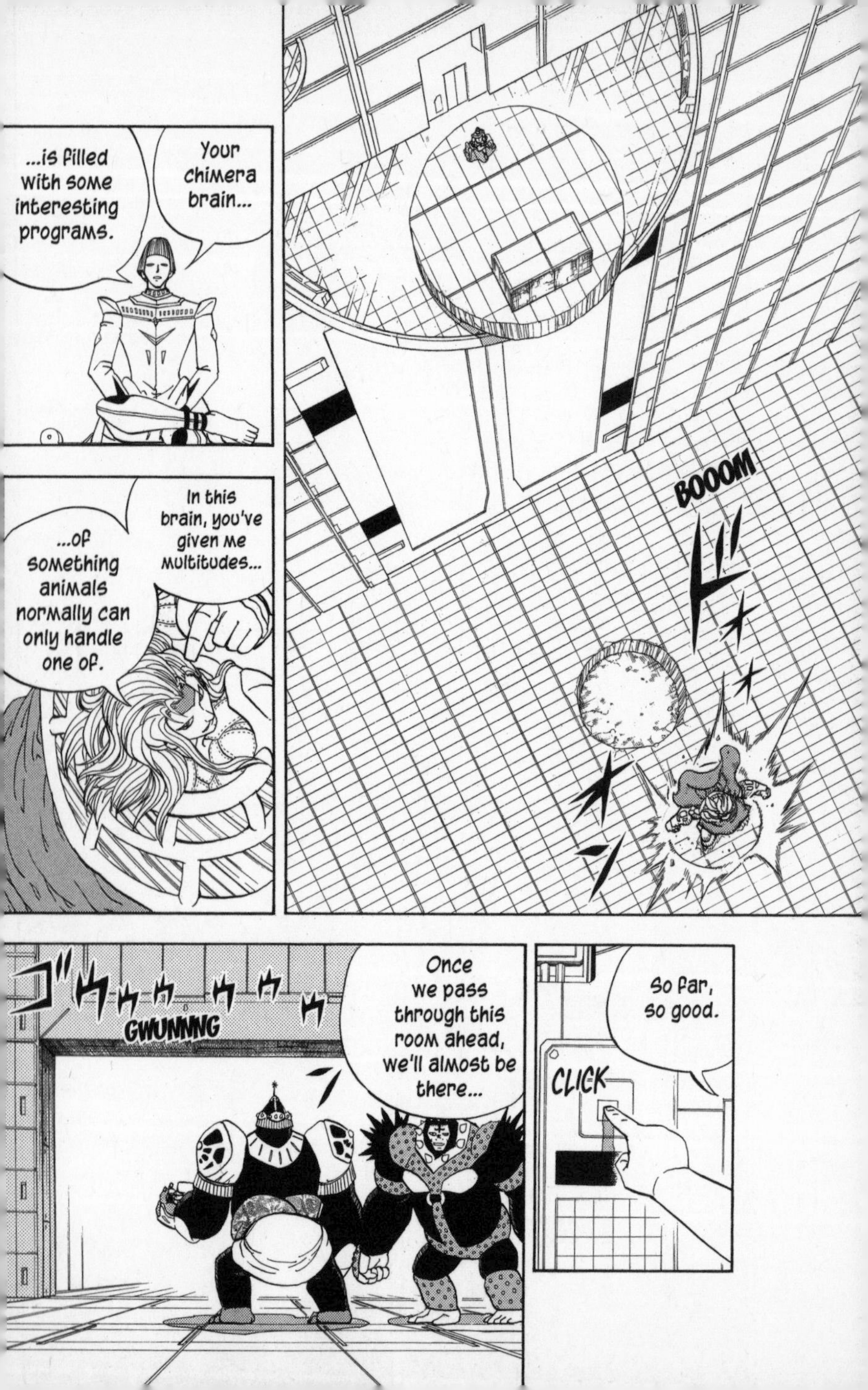
BOOOM
Your chimera brain...
...is filled with some interesting programs.
In this brain, you've given me multitudes...
...of something animals normally can only handle one of.
So far, so good.
CLICK
Once we pass through this room ahead, we'll almost be there...
GWUNNNG

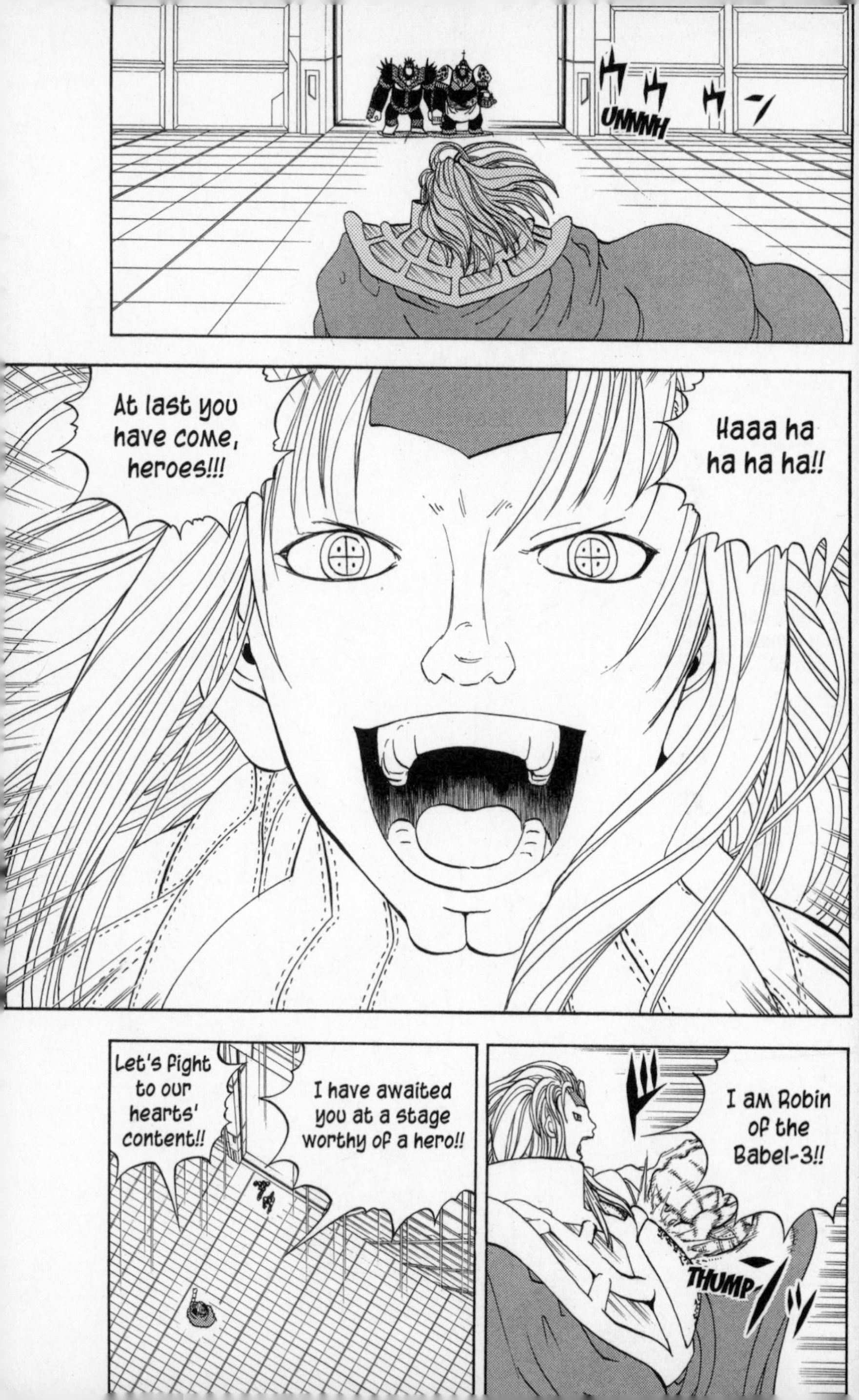
UNNNH
Haaa ha ha ha ha!!
At last you have come, heroes!!!
I am Robin of the Babel-3!!
THUMP
I have awaited you at a stage worthy of a hero!!
Let's fight to our hearts' content!!

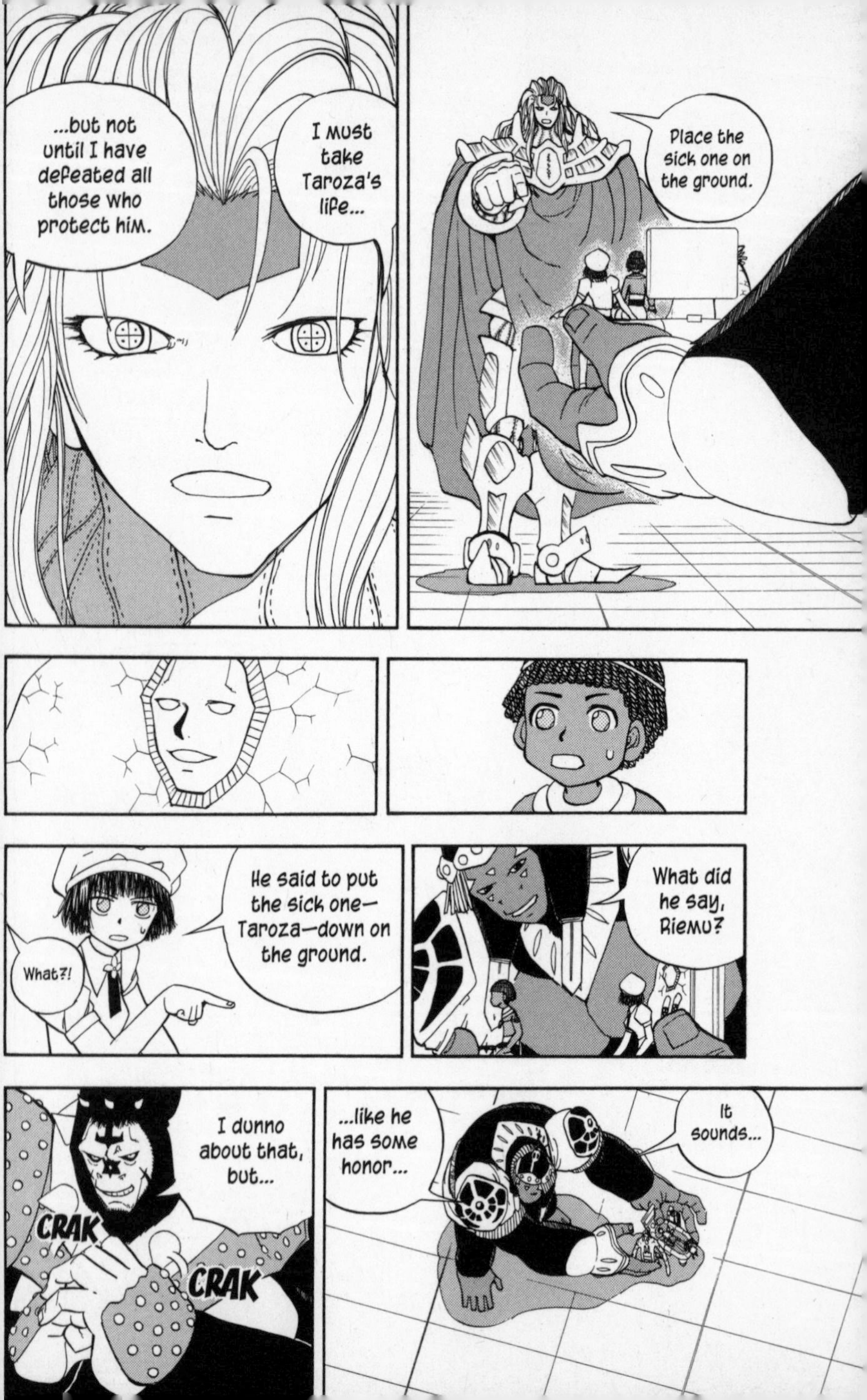
Place the sick one on the ground.
I must take Taroza's life...
...but not until I have defeated all those who protect him.
What did he say, Riemu?
He said to put the sick one—Taroza—down on the ground.
What?!
It sounds...
...like he has some honor...
I dunno about that, but...
CRAK
CRAK

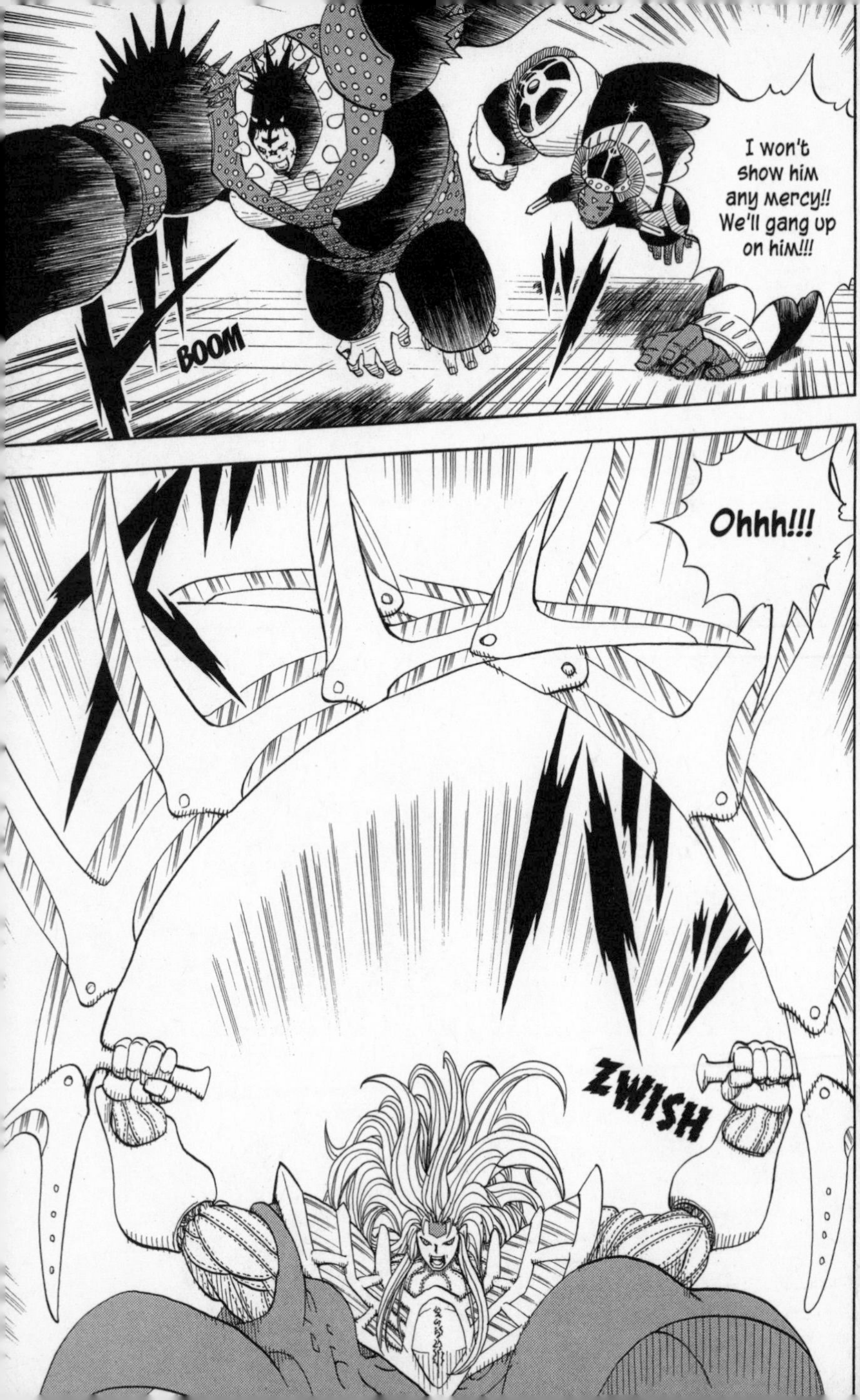
I won't show him any mercy!! We'll gang up on him!!!
BOOM
Ohhh!!!
ZWISH

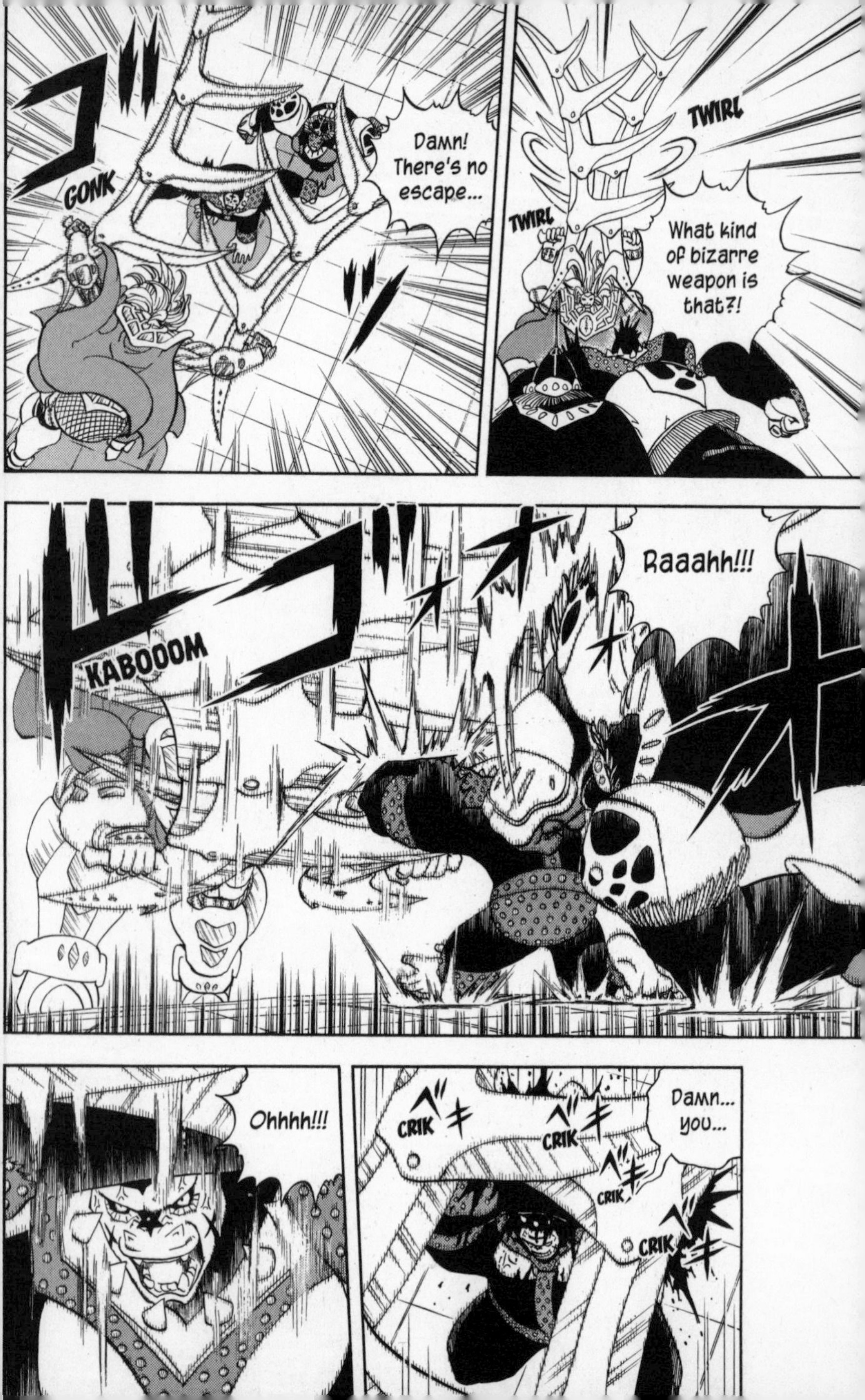
TWIRL
What kind of bizarre weapon is that?!
TWIRL
Damn! There's no escape...
GONK
Raaahh!!!
KABOOOM
Damn... you...
CRIK
CRIK
CRIK
CRIK
Ohhhh!!!

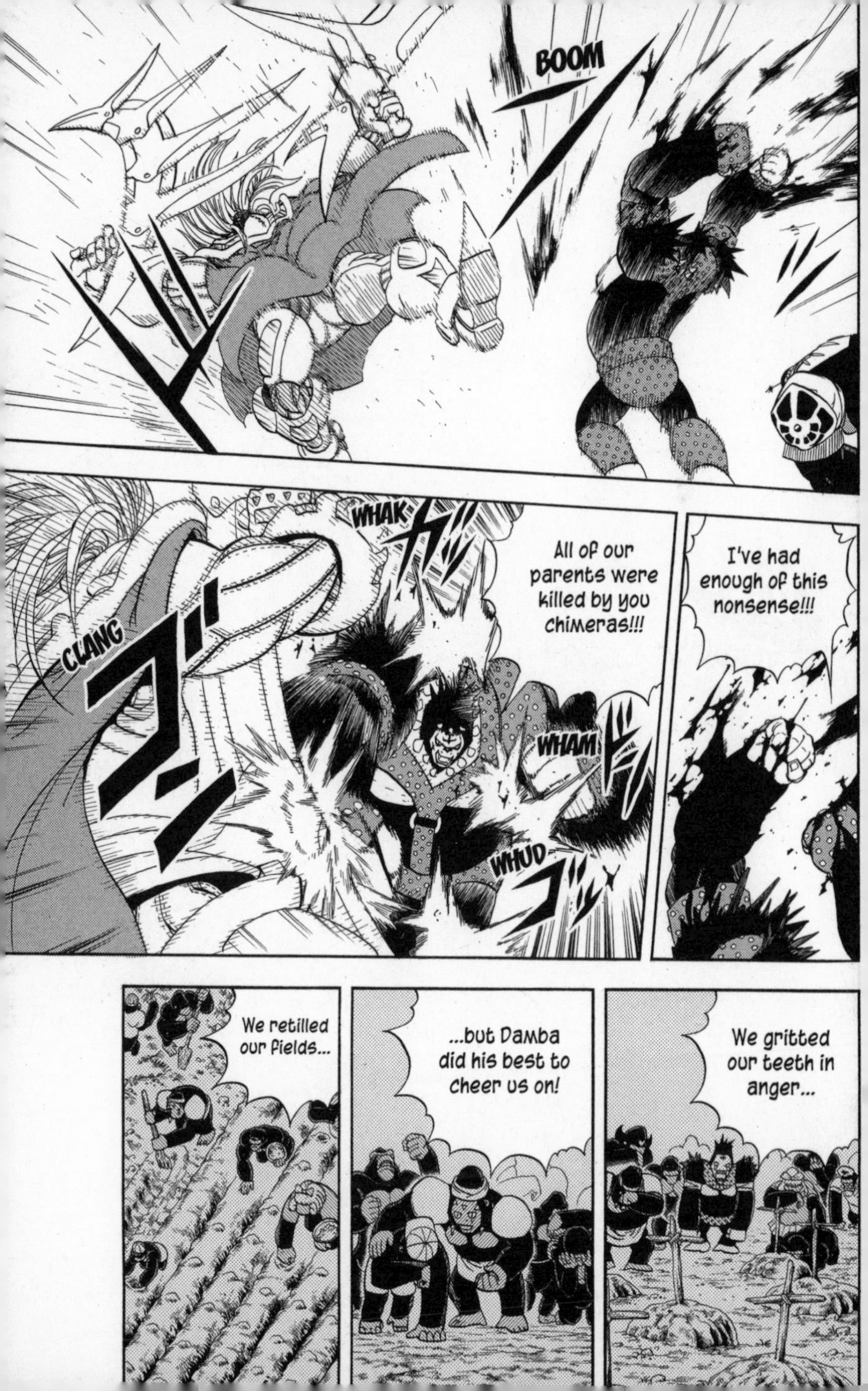
BOOM
I've had enough of this nonsense!!!
All of our parents were killed by you chimeras!!!
WHAK
WHAM
CLANG
WHUD
We gritted our teeth in anger...
...but Damba did his best to cheer us on!
We retilled our fields...

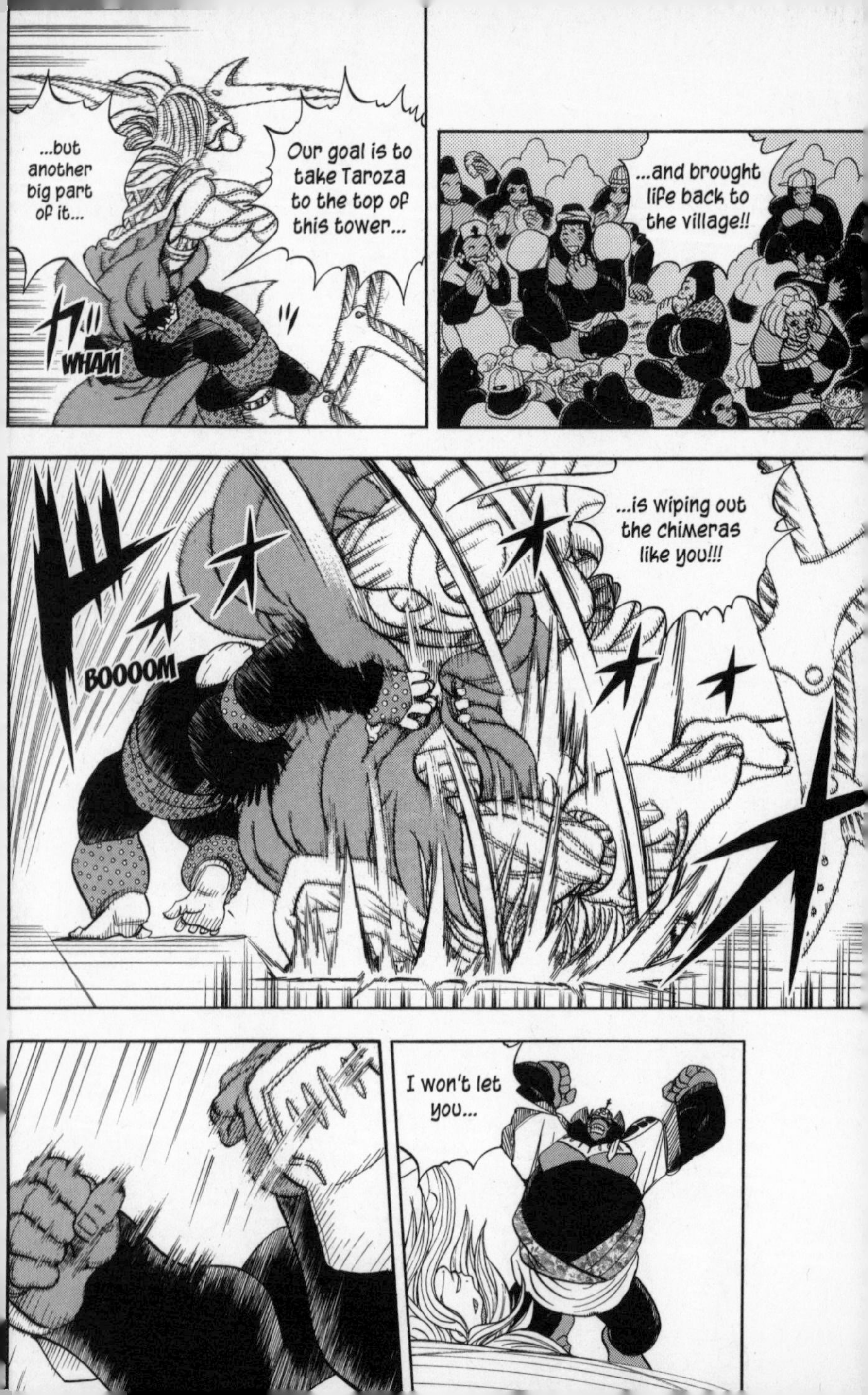
...and brought life back to the village!!
Our goal is to take Taroza to the top of this tower...
...but another big part of it...
WHAM
...is wiping out the chimeras like you!!!
BOOOOM
I won't let you...

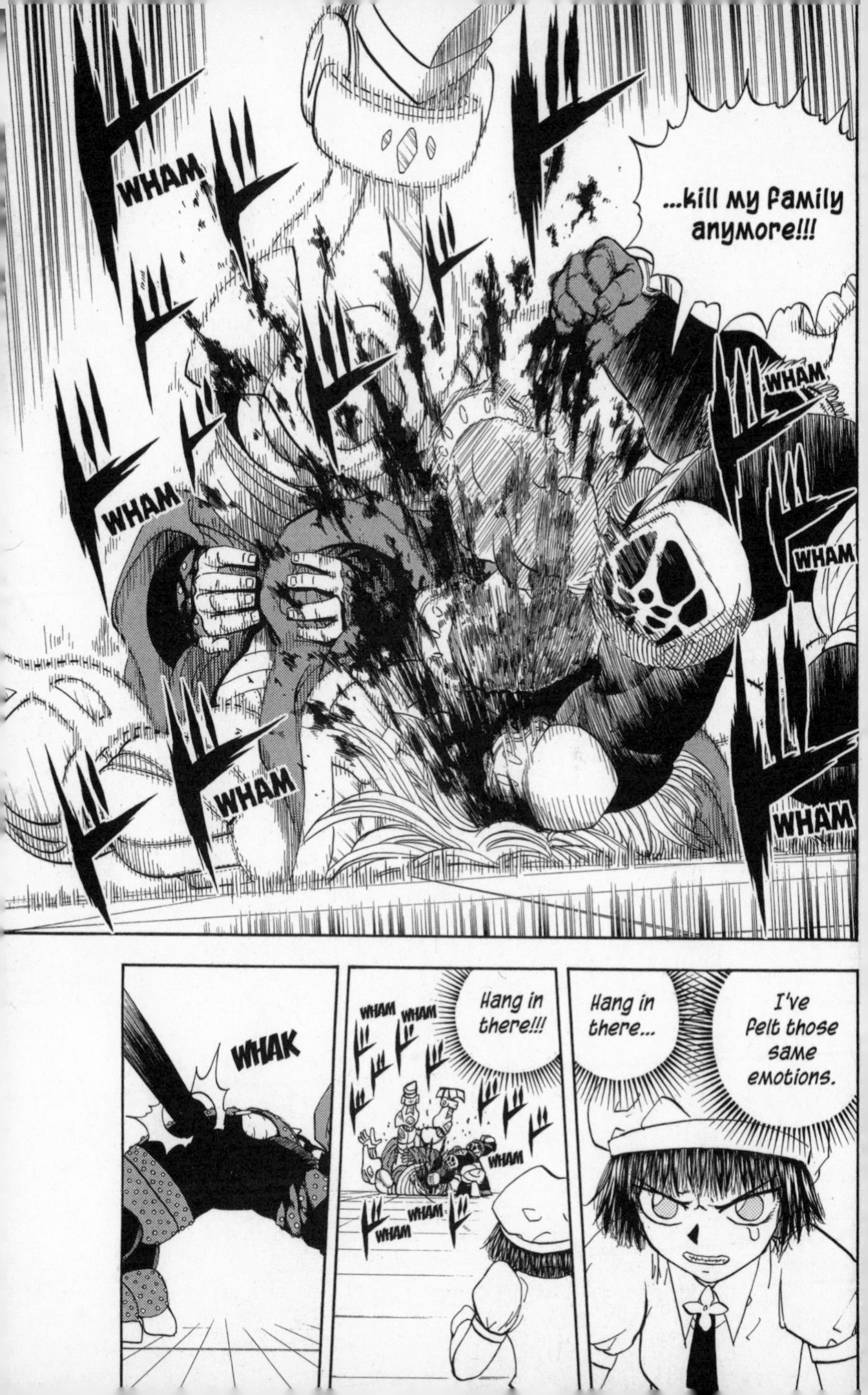
...kill my family anymore!!!
WHAM
WHAM
WHAM
WHAM
WHAM
WHAM
I've felt those same emotions.
Hang in there...
Hang in there!!!
WHAM WHAM
WHAM
WHAM
WHAM
WHAK

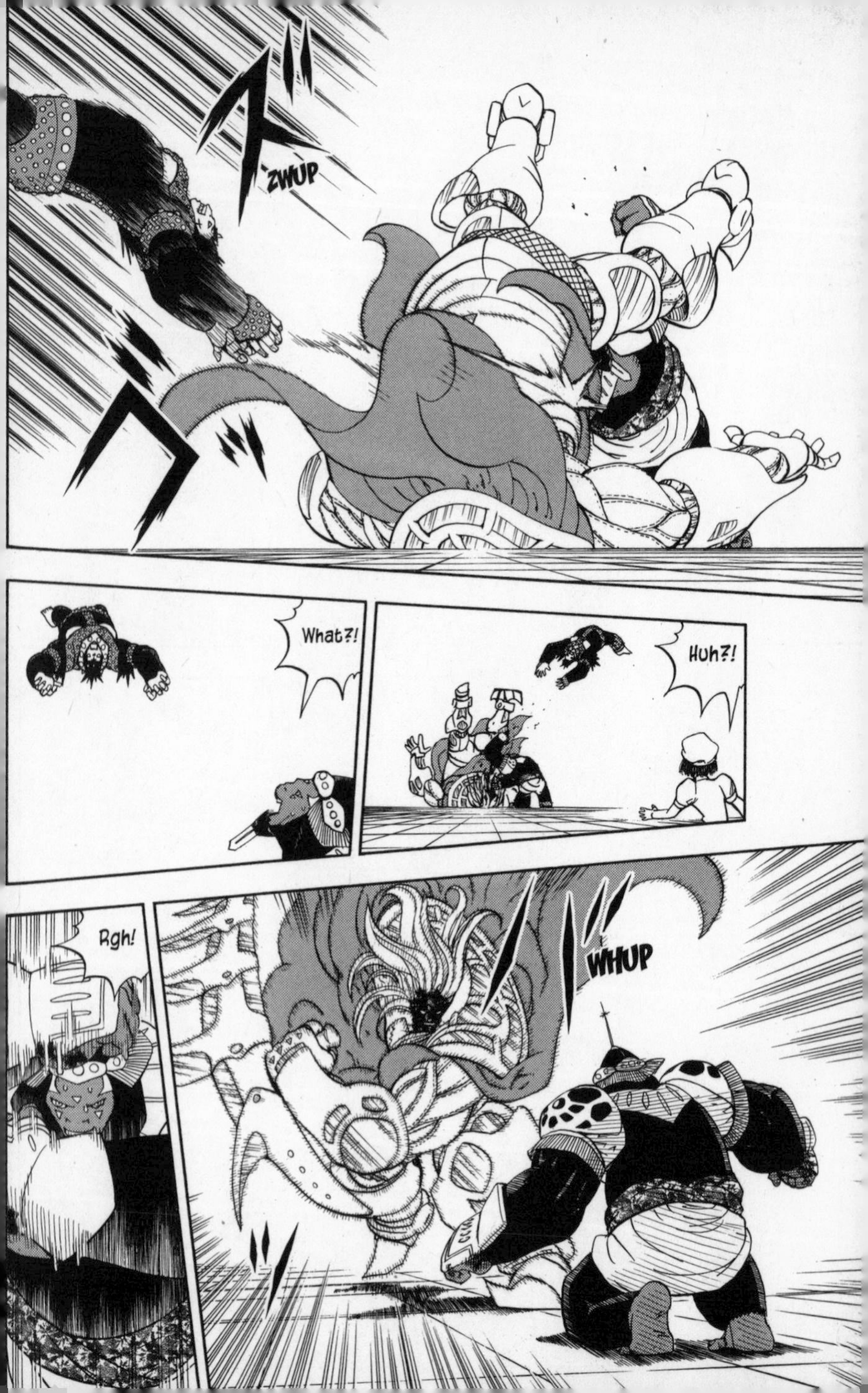
ZWUP
Huh?!
What?!
WHUP
Rgh!

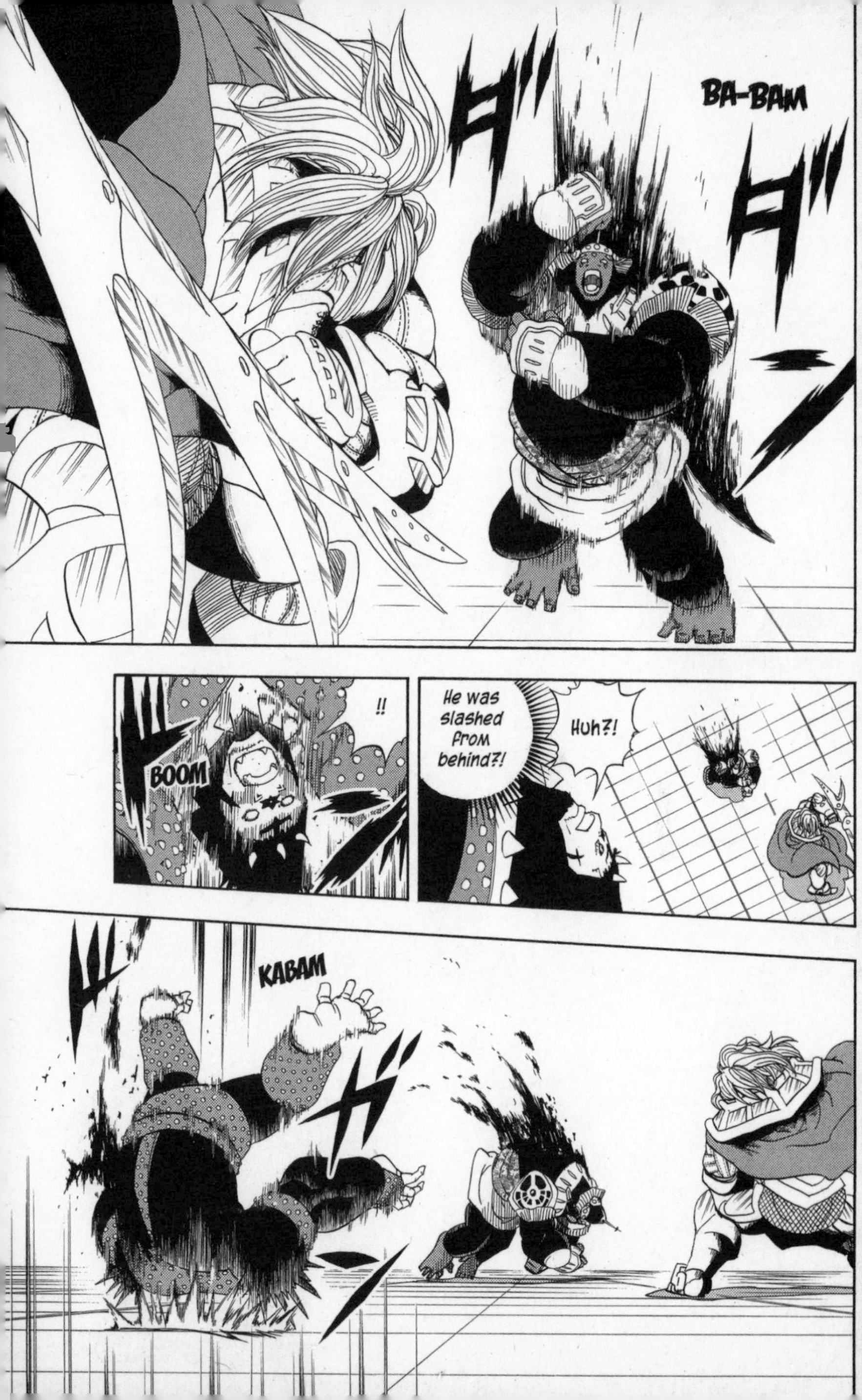
BA-BAM
Huh?!
He was slashed from behind?!
!!
BOOM
KABAM

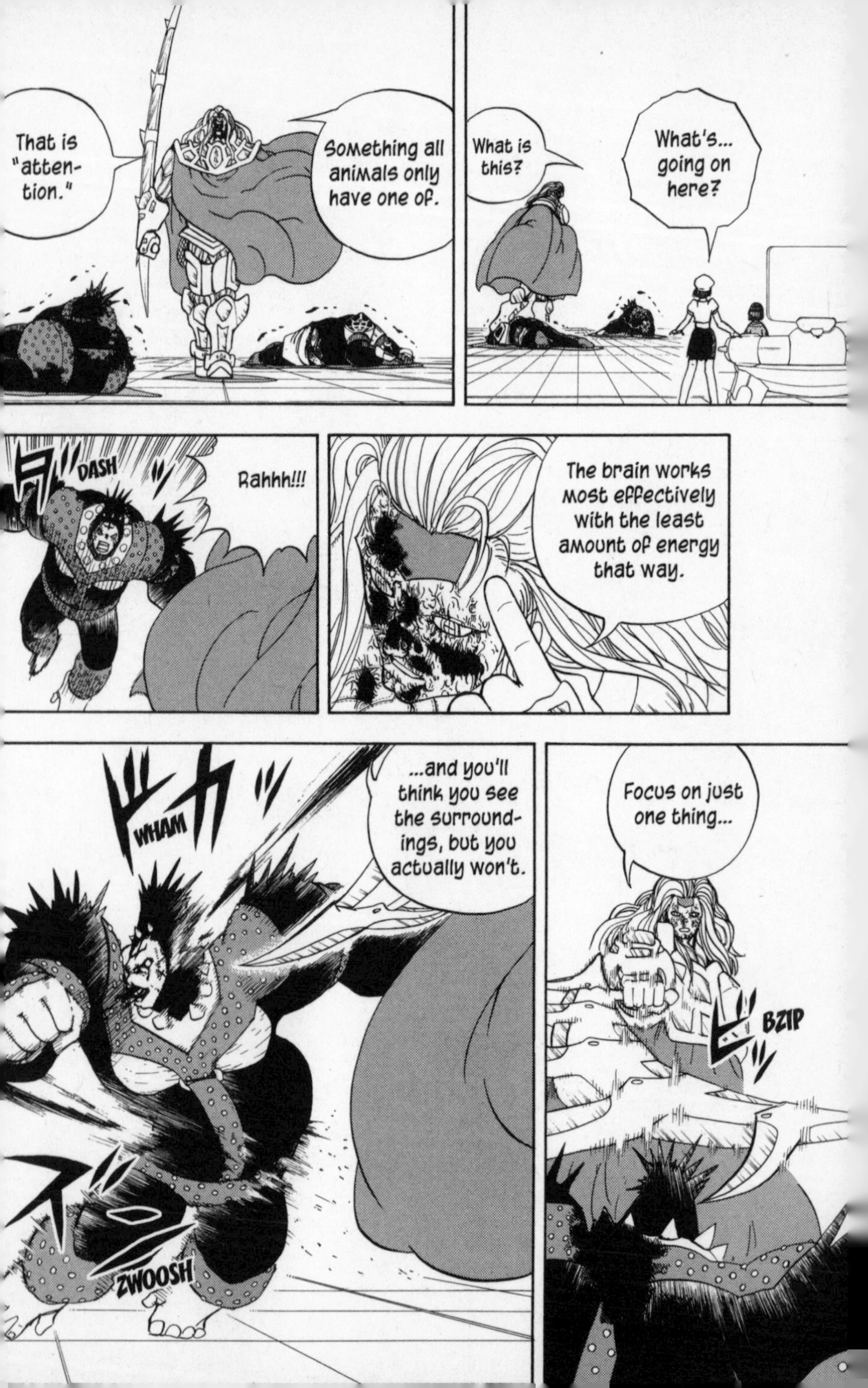
What's... going on here?
What is this?
Something all animals only have one of.
That is "atten- tion."
The brain works most effectively with the least amount of energy that way.
Rahhh!!!
DASH
Focus on just one thing...
BZIP
...and you'll think you see the surround- ings, but you actually won't.
WHAM
ZWOOSH

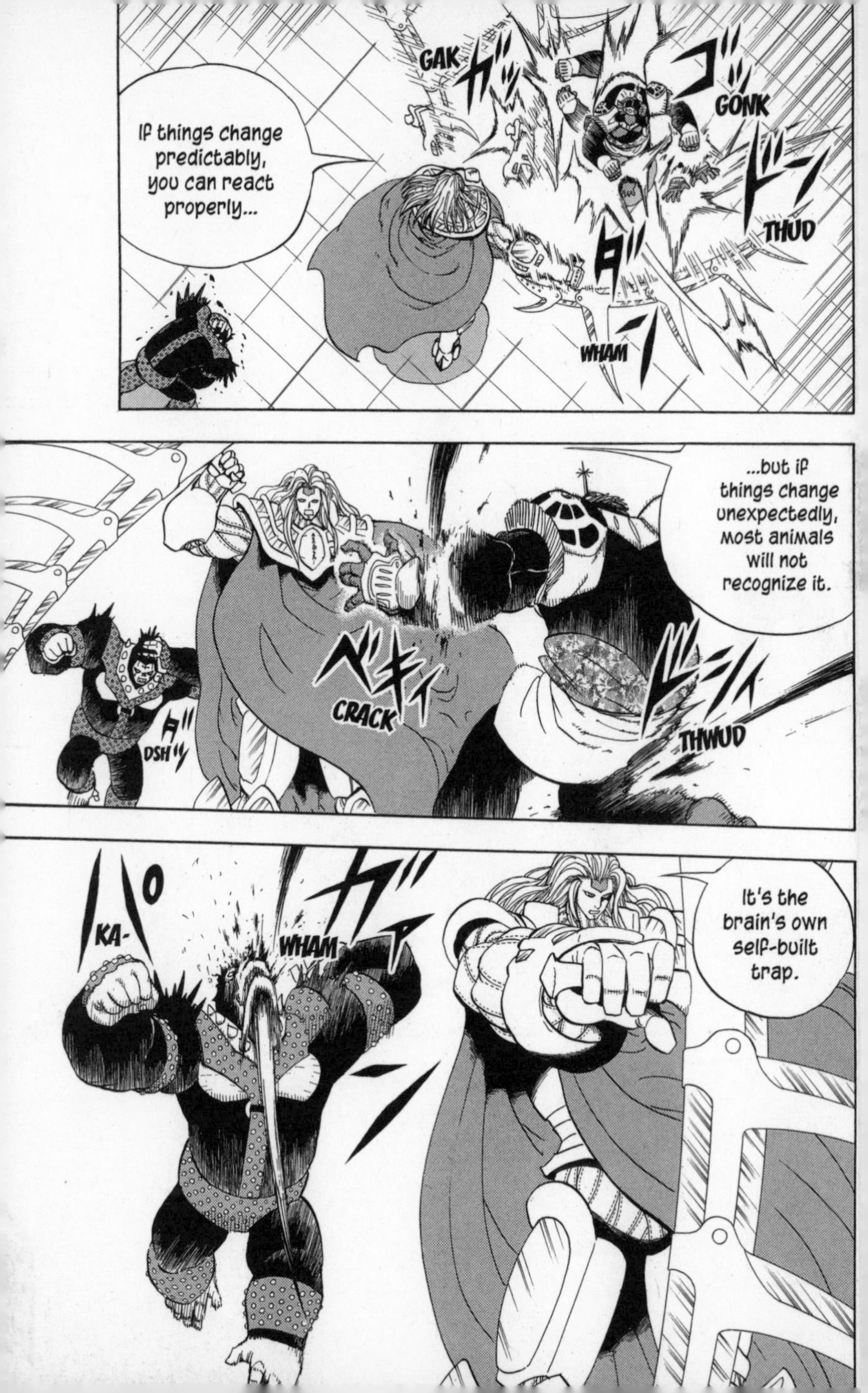
GONK
GAK
THUD
If things change predictably, you can react properly...
WHAM
...but if things change unexpectedly, most animals will not recognize it.
THWUD
CRACK
DSH
It's the brain's own self-built trap.
WHAM
KA-

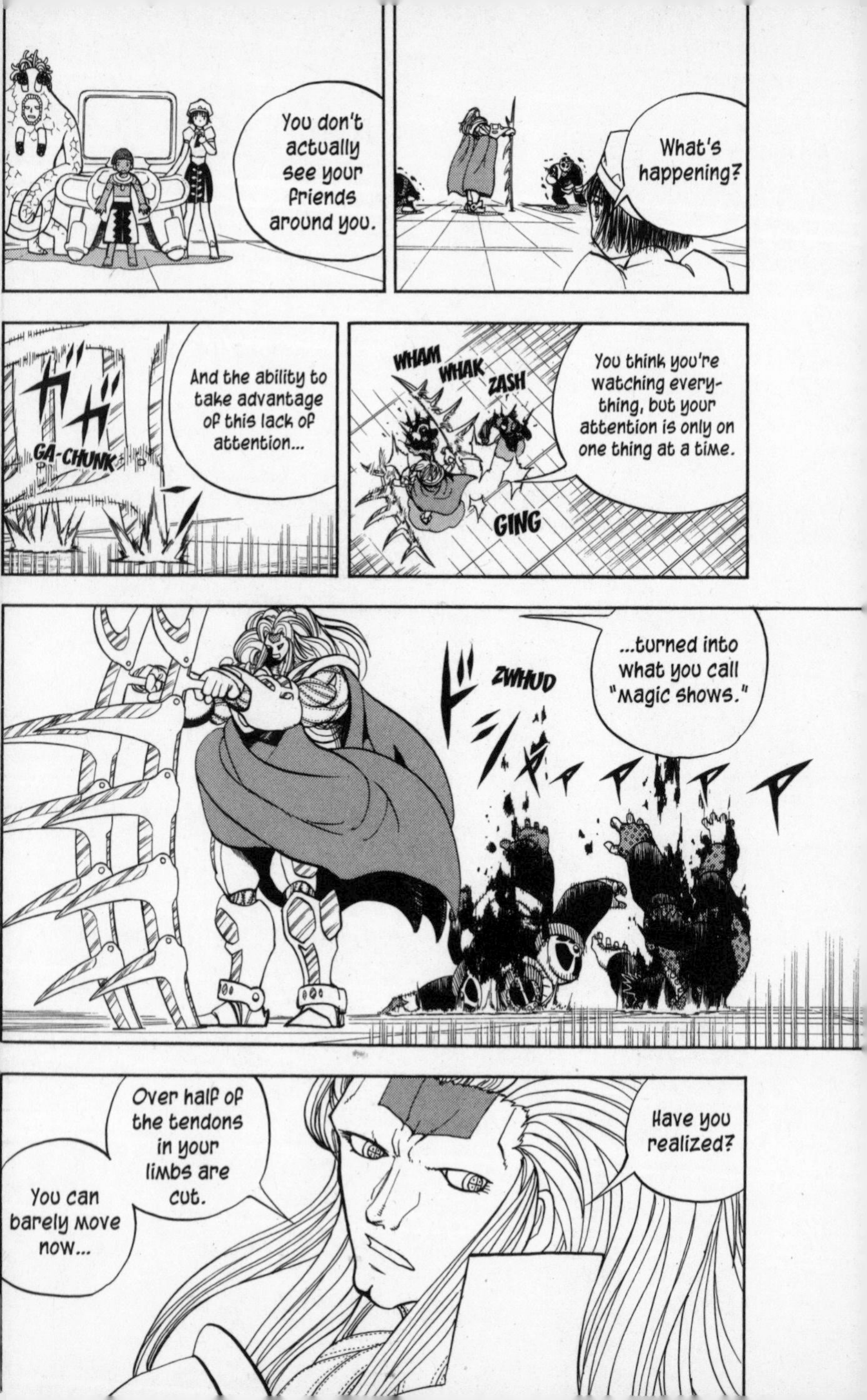
What's happening?
You don't actually see your friends around you.
WHAM
WHAK
ZASH
You think you're watching every-thing, but your attention is only on one thing at a time.
GING
And the ability to take advantage of this lack of attention...
GA-CHUNK
...turned into what you call "Magic shows."
ZWHUD
Have you realized?
Over half of the tendons in your limbs are cut.
You can barely move now...

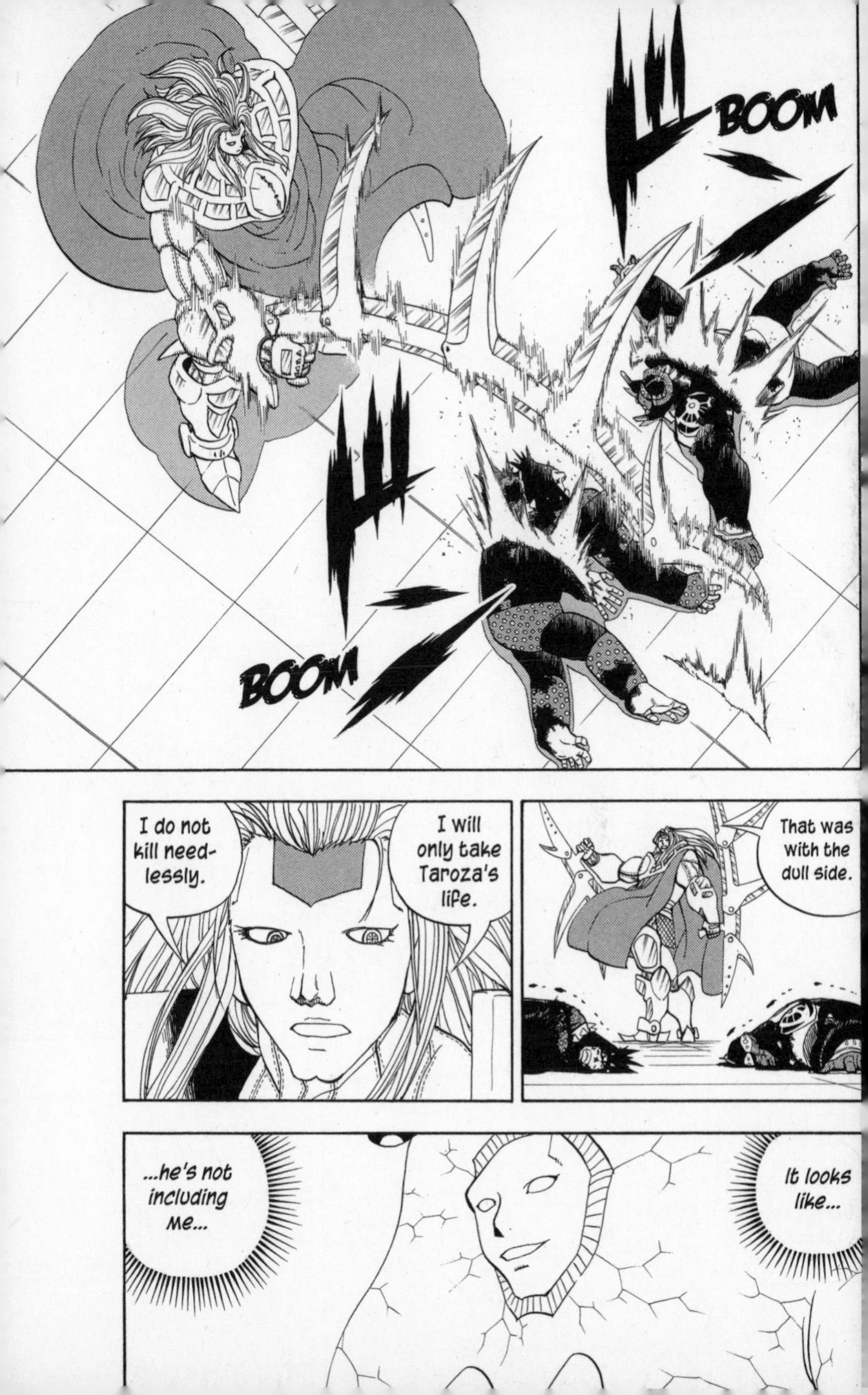
BOOM
BOOM
That was with the dull side.
I will only take Taroza's life.
I do not kill needlessly.
It looks like...
...he's not including me...

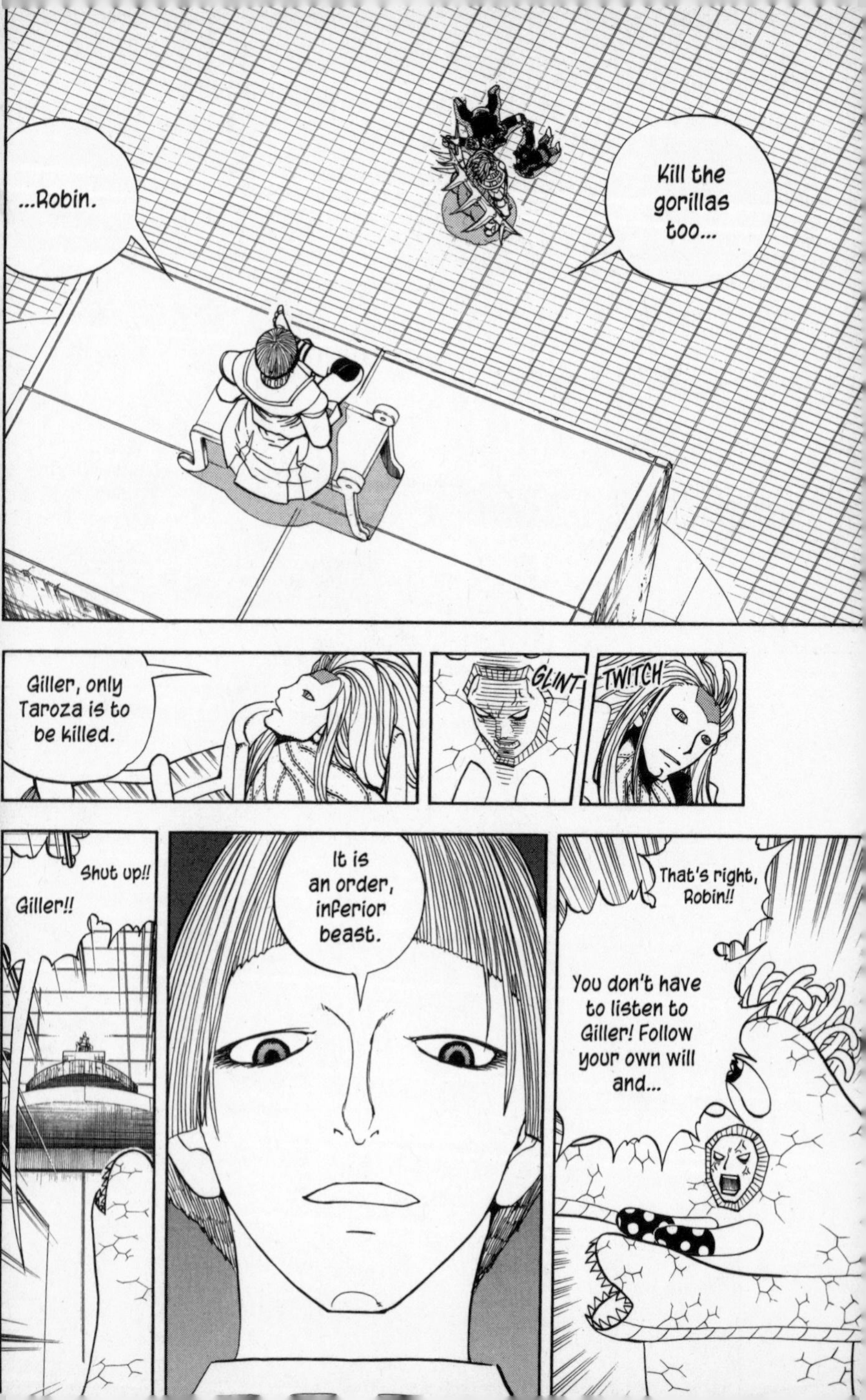
Kill the gorillas too...
...Robin.
TWITCH
GLINT
Giller, only Taroza is to be killed.
That's right, Robin!!
You don't have to listen to Giller! Follow your own will and...
It is an order, inferior beast.
Shut up!!
Giller!!

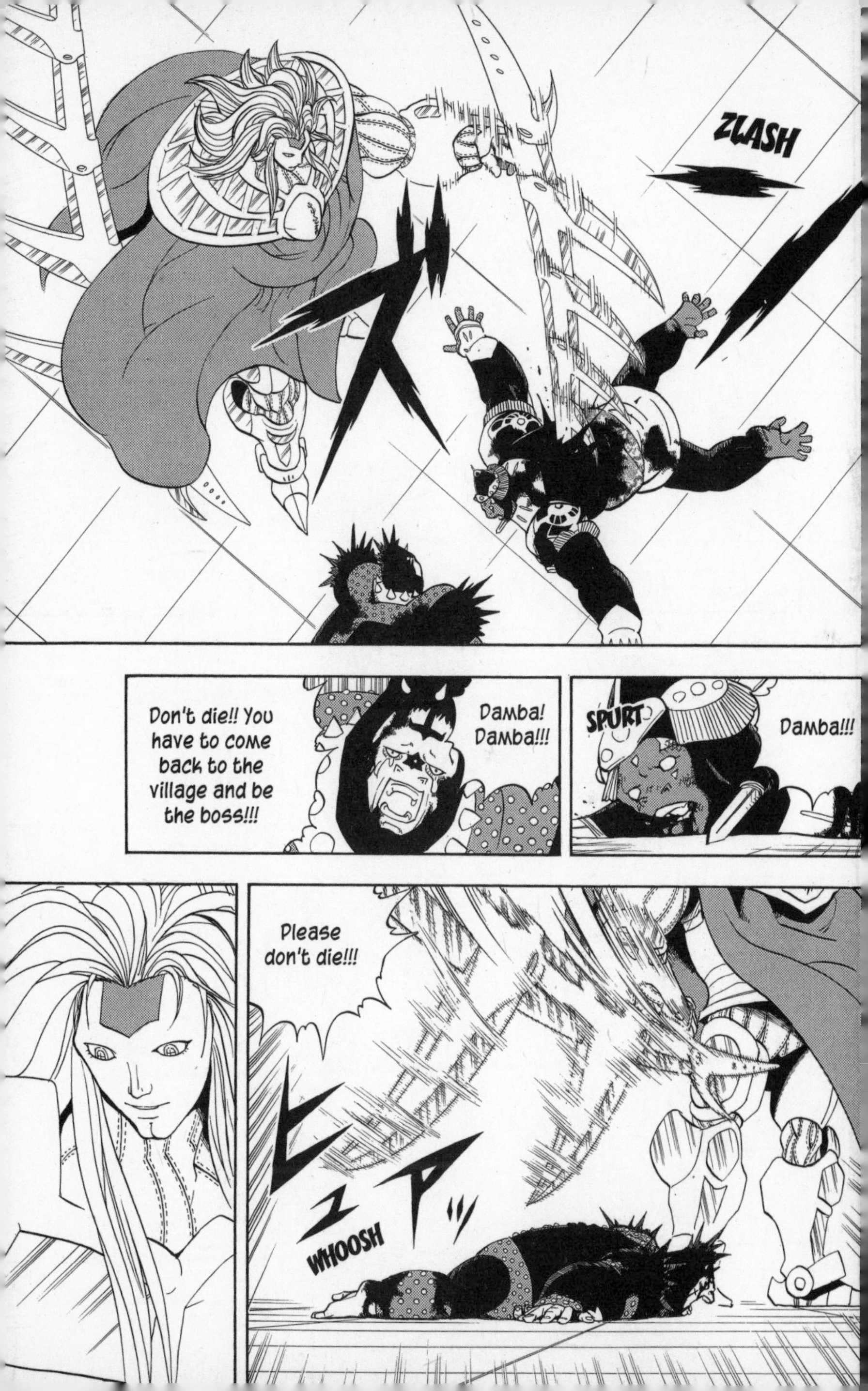
ZLASH
Damba!!!
SPURT
Damba! Damba!!!
Don't die!! You have to come back to the village and be the boss!!!
Please don't die!!!
WHOOSH

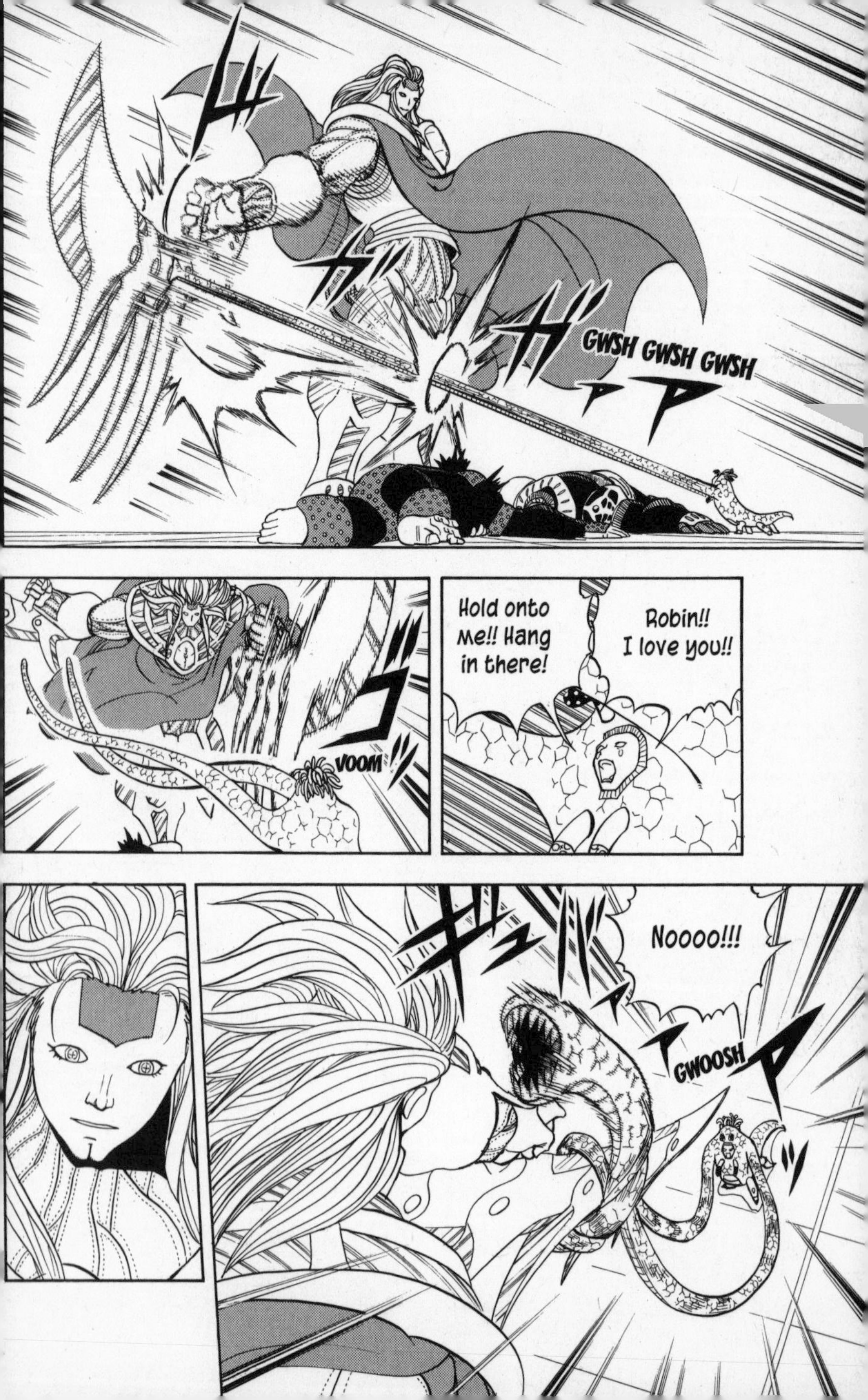
GWSH GWSH GWSH
Robin!! I love you!!
Hold onto me!! Hang in there!
VOOM
Noooo!!!
GWOOSH

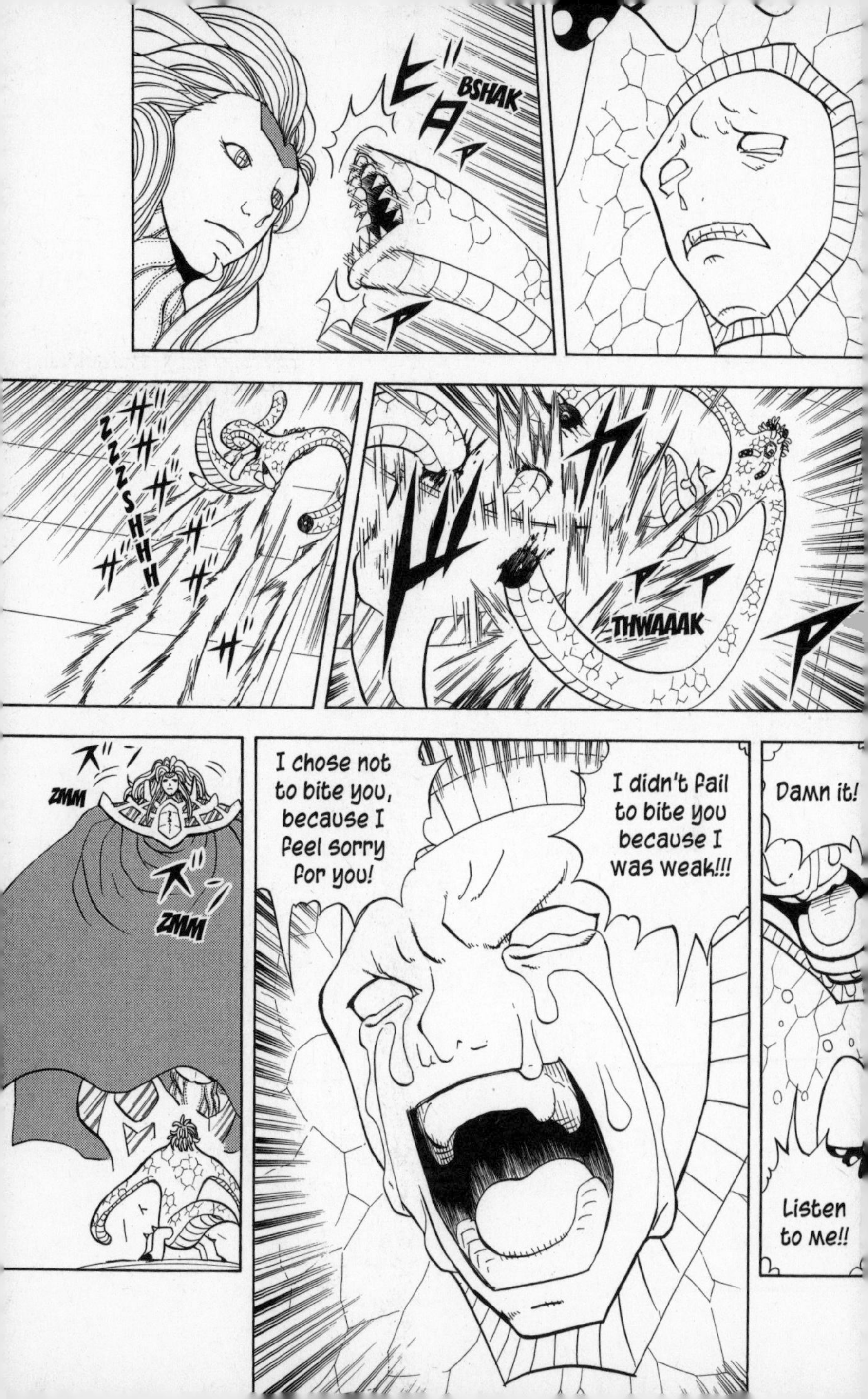
BSHAK
THWAAAK
ZZZSHHH
Damn it!
Listen to me!!
I didn't fail to bite you because I was weak!!!
I chose not to bite you, because I feel sorry for you!
ZMM
ZMM

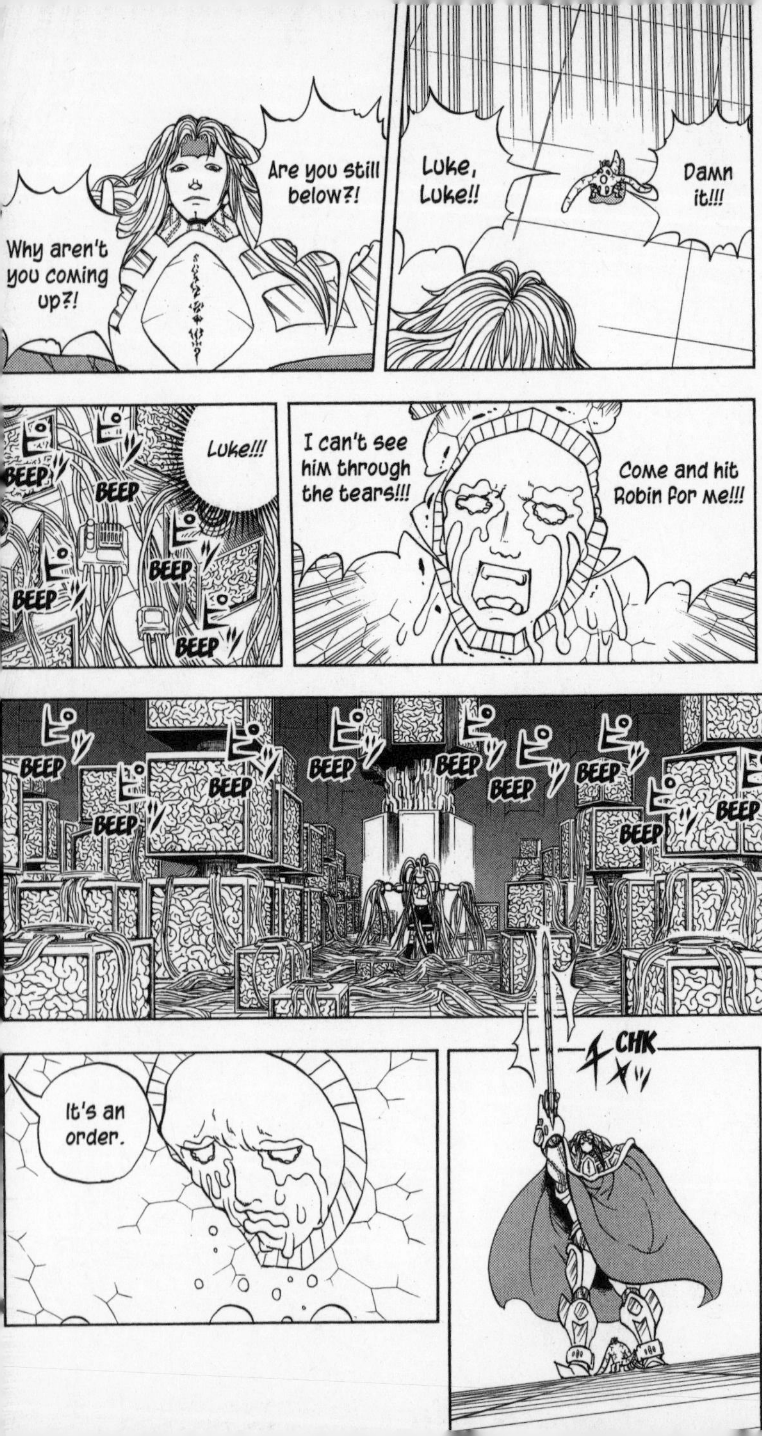

Damn it!!!
Luke, Luke!!
Are you still below?!
Why aren't you coming up?!
Come and hit Robin for me!!!
I can't see him through the tears!!!
Luke!!!
ピッ BEEP
ピッ BEEP
ピッ BEEP
ピッ BEEP
ピッ BEEP
ピッ BEEP
ピッ BEEP
ピッ BEEP
ピッ BEEP
ピッ BEEP
ピッ BEEP
ピッ BEEP
ピッ BEEP
ピッ BEEP
チャッ CHK
It's an order.

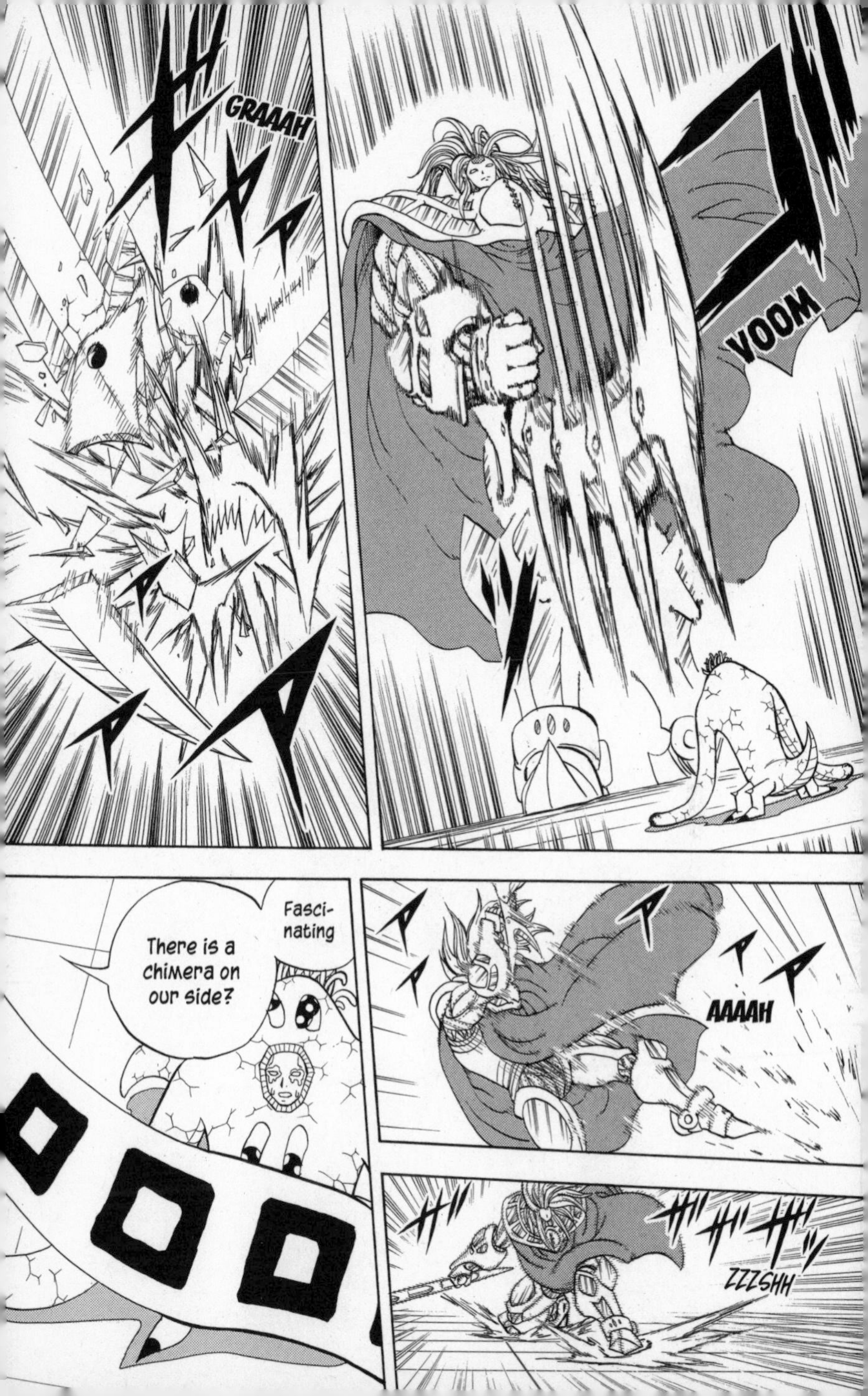
VOOM
GRAAAH
AAAAH
ZZZSHH
Fasci-nating
There is a chimera on our side?

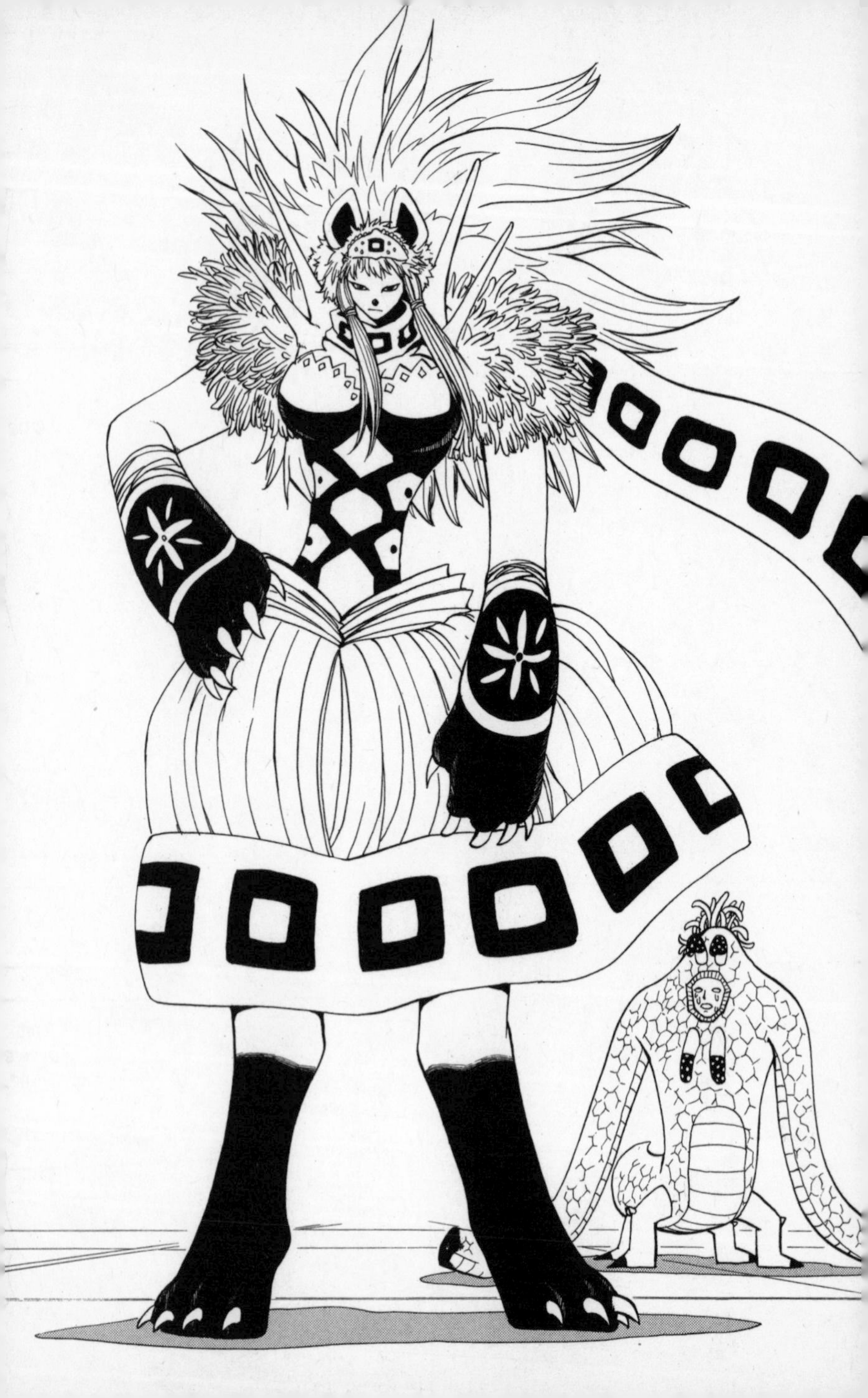

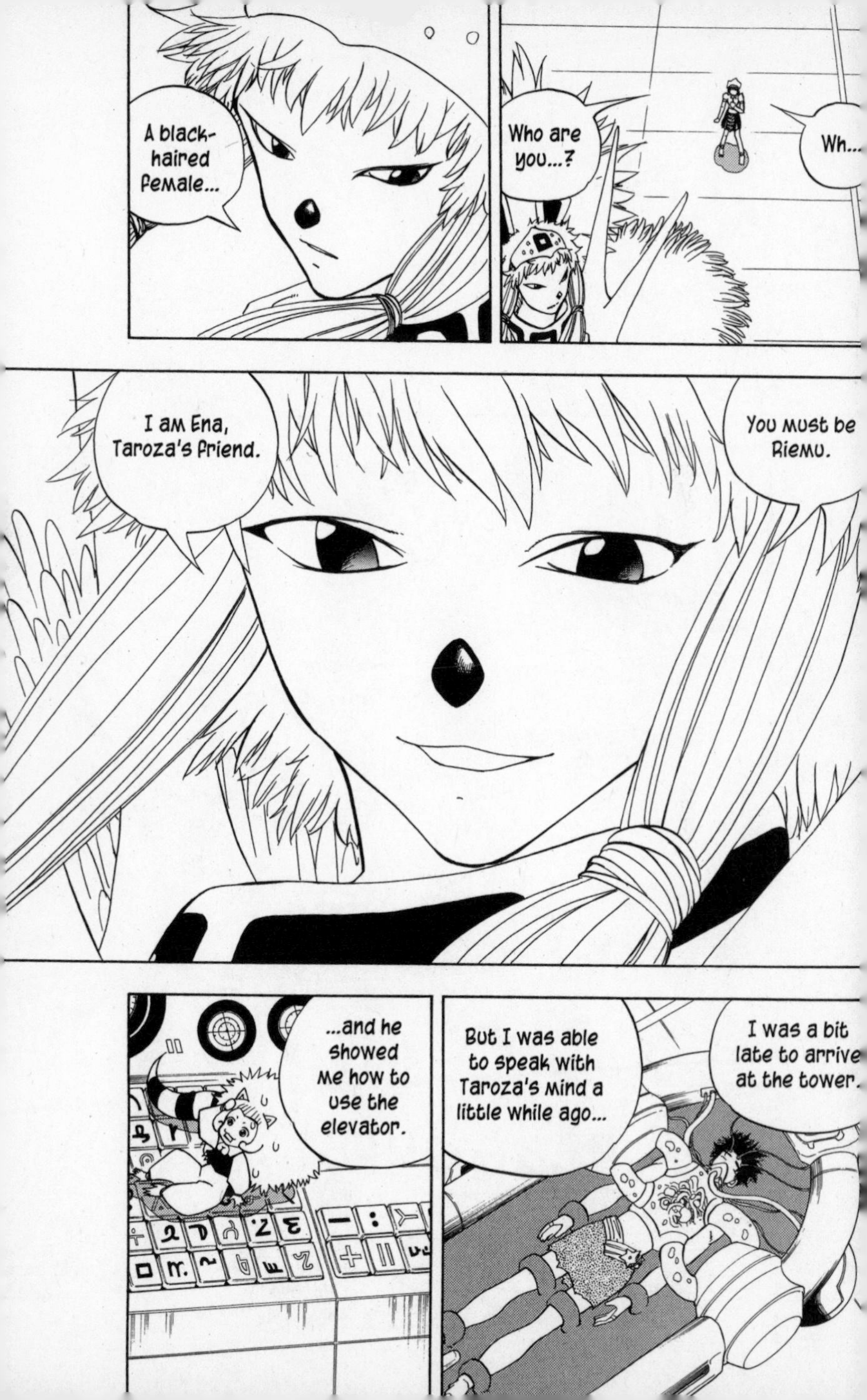
Wh...
Who are you...?
A black-haired female...
You must be Riemu.
I am Ena, Taroza's friend.
I was a bit late to arrive at the tower.
But I was able to speak with Taroza's mind a little while ago...
...and he showed me how to use the elevator.

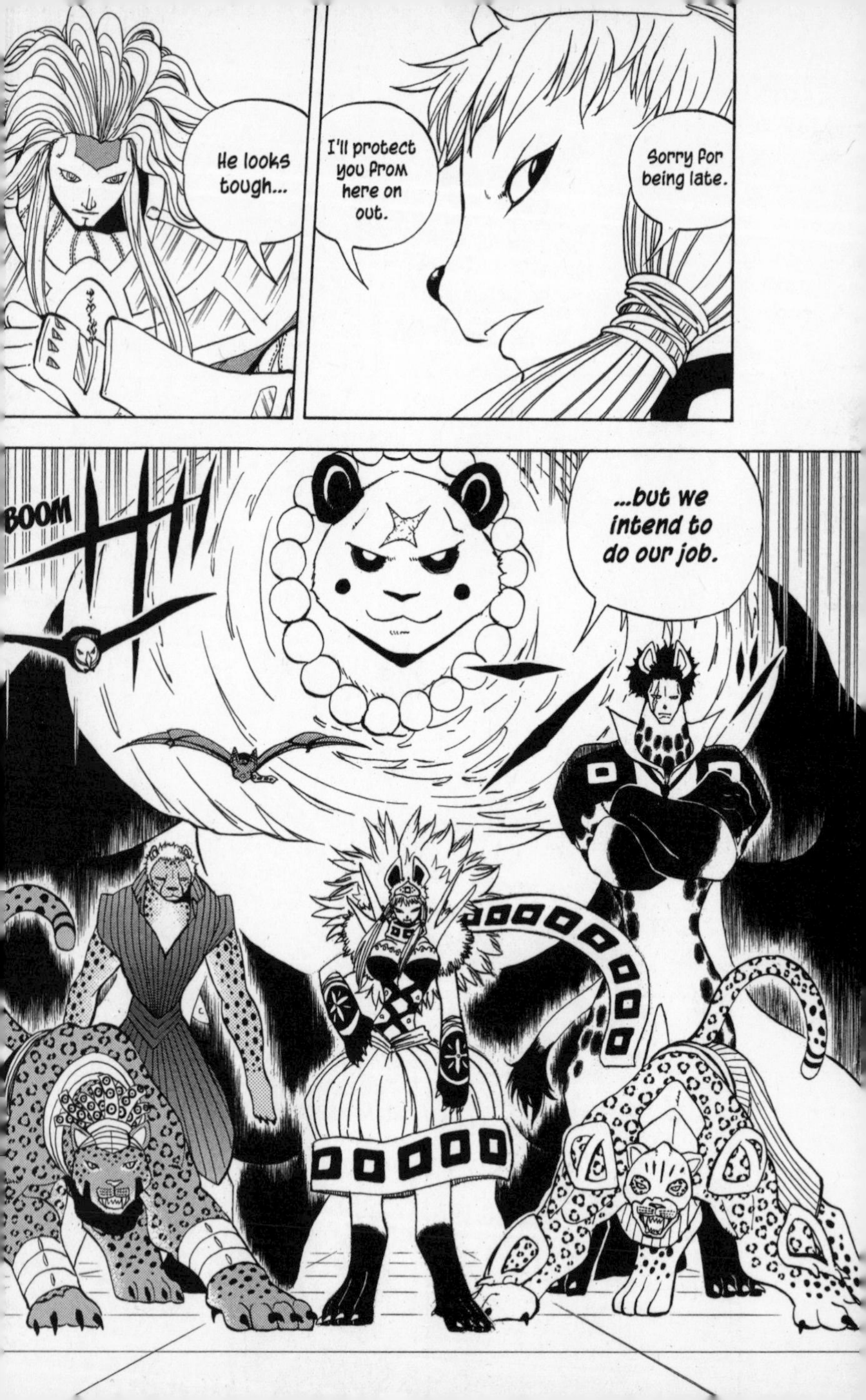
Sorry for being late.
I'll protect you from here on out.
He looks tough...
...but we intend to do our job.
BOOM

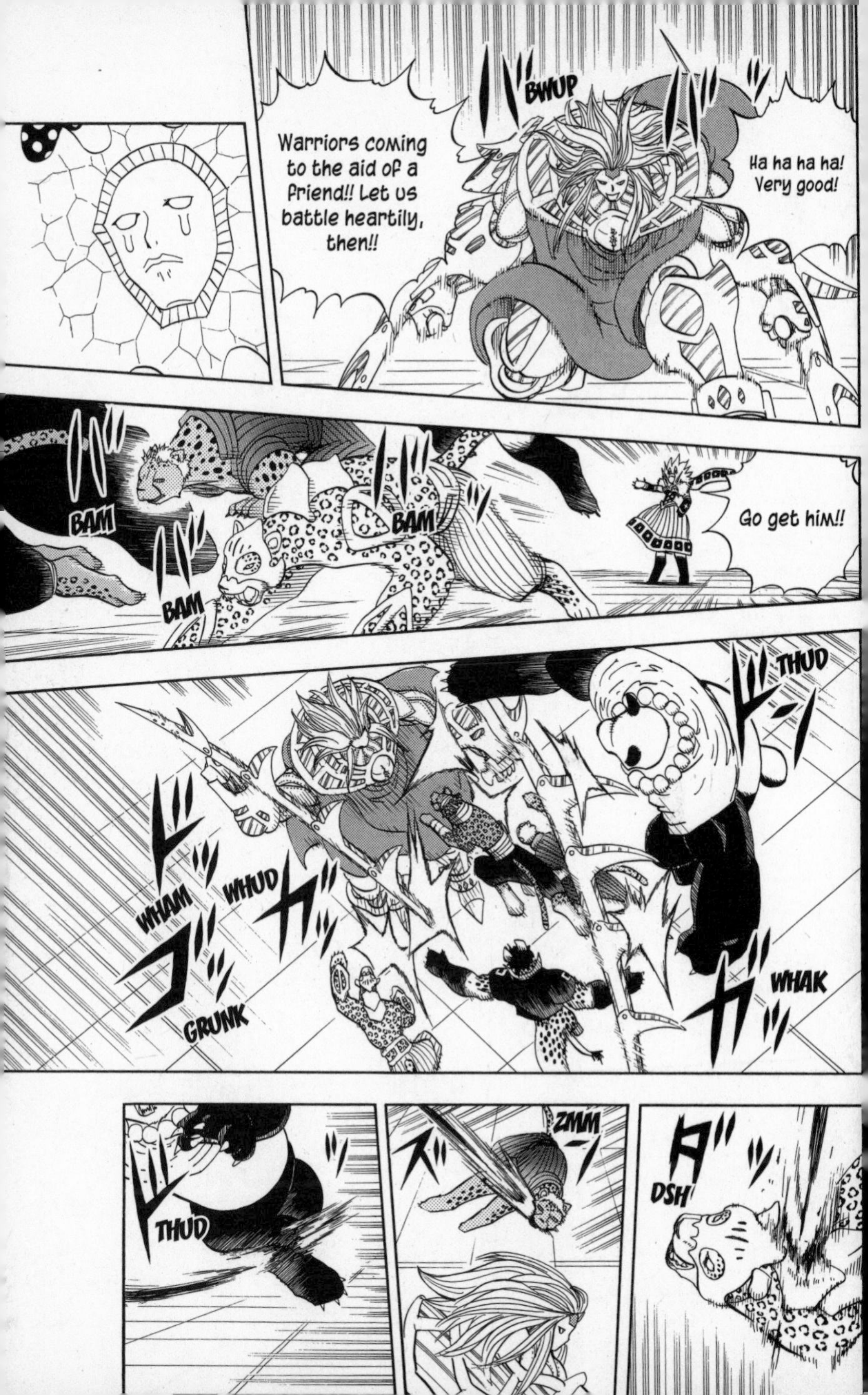
BWUP
Ha ha ha ha! Very good!
Warriors coming to the aid of a friend!! Let us battle heartily, then!!
Go get him!!
BAM
BAM
BAM
THUD
WHAK
WHUD
WHAM
GRUNK
DSH
ZMM
THUD

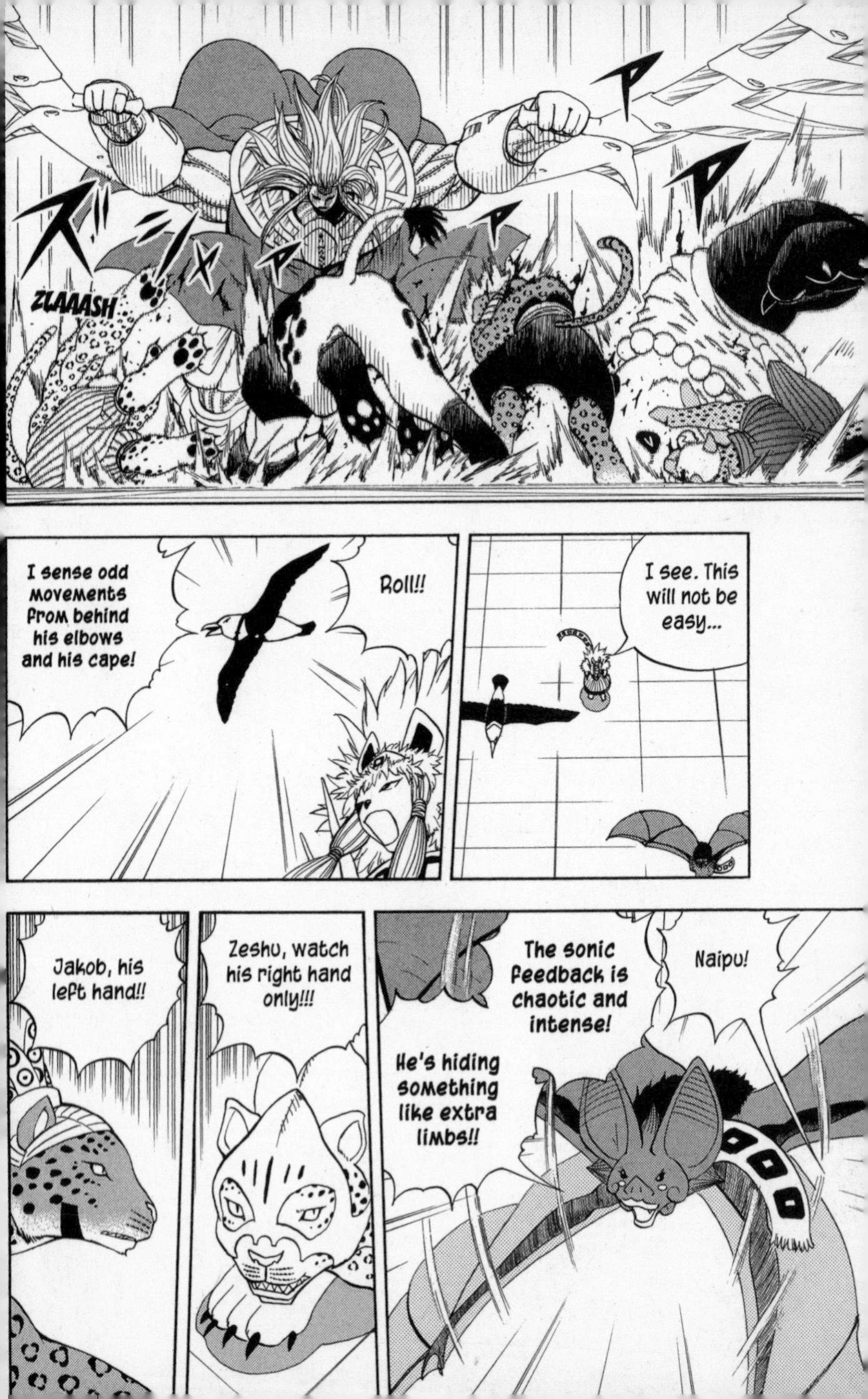
ZLAAASH
I sense odd movements from behind his elbows and his cape!
Roll!!
I see. This will not be easy...
Jakob, his left hand!!
Zeshu, watch his right hand only!!!
The sonic feedback is chaotic and intense!
He's hiding something like extra limbs!!
Naipu!

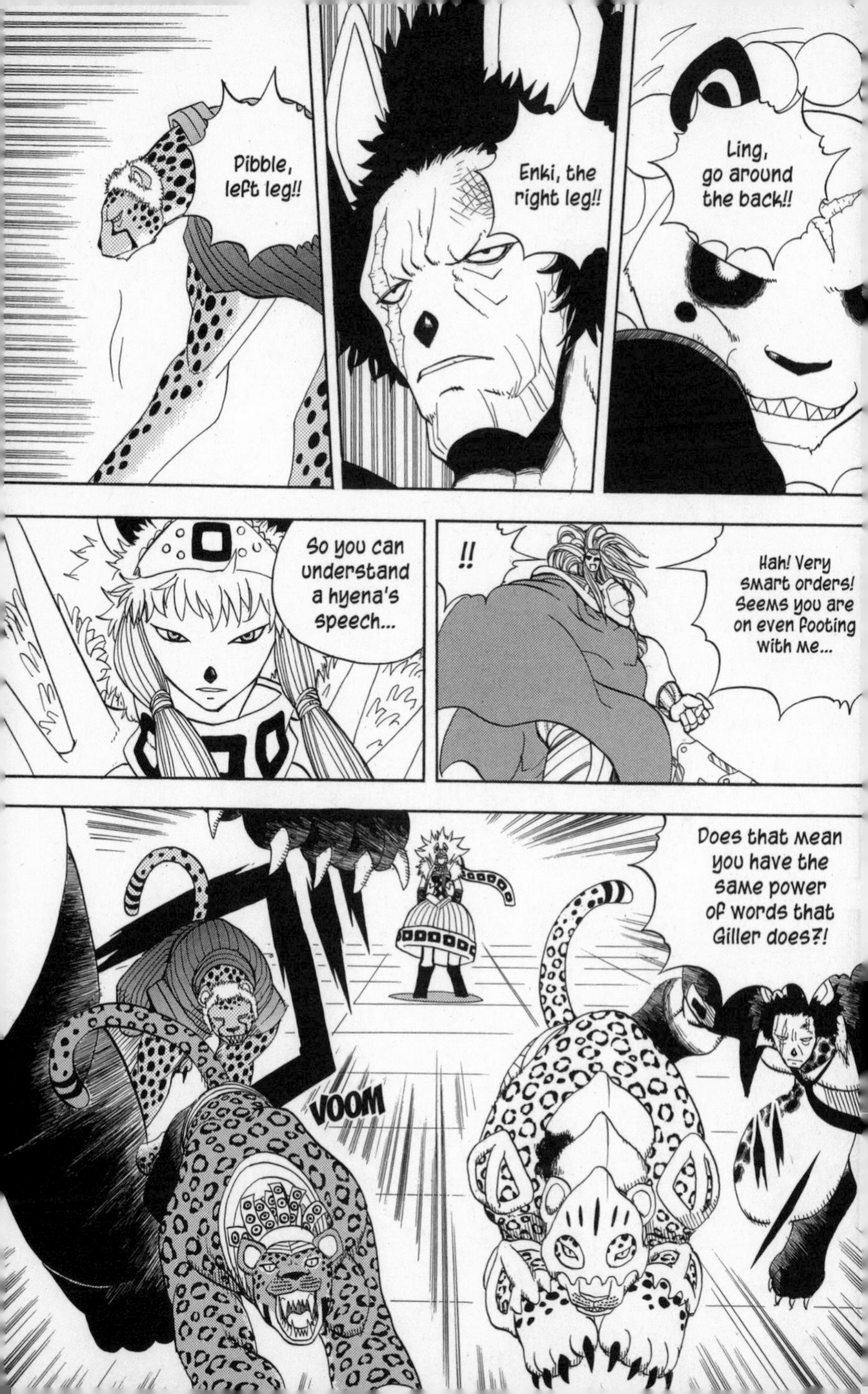
Ling, go around the back!!
Enki, the right leg!!
Pibble, left leg!!
Hah! Very smart orders! Seems you are on even footing with me...
!!
So you can understand a hyena's speech...
Does that mean you have the same power of words that Giller does?!
VOOM

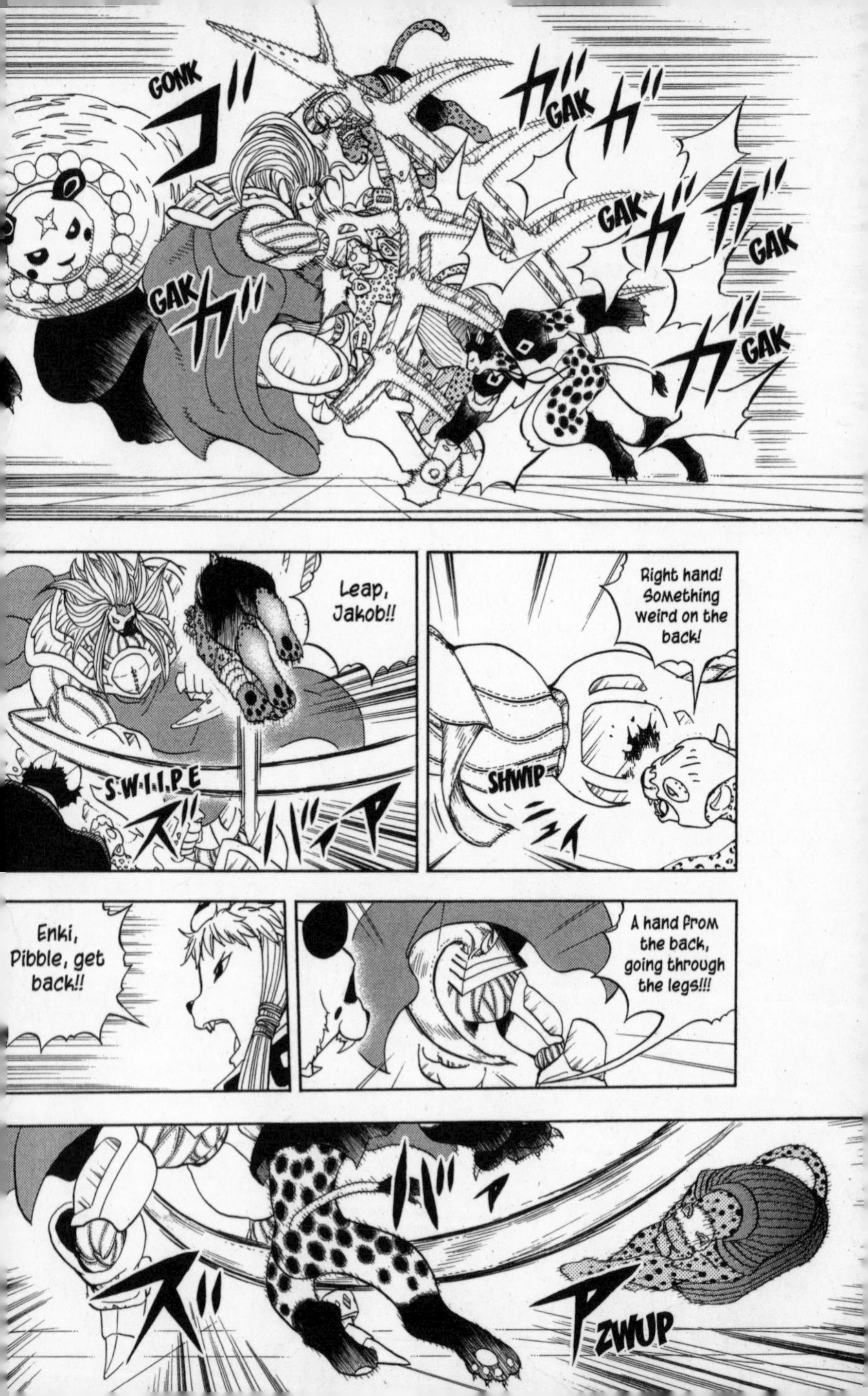
GAK
GAK
GAK
GAK
GONK
GAK
Right hand! Something weird on the back!
SHWIP
Leap, Jakob!!
S-W-I-I-P-E
A hand from the back, going through the legs!!!
Enki, Pibble, get back!!
ZWUP

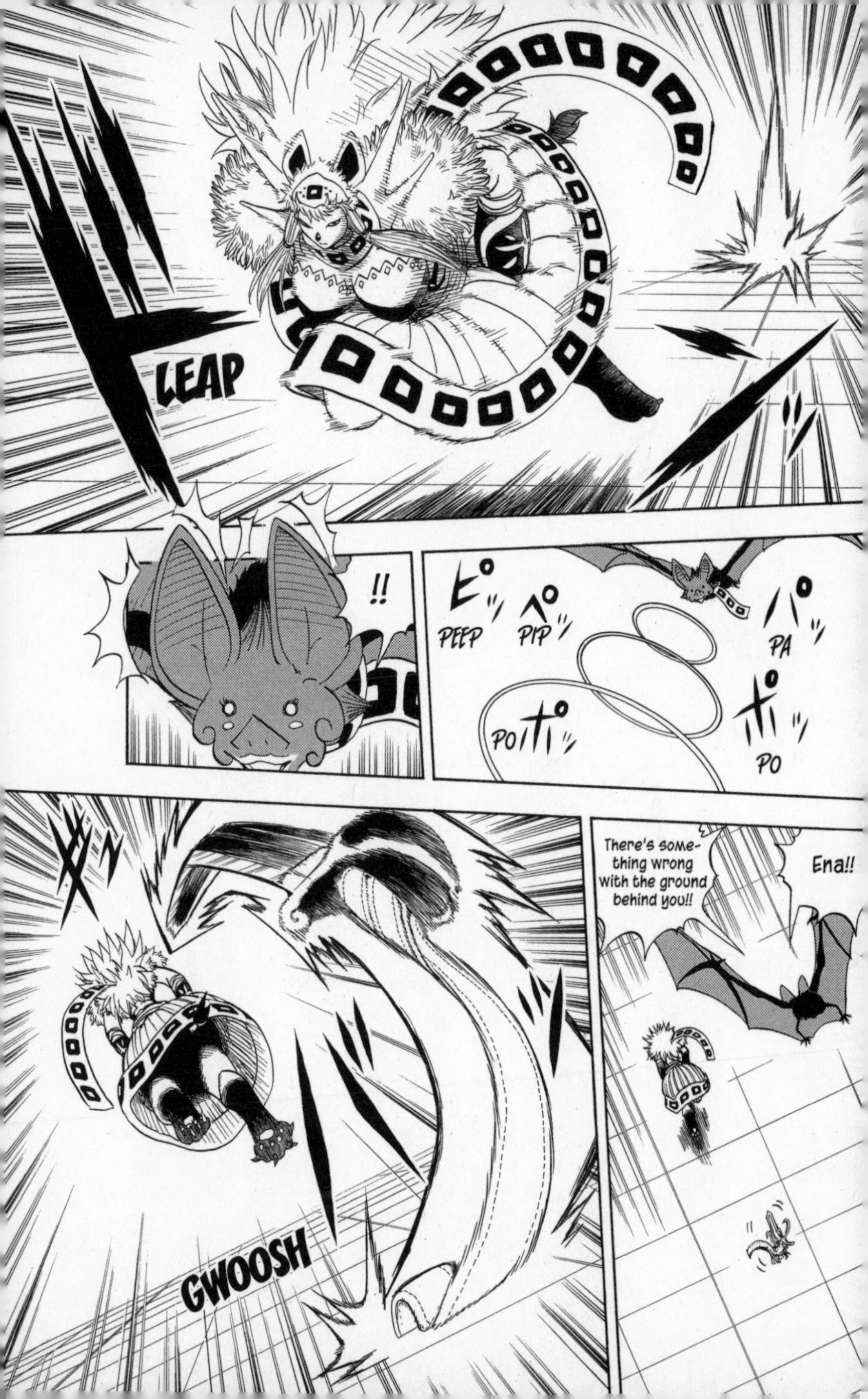

LEAP
PA
PIP
PEEP
PO
POI
!!
Ena!!
There's some-thing wrong with the ground behind you!!
GWOOSH

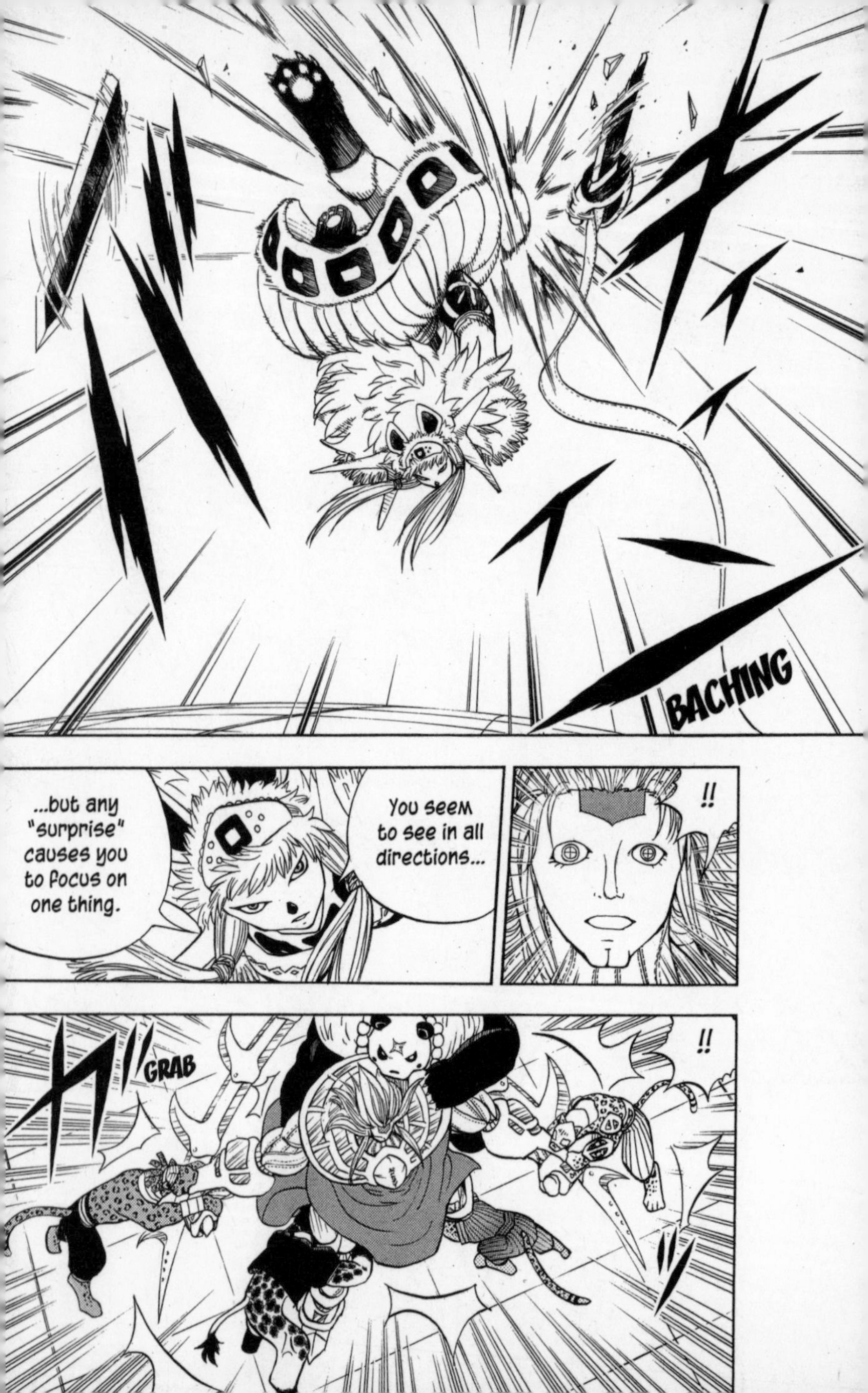
BACHING
!!
You seem to see in all directions...
...but any "surprise" causes you to focus on one thing.
!!
GRAB

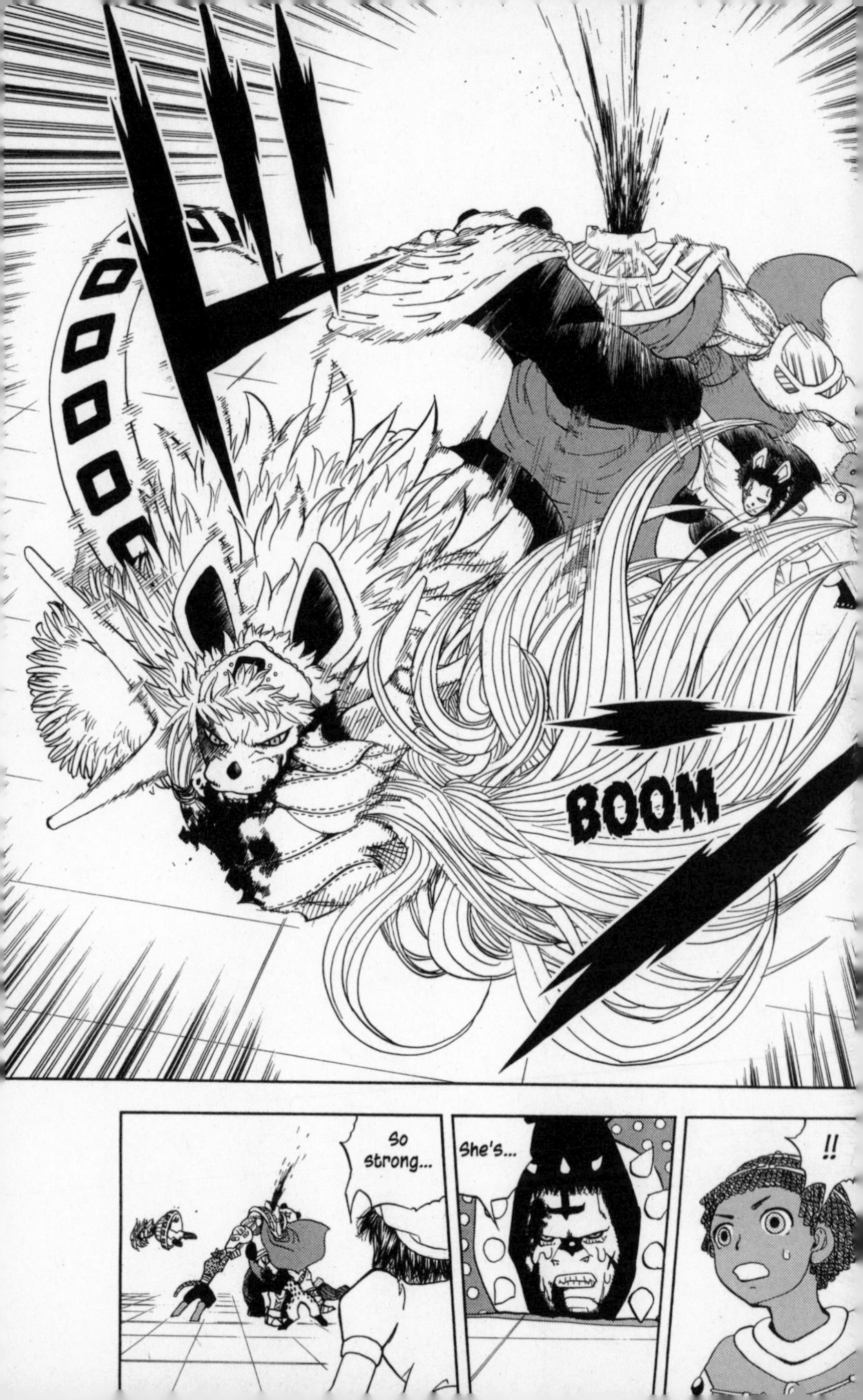
BOOM
!!
She's...
So strong...

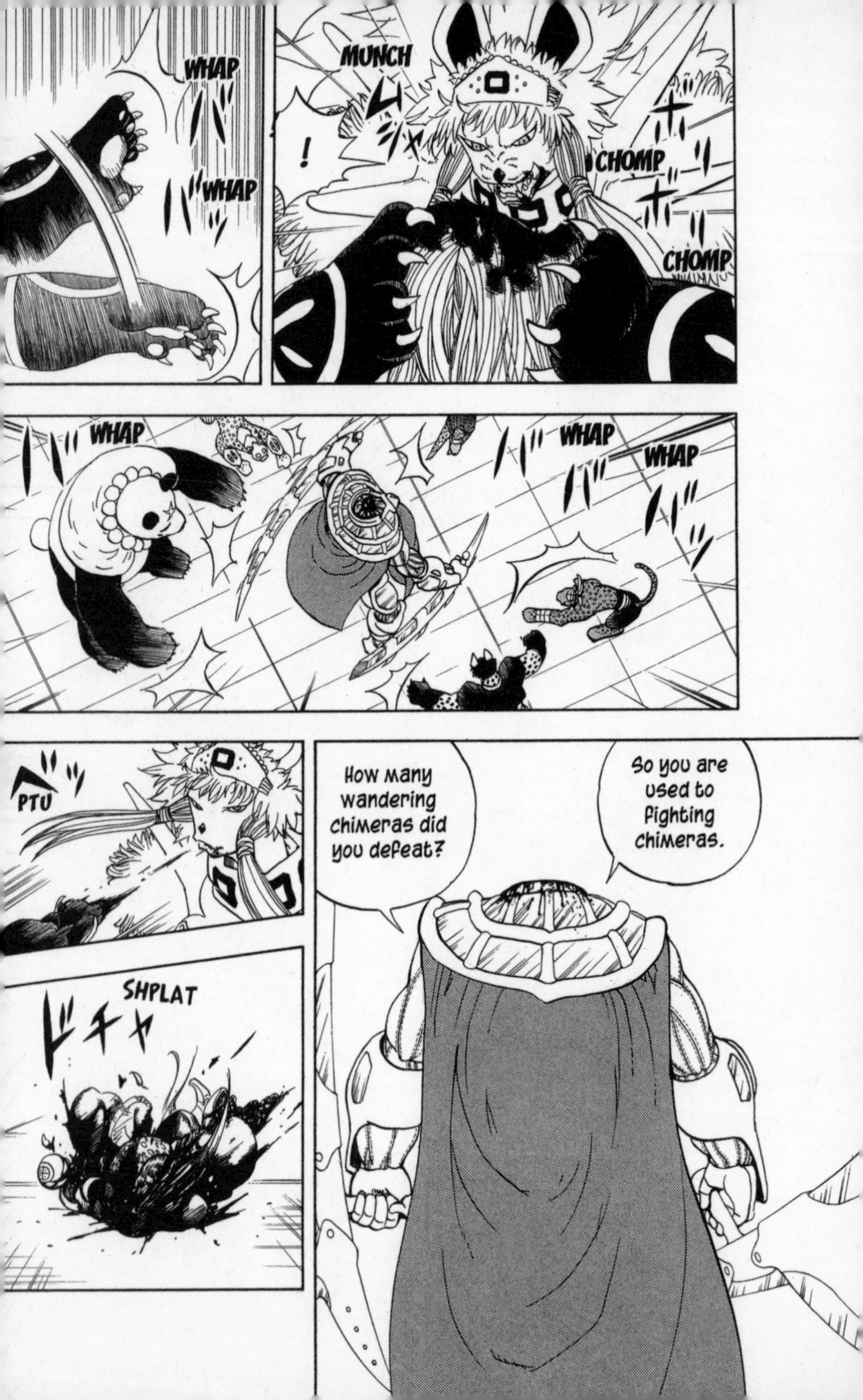
MUNCH
!
CHOMP
CHOMP
WHAP
WHAP
WHAP
WHAP
WHAP
So you are used to fighting chimeras.
How many wandering chimeras did you defeat?
PTU
SHPLAT
ドチャ

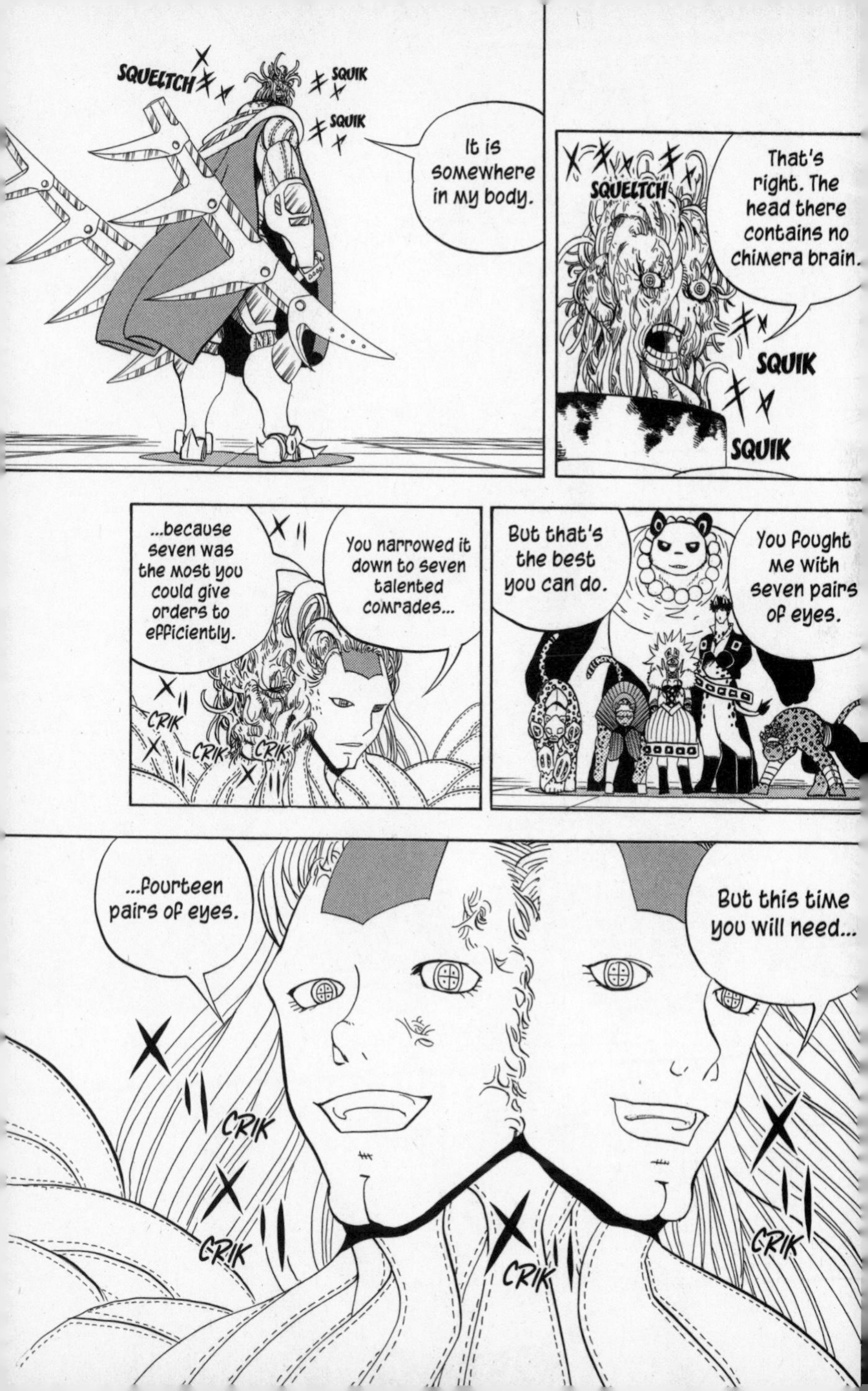
SQUELTCH
That's right. The head there contains no chimera brain.
SQUIK
SQUIK
SQUELTCH
SQUIK
SQUIK
It is somewhere in my body.
You fought me with seven pairs of eyes.
But that's the best you can do.
You narrowed it down to seven talented comrades...
...because seven was the most you could give orders to efficiently.
CRIK
CRIK
CRIK
But this time you will need...
...fourteen pairs of eyes.
CRIK
CRIK
CRIK
CRIK

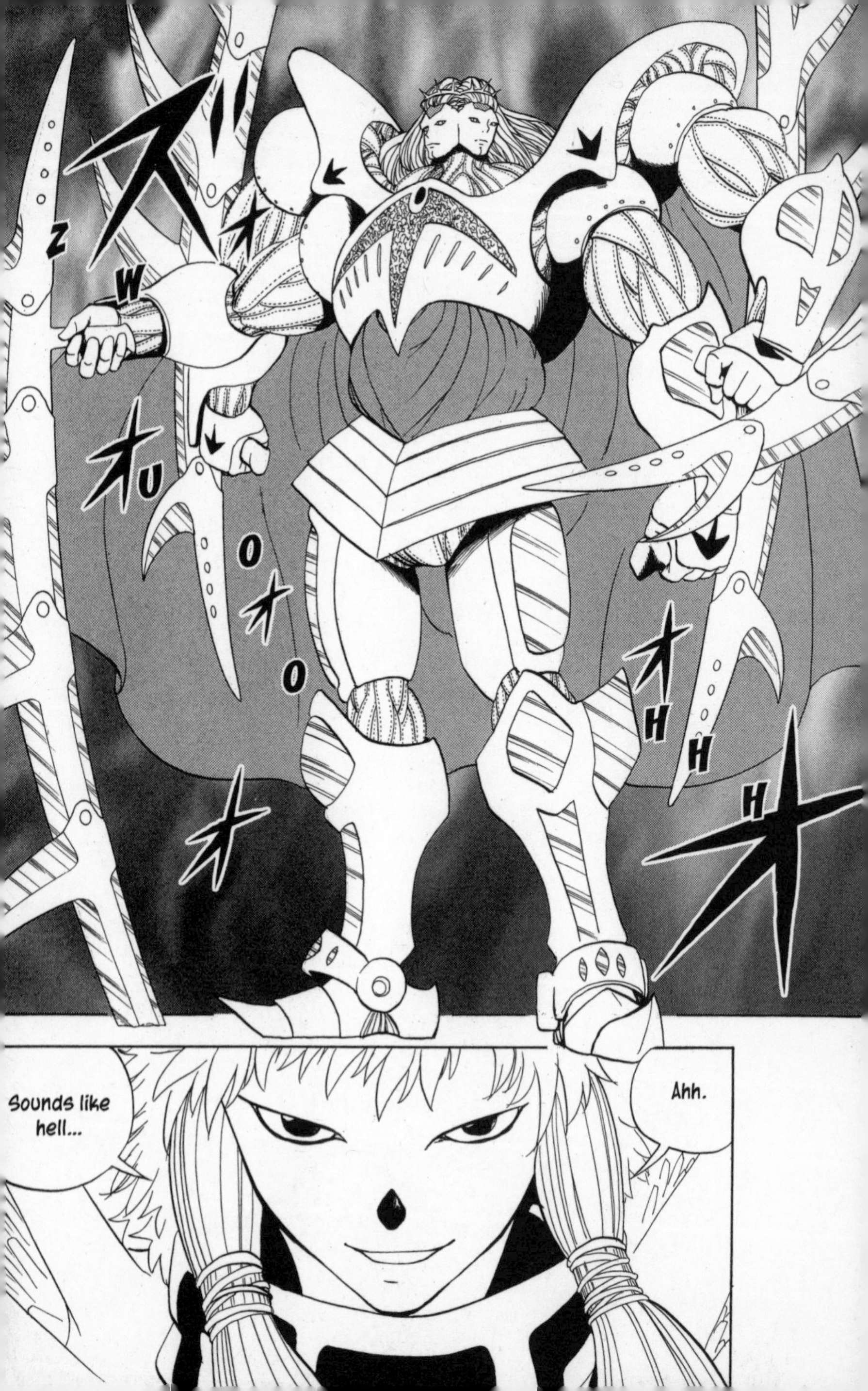
ZWUOOHHH
Ahh.
Sounds like hell...

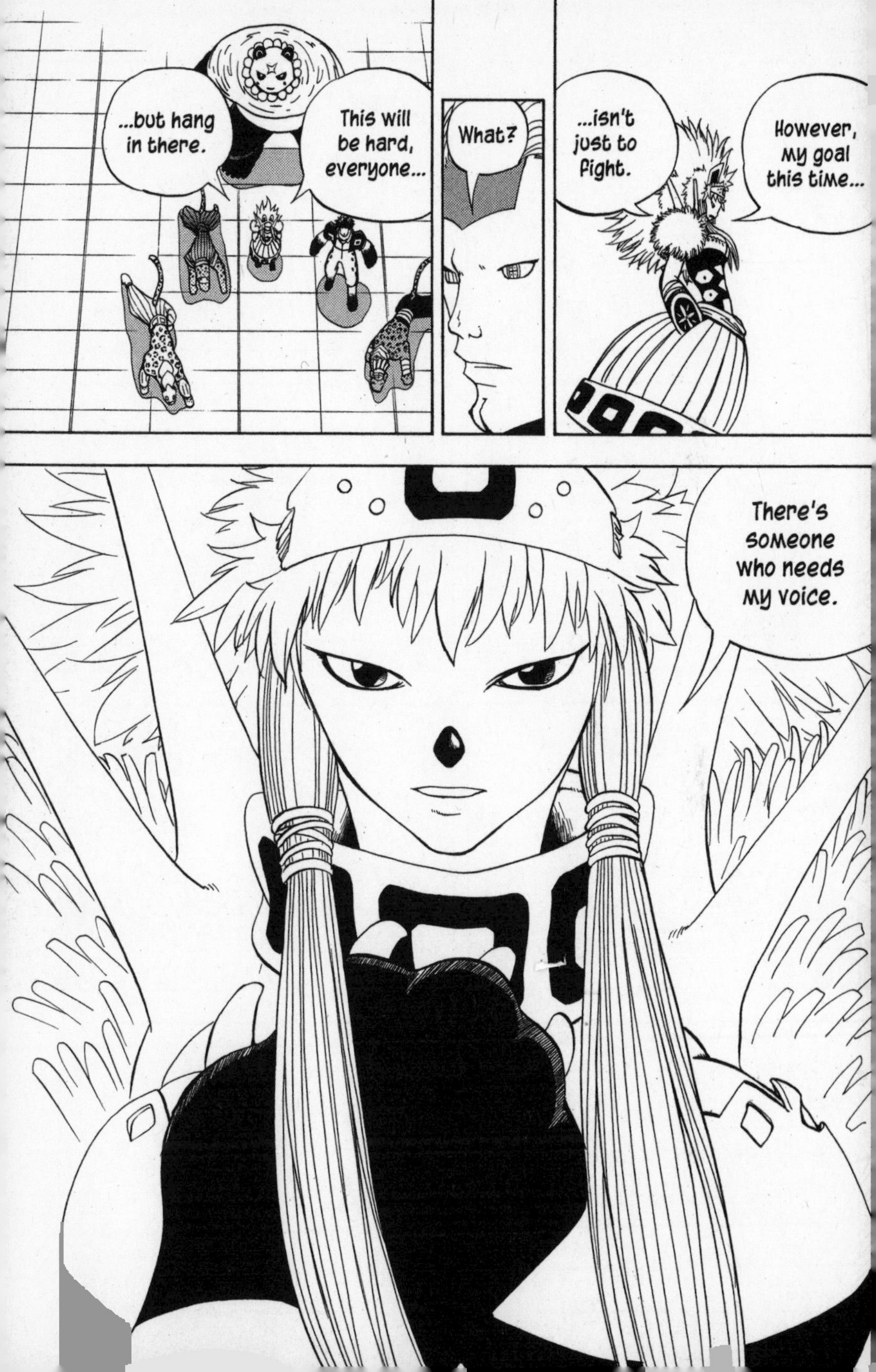
However, my goal this time...
...isn't just to fight.
What?
This will be hard, everyone...
...but hang in there.
There's someone who needs my voice.

Bonus Page

BAP
BOOM
BAP
BABAP
1
K THUNK
K THUNK
K THUNK
K THUNK
2
VWEEE
GAK
GAK
GAK
GAK
3
VWEEE
VWEEE
VWEEE
4
TUG
5
6
THUNK
7
Yep...
SCRITCH
SCRITCH
SCRITCH
SCRITCH
Broke it again...
8

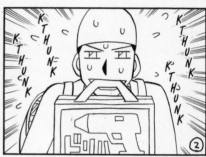

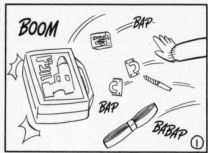

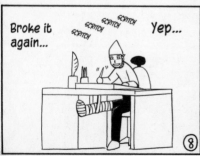

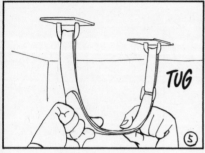

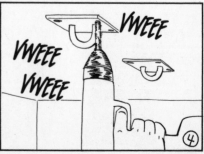

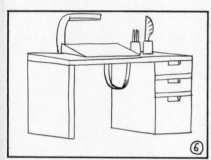

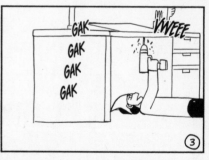

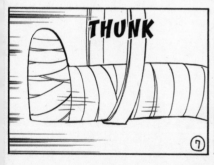

But I didn't miss an issue!
Well, it's my job, after all (sweats).

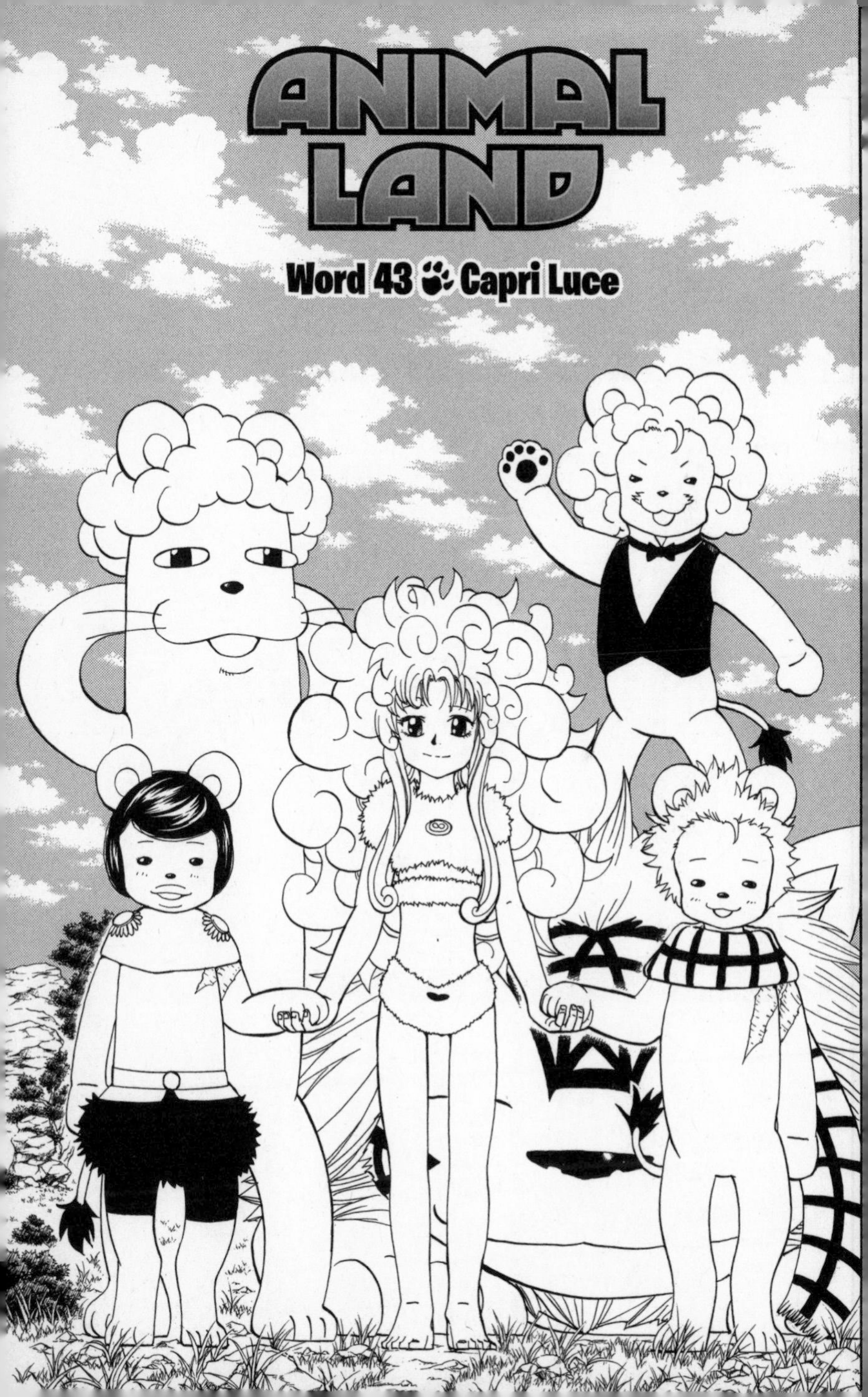
ANIMAL LAND
Word 43 Capri Luce

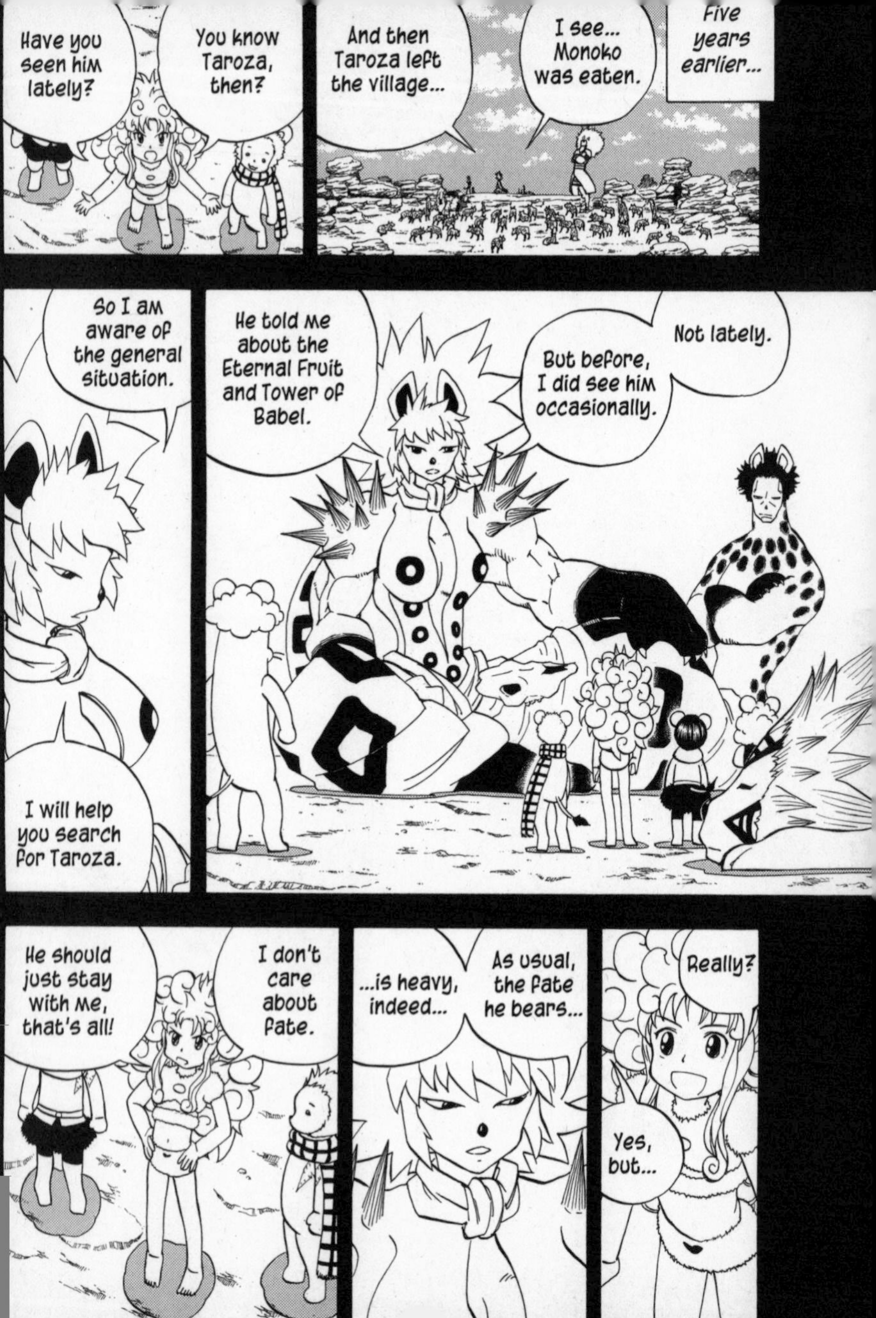
Five years earlier...
I see... Monoko was eaten.
And then Taroza left the village...
You know Taroza, then?
Have you seen him lately?
Not lately.
But before, I did see him occasionally.
He told me about the Eternal Fruit and Tower of Babel.
So I am aware of the general situation.
I will help you search for Taroza.
Really?
Yes, but...
As usual, the fate he bears...
...is heavy, indeed...
I don't care about fate.
He should just stay with me, that's all!

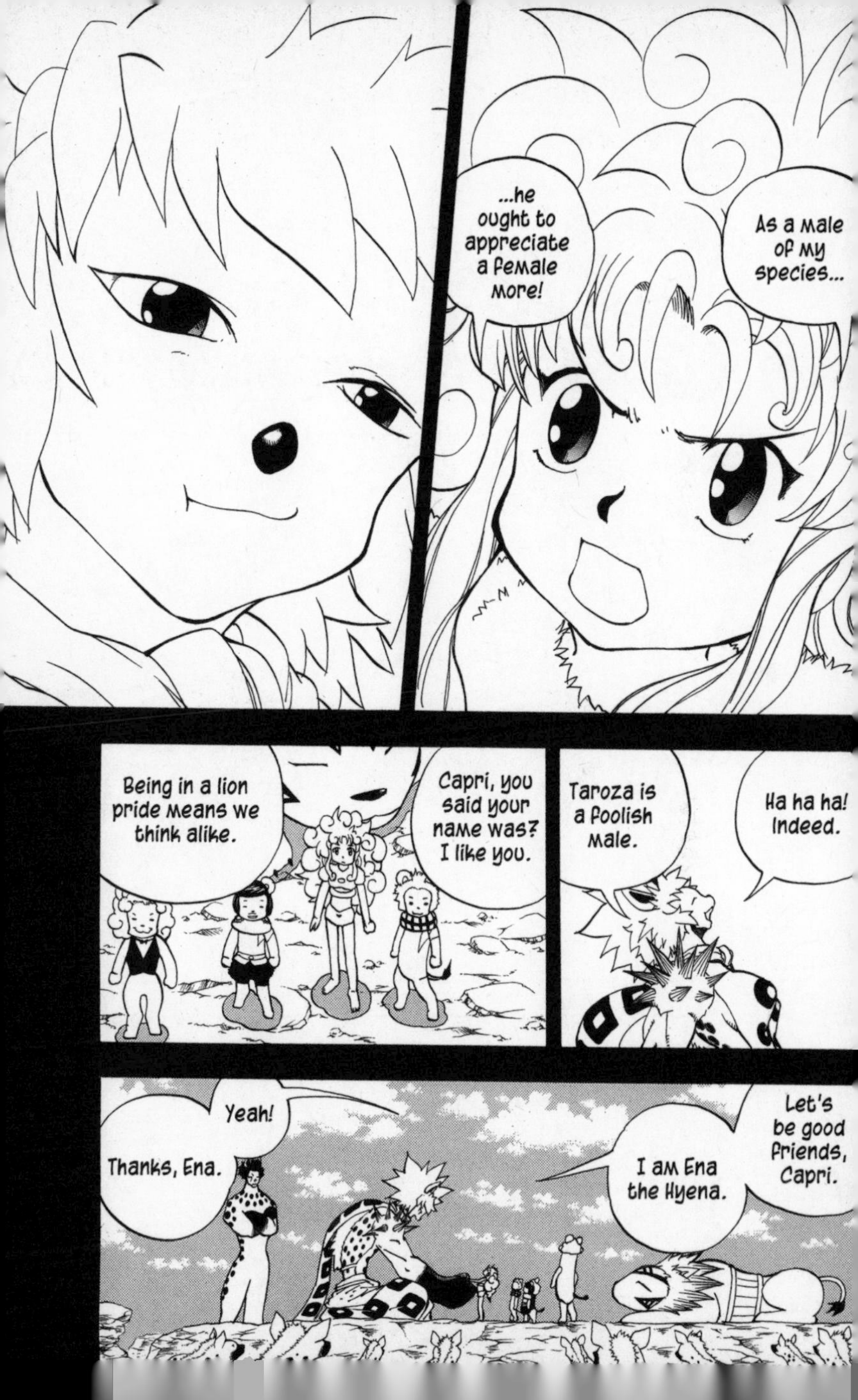
As a male of my species...
...he ought to appreciate a female more!
Ha ha ha! Indeed.
Taroza is a foolish male.
Capri, you said your name was? I like you.
Being in a lion pride means we think alike.
Let's be good friends, Capri.
I am Ena the Hyena.
Yeah!
Thanks, Ena.

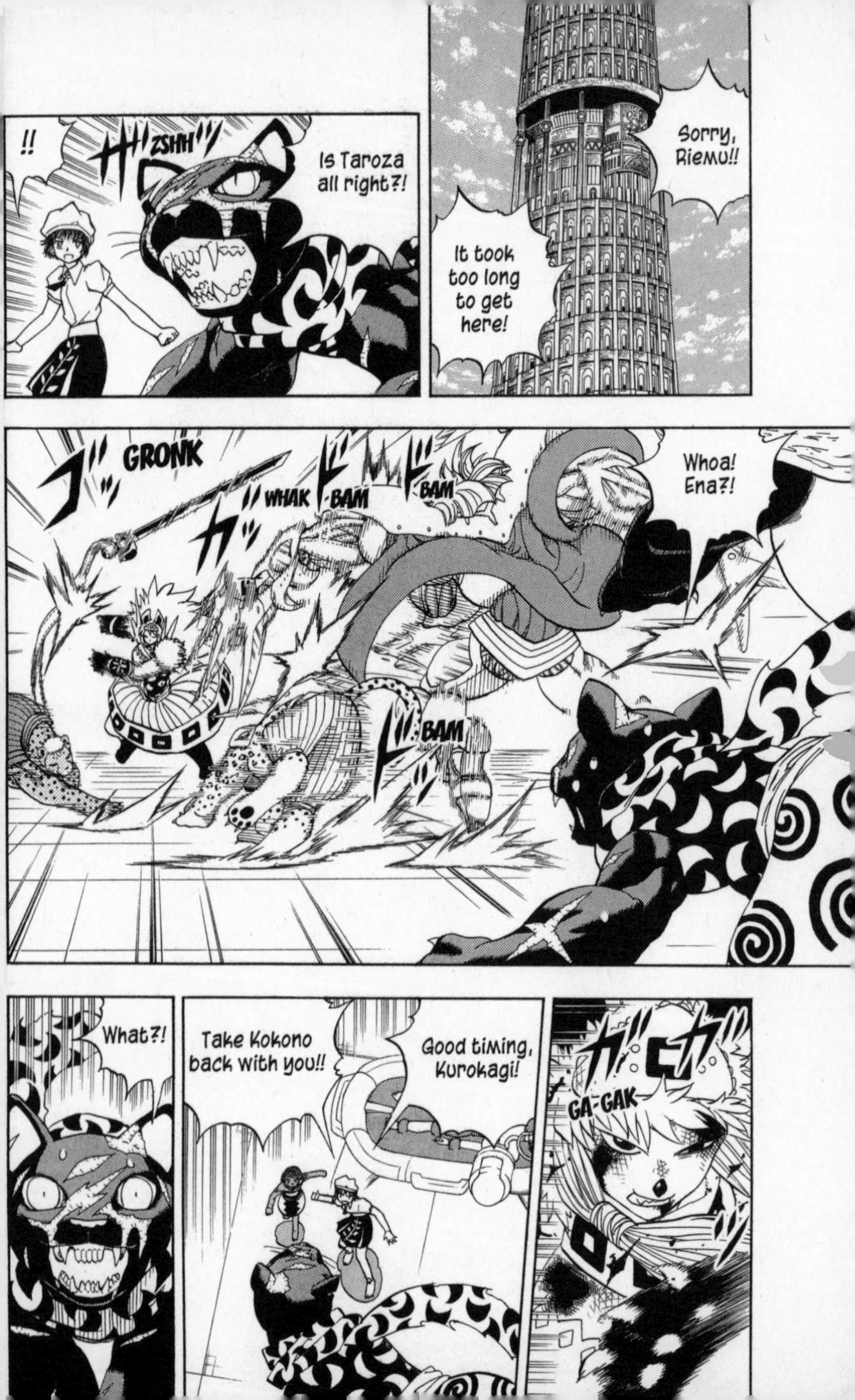
Sorry, Riemu!!
It took too long to get here!
Is Taroza all right?!
ZSHH
!!
Whoa! Ena?!
BAM
WHAK BAM
GRONK
BAM
GA-GAK
Good timing, Kurokagi!
Take Kokono back with you!!
What?!

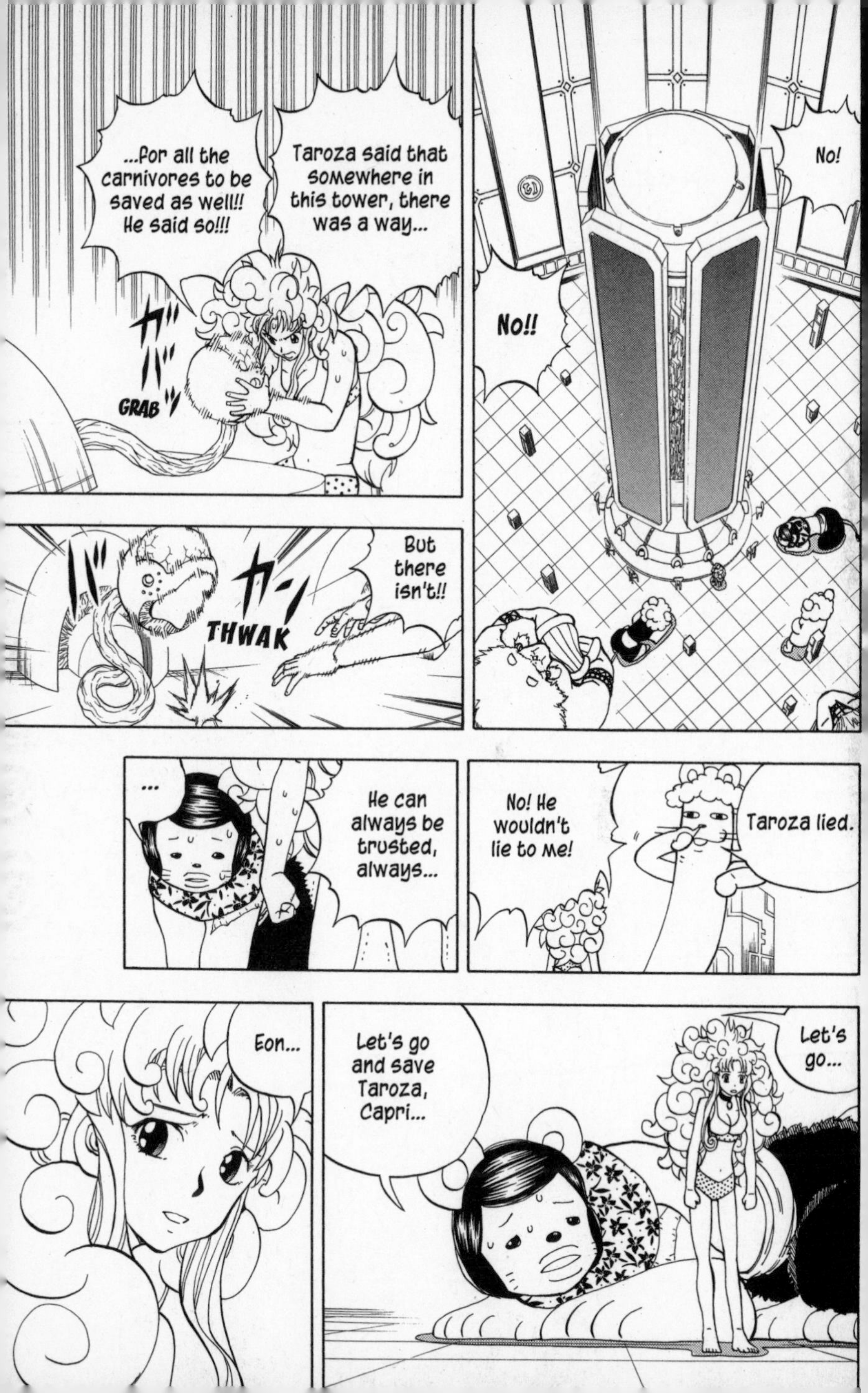
No!
No!!
Taroza said that somewhere in this tower, there was a way...
...for all the carnivores to be saved as well!! He said so!!!
GRAB
But there isn't!!
THWAK
Taroza lied.
No! He wouldn't lie to me!
He can always be trusted, always...
...
Let's go...
Let's go and save Taroza, Capri...
Eon...

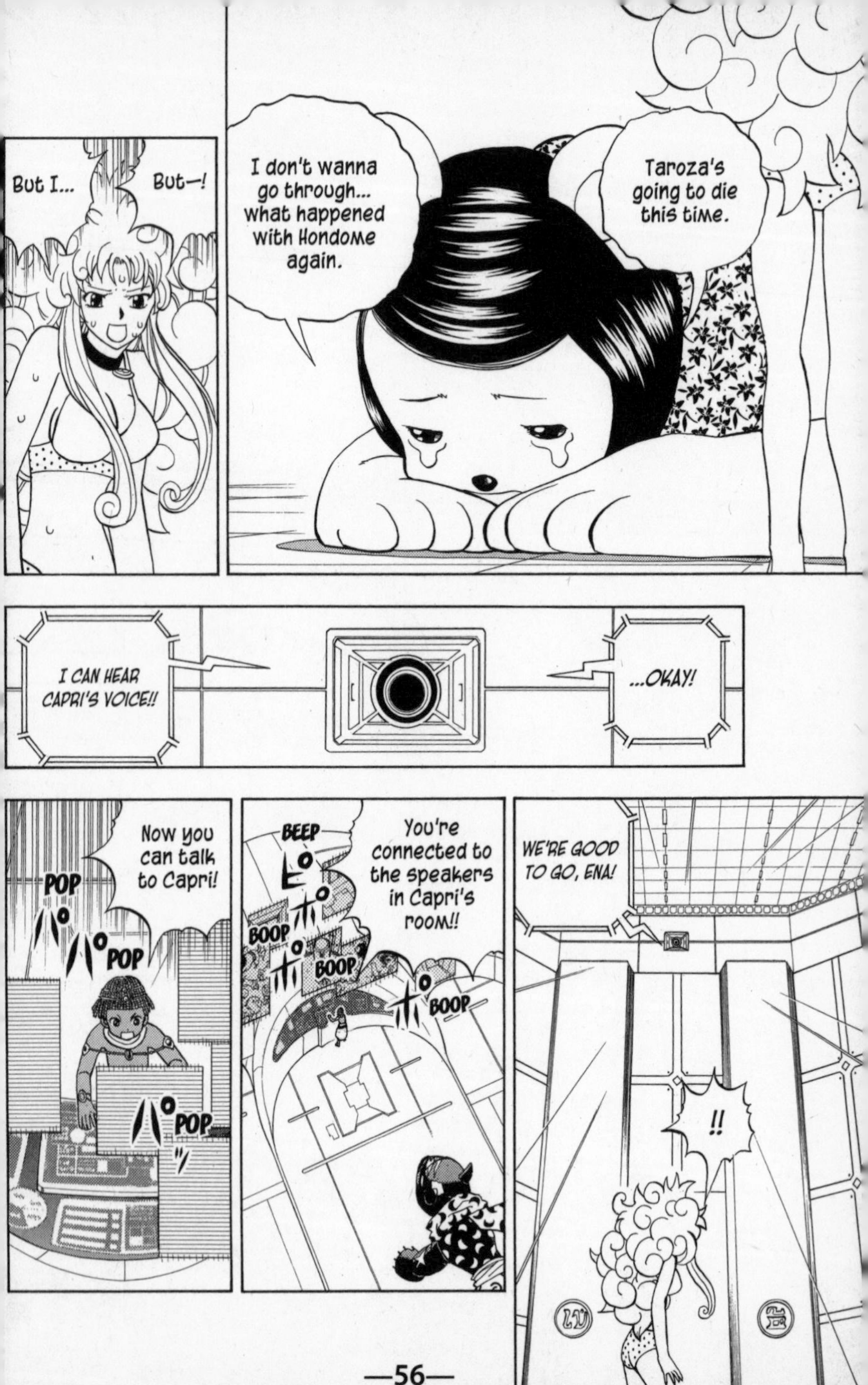

Taroza's going to die this time.
I don't wanna go through... what happened with Hondome again.
But I... But—!
...OKAY!
I CAN HEAR CAPRI'S VOICE!!
WE'RE GOOD TO GO, ENA!
!!
You're connected to the speakers in Capri's room!!
BEEP
BOOP
BOOP
BOOP
Now you can talk to Capri!
POP
POP
POP

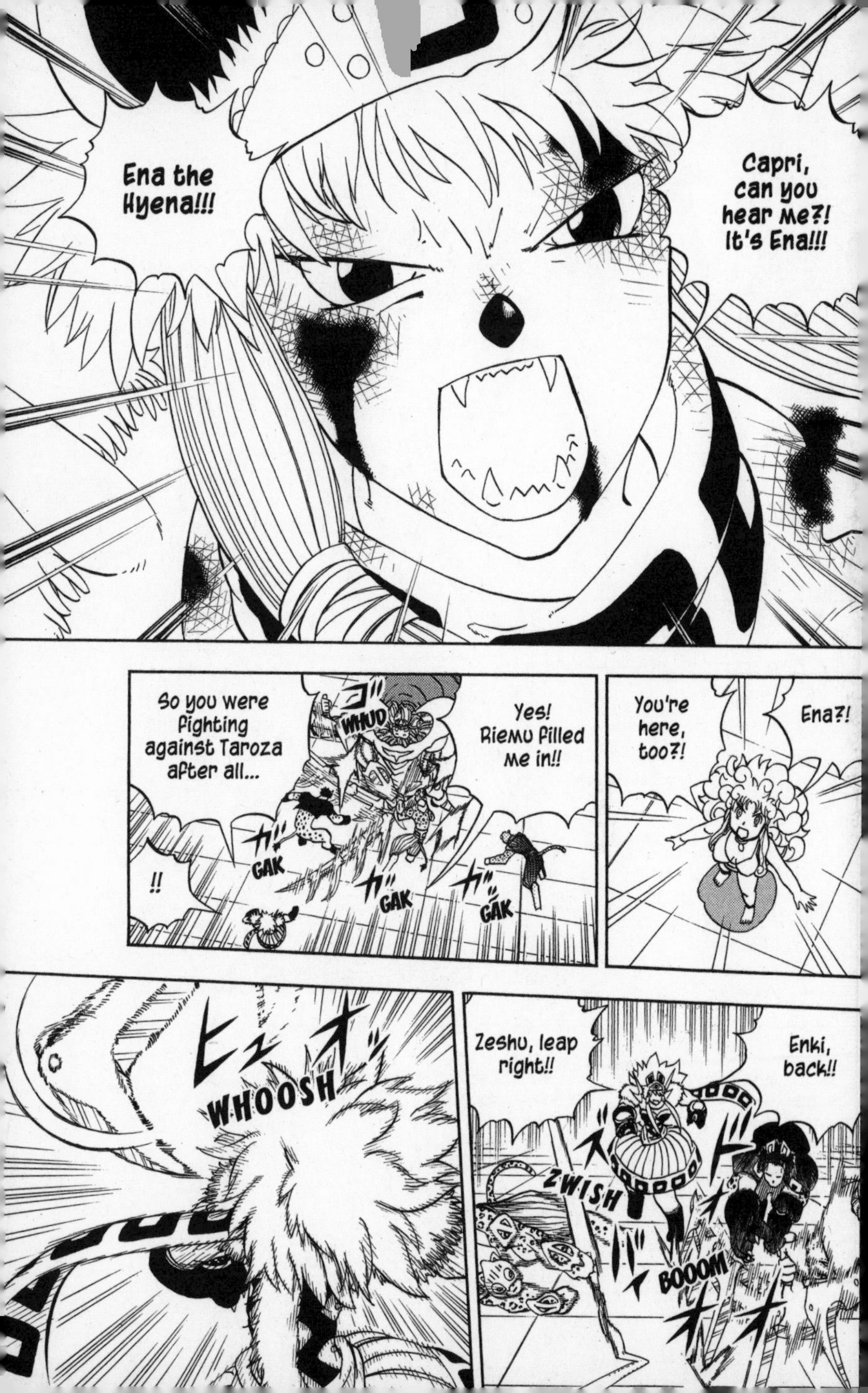
Capri, can you hear me?! It's Ena!!!
Ena the Hyena!!!
Ena?!
You're here, too?!
Yes! Riemu filled me in!!
So you were fighting against Taroza after all...
WHUD
GAK
GAK
GAK
!!
Enki, back!!
Zeshu, leap right!!
ZWISH
BOOOM
WHOOSH

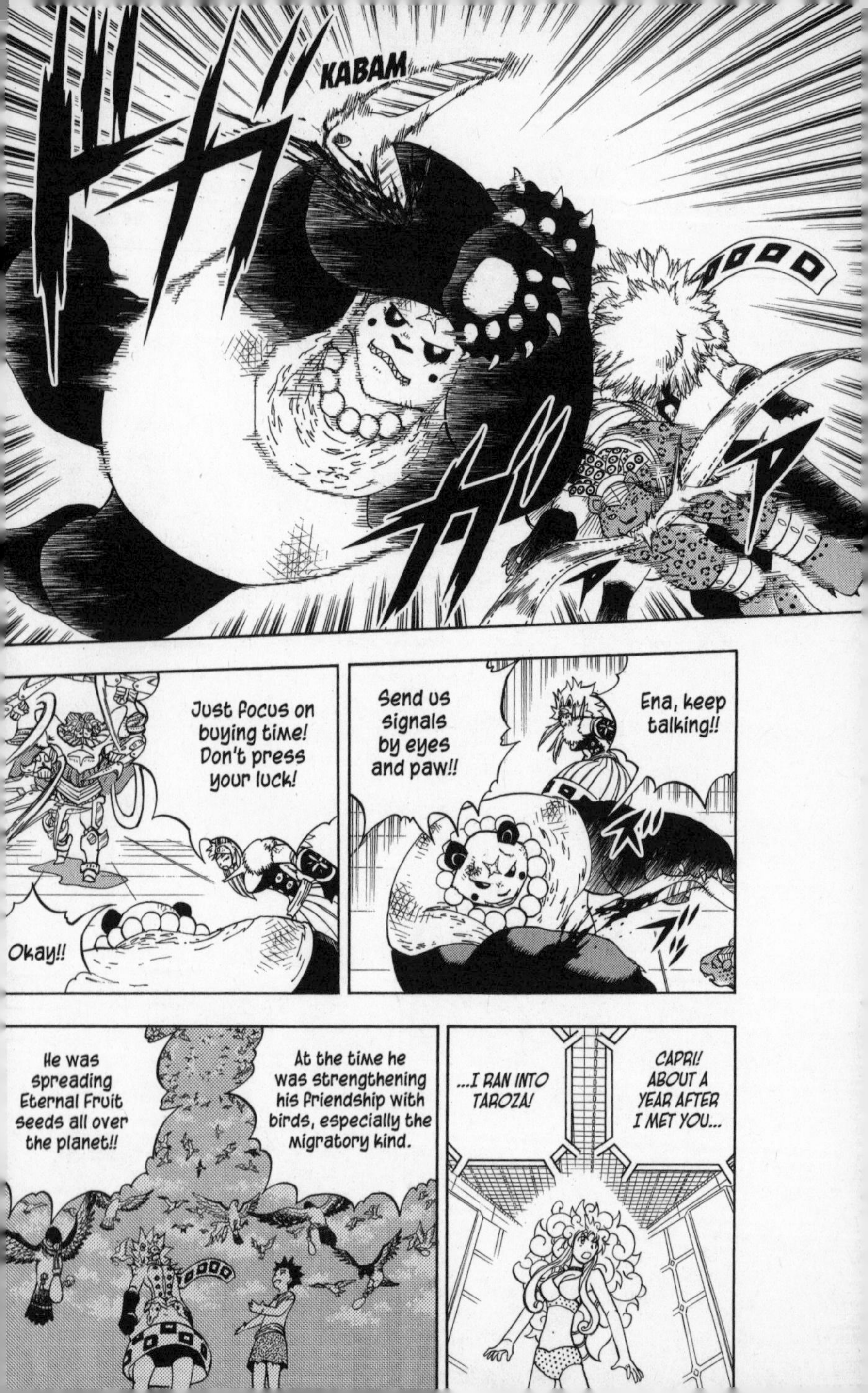
KABAM
Ena, keep talking!!
Send us signals by eyes and paw!!
Just focus on buying time! Don't press your luck!
Okay!!
CAPRI! ABOUT A YEAR AFTER I MET YOU...
...I RAN INTO TAROZA!
At the time he was strengthening his friendship with birds, especially the migratory kind.
He was spreading Eternal Fruit seeds all over the planet!!

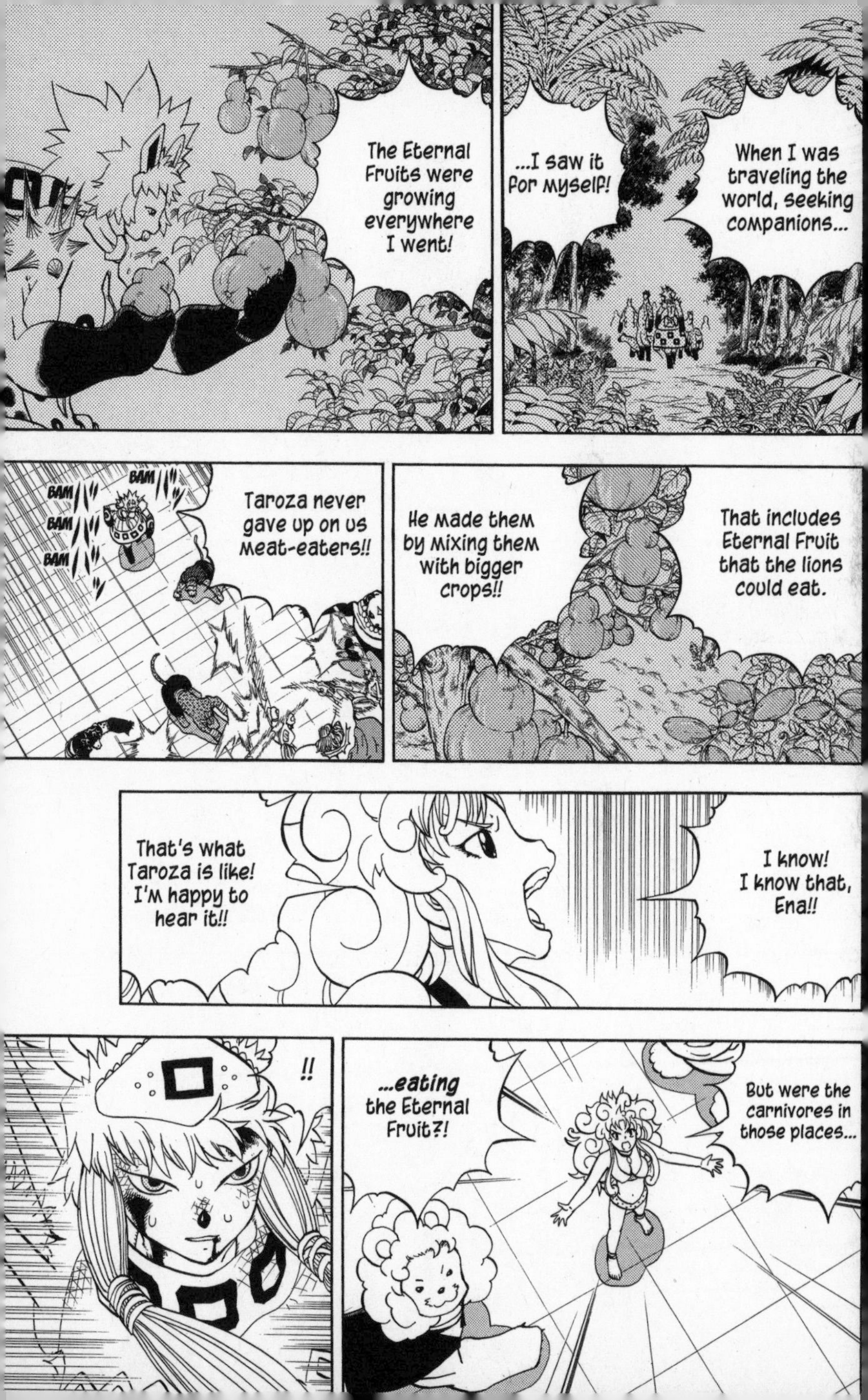
When I was traveling the world, seeking companions...
...I saw it for myself!
The Eternal Fruits were growing everywhere I went!
That includes Eternal Fruit that the lions could eat.
He made them by mixing them with bigger crops!!
Taroza never gave up on us Meat-eaters!!
BAM
BAM
BAM
BAM
I know! I know that, Ena!!
That's what Taroza is like! I'm happy to hear it!!
But were the carnivores in those places...
...eating the Eternal Fruit?!
!!

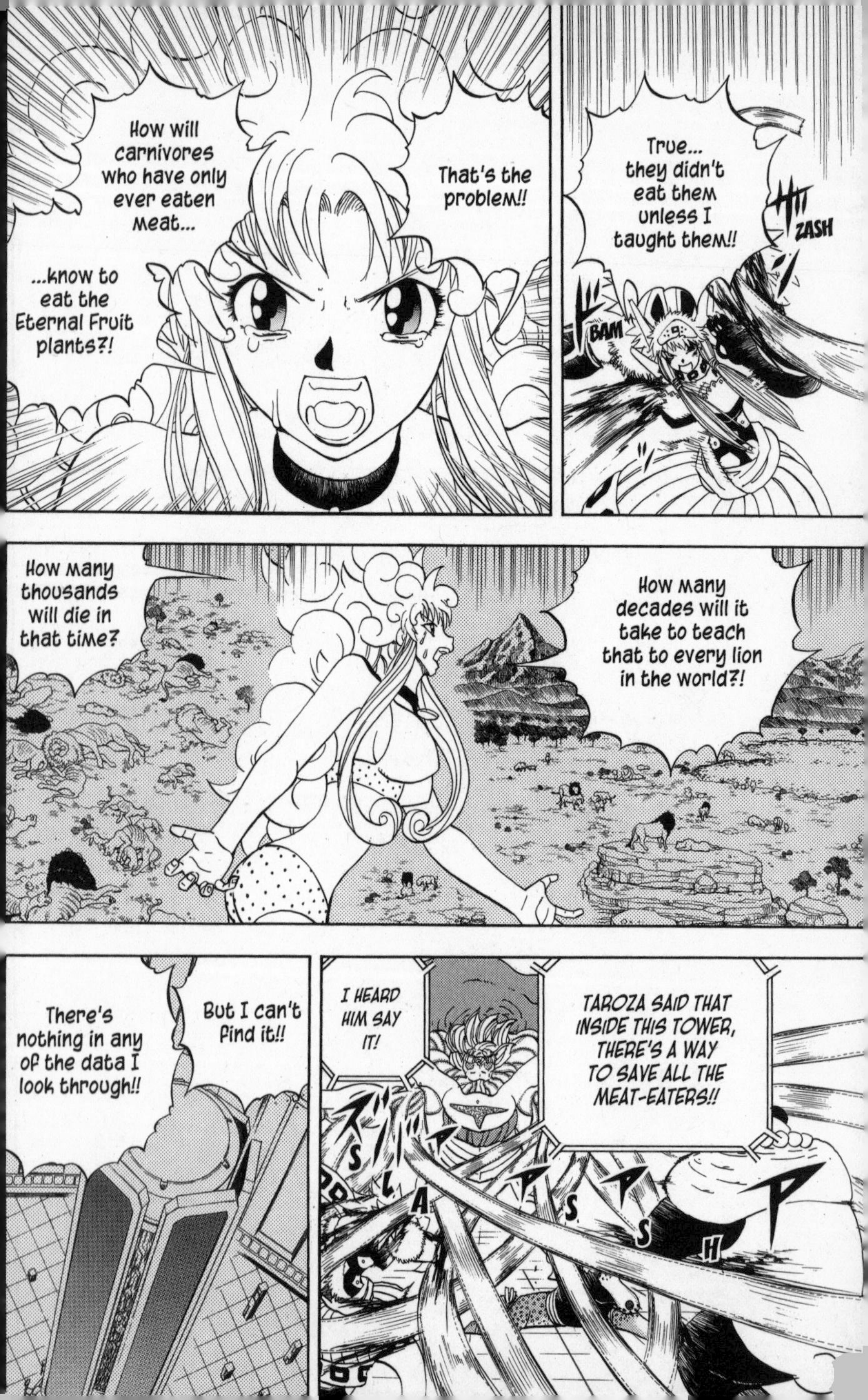
True... they didn't eat them unless I taught them!!
ZASH
BAM
That's the problem!!
How will carnivores who have only ever eaten meat...
...know to eat the Eternal Fruit plants?!
How many decades will it take to teach that to every lion in the world?!
How many thousands will die in that time?
TAROZA SAID THAT INSIDE THIS TOWER, THERE'S A WAY TO SAVE ALL THE MEAT-EATERS!!
I HEARD HIM SAY IT!
But I can't find it!!
There's nothing in any of the data I look through!!

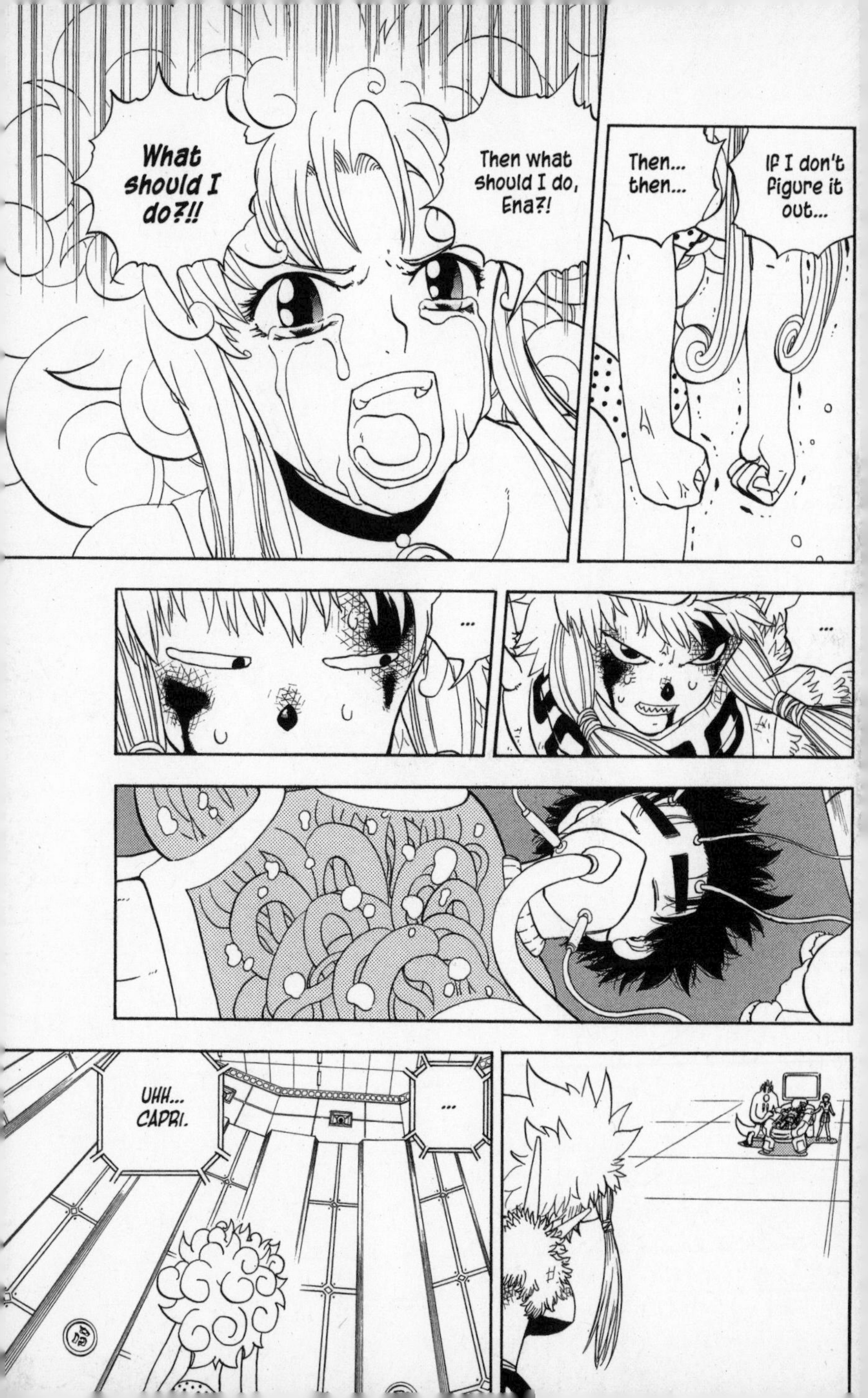
If I don't figure it out...
Then... then...
Then what should I do, Ena?!
What should I do?!!
...
...
...
UHH... CAPRI.

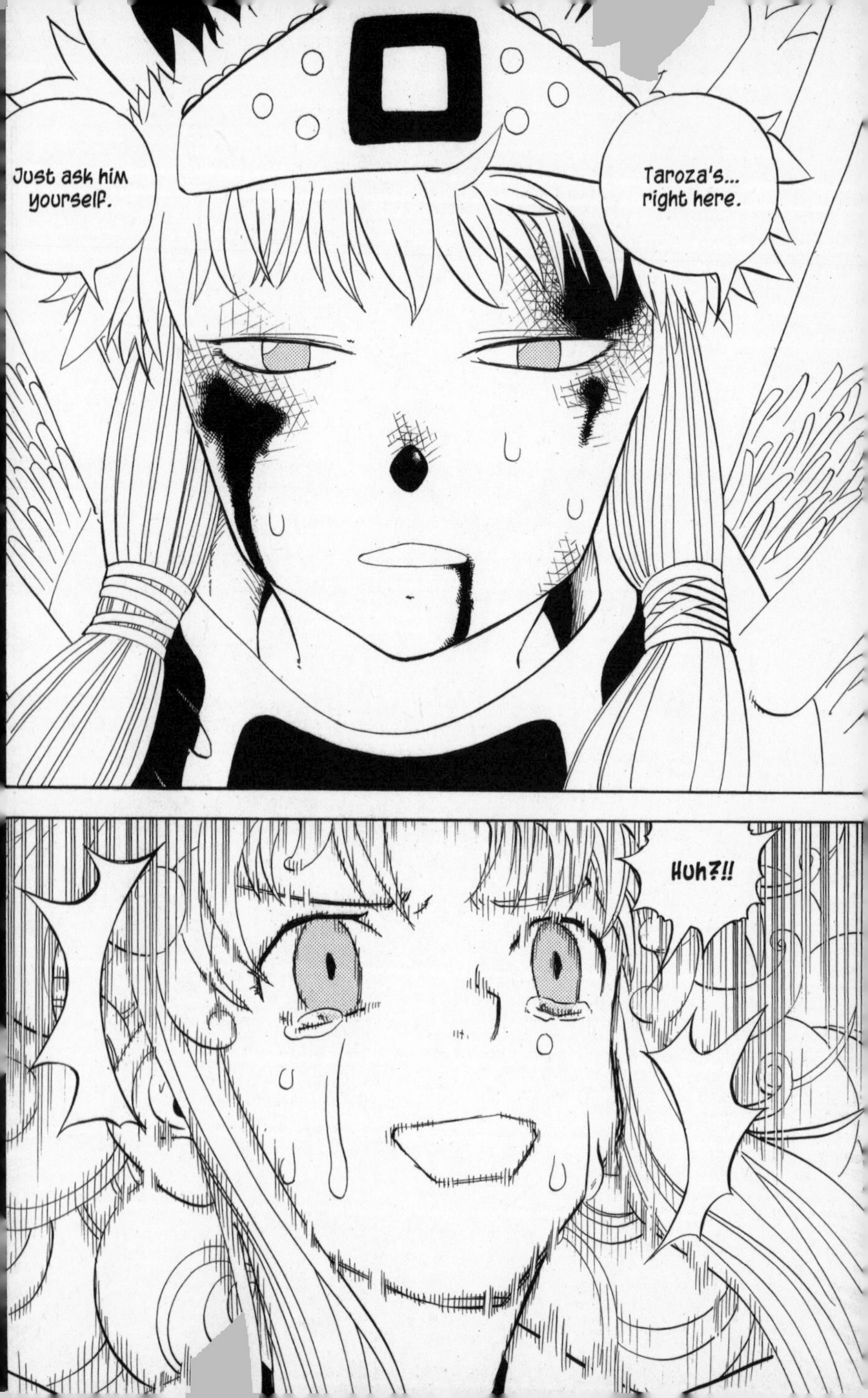
Taroza's... right here.
Just ask him yourself.
Huh?!!

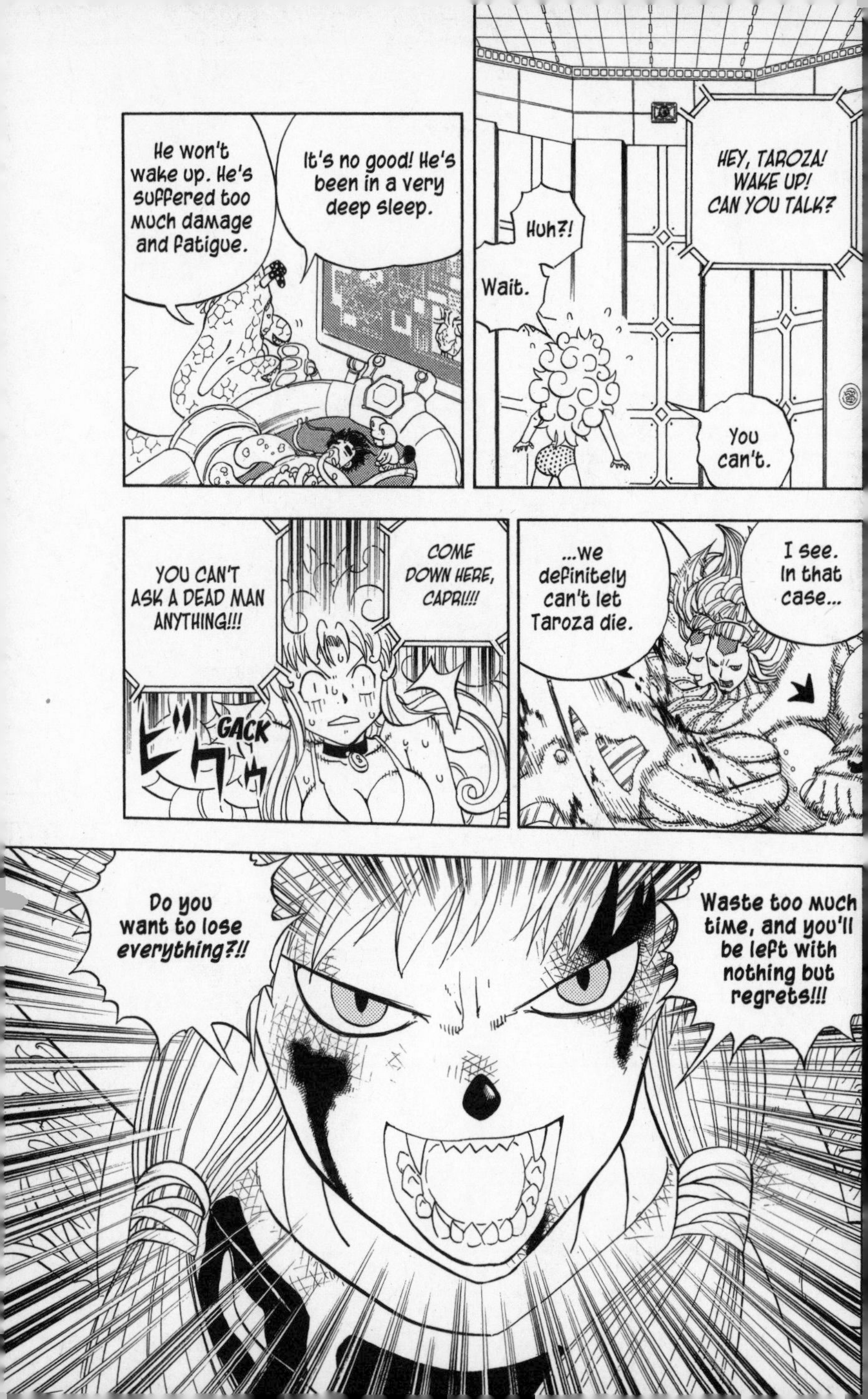
HEY, TAROZA! WAKE UP! CAN YOU TALK?
Huh?!
Wait.
You can't.
It's no good! He's been in a very deep sleep.
He won't wake up. He's suffered too much damage and fatigue.
I see. In that case...
...we definitely can't let Taroza die.
COME DOWN HERE, CAPRI!!!
YOU CAN'T ASK A DEAD MAN ANYTHING!!!
ビクッ
GACK
Waste too much time, and you'll be left with nothing but regrets!!!
Do you want to lose everything?!!

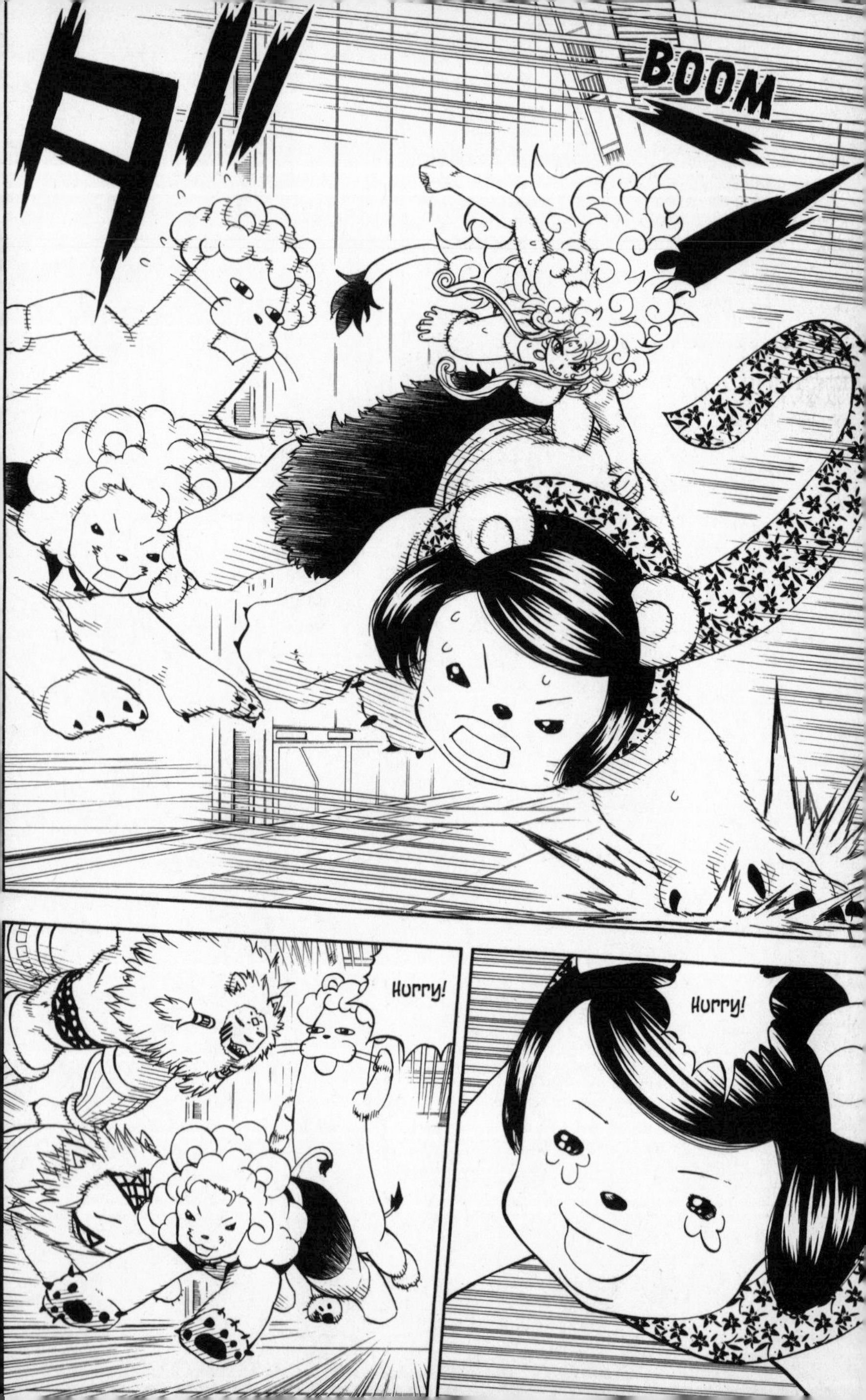
BOOM
ダ
Hurry!
Hurry!

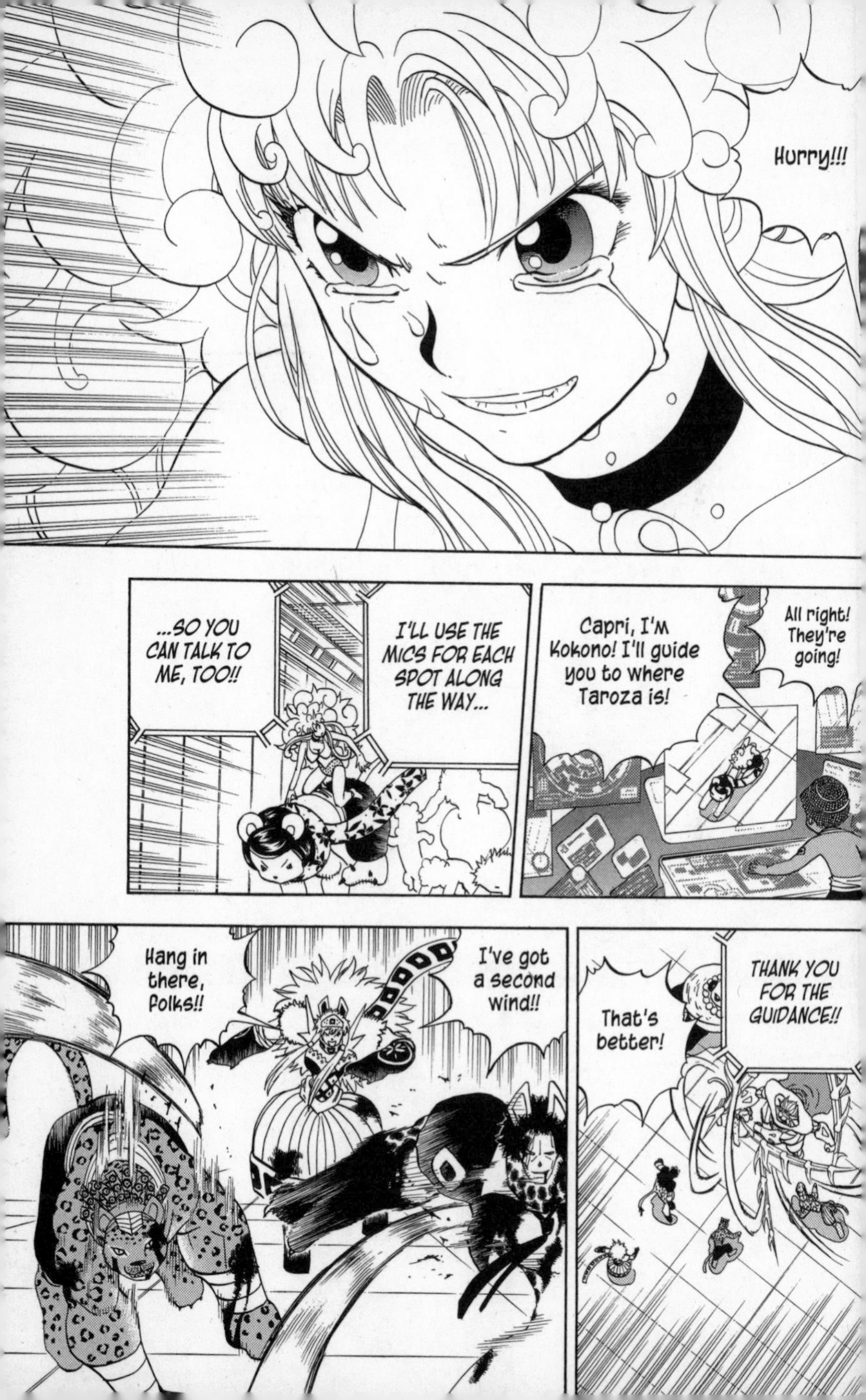
Hurry!!!
All right! They're going!
Capri, I'm Kokono! I'll guide you to where Taroza is!
I'LL USE THE MICS FOR EACH SPOT ALONG THE WAY...
...SO YOU CAN TALK TO ME, TOO!!
THANK YOU FOR THE GUIDANCE!!
That's better!
I've got a second wind!!
Hang in there, folks!!

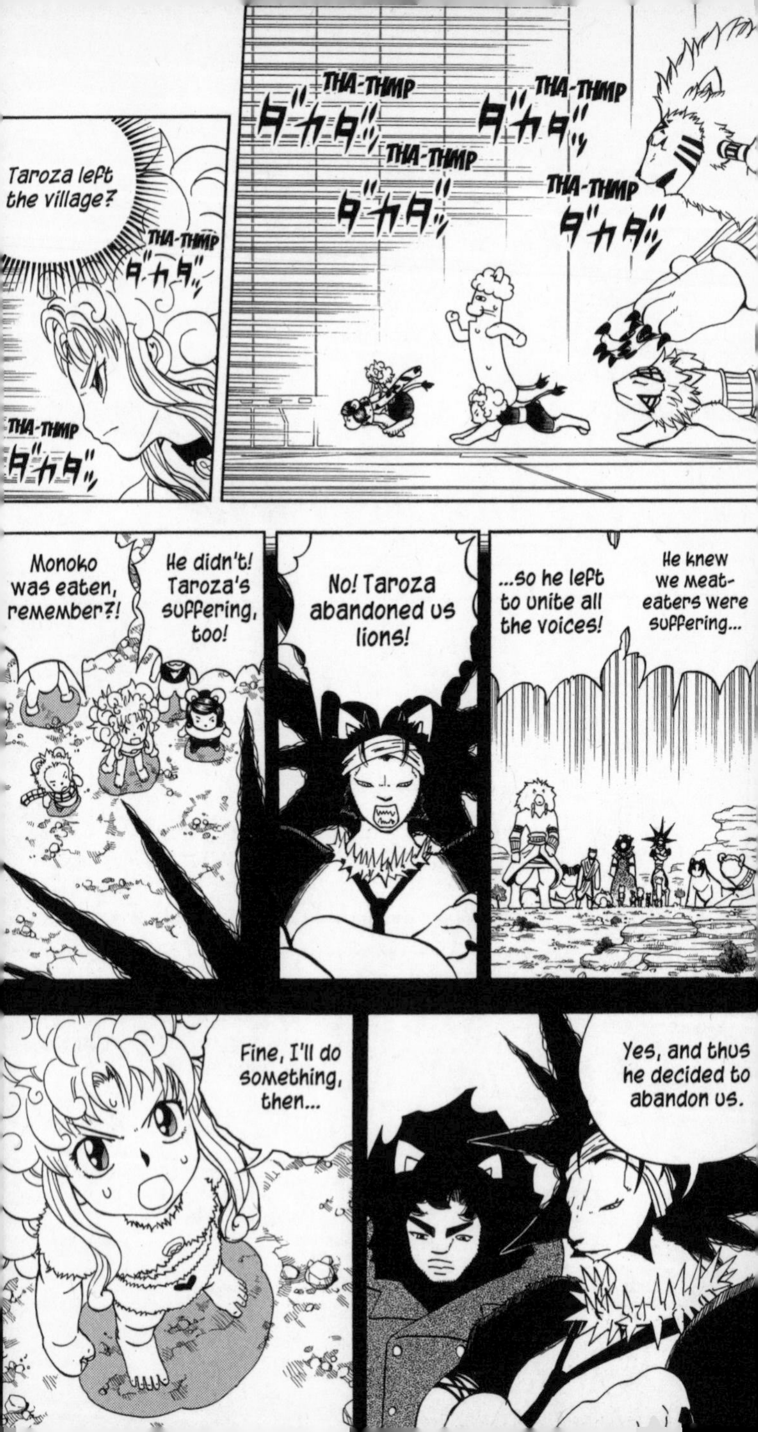
THA-THMP
ダカダッ
THA-THMP
ダカダッ
THA-THMP
ダカダッ
THA-THMP
ダカダッ
Taroza left the village?
THA-THMP
ダカダッ
THA-THMP
ダカダッ
He knew we meat-eaters were suffering...
...so he left to unite all the voices!
No! Taroza abandoned us lions!
He didn't! Taroza's suffering, too!
Monoko was eaten, remember?!
Yes, and thus he decided to abandon us.
Fine, I'll do something, then...

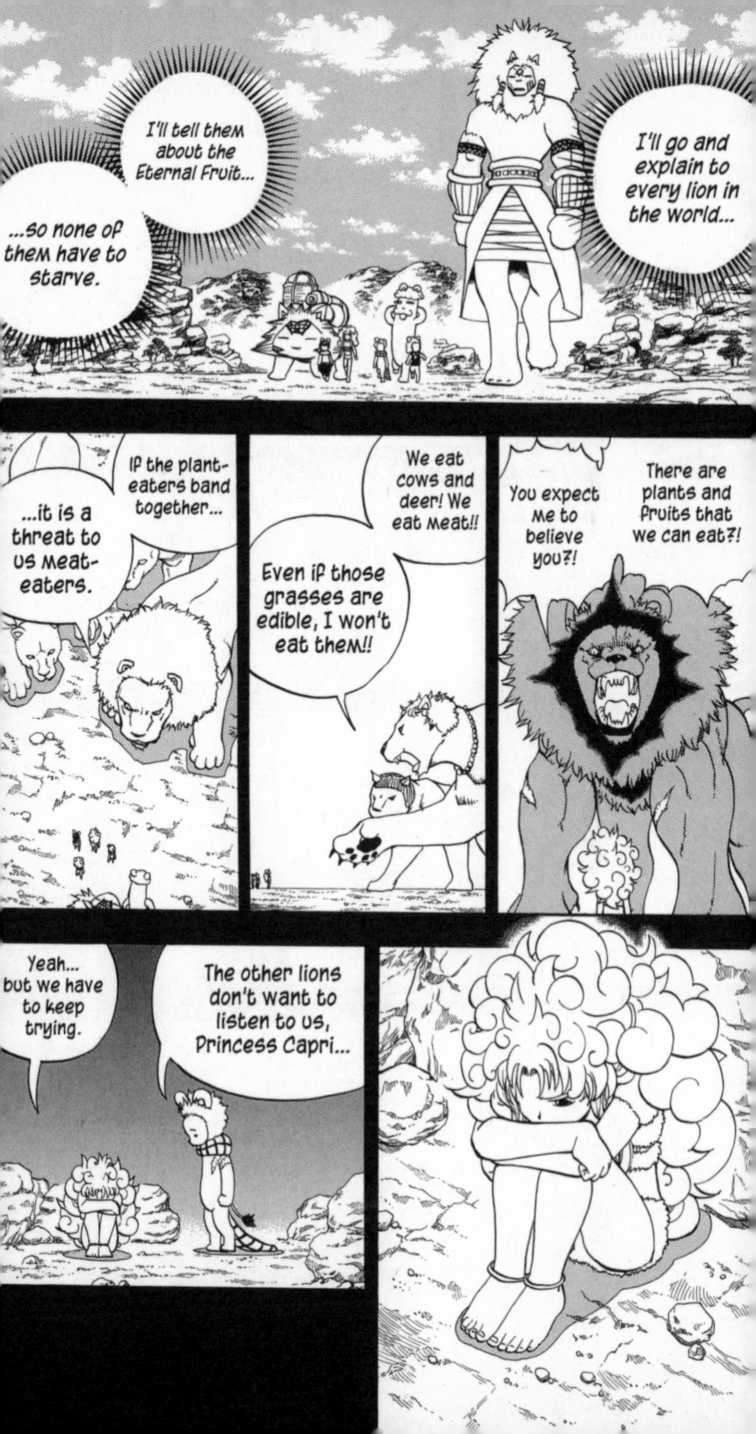
I'll go and explain to every lion in the world...
I'll tell them about the Eternal Fruit...
...so none of them have to starve.
There are plants and fruits that we can eat?!
You expect me to believe you?!
We eat cows and deer! We eat meat!!
Even if those grasses are edible, I won't eat them!!
If the plant-eaters band together...
...it is a threat to us meat-eaters.
The other lions don't want to listen to us, Princess Capri...
Yeah... but we have to keep trying.

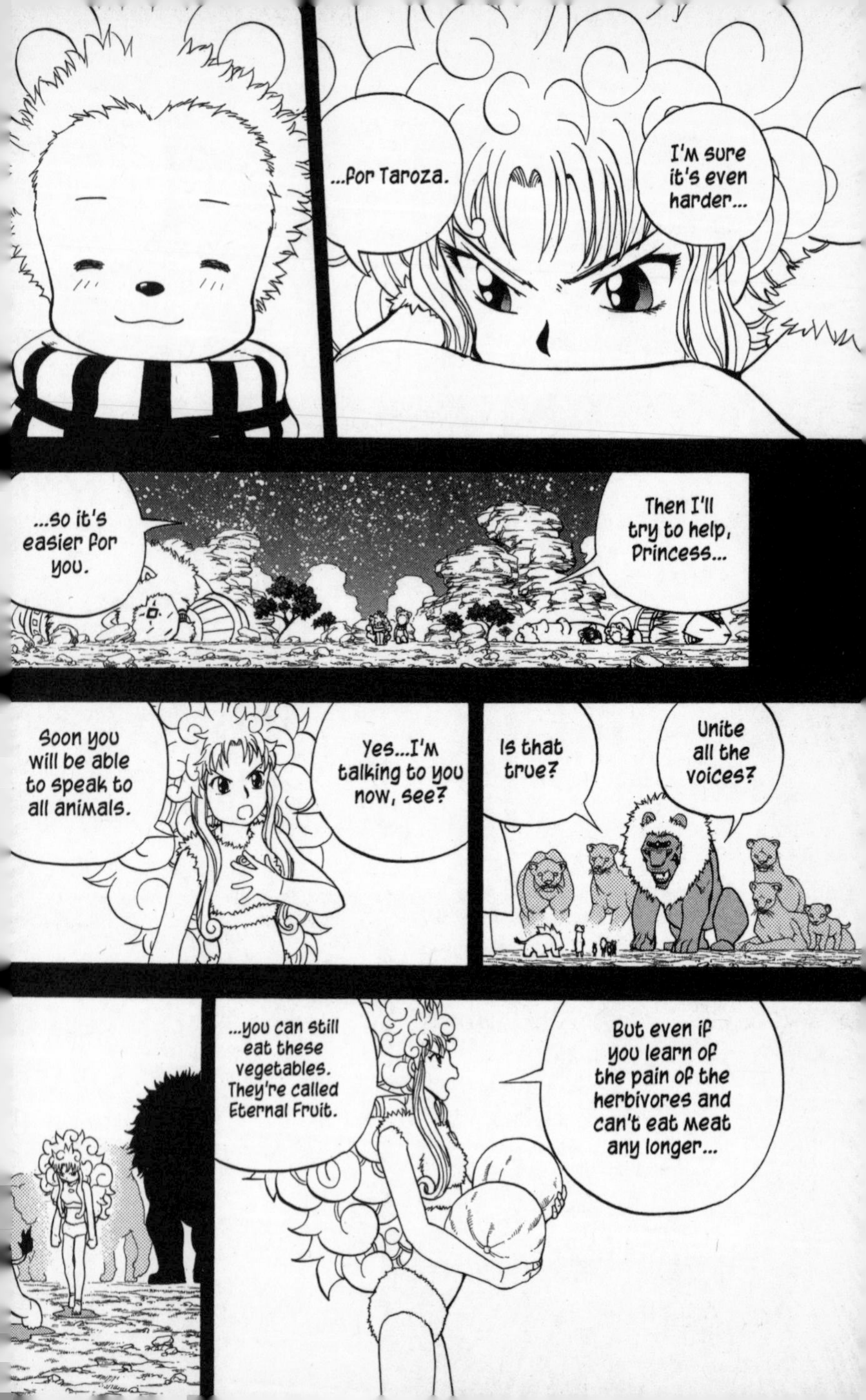
I'm sure it's even harder...
...for Taroza.
Then I'll try to help, Princess...
...so it's easier for you.
Unite all the voices?
Is that true?
Yes...I'm talking to you now, see?
Soon you will be able to speak to all animals.
But even if you learn of the pain of the herbivores and can't eat meat any longer...
...you can still eat these vegetables. They're called Eternal Fruit.

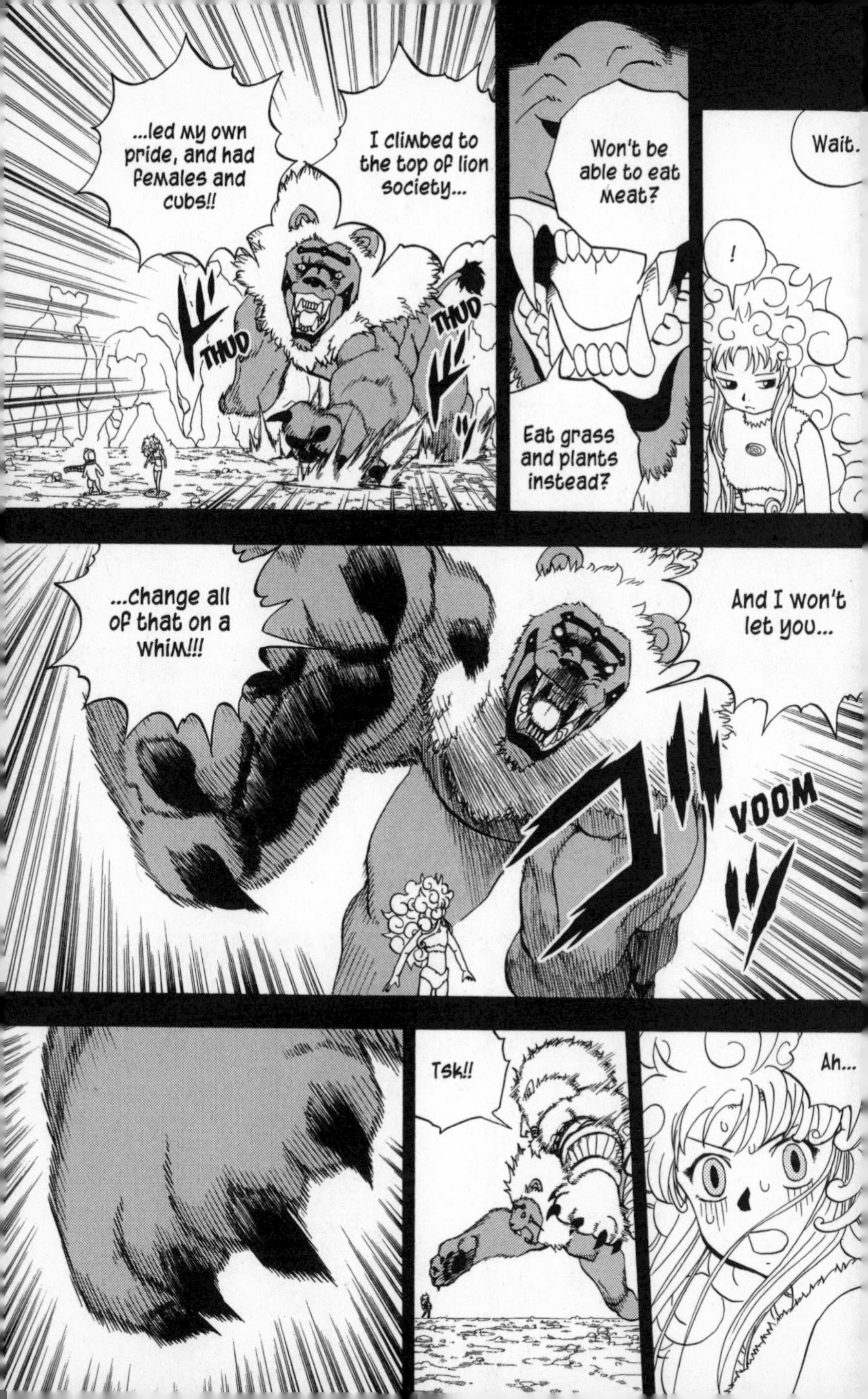
Wait.
!
Won't be able to eat meat?
Eat grass and plants instead?
I climbed to the top of lion society...
...led my own pride, and had females and cubs!!
THUD
THUD
And I won't let you...
VOOM
...change all of that on a whim!!!
Ah...
Tsk!!

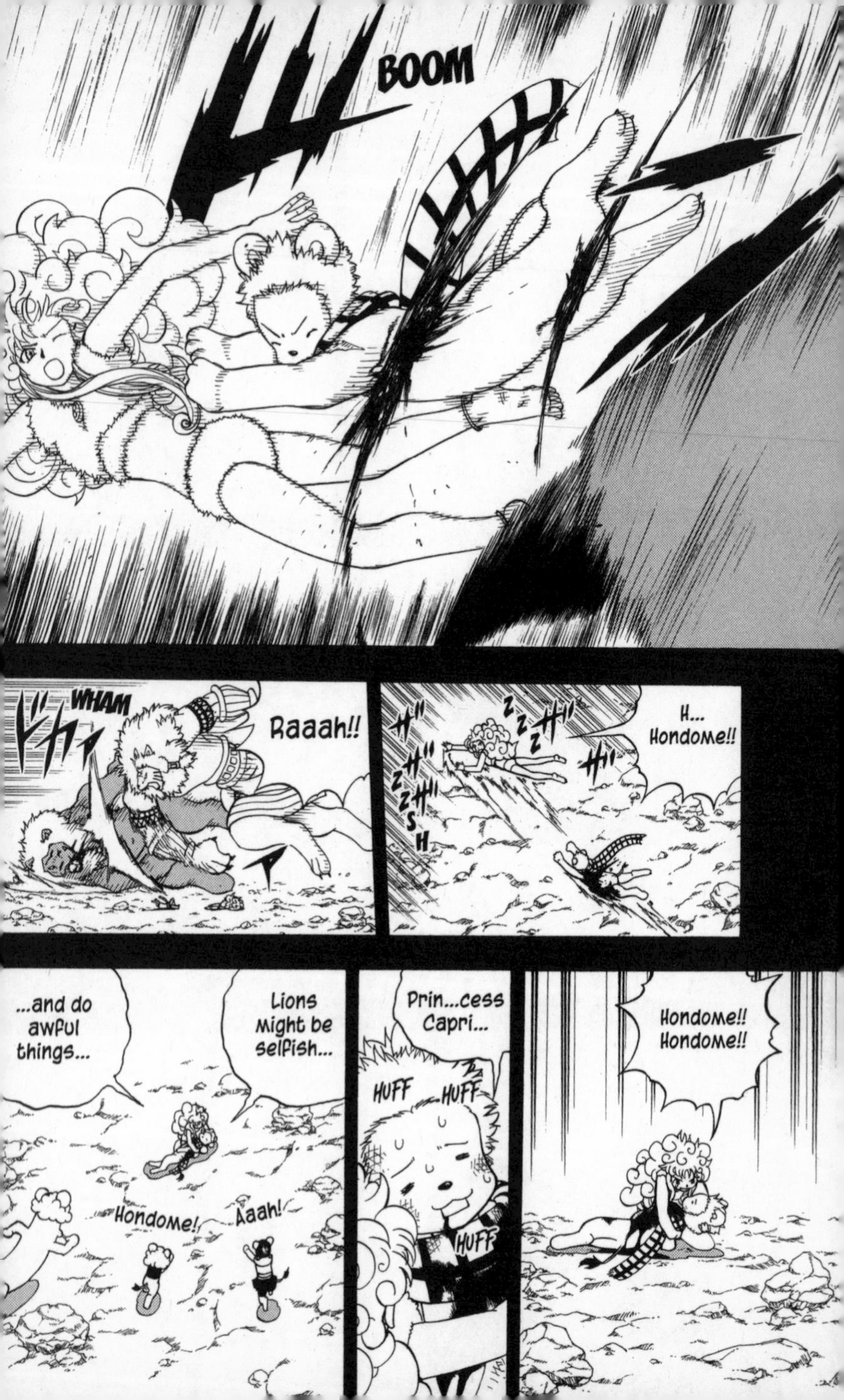

BOOM
ZZZ
ZZSH
H... Hondome!!
WHAM
Raaah!!
Hondome!! Hondome!!
Prin...cess Capri...
HUFF
HUFF
HUFF
Lions might be selfish...
...and do awful things...
Aaah!
Hondome!

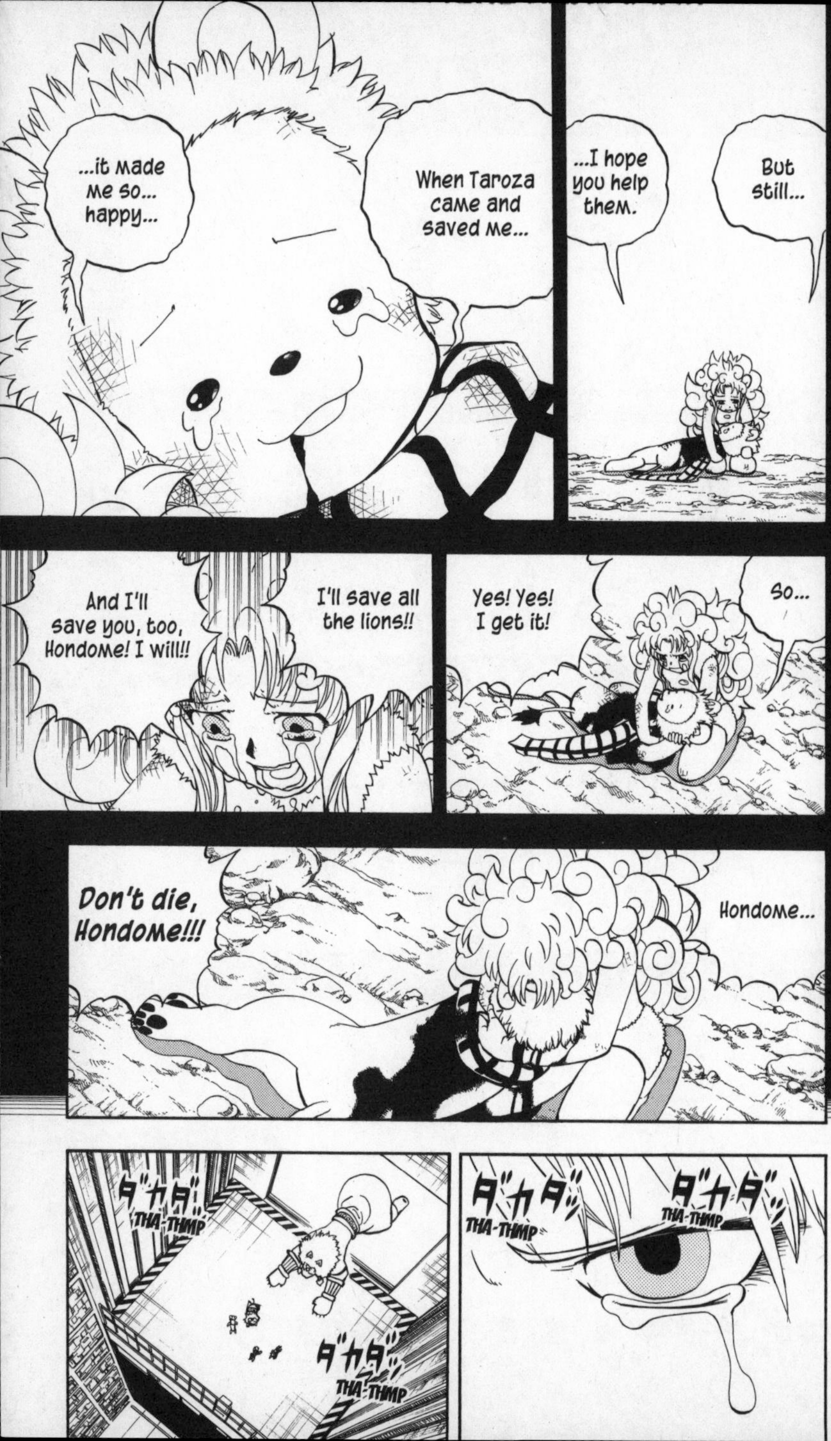
But still...
...I hope you help them.
When Taroza came and saved me...
...it made me so... happy...
So...
Yes! Yes! I get it!
I'll save all the lions!!
And I'll save you, too, Hondome! I will!!
Hondome...
Don't die, Hondome!!!
ダカダッ
THA-THMP
ダカダッ
THA-THMP
ダカダ
THA-THMP
ダカダ
THA-THMP

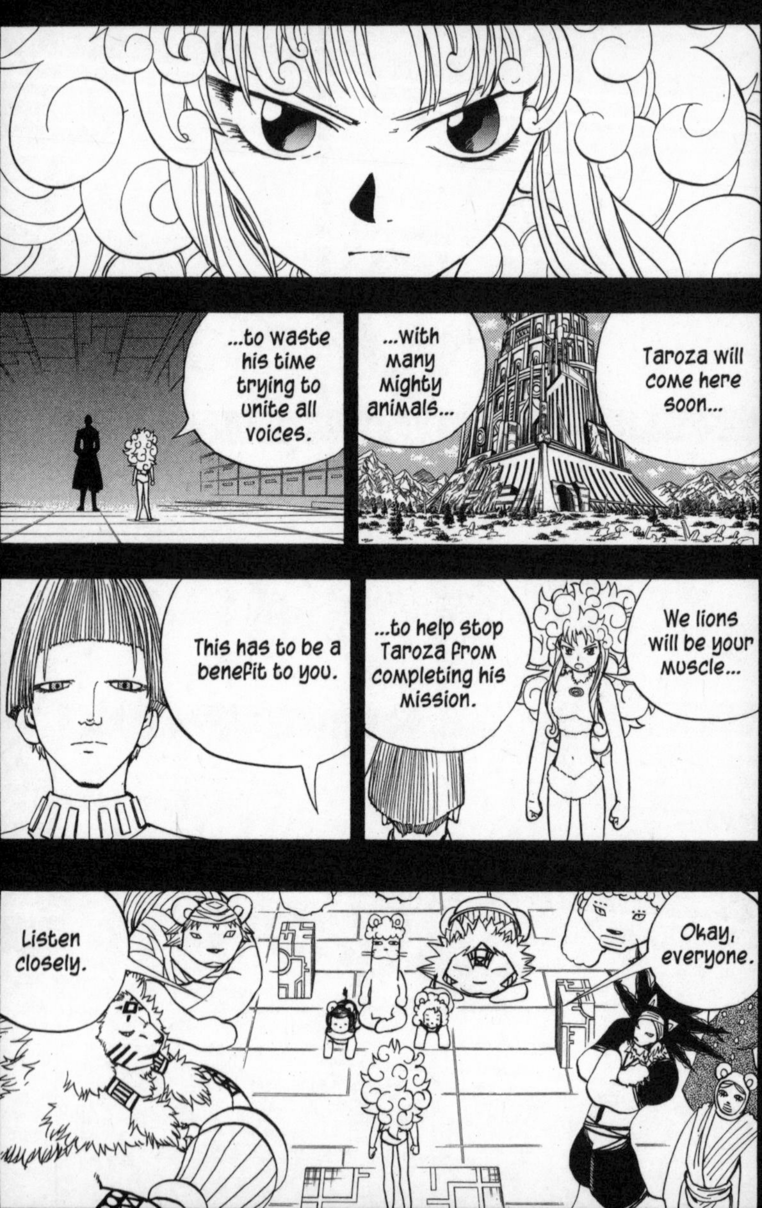
Taroza will come here soon...
...with many mighty animals...
...to waste his time trying to unite all voices.
We lions will be your muscle...
...to help stop Taroza from completing his mission.
This has to be a benefit to you.
Okay, everyone.
Listen closely.

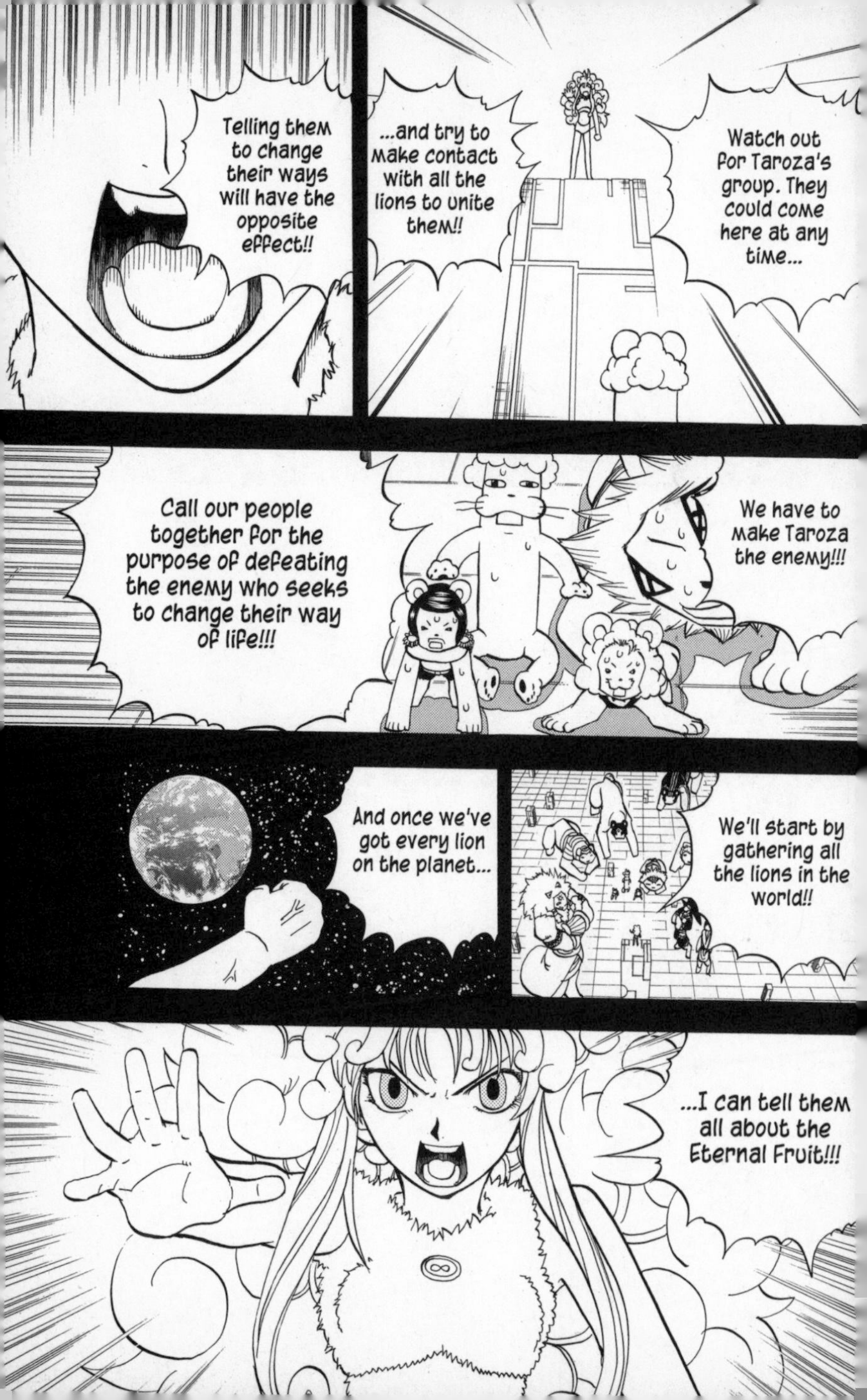
Watch out for Taroza's group. They could come here at any time...
...and try to make contact with all the lions to unite them!!
Telling them to change their ways will have the opposite effect!!
We have to make Taroza the enemy!!!
Call our people together for the purpose of defeating the enemy who seeks to change their way of life!!!
We'll start by gathering all the lions in the world!!
And once we've got every lion on the planet...
...I can tell them all about the Eternal Fruit!!!

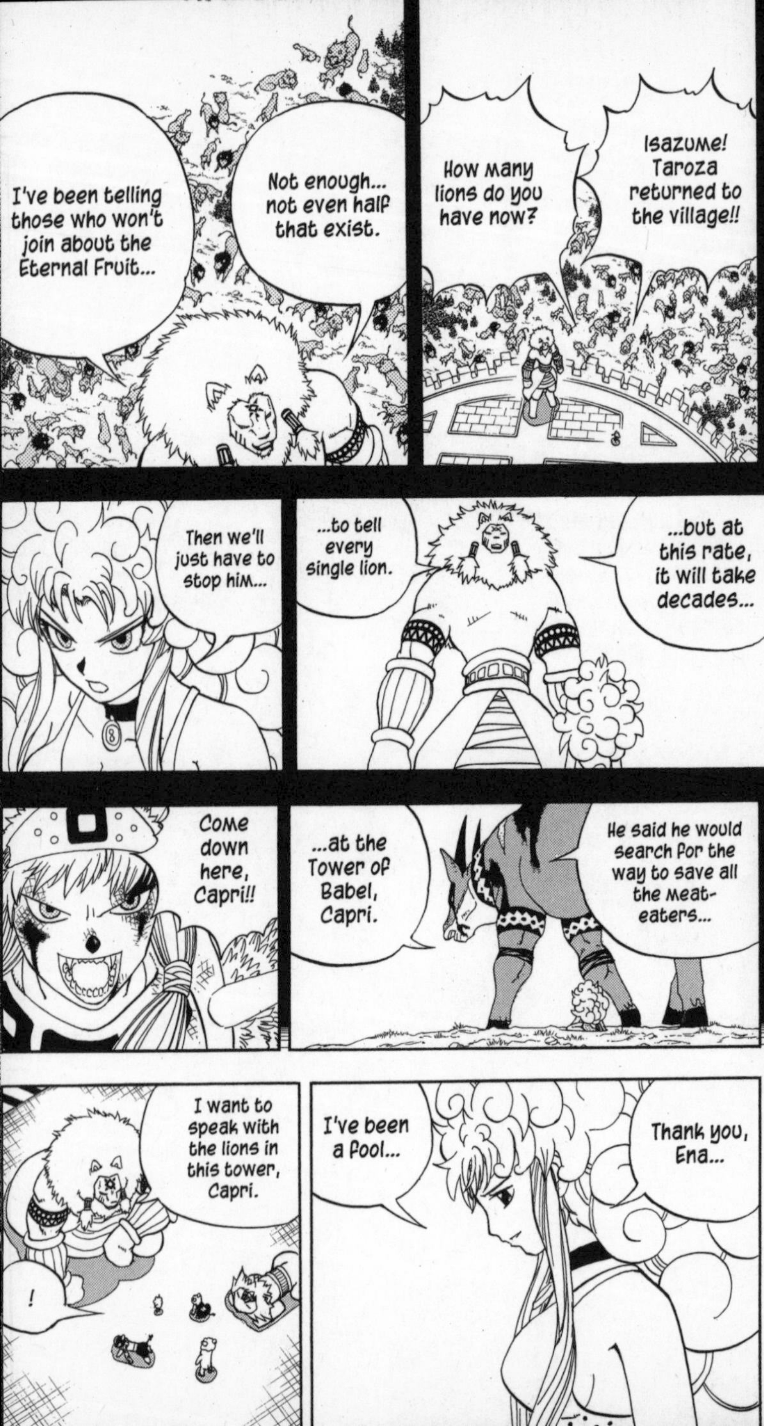
Isazume! Taroza returned to the village!!
How many lions do you have now?
Not enough... not even half that exist.
I've been telling those who won't join about the Eternal Fruit...
...but at this rate, it will take decades...
...to tell every single lion.
Then we'll just have to stop him...
He said he would search for the way to save all the meat-eaters...
...at the Tower of Babel, Capri.
Come down here, Capri!!
Thank you, Ena...
I've been a fool...
I want to speak with the lions in this tower, Capri.
!

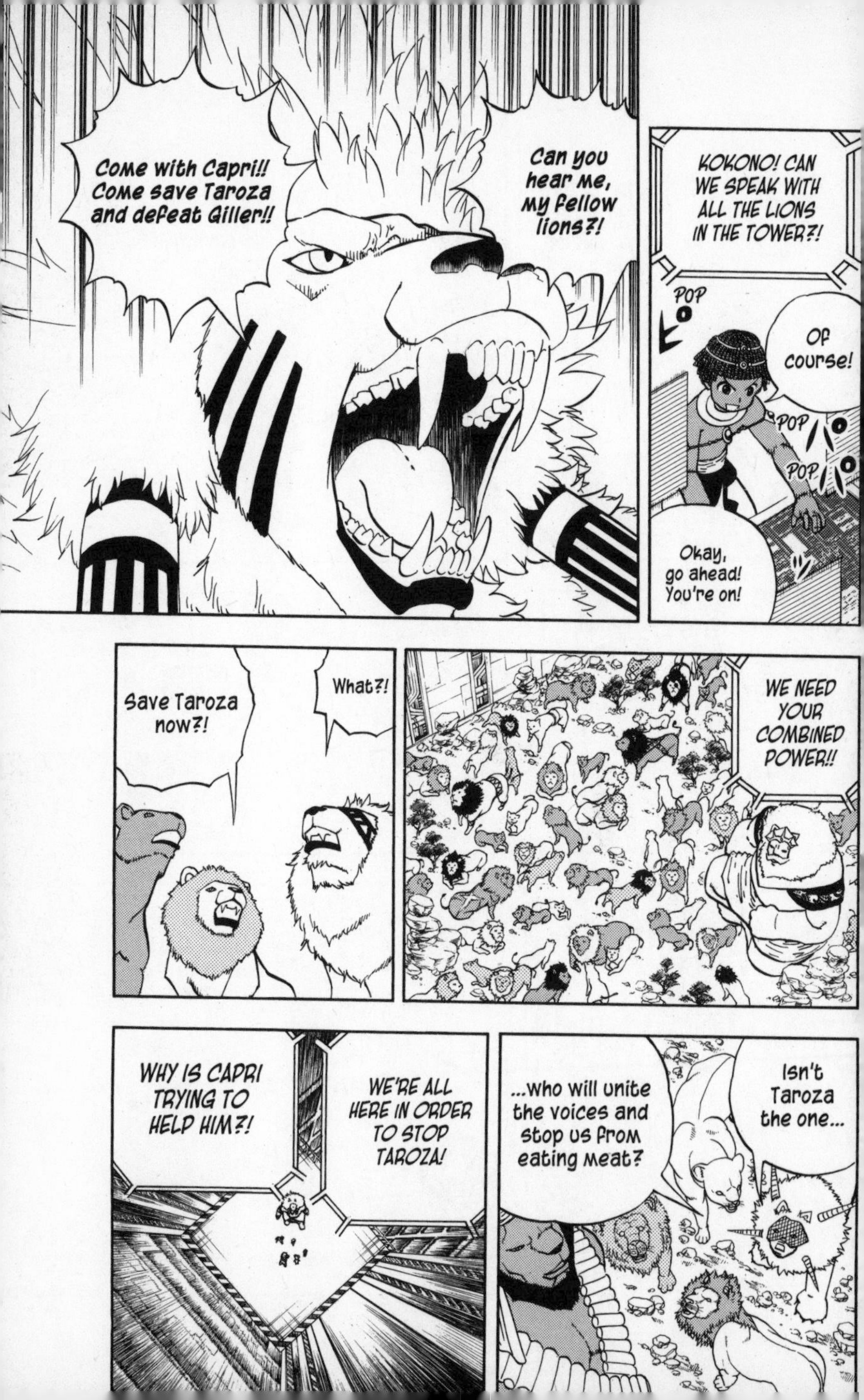
KOKONO! CAN WE SPEAK WITH ALL THE LIONS IN THE TOWER?!
POP
Of course!
POP
POP
Okay, go ahead! You're on!
Can you hear me, my fellow lions?!
Come with Capri!! Come save Taroza and defeat Giller!!
WE NEED YOUR COMBINED POWER!!
What?!
Save Taroza now?!
Isn't Taroza the one...
...who will unite the voices and stop us from eating meat?
WE'RE ALL HERE IN ORDER TO STOP TAROZA!
WHY IS CAPRI TRYING TO HELP HIM?!

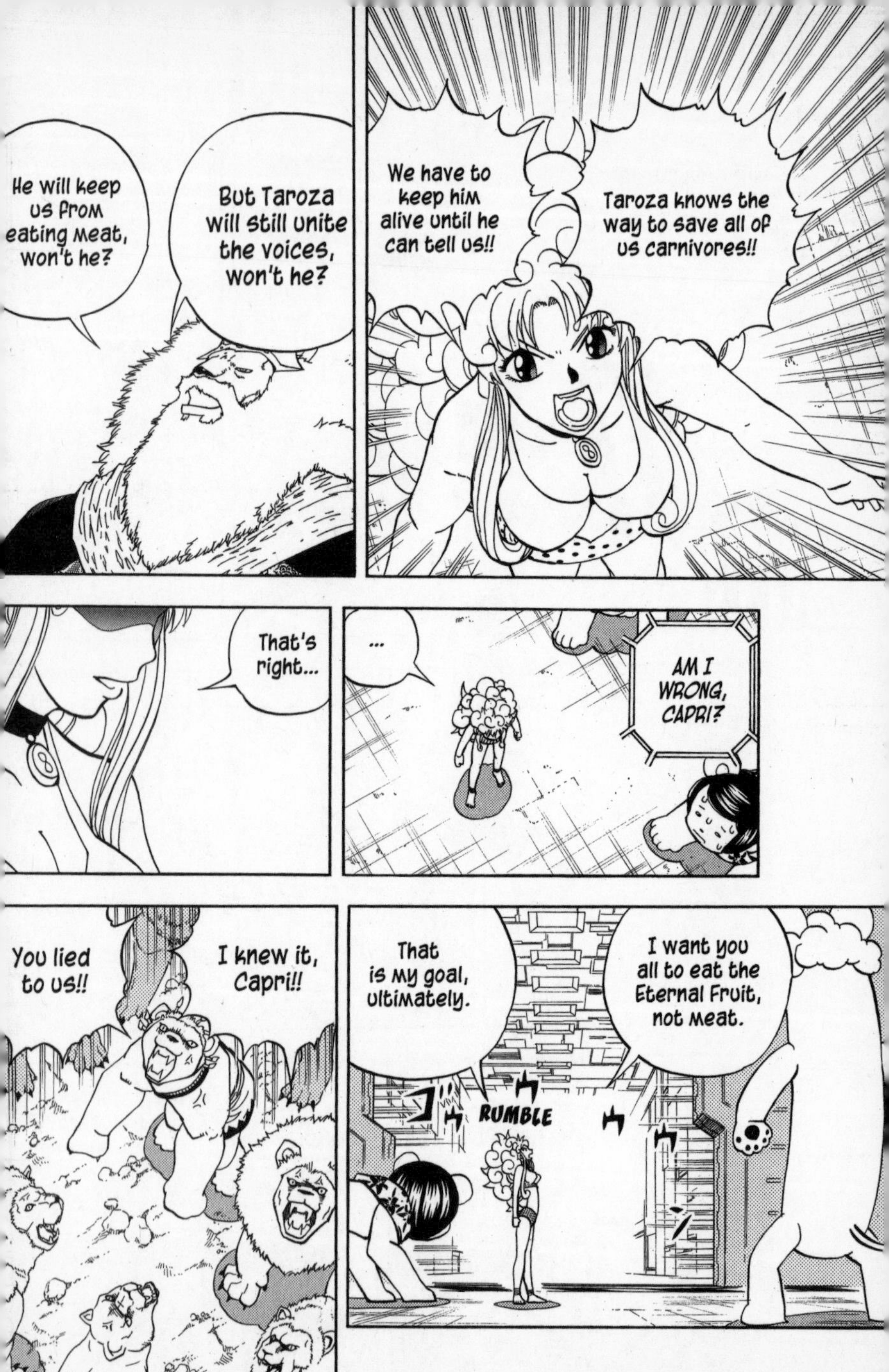
Taroza knows the way to save all of us carnivores!!
We have to keep him alive until he can tell us!!
But Taroza will still unite the voices, won't he?
He will keep us from eating meat, won't he?
AM I WRONG, CAPRI?
...
That's right...
I want you all to eat the Eternal Fruit, not meat.
That is my goal, ultimately.
RUMBLE
I knew it, Capri!!
You lied to us!!

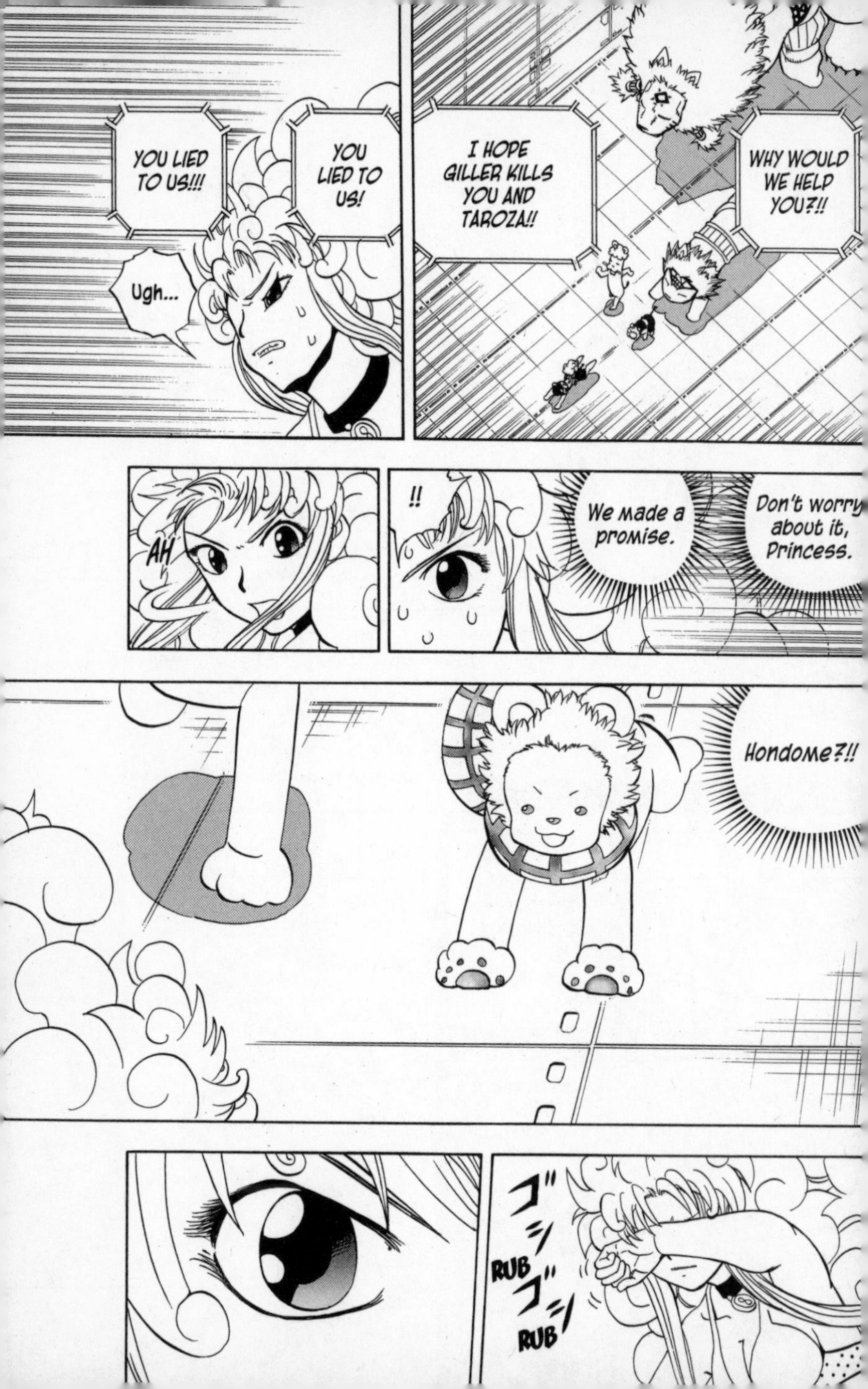

WHY WOULD WE HELP YOU?!!
I HOPE GILLER KILLS YOU AND TAROZA!!
YOU LIED TO US!
YOU LIED TO US!!!
Ugh...
Don't worry about it, Princess.
We made a promise.
!!
AH
Hondome?!!
ゴシ RUB
ゴシ RUB

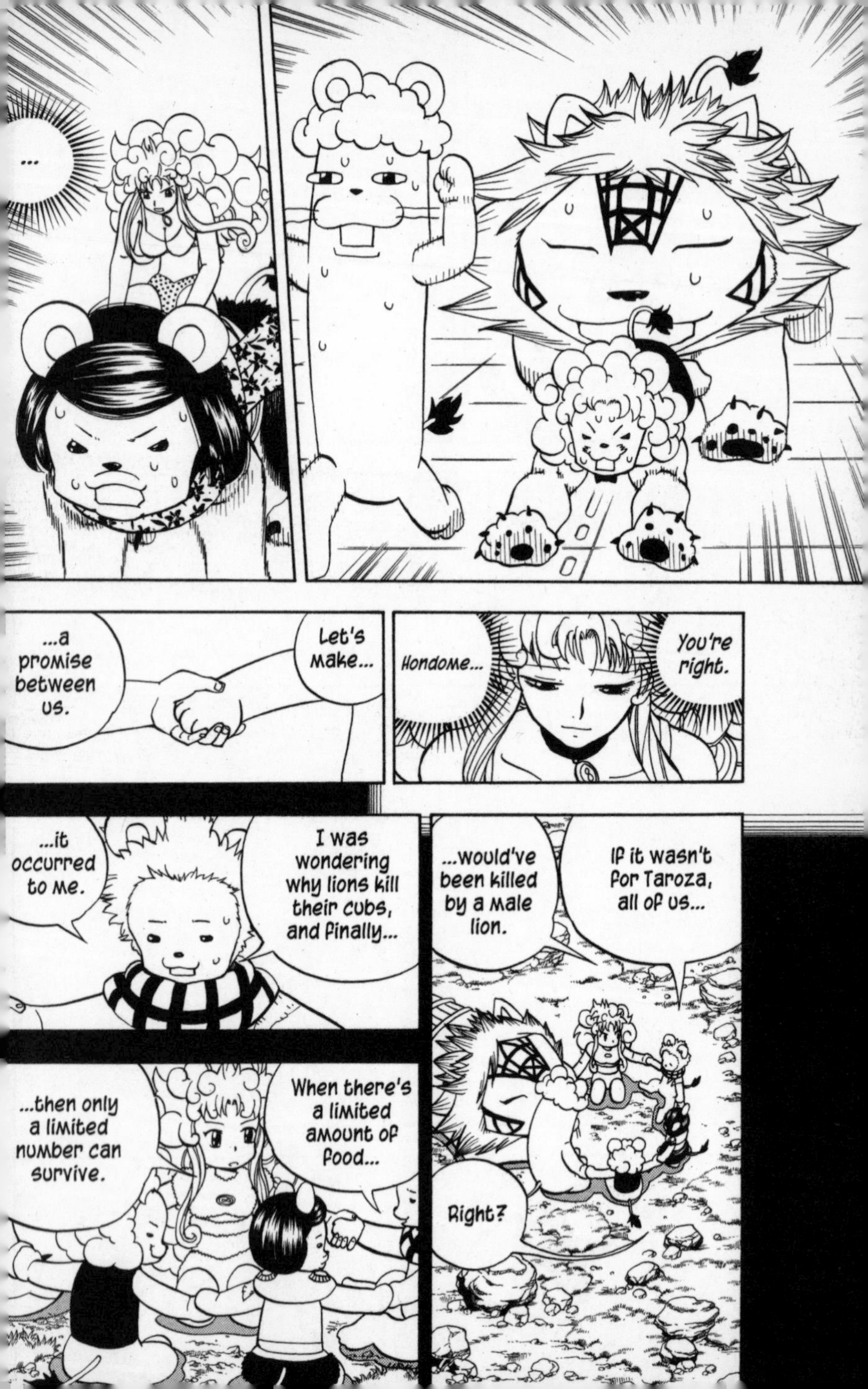
...
You're right.
Hondome...
Let's make...
...a promise between us.
If it wasn't for Taroza, all of us...
...would've been killed by a male lion.
Right?
I was wondering why lions kill their cubs, and finally...
...it occurred to me.
When there's a limited amount of food...
...then only a limited number can survive.

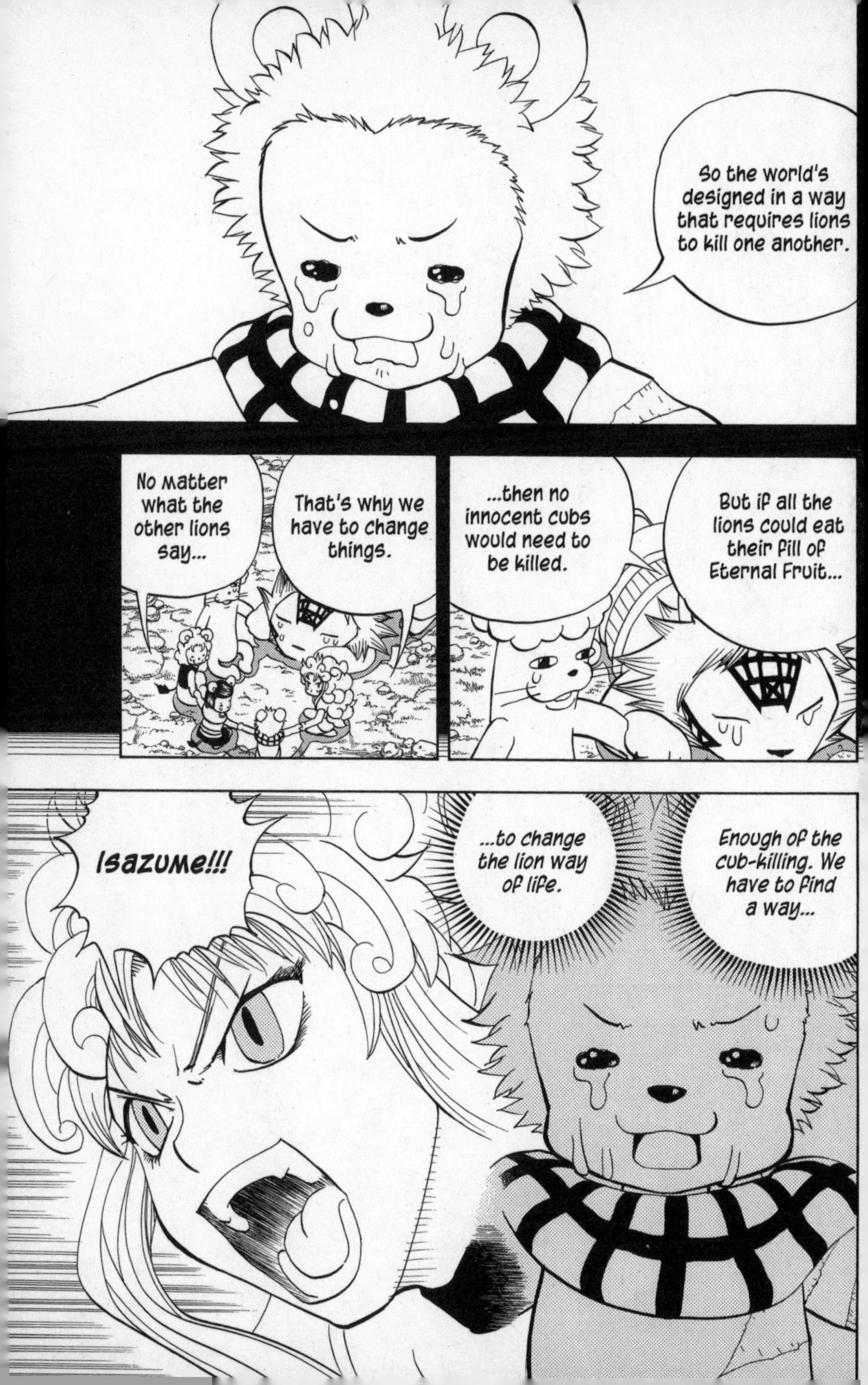
So the world's designed in a way that requires lions to kill one another.
But if all the lions could eat their fill of Eternal Fruit...
...then no innocent cubs would need to be killed.
That's why we have to change things.
No matter what the other lions say...
Enough of the cub-killing. We have to find a way...
...to change the lion way of life.
Isazume!!!

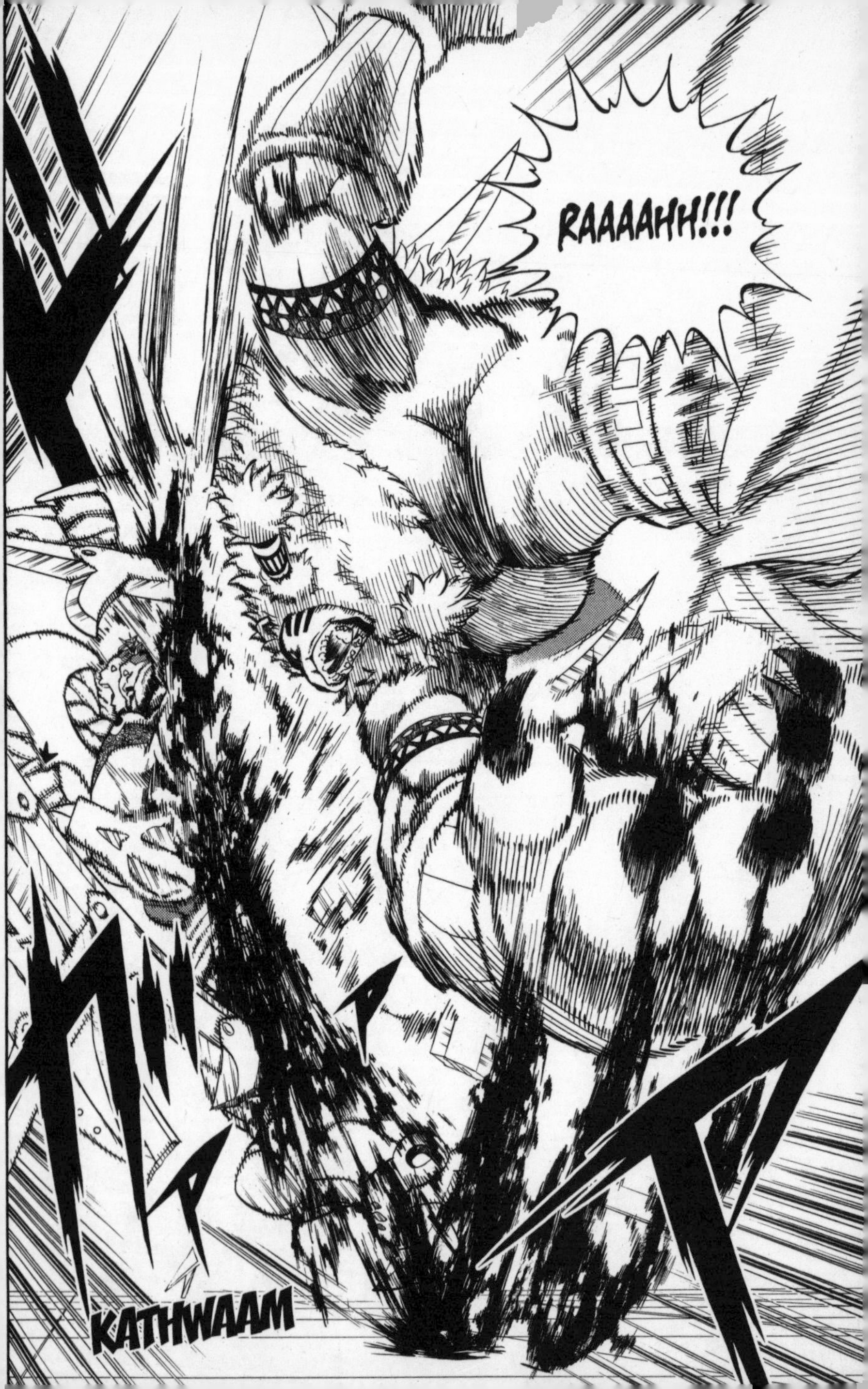
RAAAAHH!!!
KATHWAAM

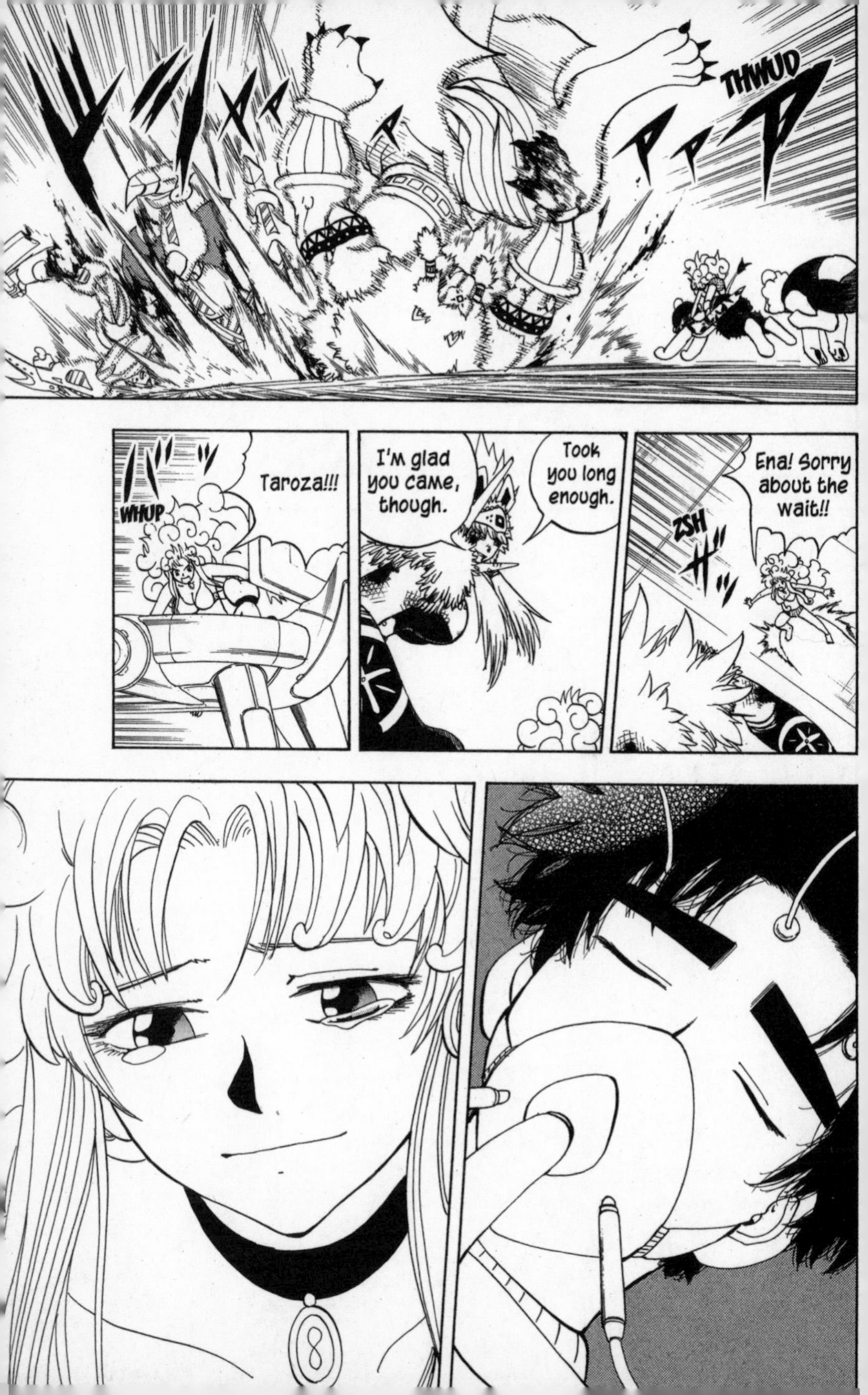
THWUD
Ena! Sorry about the wait!!
ZSH
Took you long enough.
I'm glad you came, though.
Taroza!!!
WHUP

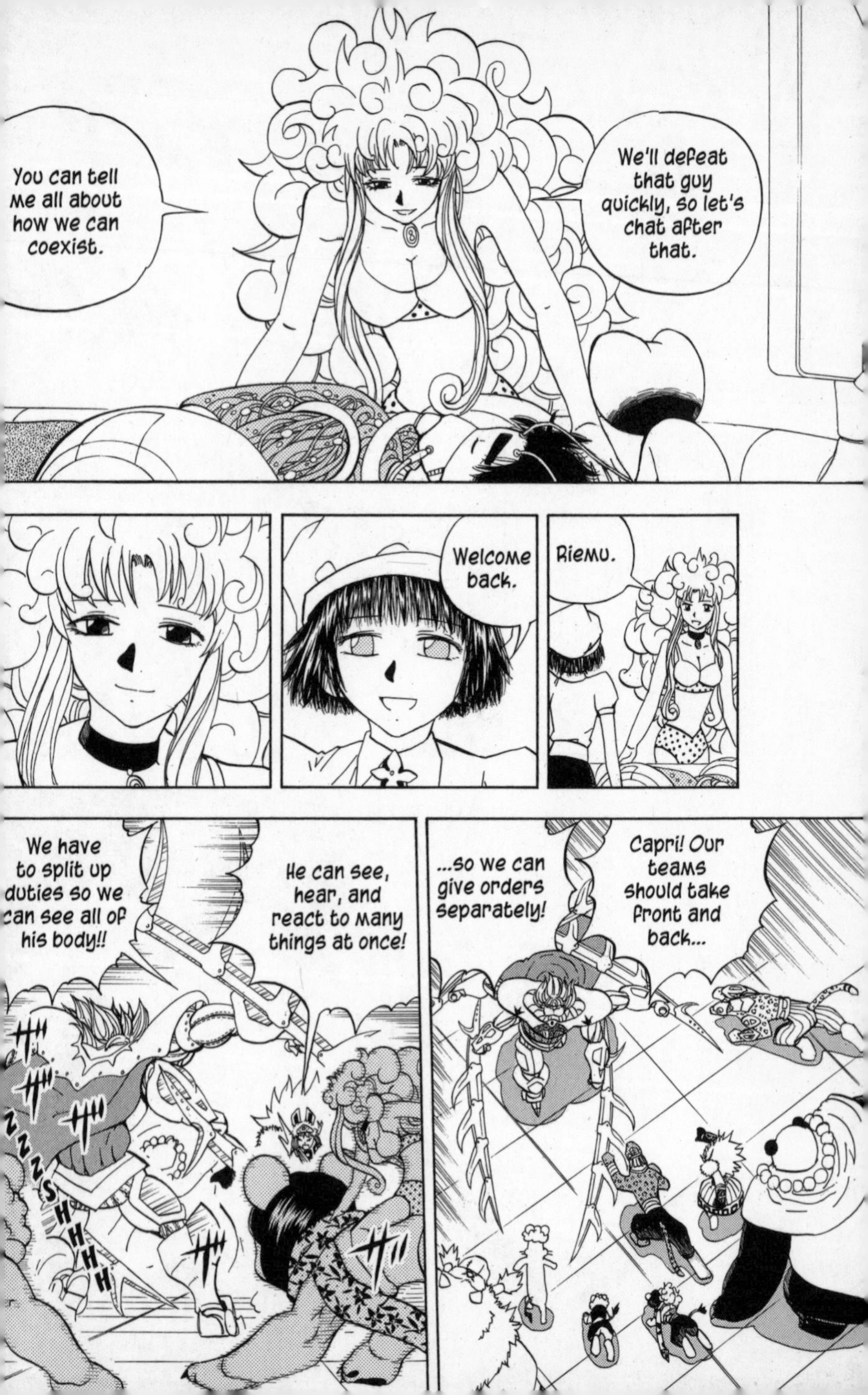
We'll defeat that guy quickly, so let's chat after that.
You can tell me all about how we can coexist.
Riemu.
Welcome back.
Capri! Our teams should take front and back...
...so we can give orders separately!
He can see, hear, and react to many things at once!
We have to split up duties so we can see all of his body!!
ZZZSHHHH

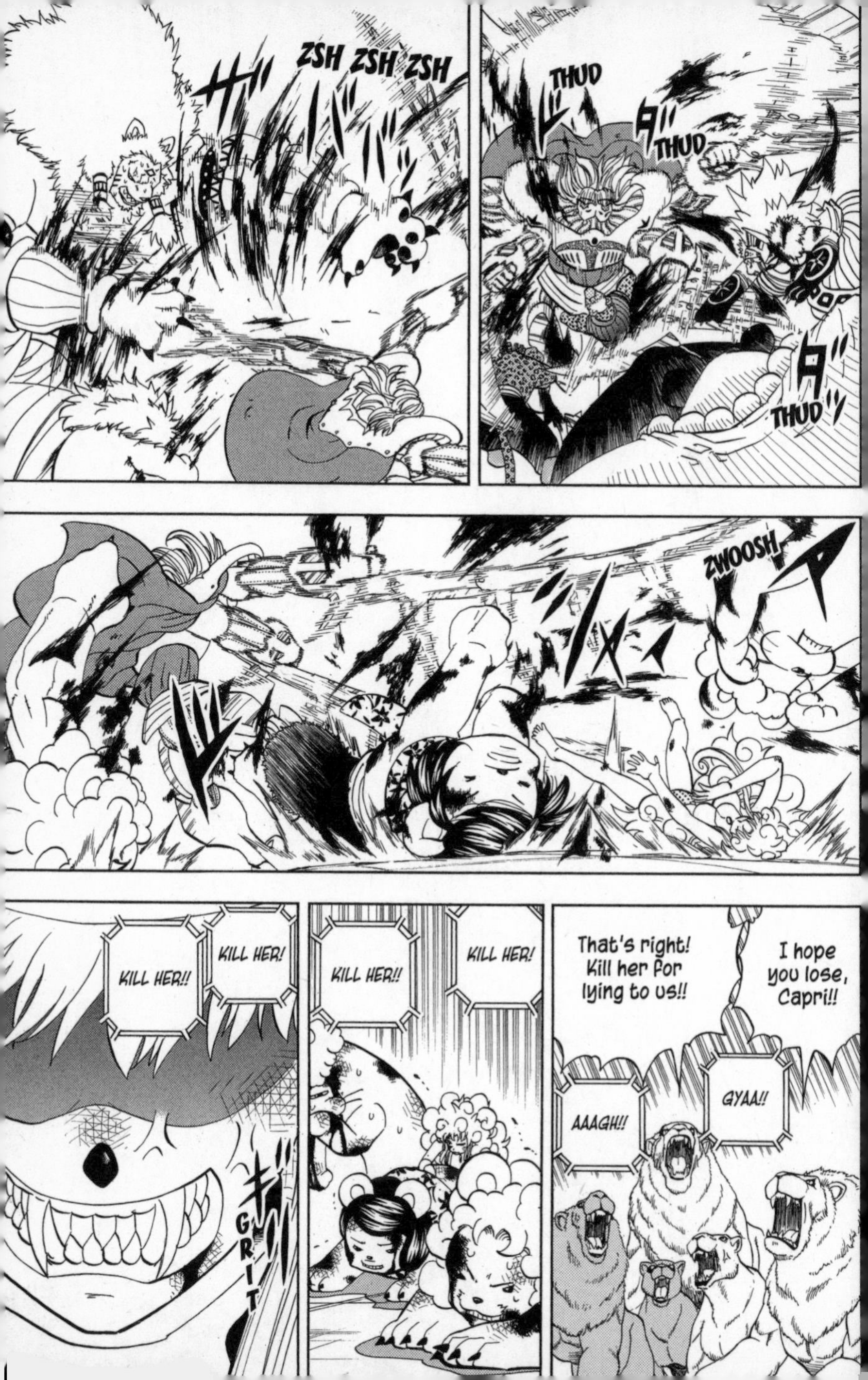
THUD
THUD
THUD
ZSH ZSH ZSH
ZWOOSH
I hope you lose, Capri!!
That's right! Kill her for lying to us!!
GYAA!!
AAAGH!!
KILL HER!
KILL HER!!
KILL HER!
KILL HER!!
GRIT

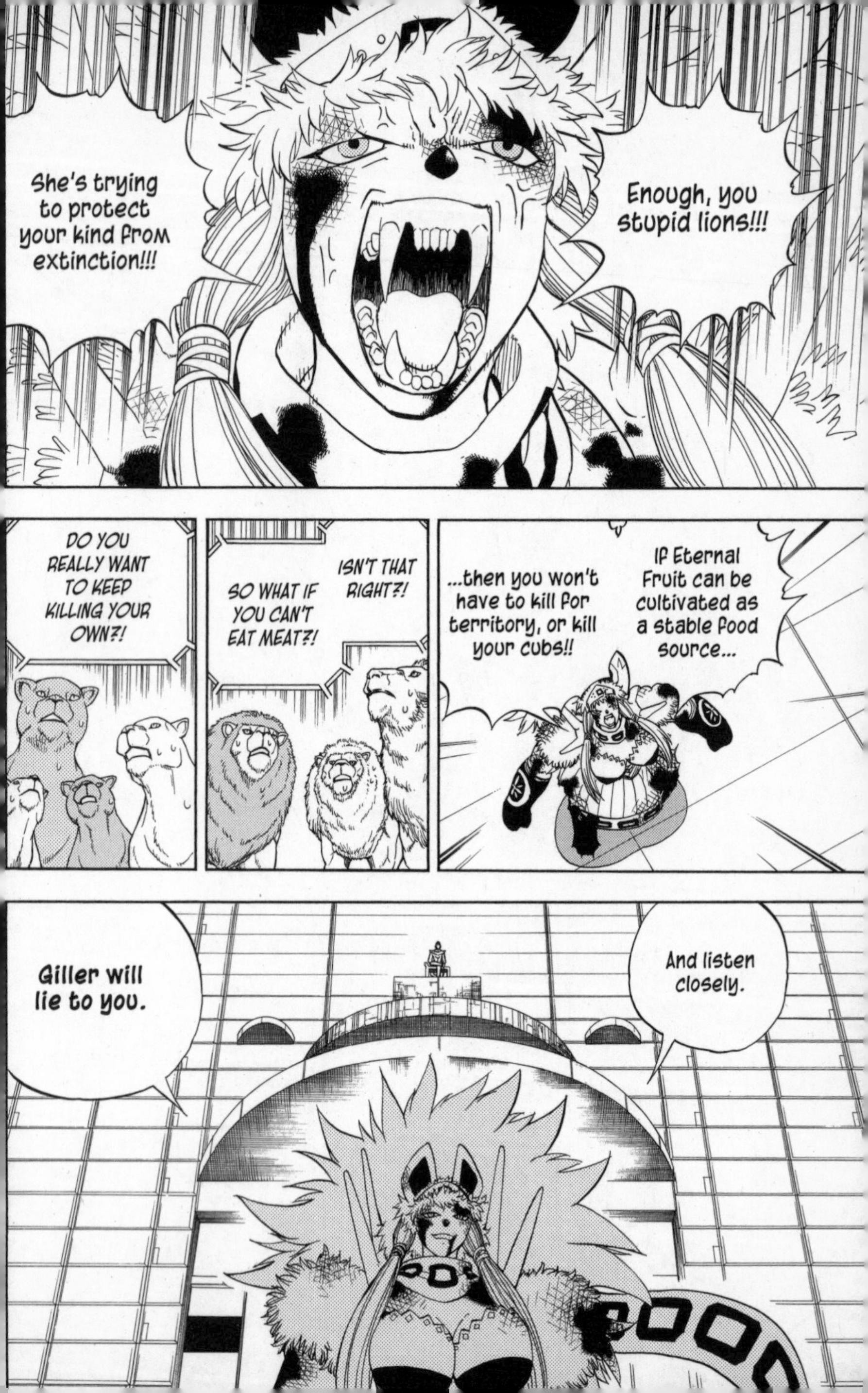
Enough, you stupid lions!!!
She's trying to protect your kind from extinction!!!
If Eternal Fruit can be cultivated as a stable food source...
...then you won't have to kill for territory, or kill your cubs!!
ISN'T THAT RIGHT?!
SO WHAT IF YOU CAN'T EAT MEAT?!
DO YOU REALLY WANT TO KEEP KILLING YOUR OWN?!
And listen closely.
Giller will lie to you.

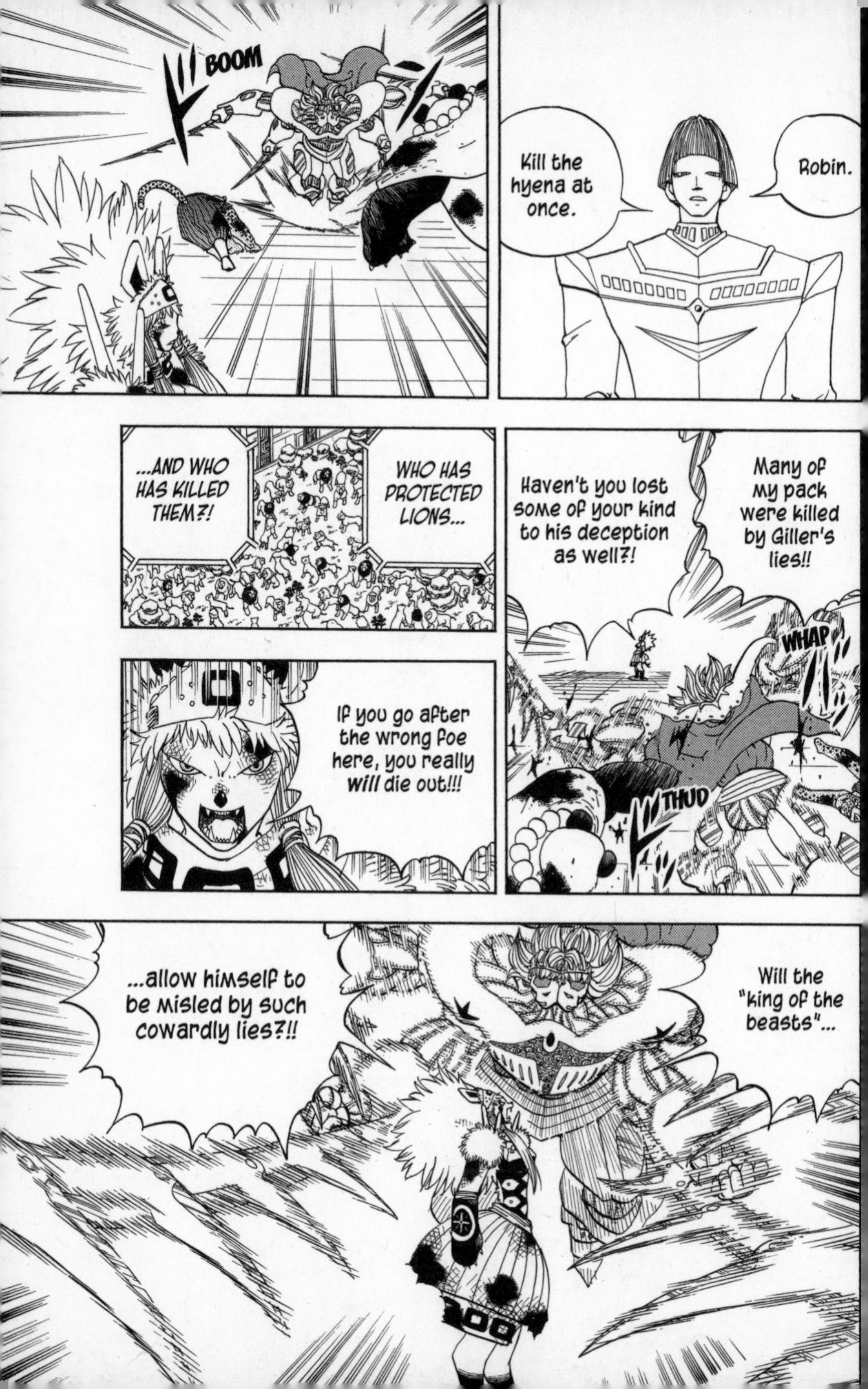
Robin.
Kill the hyena at once.
BOOM
Many of my pack were killed by Giller's lies!!
Haven't you lost some of your kind to his deception as well?!
WHAP
THUD
WHO HAS PROTECTED LIONS...
...AND WHO HAS KILLED THEM?!
If you go after the wrong foe here, you really *will* die out!!!
Will the "king of the beasts"...
...allow himself to be misled by such cowardly lies?!!

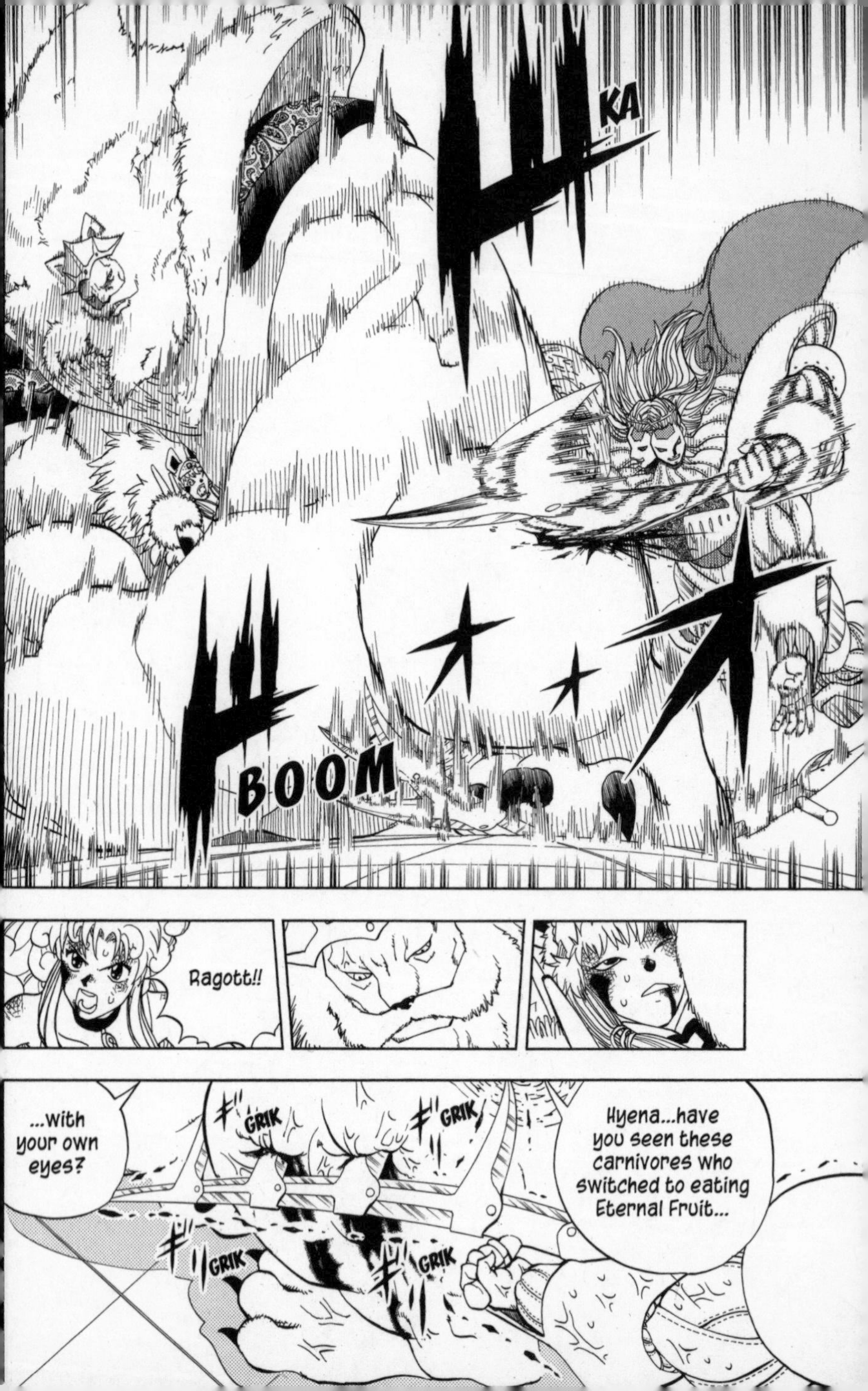
KA
BOOM
Ragott!!
Hyena...have you seen these carnivores who switched to eating Eternal Fruit...
GRIK
GRIK
...with your own eyes?
GRIK
GRIK

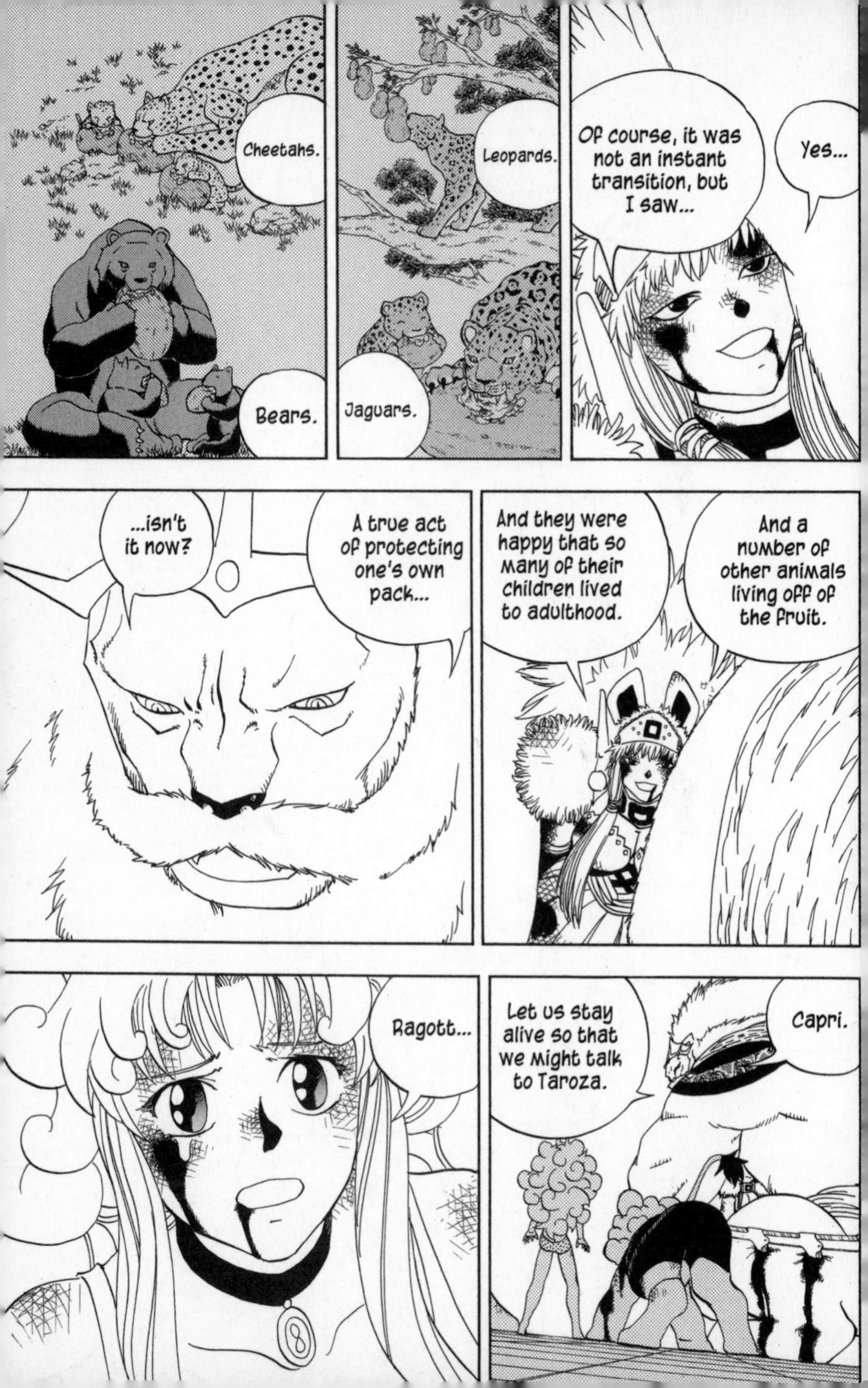
Yes...
Of course, it was not an instant transition, but I saw...
Leopards.
Jaguars.
Cheetahs.
Bears.
And a number of other animals living off of the fruit.
And they were happy that so many of their children lived to adulthood.
A true act of protecting one's own pack...
...isn't it now?
Capri.
Let us stay alive so that we might talk to Taroza.
Ragott...

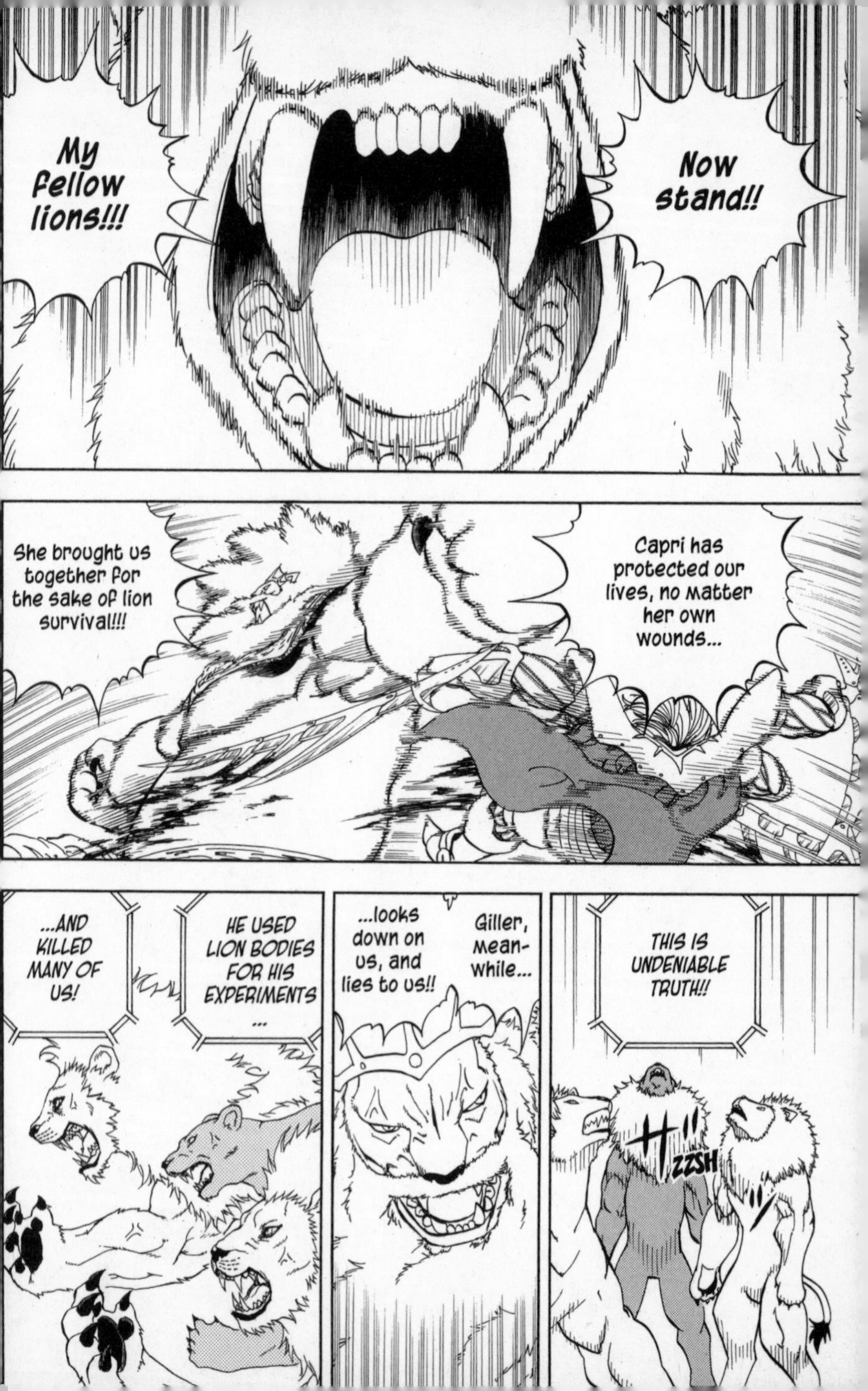
Now stand!!
My fellow lions!!!
Capri has protected our lives, no matter her own wounds...
She brought us together for the sake of lion survival!!!
THIS IS UNDENIABLE TRUTH!!
ZZSH
Giller, mean-while...
...looks down on us, and lies to us!!
HE USED LION BODIES FOR HIS EXPERIMENTS...
...AND KILLED MANY OF US!

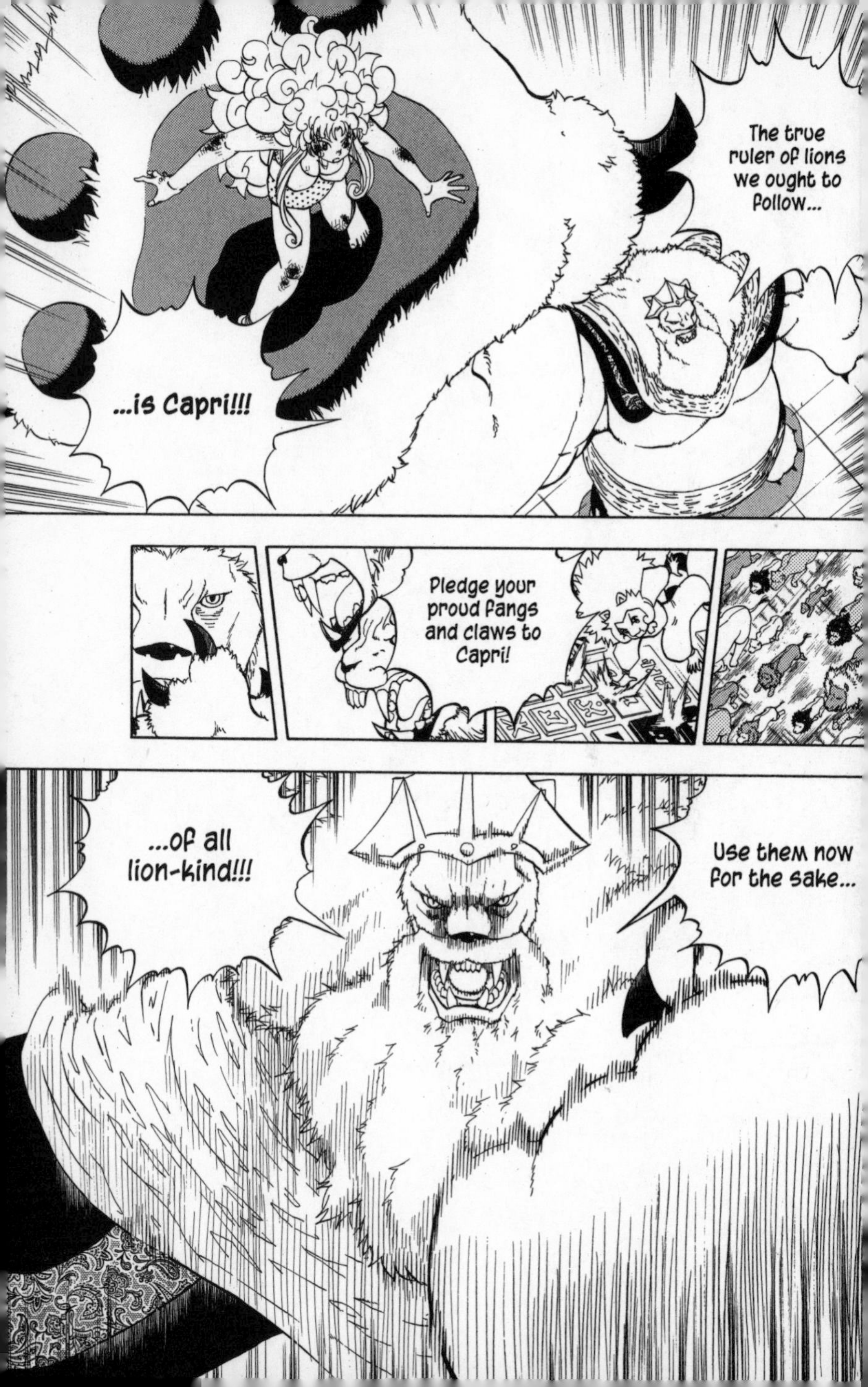

The true ruler of lions we ought to follow...
...is Capri!!!
Pledge your proud fangs and claws to Capri!
Use them now for the sake...
...of all lion-kind!!!

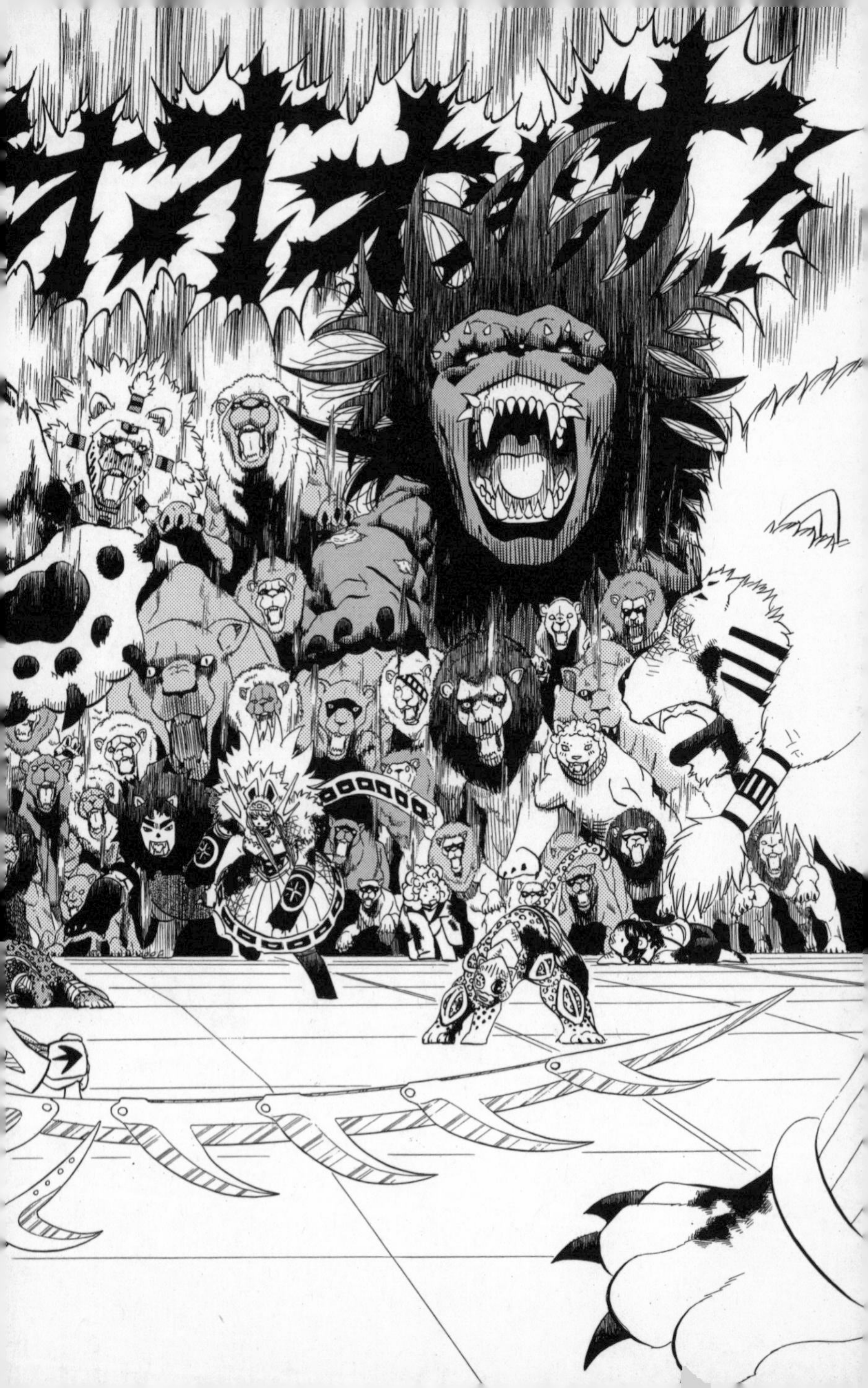

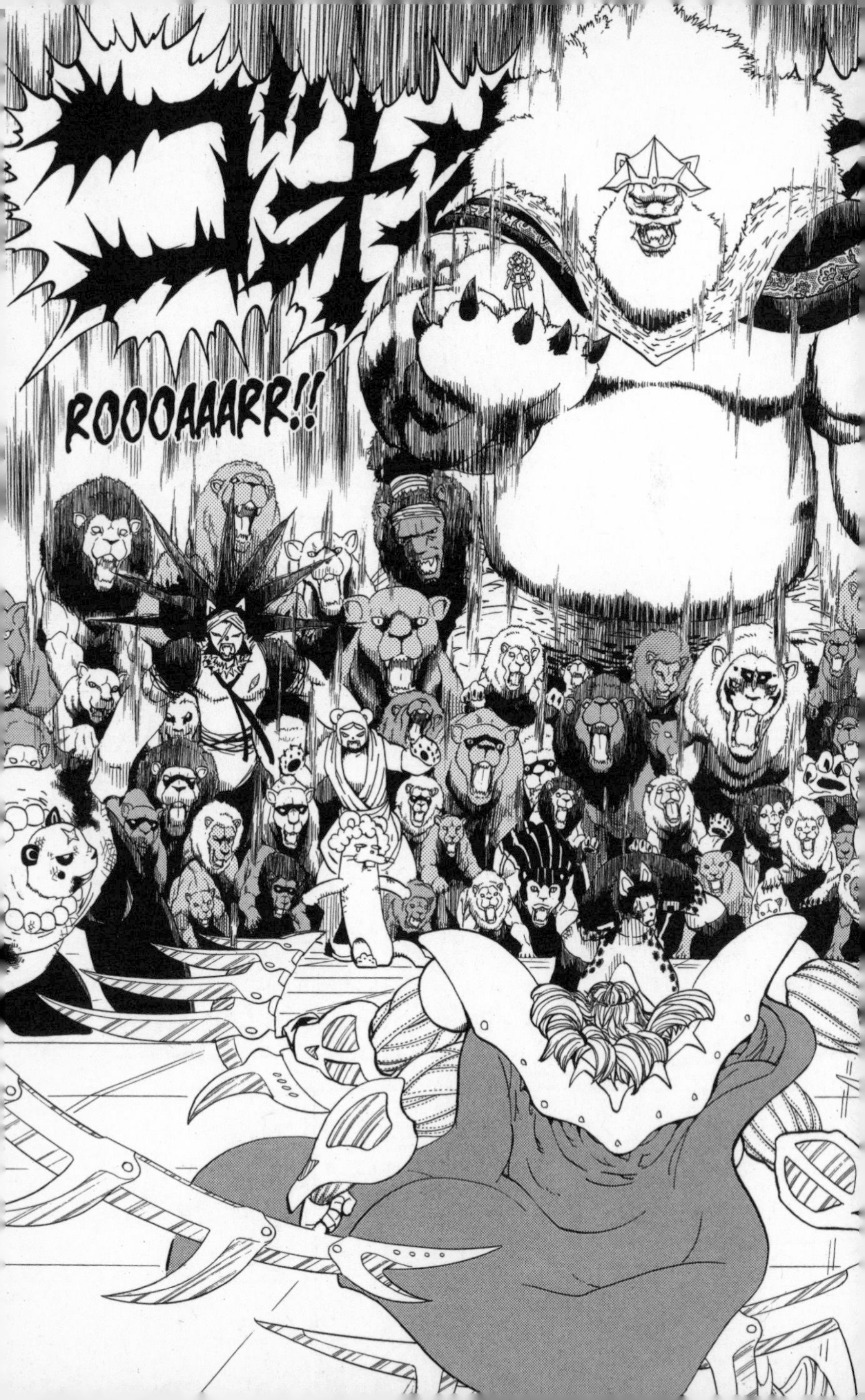
ROOOAAARR!!

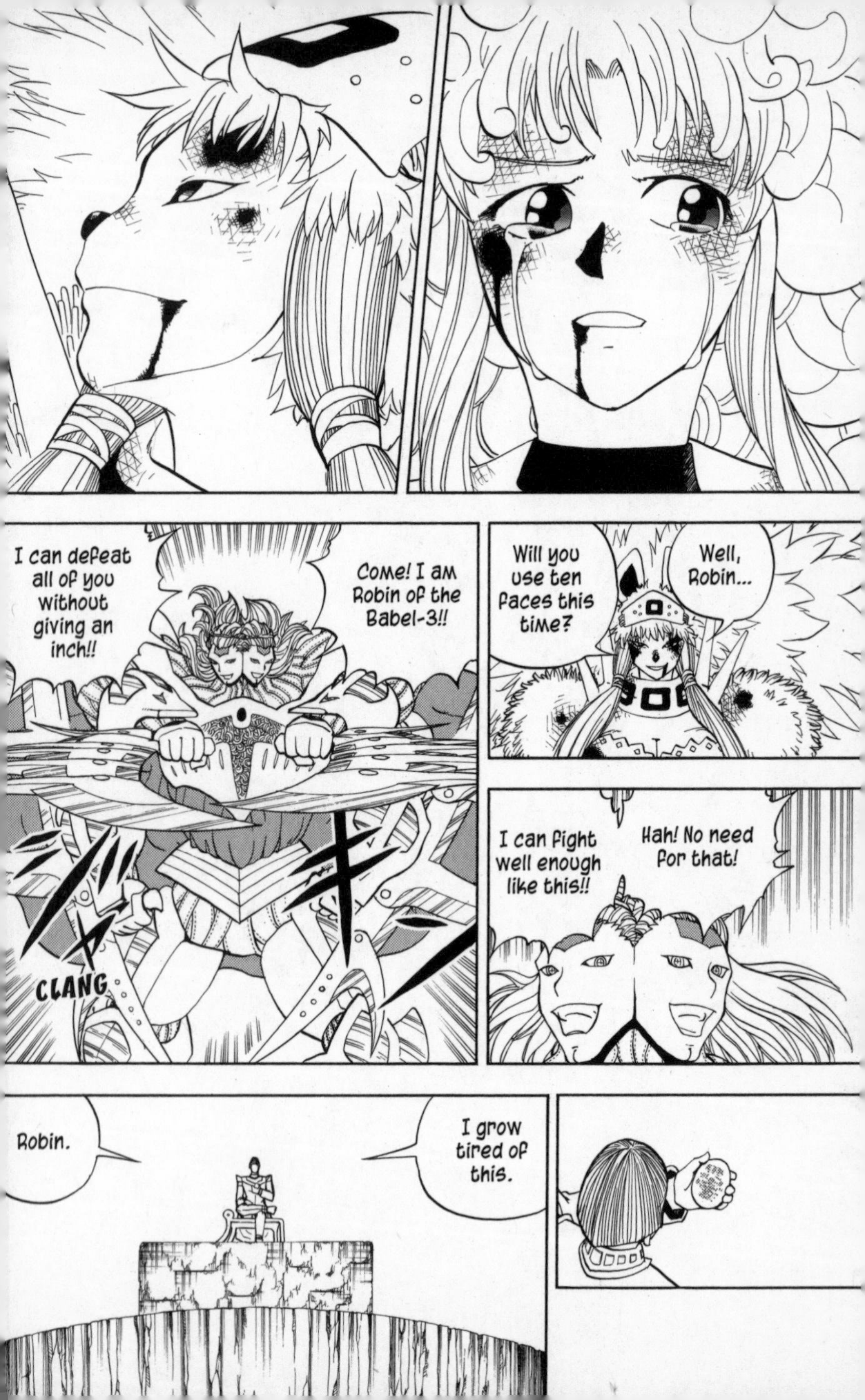
Well, Robin...
Will you use ten faces this time?
Hah! No need for that!
I can fight well enough like this!!
Come! I am Robin of the Babel-3!!
I can defeat all of you without giving an inch!!
CLANG
I grow tired of this.
Robin.

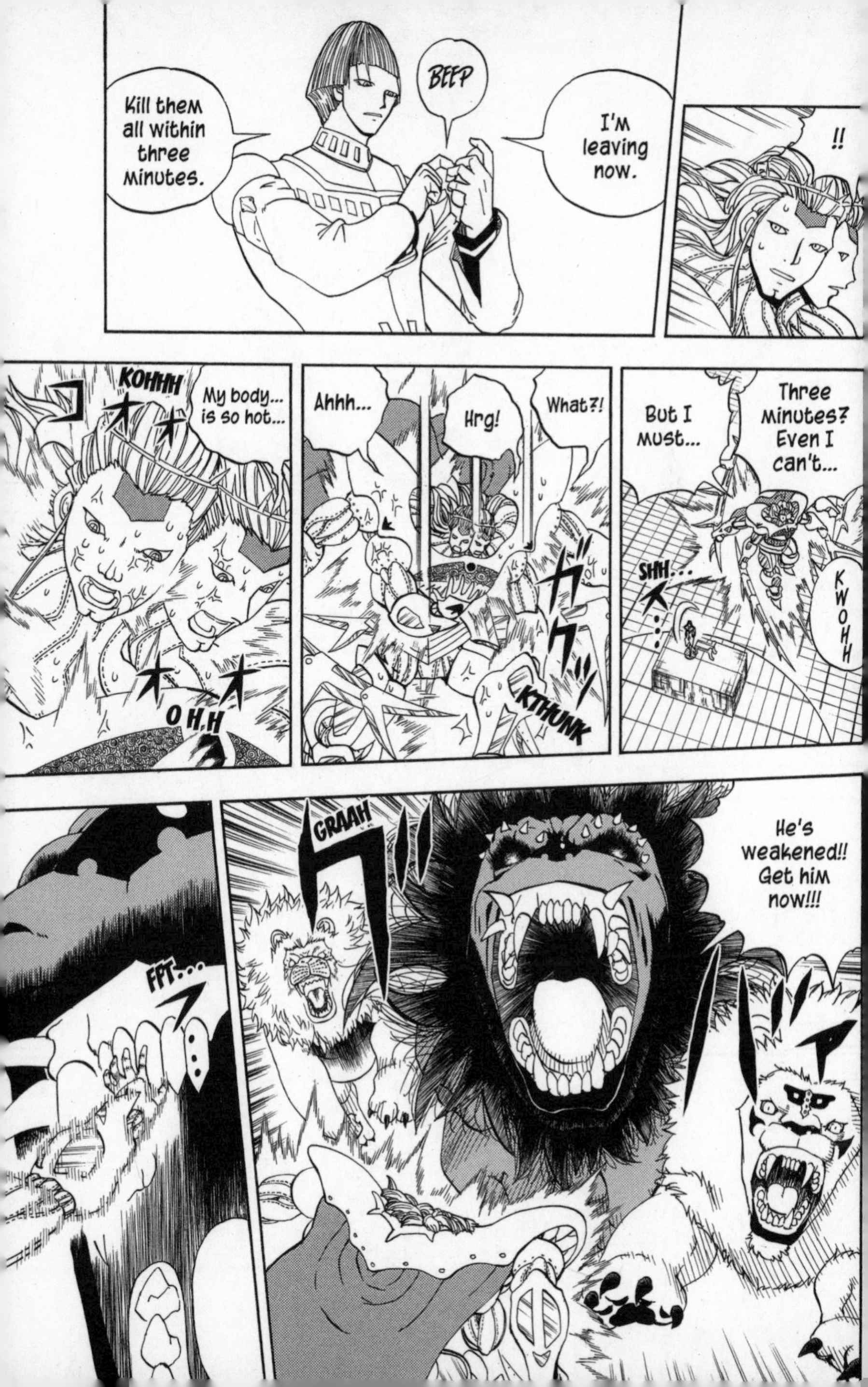
!!
I'M leaving now.
BEEP
Kill theM all within three Minutes.
Three Minutes? Even I can't...
But I Must...
KWOHH
SHH...
What?!
Hrg!
Ahhh...
KTHUNK
My body... is so hot...
KOHHH
OHH
He's weakened!! Get him now!!!
GRAAH
FFT...

BOOM

Robin.

You are the strongest of the Babel-3.

The secret to that strength lies in your brain...

...but also in the energy-creation capability of your heart.

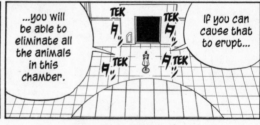

If you can cause that to erupt...

TEK TEK TEK TEK

...you will be able to eliminate all the animals in this chamber.

Erupt...?

That means your body will explode within three minutes...

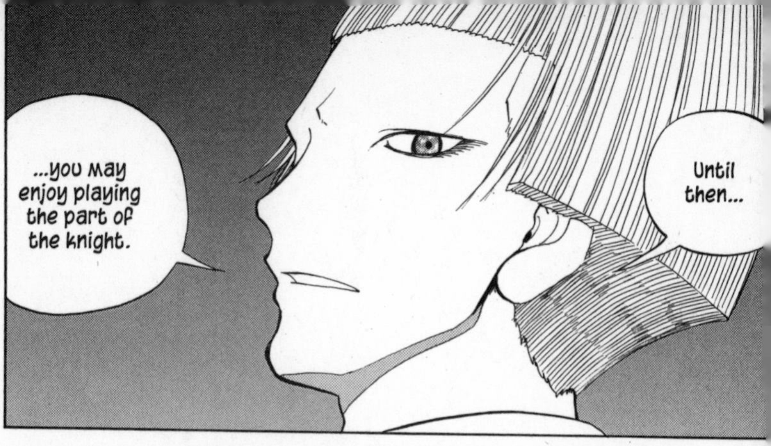
Until then...
...you may enjoy playing the part of the knight.

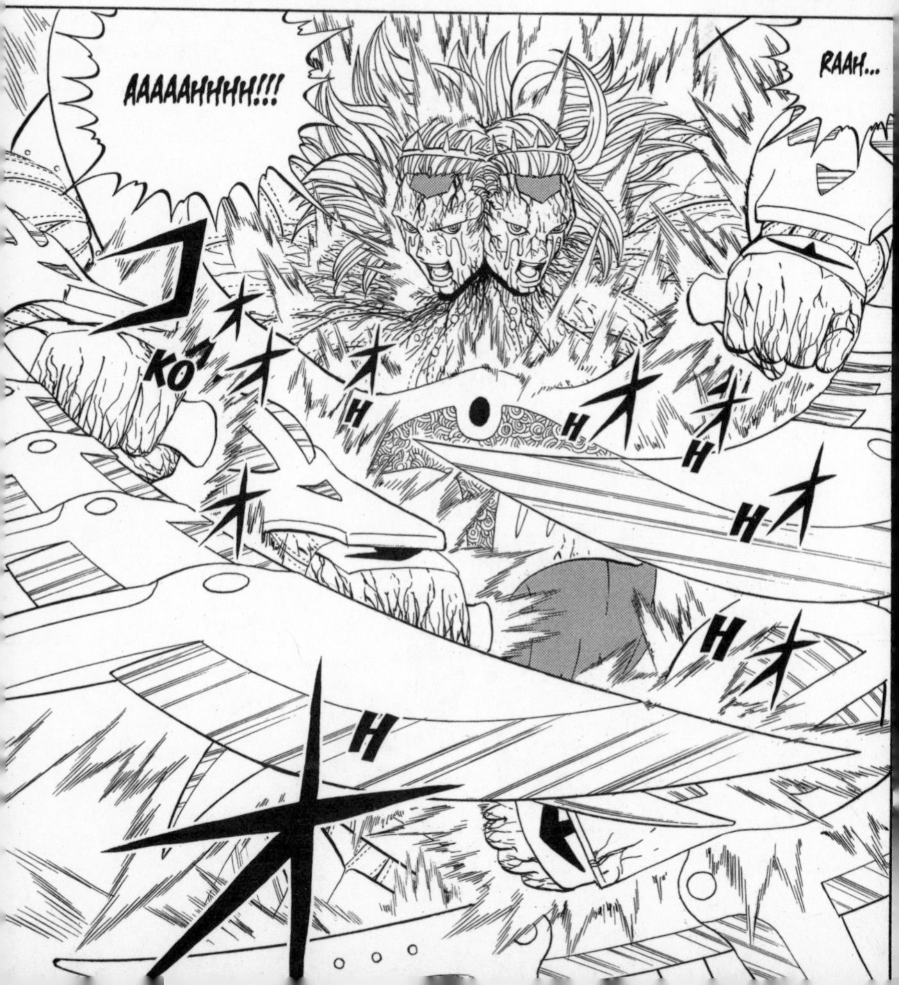
RAAH...
AAAAAHHHH!!!
KO

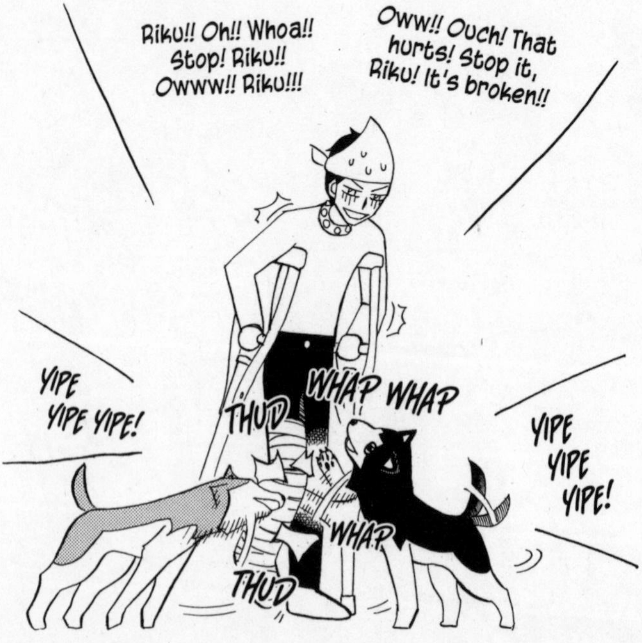
Oww!! Ouch! That hurts! Stop it, Riku! It's broken!!
Riku!! Oh!! Whoa!! Stop! Riku!! Owww!! Riku!!!
YIPE YIPE YIPE!
WHAP WHAP
THUD
YIPE YIPE YIPE!
WHAP
THUD

Raaah!

Aaaahhh!!!

Just three minutes.

Aah... aaaah...

Just three...

In three minutes, your body will explode...

TUG

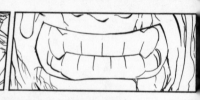

...these three minutes...

In that case...

FWAAP

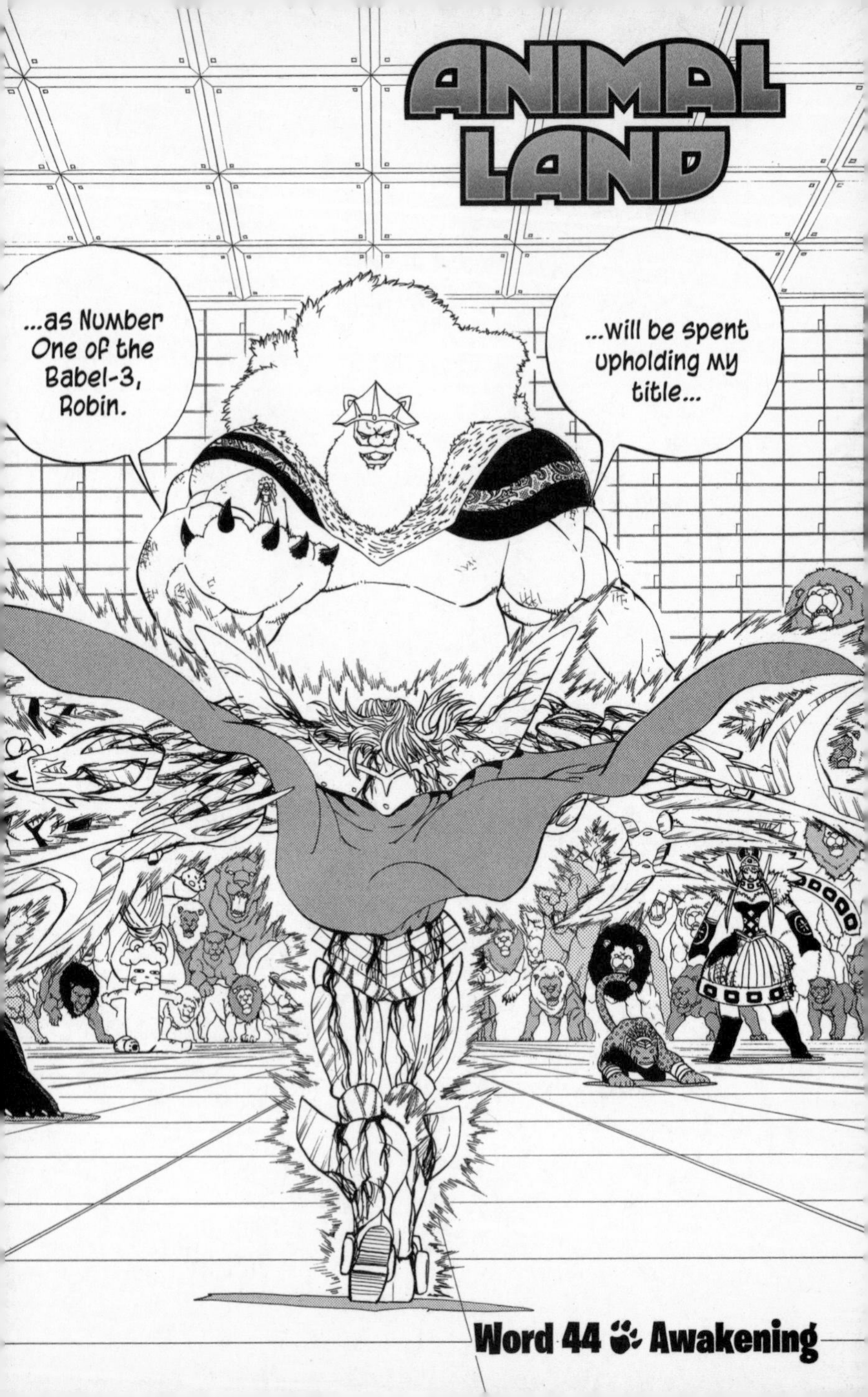
ANIMAL LAND
...will be spent upholding my title...
...as Number One of the Babel-3, Robin.
Word 44 Awakening

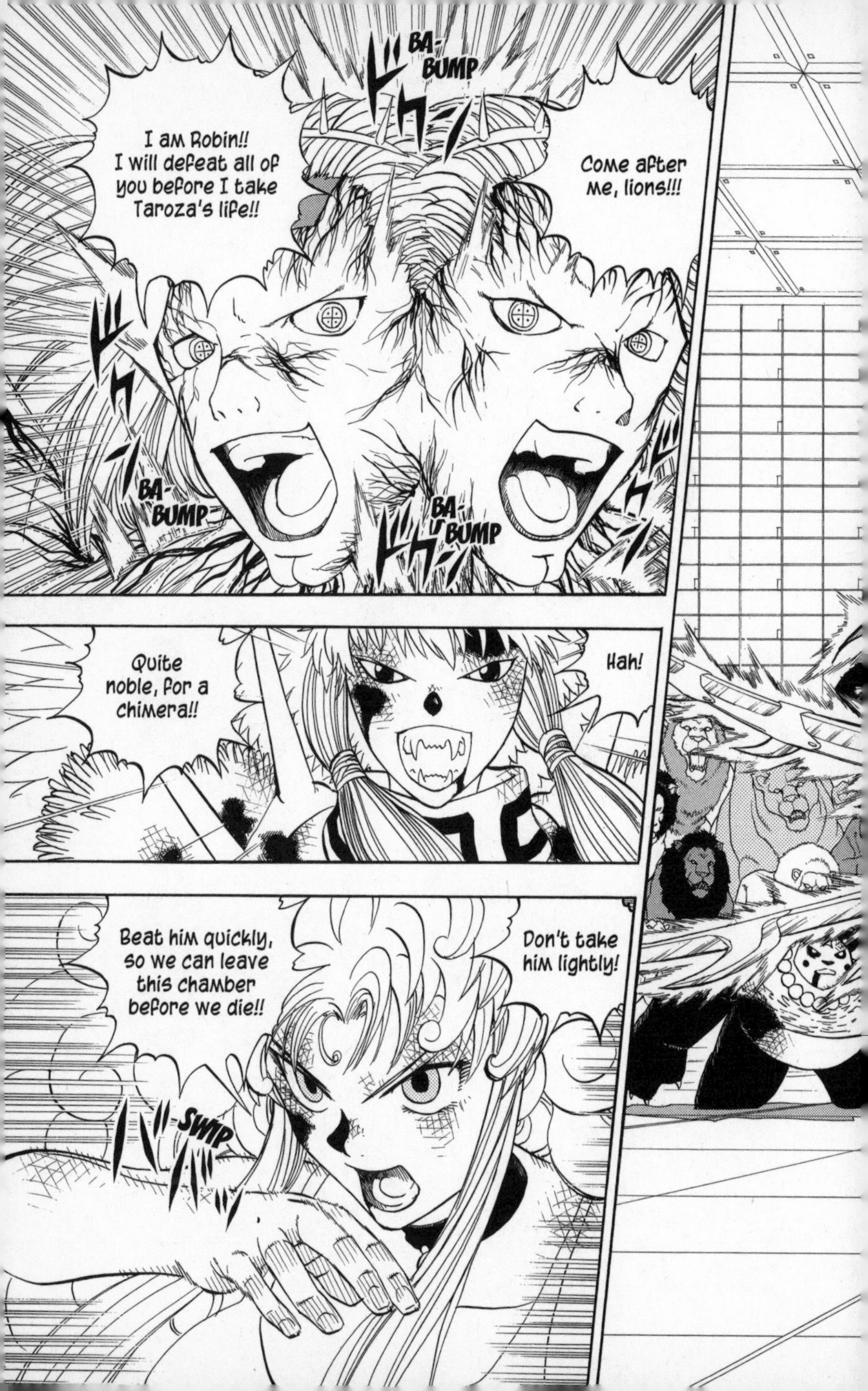

BA-BUMP
Come after me, lions!!!
I am Robin!! I will defeat all of you before I take Taroza's life!!
BA-BUMP
BA-BUMP
Hah!
Quite noble, for a chimera!!
Don't take him lightly!
Beat him quickly, so we can leave this chamber before we die!!
SWIP

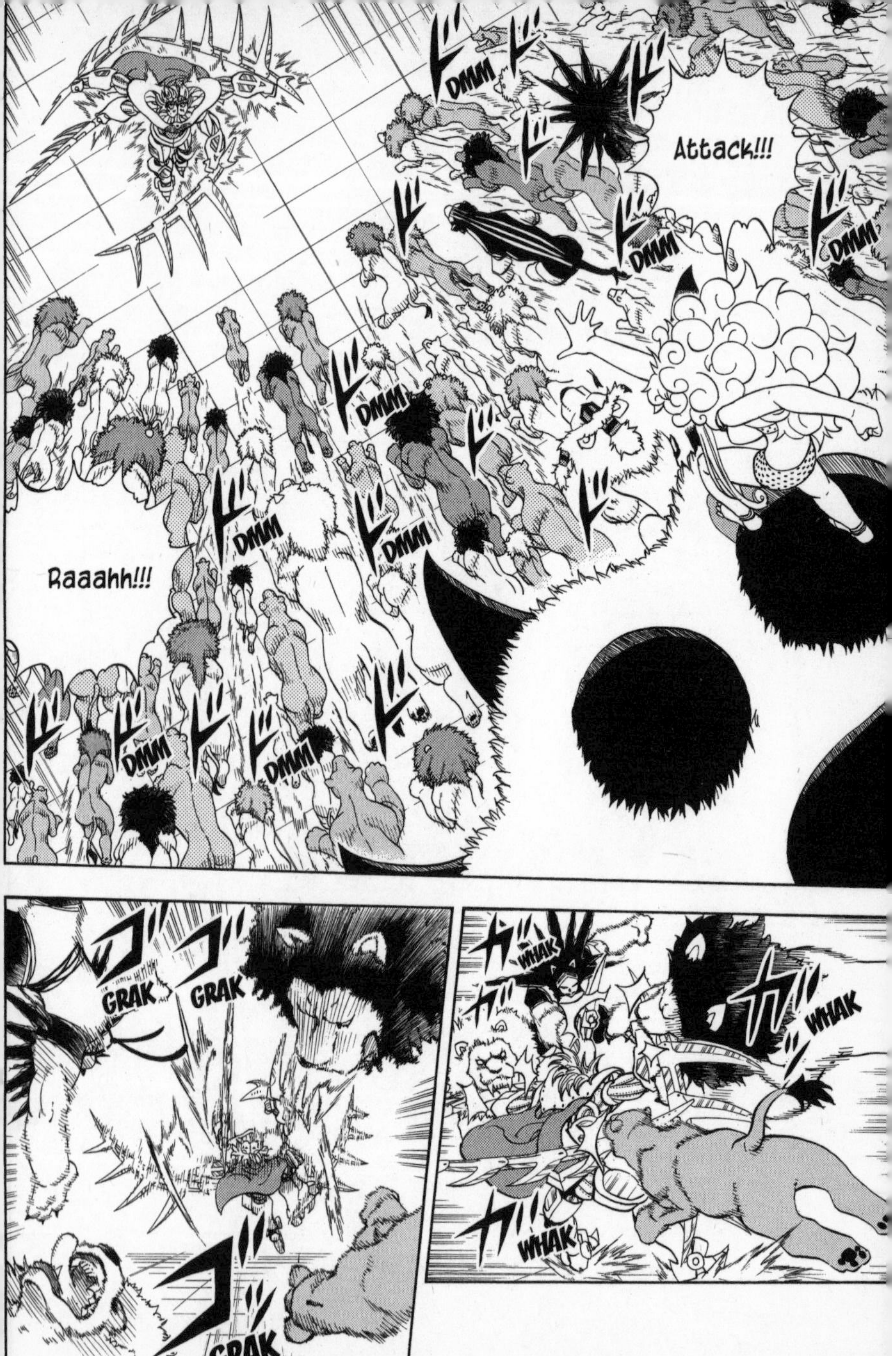
Attack!!!
DMM
DMM
DMM
DMM
DMM
DMM
DMM
DMM
DMM
Raaahh!!!
WHAK
WHAK
WHAK
GRAK
GRAK
GRAK

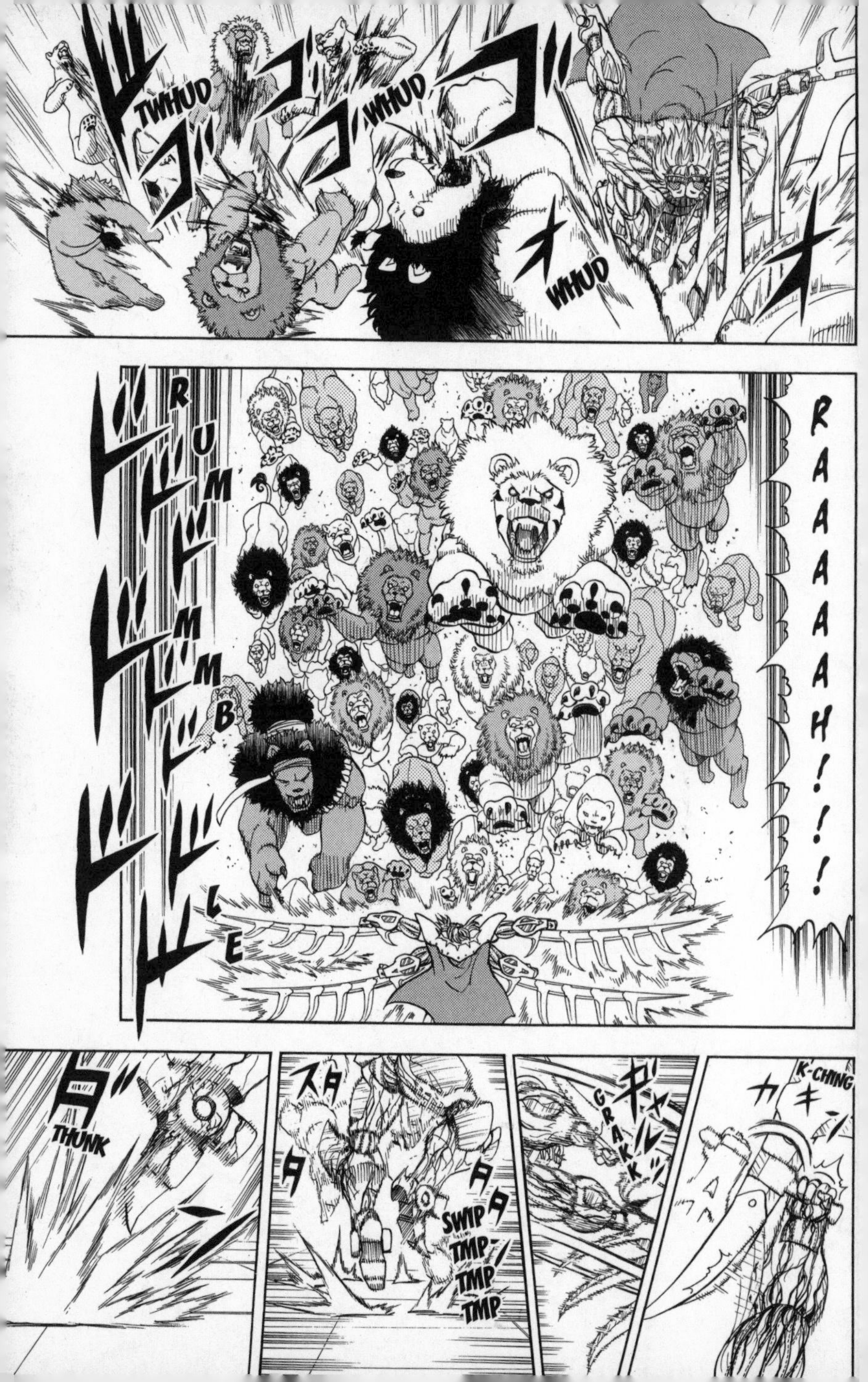
WHUD
TWHUD
WHUD
RAAAAAAH!!!
RUMMMBLE
K-CHING
GRAKK
SWIP
TMP-
TMP
TMP
THUNK

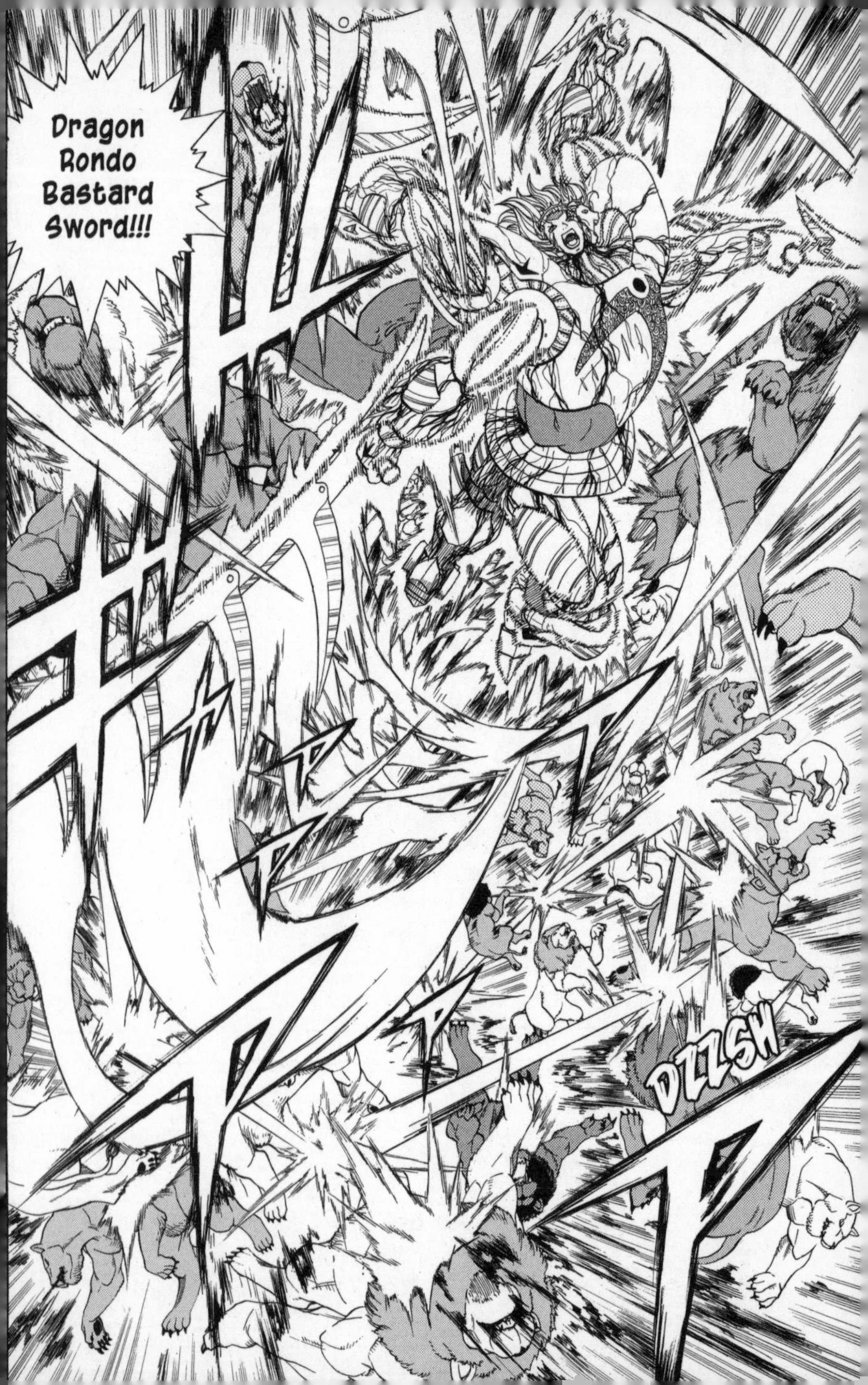
Dragon Rondo Bastard Sword!!!
DZZSH

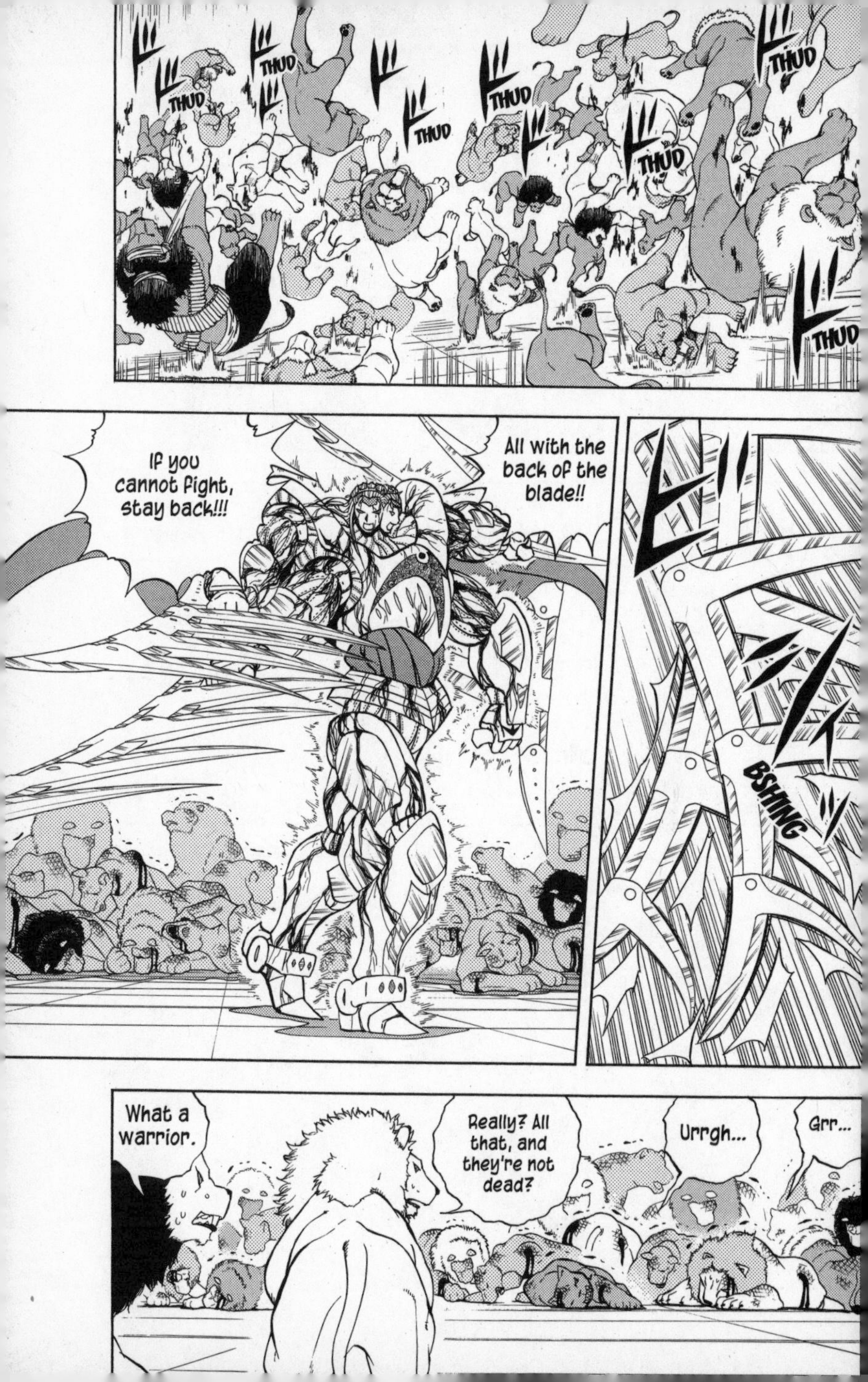
THUD
THUD
THUD
THUD
THUD
THUD
THUD
BSHING
All with the back of the blade!!
If you cannot fight, stay back!!!
Grr...
Urrgh...
Really? All that, and they're not dead?
What a warrior.

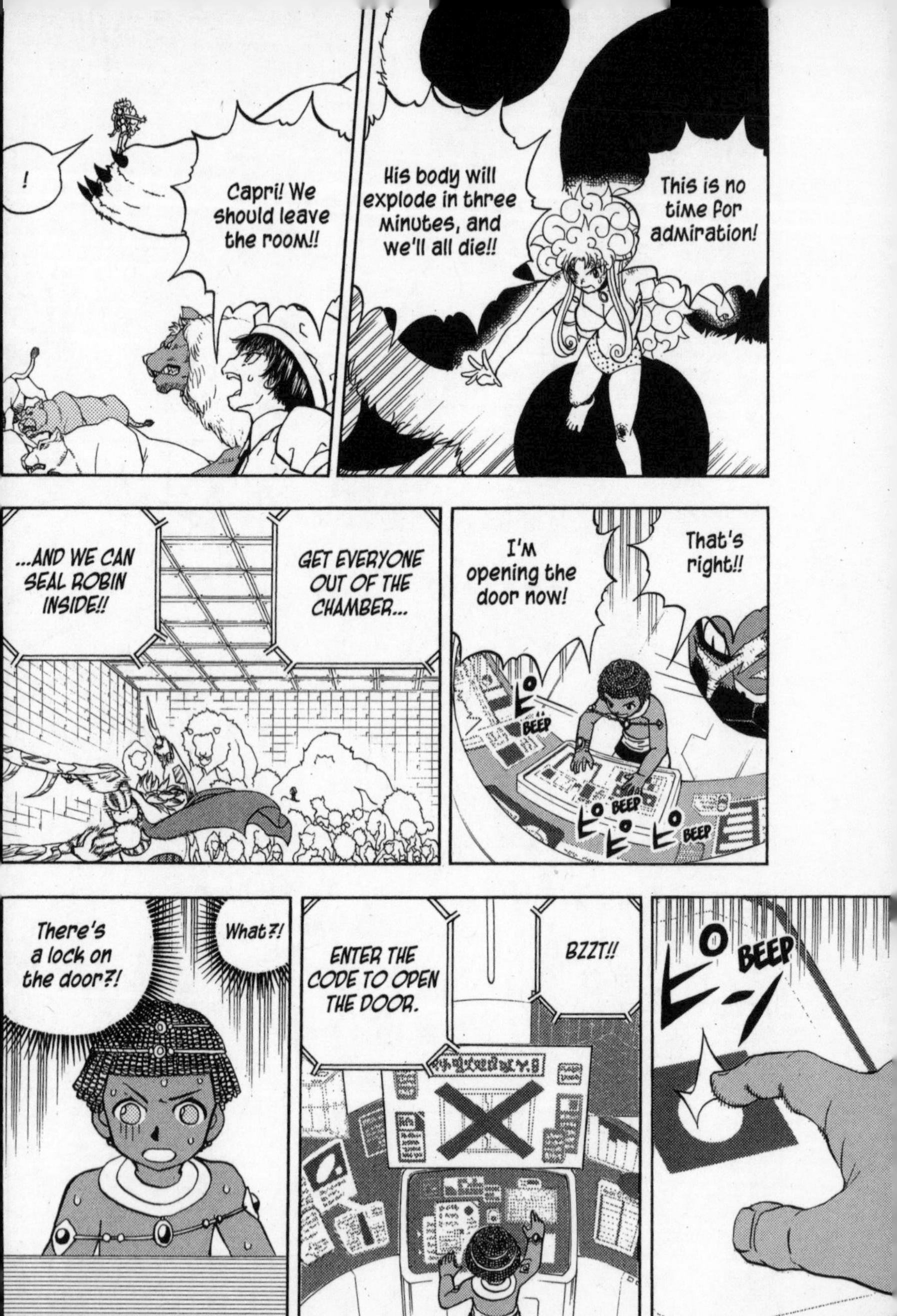
This is no time for admiration!
His body will explode in three minutes, and we'll all die!!
Capri! We should leave the room!!
!
That's right!!
I'M opening the door now!
BEEP
BEEP
BEEP
GET EVERYONE OUT OF THE CHAMBER...
...AND WE CAN SEAL ROBIN INSIDE!!
BEEP
BZZT!!
ENTER THE CODE TO OPEN THE DOOR.
What?!
There's a lock on the door?!

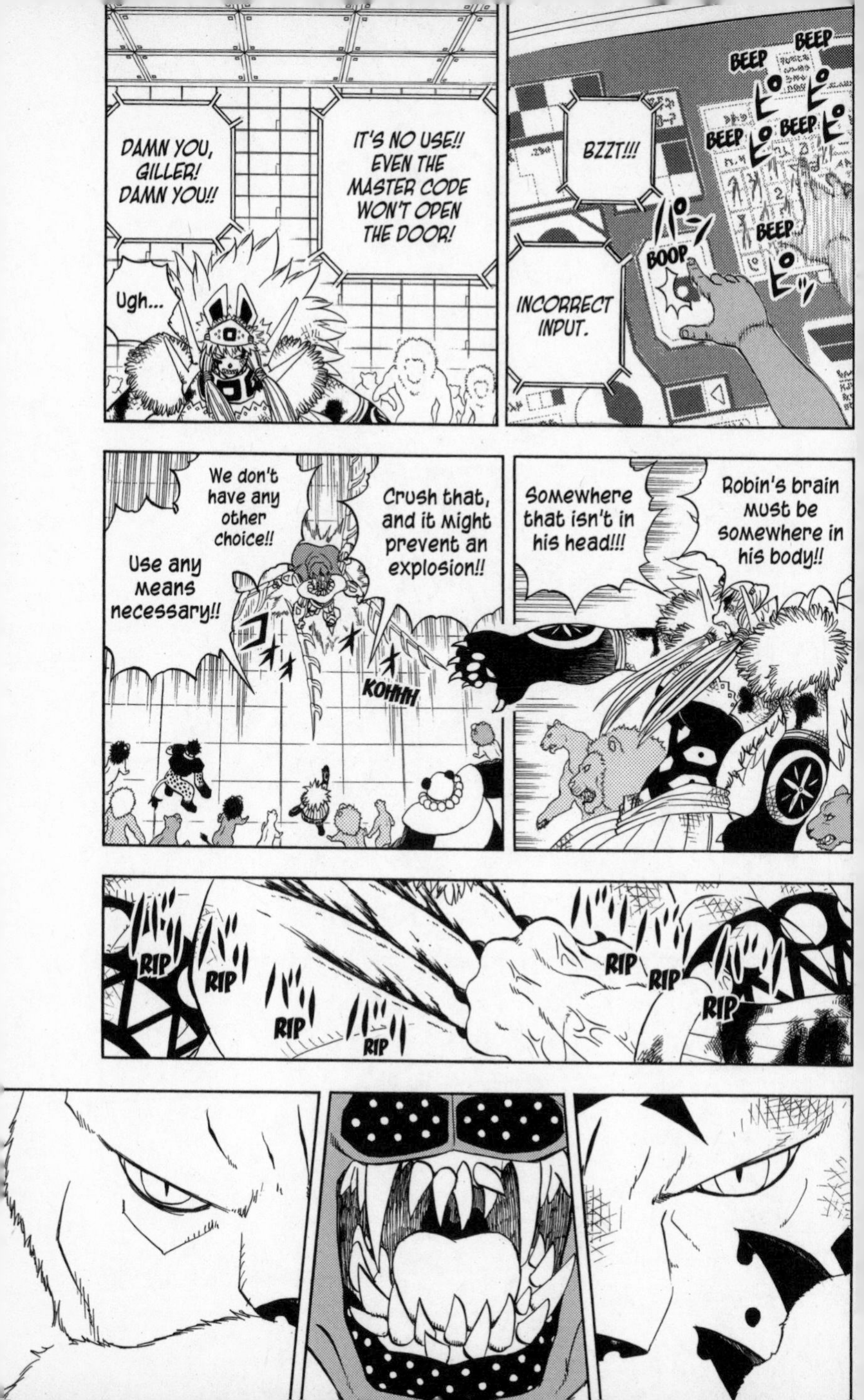
BEEP
BEEP
BEEP
BEEP
BEEP
BZZT!!!
BOOP
INCORRECT INPUT.
IT'S NO USE!! EVEN THE MASTER CODE WON'T OPEN THE DOOR!
DAMN YOU, GILLER! DAMN YOU!!
Ugh...
Robin's brain must be somewhere in his body!!
Somewhere that isn't in his head!!!
Crush that, and it might prevent an explosion!!
We don't have any other choice!!
Use any means necessary!!
KOHHH
RIP
RIP
RIP
RIP
RIP
RIP
RIP

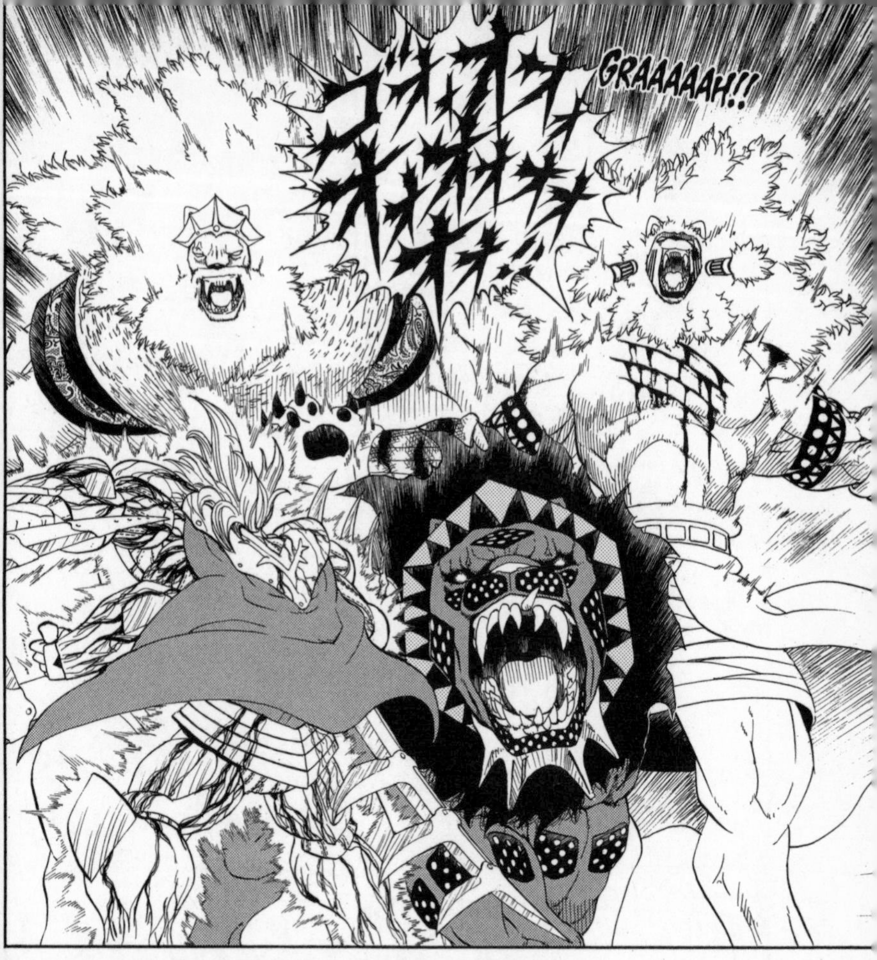
GRAAAAAH!!
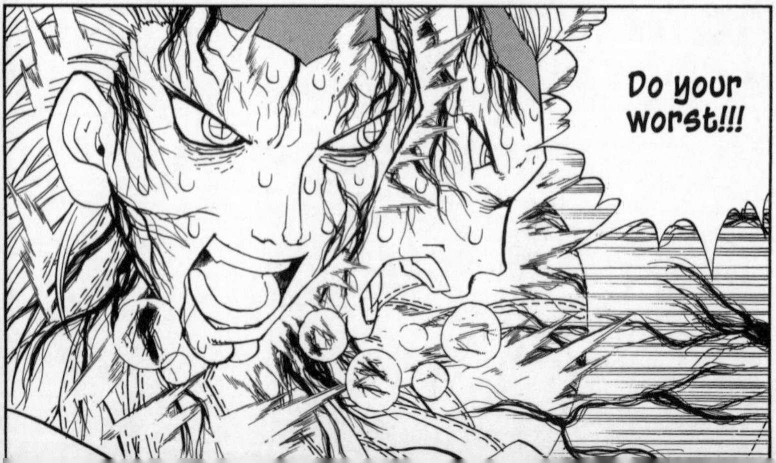
Do your worst!!!

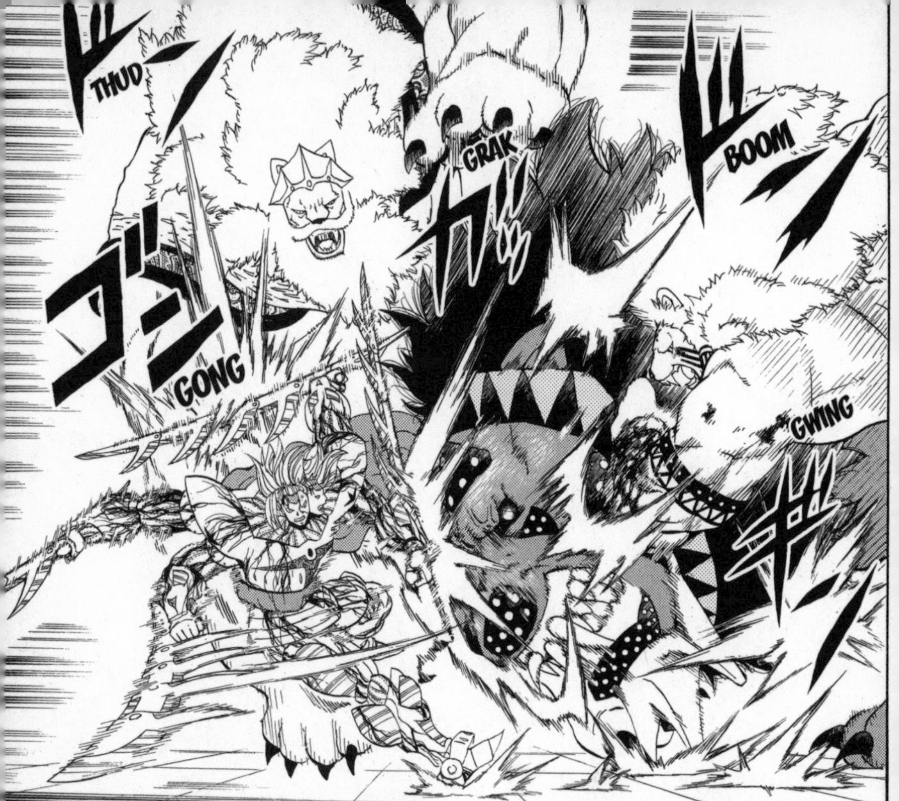
BOOM
GRAK
THUD
GWING
GONG
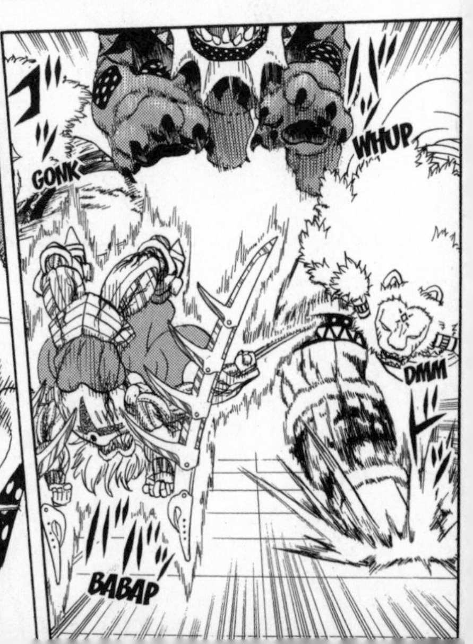
WHUP
GONK
DMM
BABAP
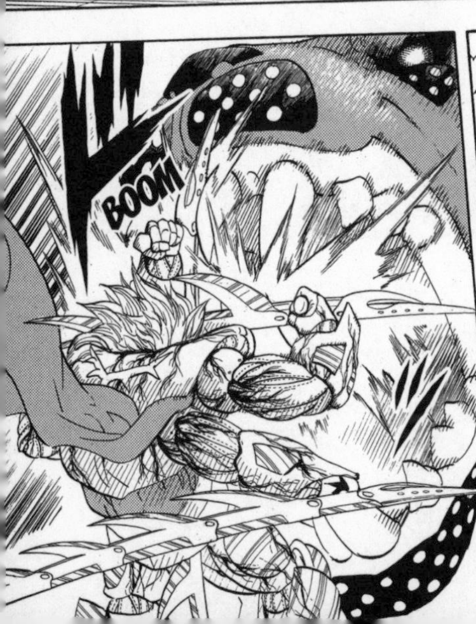
BOOM

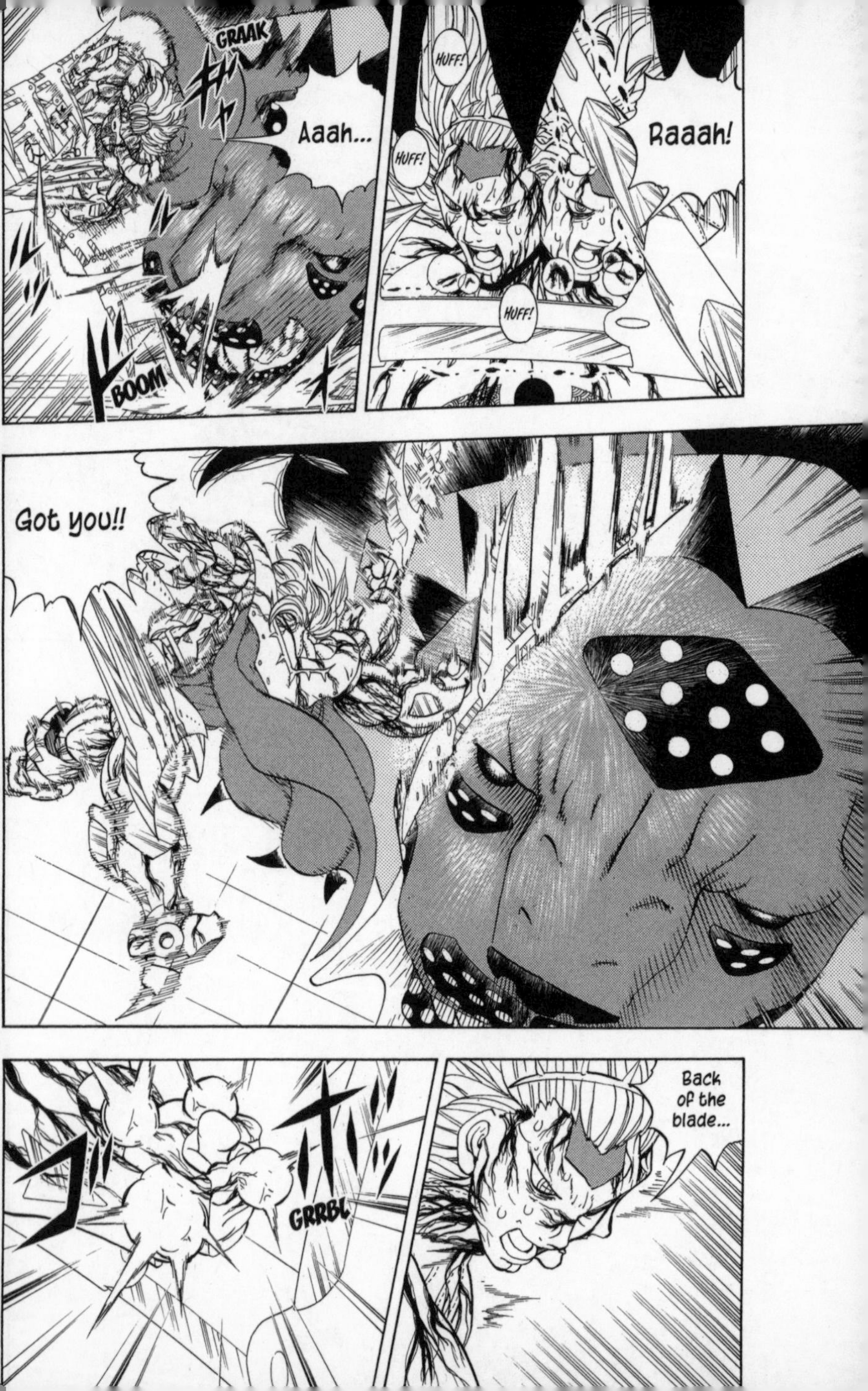
HUFF!
HUFF!
HUFF!
Raaah!
GRAAK
Aaah...
BOOM
Got you!!
Back of the blade...
GRRBL

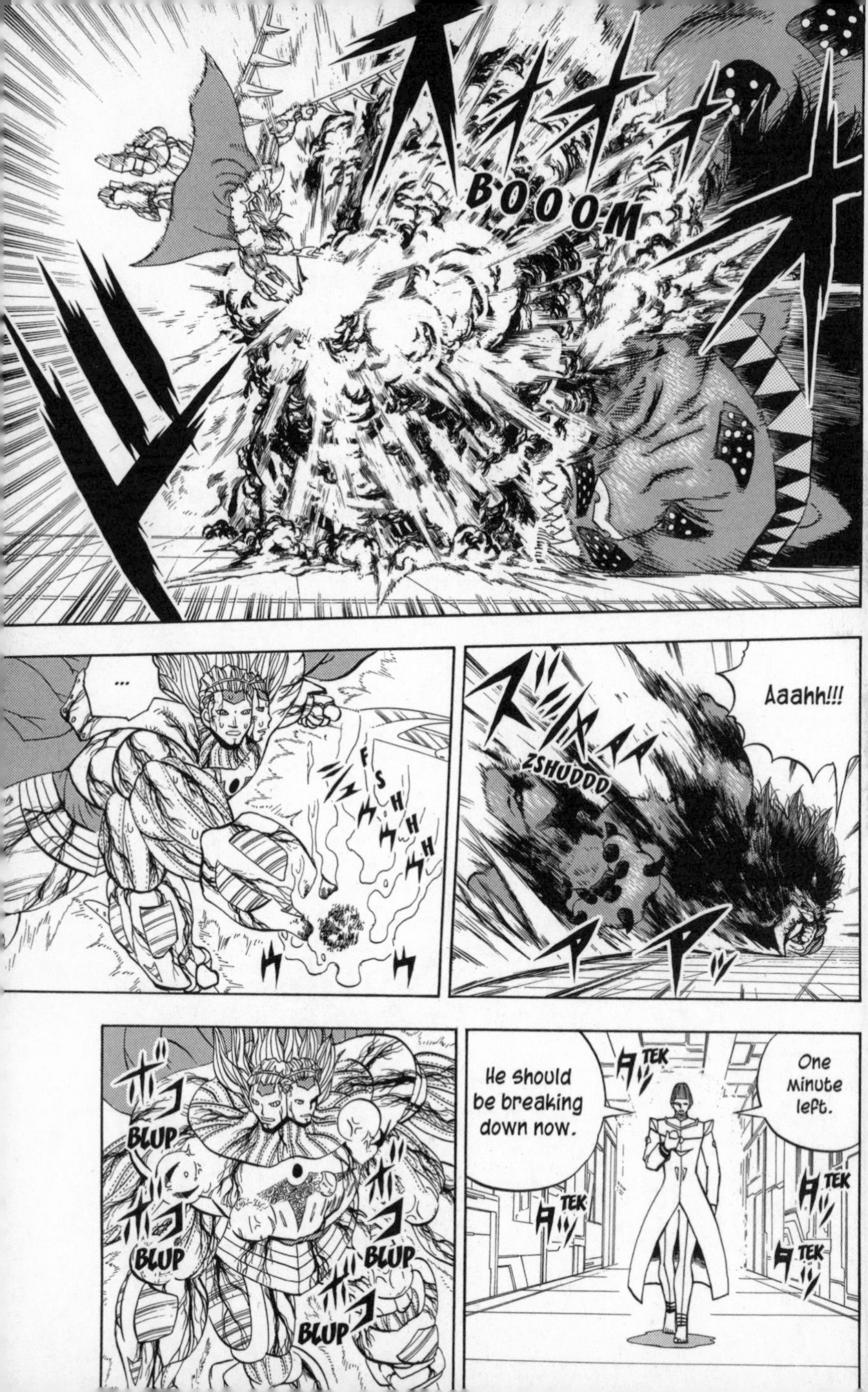
BOOOM
Aaahh!!!
ZSHUDDD
...
FSHHHH
One minute left.
TEK
He should be breaking down now.
TEK
TEK
TEK
BLUP
BLUP
BLUP
BLUP

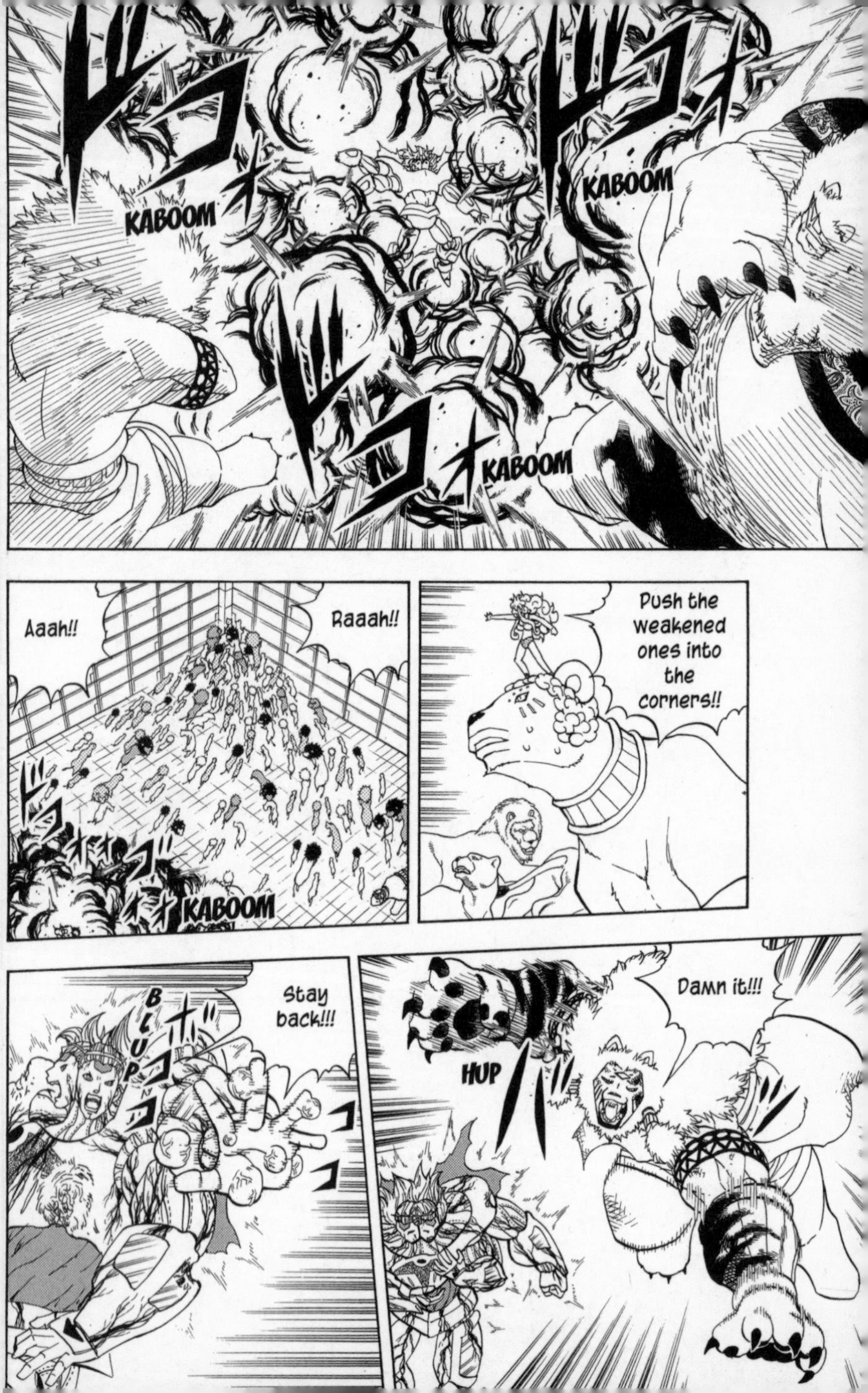
KABOOM
KABOOM
KABOOM
Push the weakened ones into the corners!!
Raaah!!
Aaah!!
KABOOM
Damn it!!!
HUP
Stay back!!!
BLUP

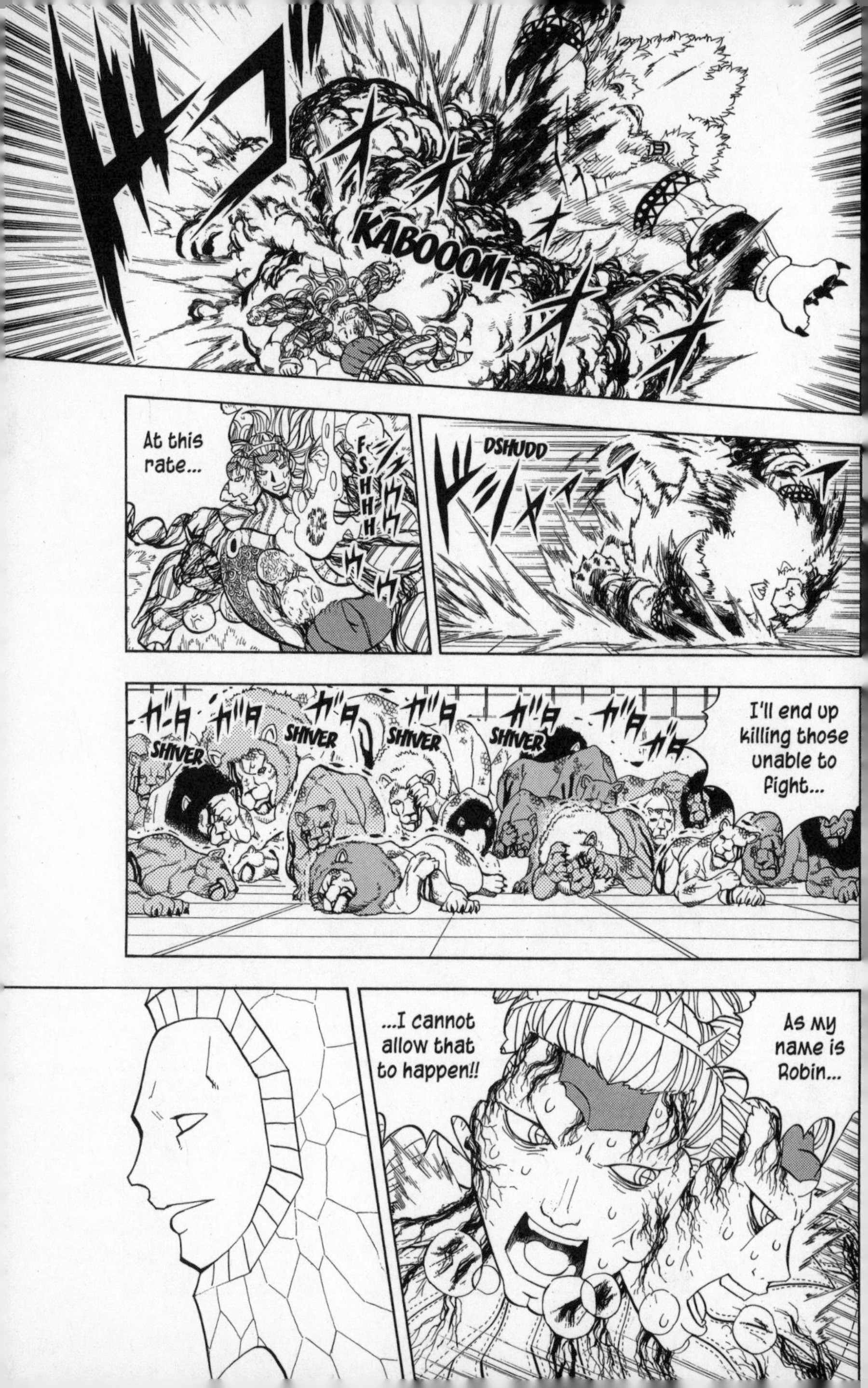
KABOOOM
DSHUDD
At this rate...
FSHHH
SHIVER
SHIVER
SHIVER
SHIVER
I'll end up killing those unable to fight...
As my name is Robin...
...I cannot allow that to happen!!

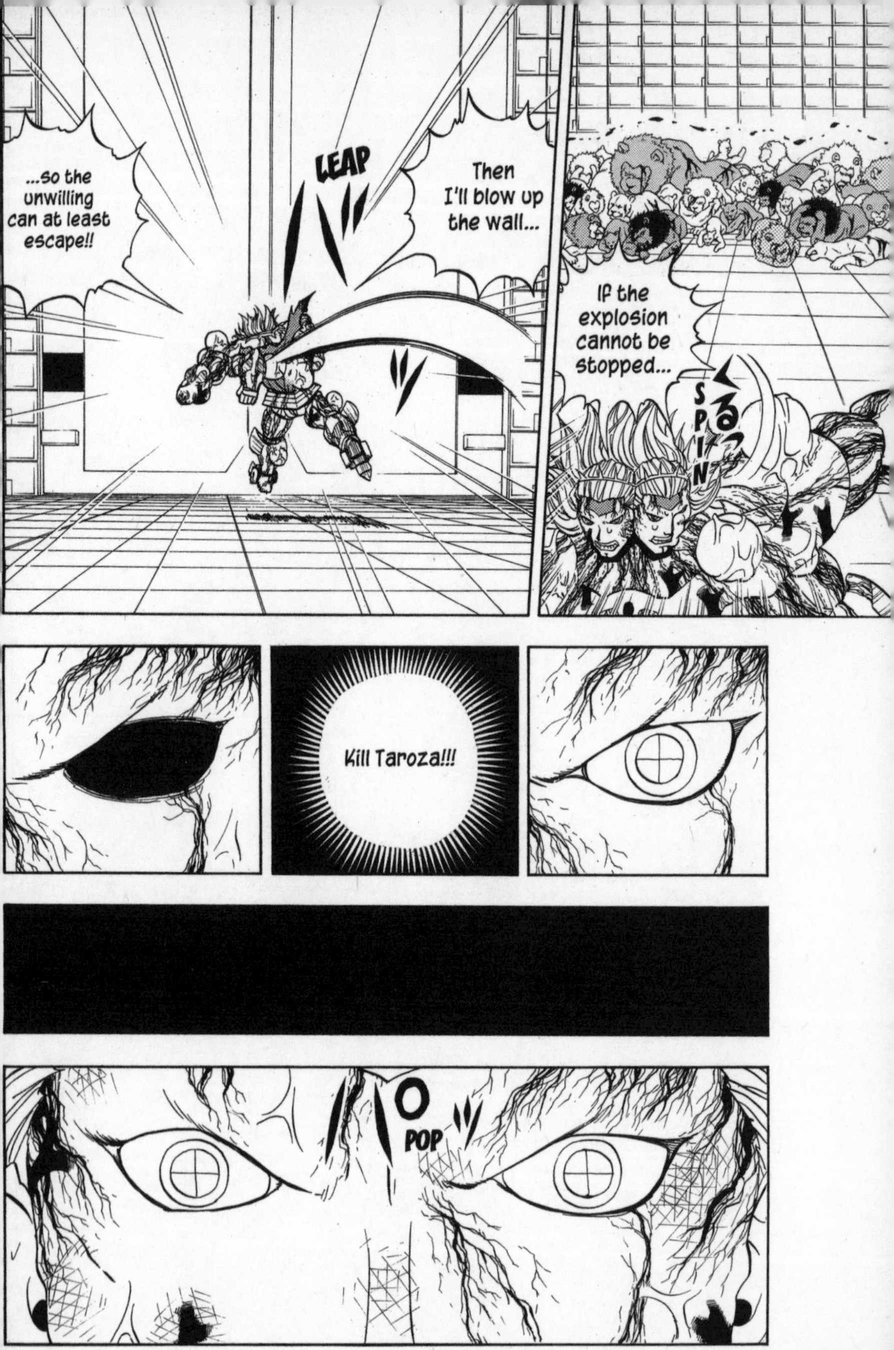
If the explosion cannot be stopped...
くるっ
SPIN
Then I'll blow up the wall...
LEAP
...so the unwilling can at least escape!!
Kill Taroza!!!
POP

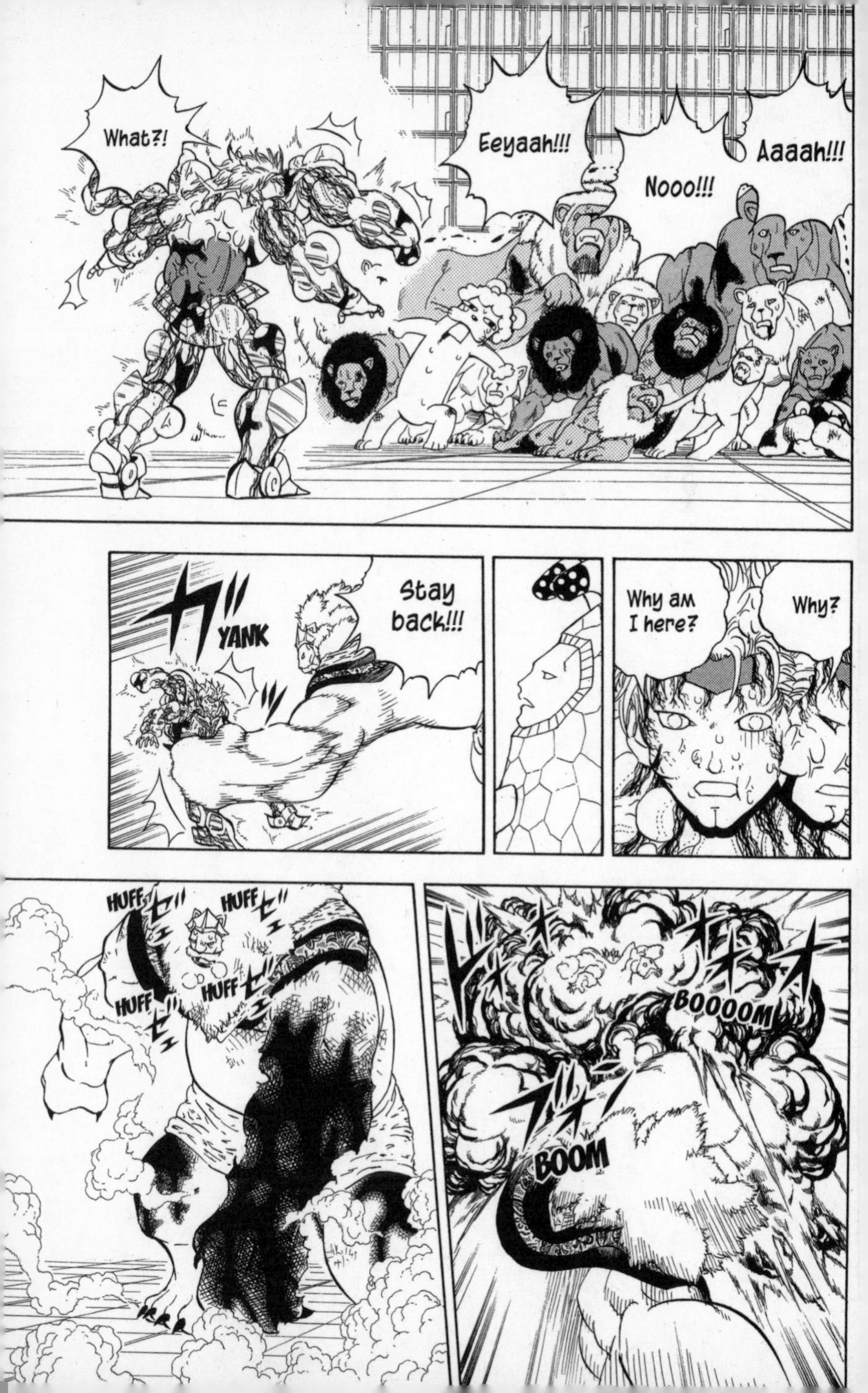
Aaaah!!!
Nooo!!!
Eeyaah!!!
What?!
Why?
Why am I here?
Stay back!!!
YANK
BOOOOM
BOOM
HUFF
HUFF
HUFF
HUFF

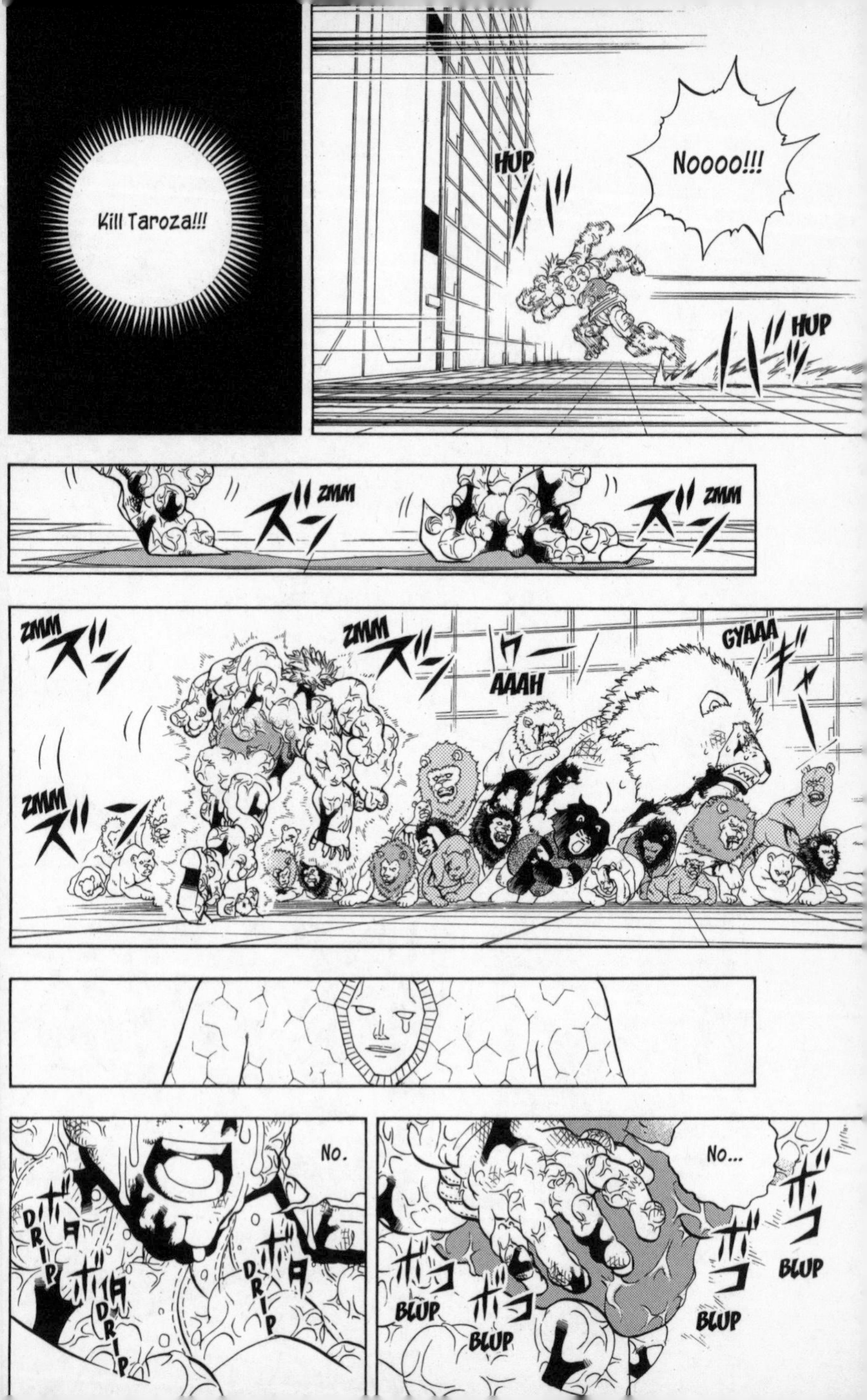

Noooo!!!
HUP
HUP
Kill Taroza!!!
ZMM
ZMM
GYAAA
AAAH
ZMM
ZMM
ZMM
No...
BLUP
BLUP
BLUP
BLUP
No.
DRIP
DRIP
DRIP

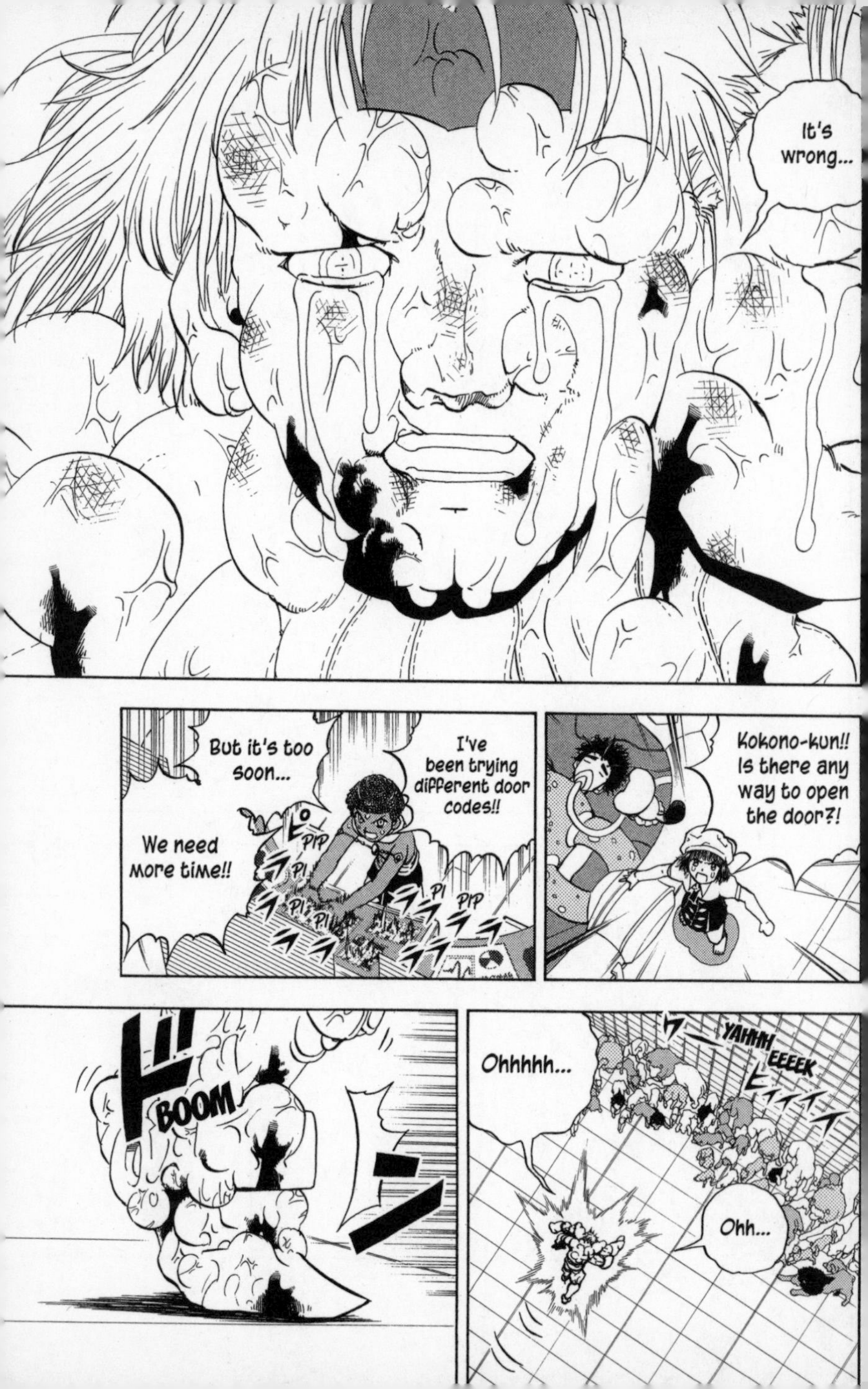
It's wrong...
Kokono-kun!! Is there any way to open the door?!
I've been trying different door codes!!
But it's too soon...
We need more time!!
PIP
PI
PI
PI
PI
PIP
YAHHH EEEEK
Ohhhhh...
Ohh...
BOOM

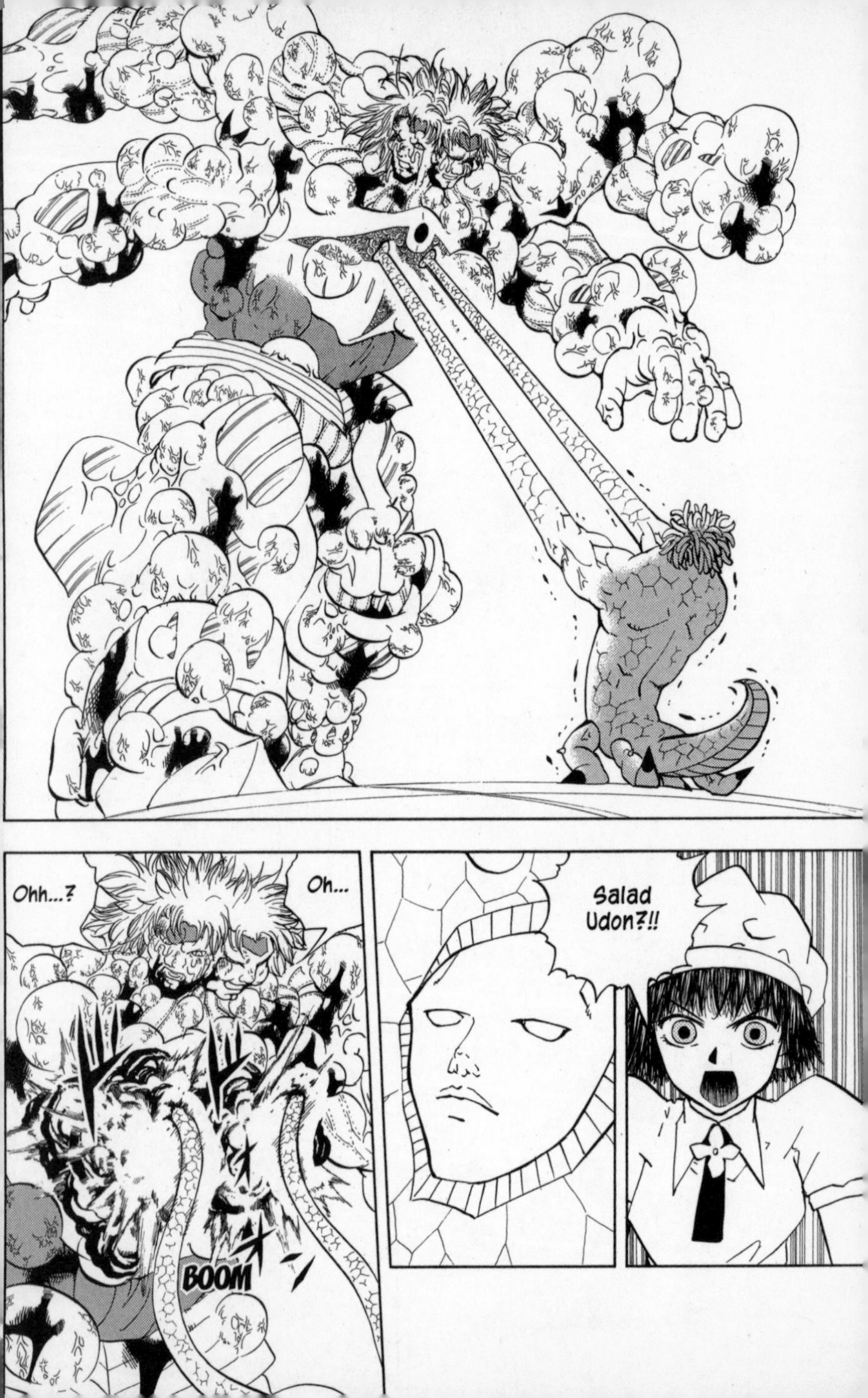
Salad Udon?!!
Oh...
Ohh...?
BOOM

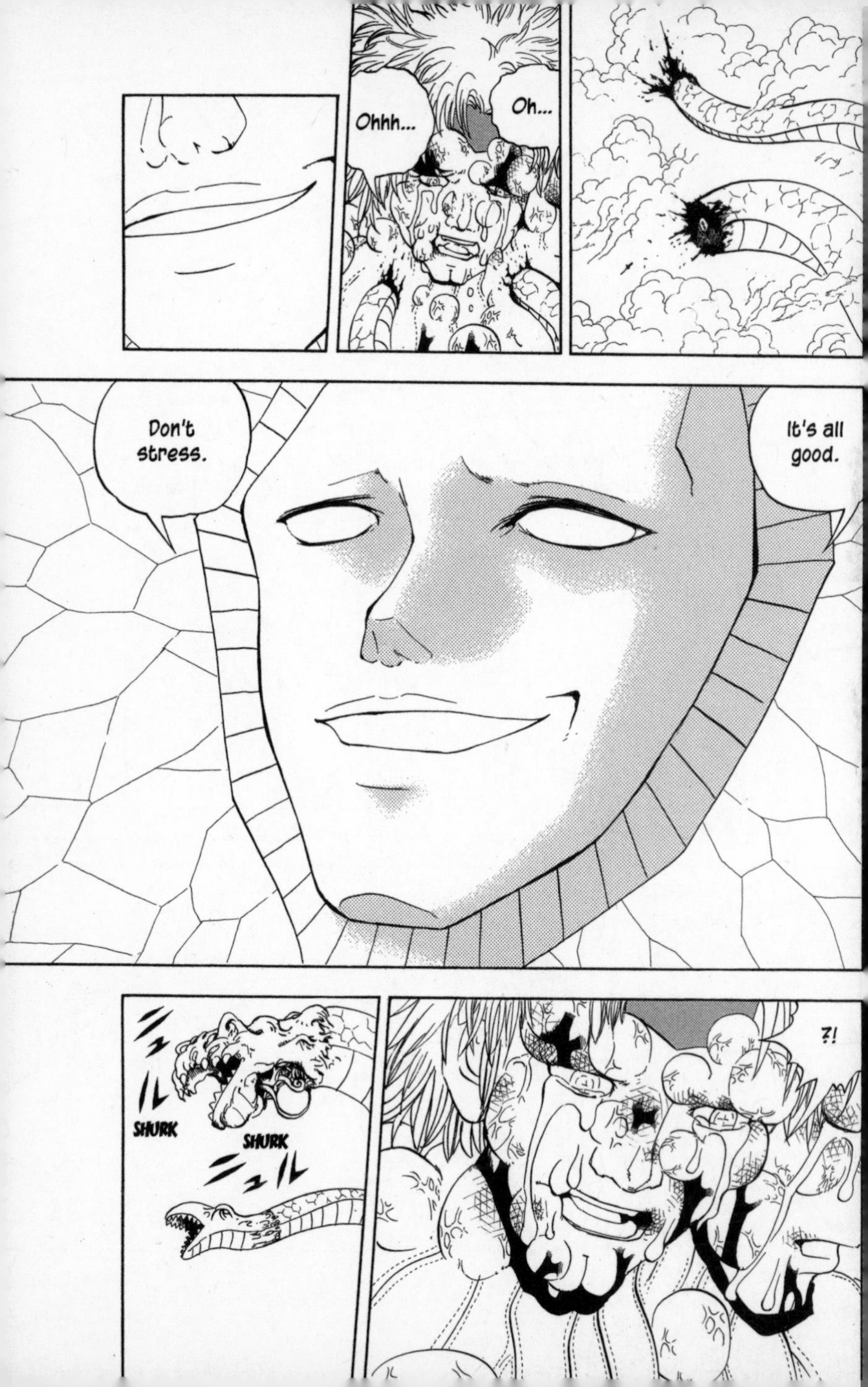
Oh...
Ohhh...
It's all good.
Don't stress.
?!
SHURK
SHURK

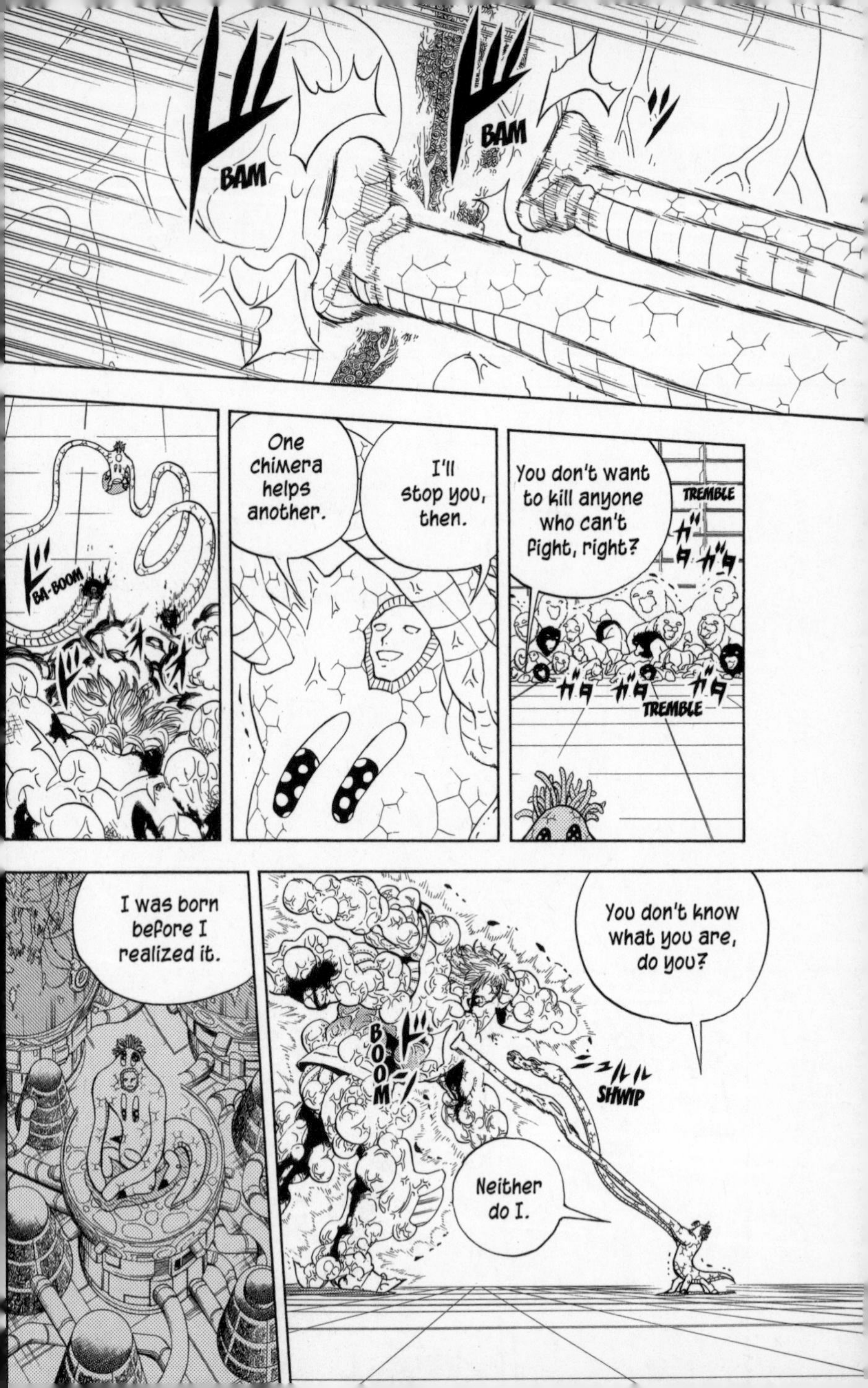
BAM
BAM
You don't want to kill anyone who can't fight, right?
TREMBLE
TREMBLE
I'll stop you, then.
One chimera helps another.
BA-BOOM
You don't know what you are, do you?
SHWIP
BOOM
Neither do I.
I was born before I realized it.

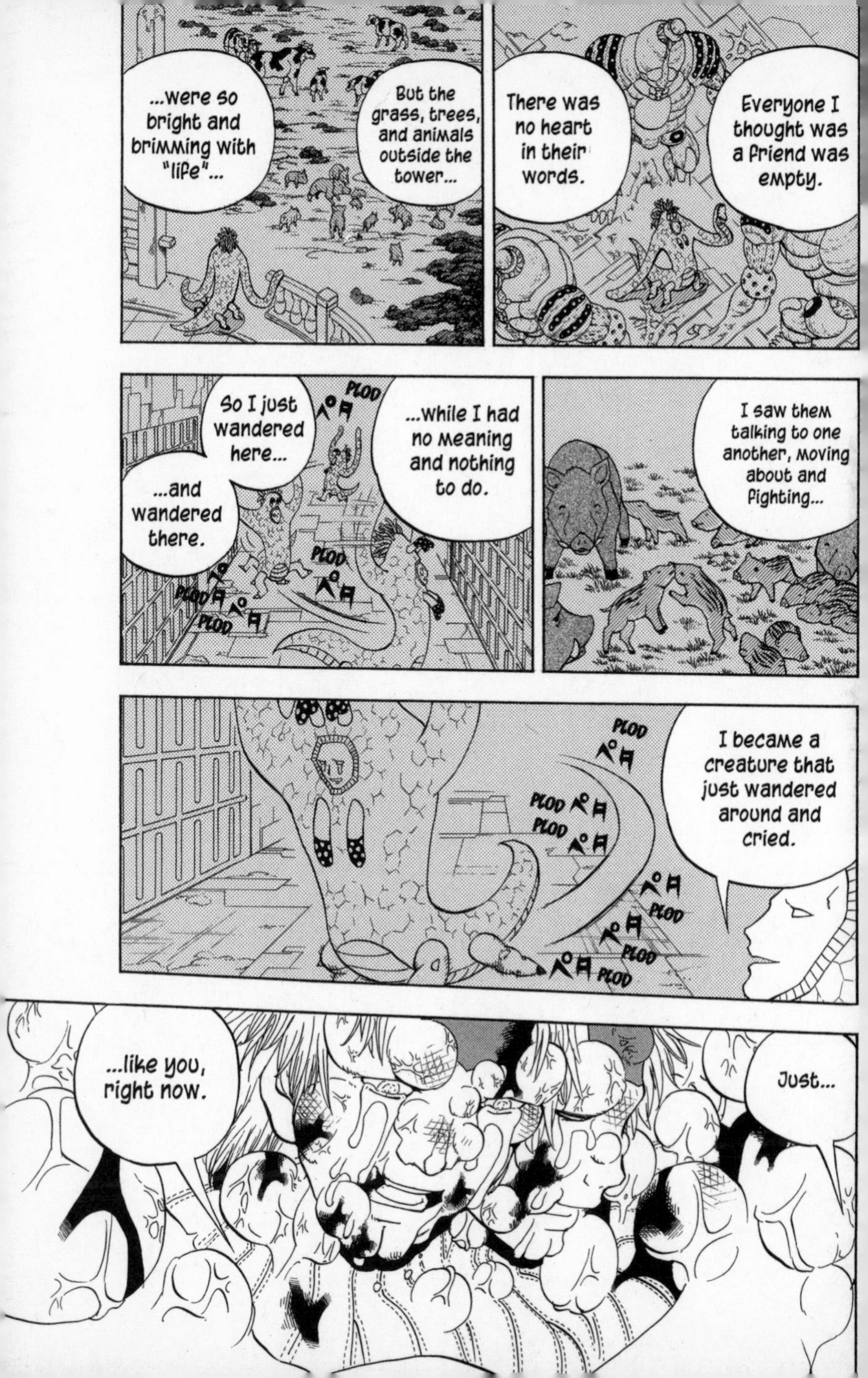
Everyone I thought was a friend was empty.
There was no heart in their words.
But the grass, trees, and animals outside the tower...
...were so bright and brimming with "life"...
I saw them talking to one another, moving about and fighting...
...while I had no meaning and nothing to do.
PLOD
So I just wandered here...
...and wandered there.
PLOD
PLOD
PLOD
PLOD
I became a creature that just wandered around and cried.
PLOD
PLOD
PLOD
PLOD
PLOD
PLOD
Just...
...like you, right now.

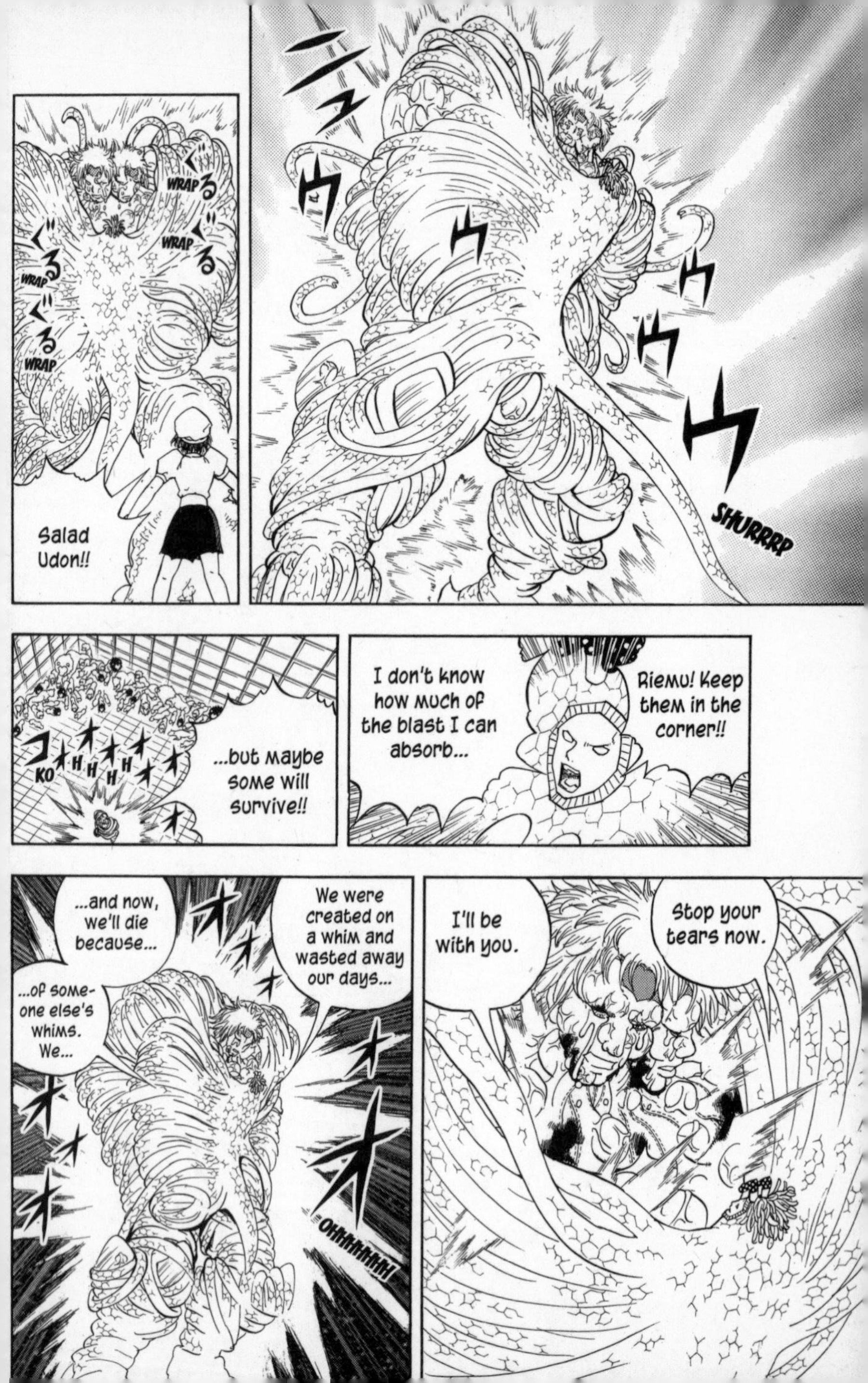
SHURRRP
WRAP
WRAP
WRAP
WRAP
ぐるぐる
ぐるぐる
ぐるぐる
ぐるぐる
Salad Udon!!
Riemu! Keep them in the corner!!
I don't know how much of the blast I can absorb...
...but maybe some will survive!!
KOHHHH
Stop your tears now.
I'll be with you.
We were created on a whim and wasted away our days...
...and now, we'll die because...
...of some-one else's whims. We...
OHHHHHHH

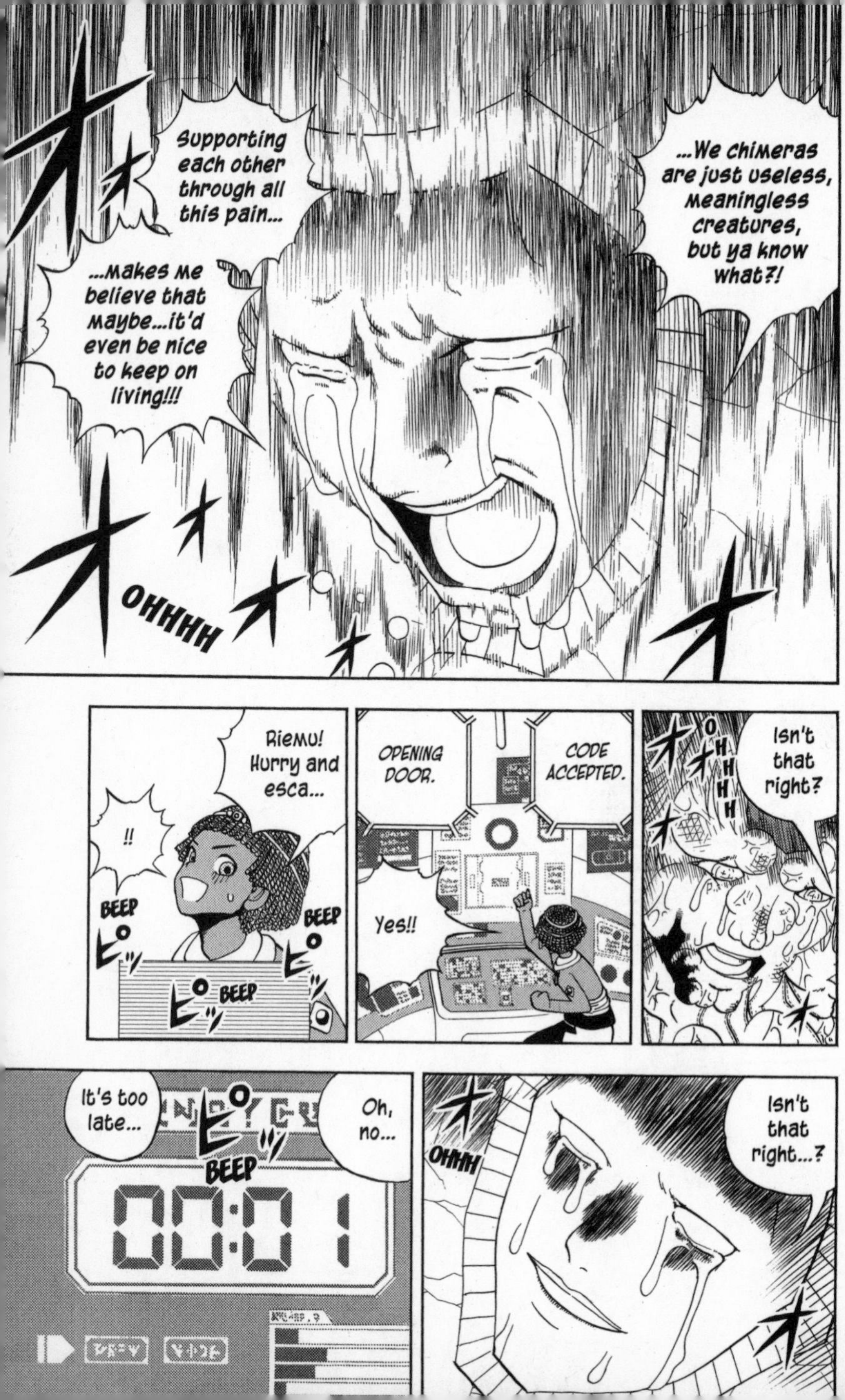
...We chimeras are just useless, meaningless creatures, but ya know what?!
Supporting each other through all this pain...
...makes me believe that maybe...it'd even be nice to keep on living!!!
OHHHH
OHHHH
Isn't that right?
CODE ACCEPTED.
OPENING DOOR.
Yes!!
Riemu! Hurry and esca...
!!
BEEP
BEEP
BEEP
Isn't that right...?
OHHH
Oh, no...
It's too late...
BEEP
00:01

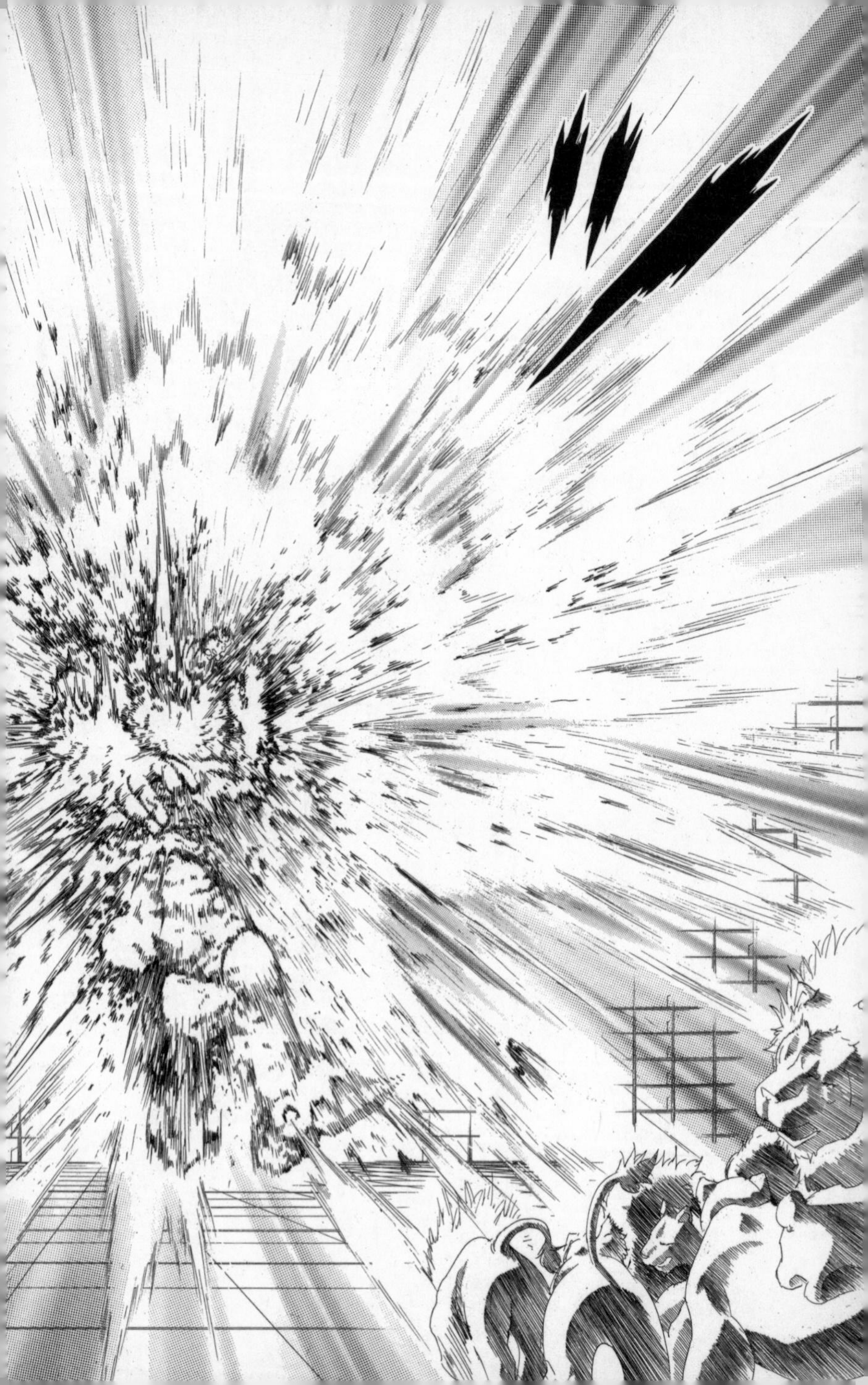

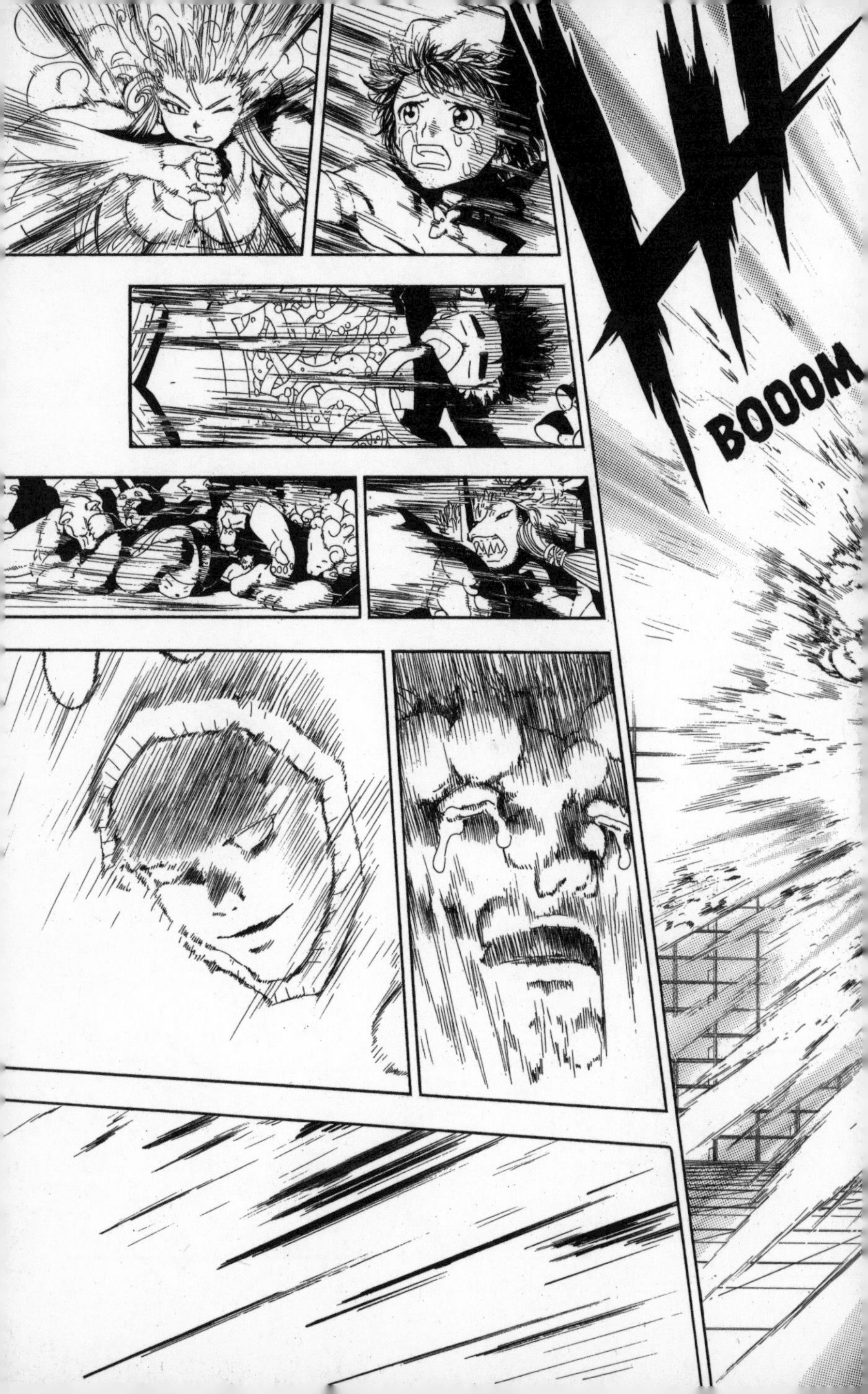
BOOOM

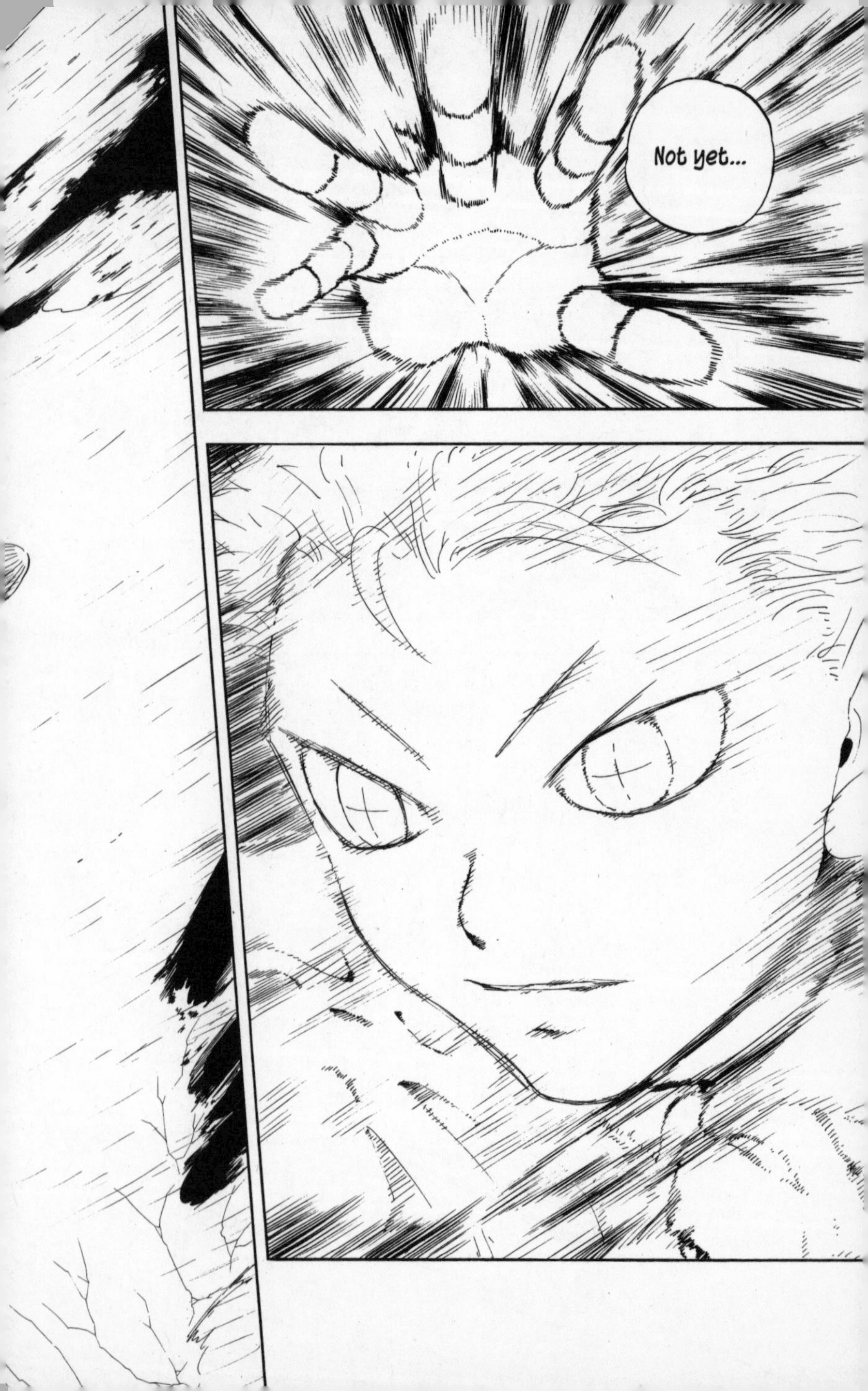
Not yet...

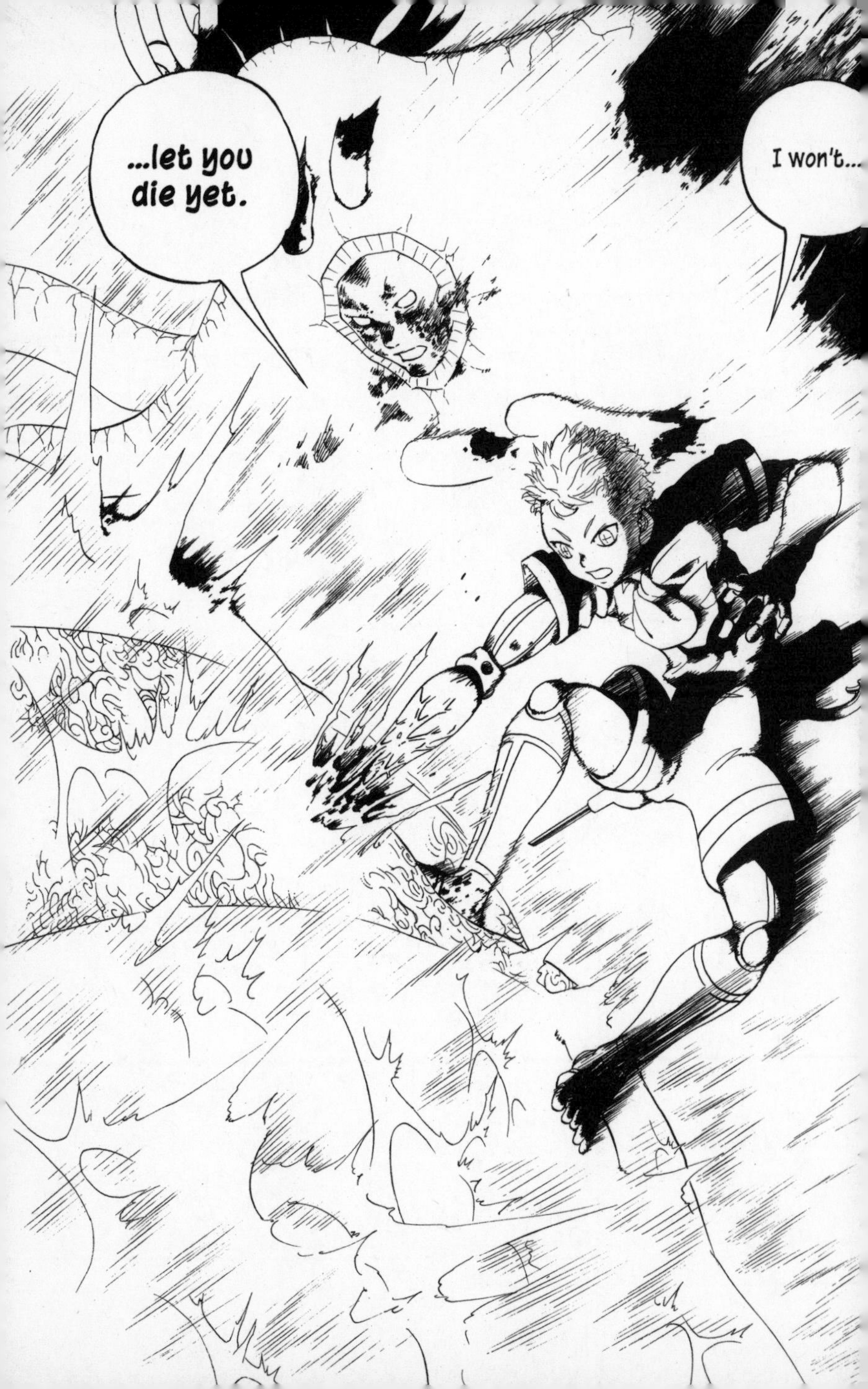
I won't...
...let you die yet.

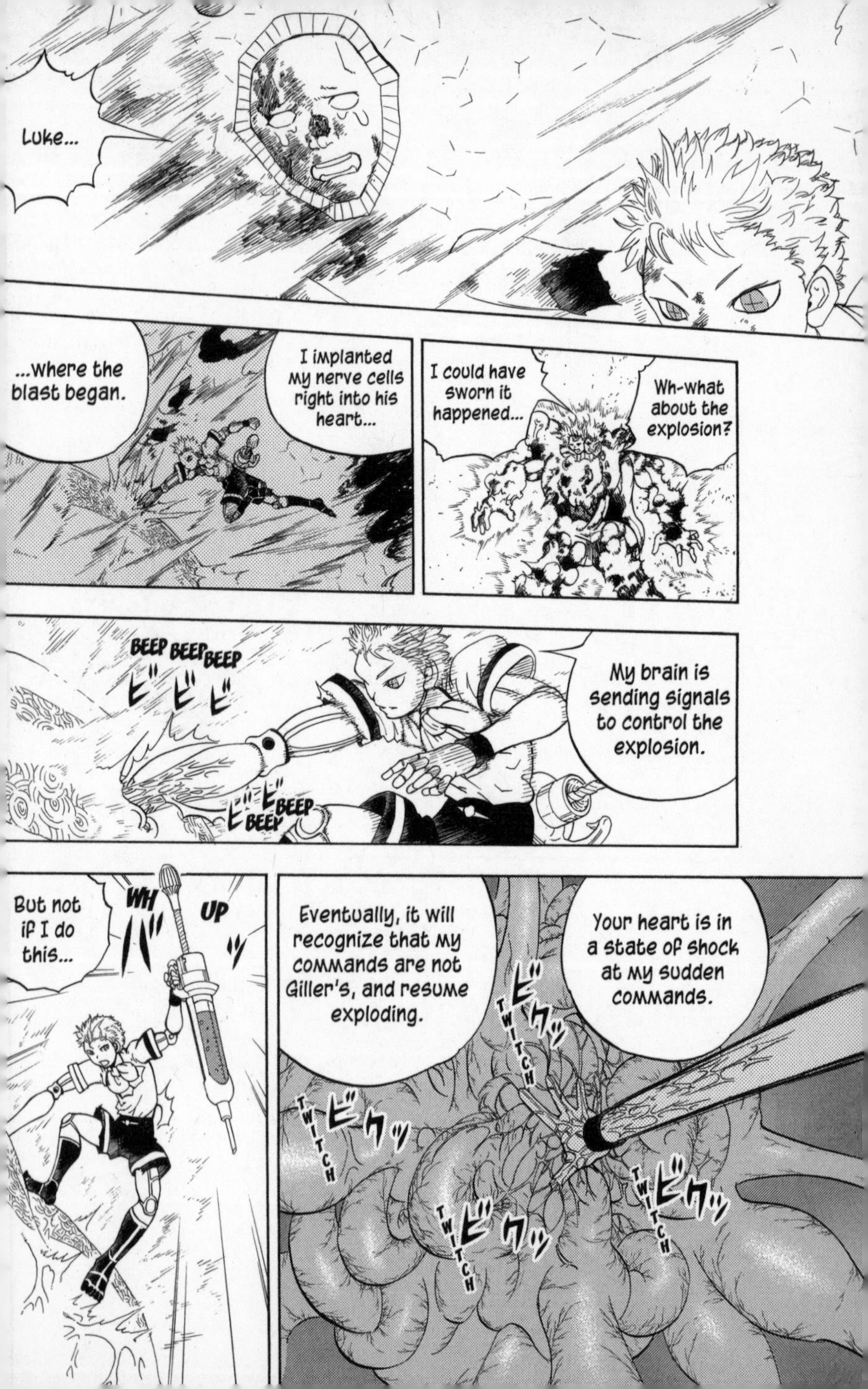
Luke...
Wh-what about the explosion?
I could have sworn it happened...
I implanted my nerve cells right into his heart...
...where the blast began.
My brain is sending signals to control the explosion.
BEEP BEEP BEEP
ビビビ
BEEP BEEP
ビビビ
Your heart is in a state of shock at my sudden commands.
Eventually, it will recognize that my commands are not Giller's, and resume exploding.
TWITCH
ビクッ
TWITCH
ビクッ
TWITCH
ビクッ
TWITCH
ビクッ
But not if I do this...
WHUP
バッ

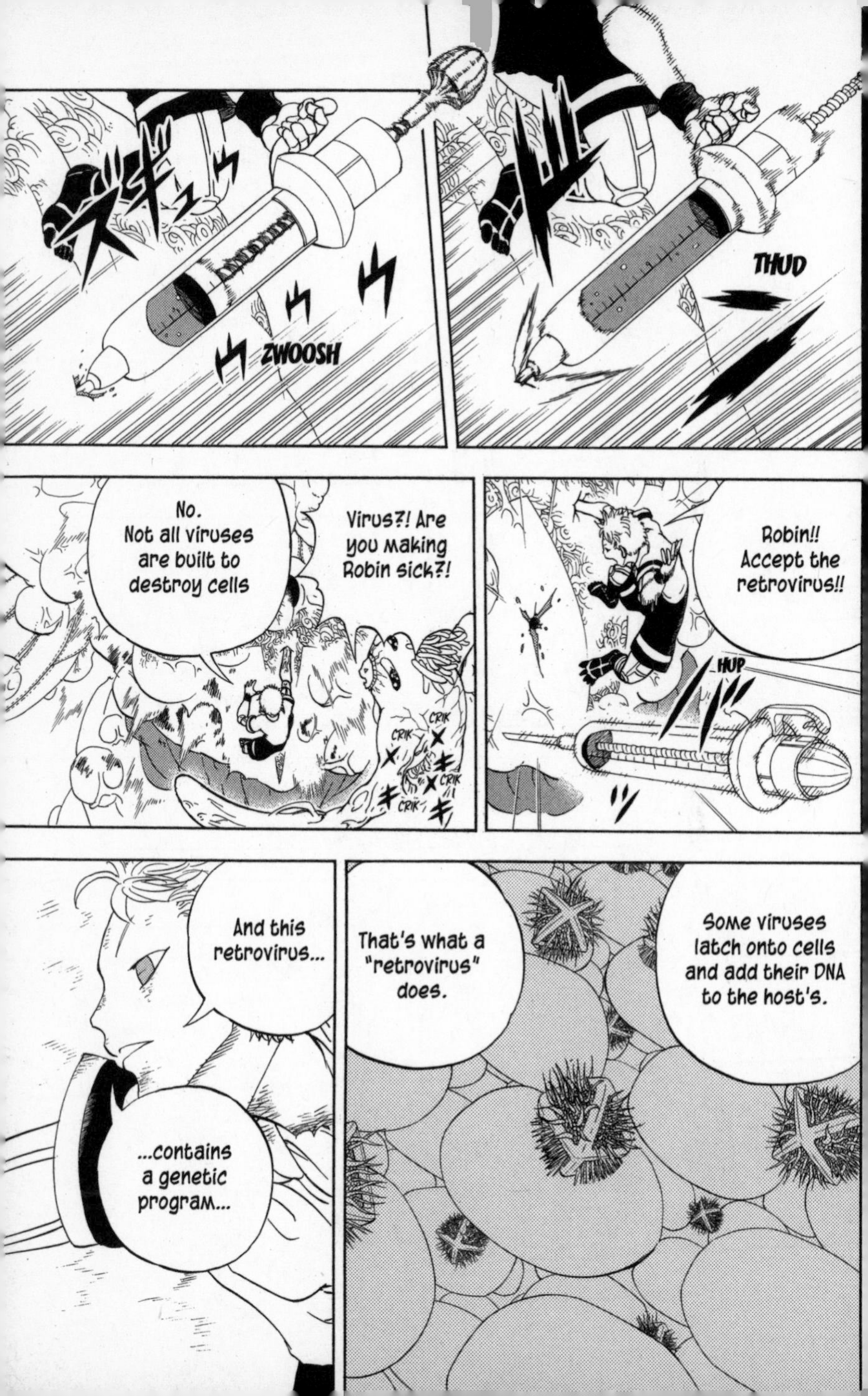
THUD
ZWOOSH
HUP
Robin!! Accept the retrovirus!!
Virus?! Are you making Robin sick?!
No. Not all viruses are built to destroy cells
CRIK
CRIK
CRIK
CRIK
Some viruses latch onto cells and add their DNA to the host's.
That's what a "retrovirus" does.
And this retrovirus...
...contains a genetic program...

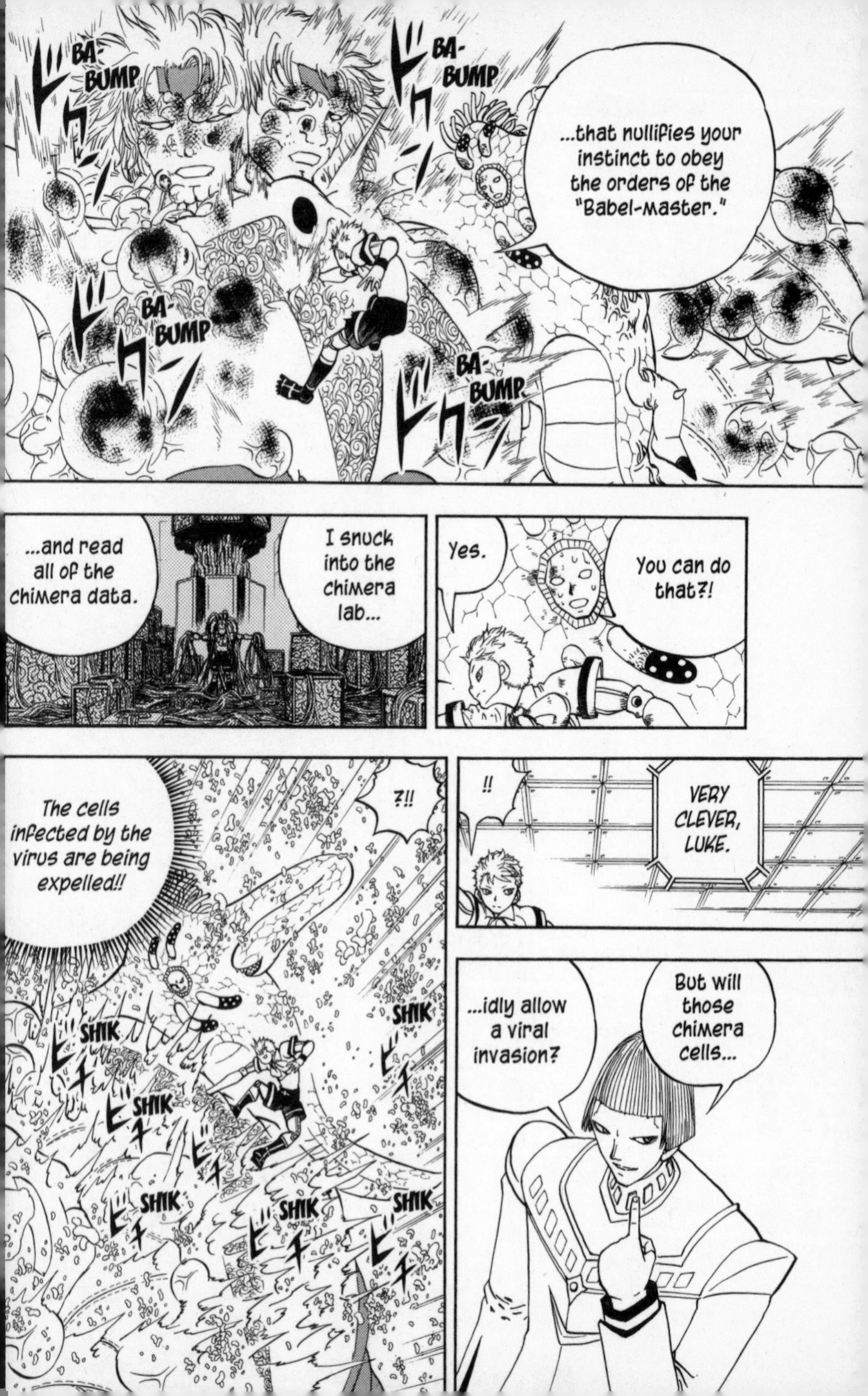
BA-BUMP
BA-BUMP
...that nullifies your instinct to obey the orders of the "Babel-master."
BA-BUMP
BA-BUMP
You can do that?!
Yes.
I snuck into the chimera lab...
...and read all of the chimera data.
VERY CLEVER, LUKE.
!!
But will those chimera cells...
...idly allow a viral invasion?
?!!
The cells infected by the virus are being expelled!!
SHIK
SHIK
SHIK
SHIK
SHIK
SHIK

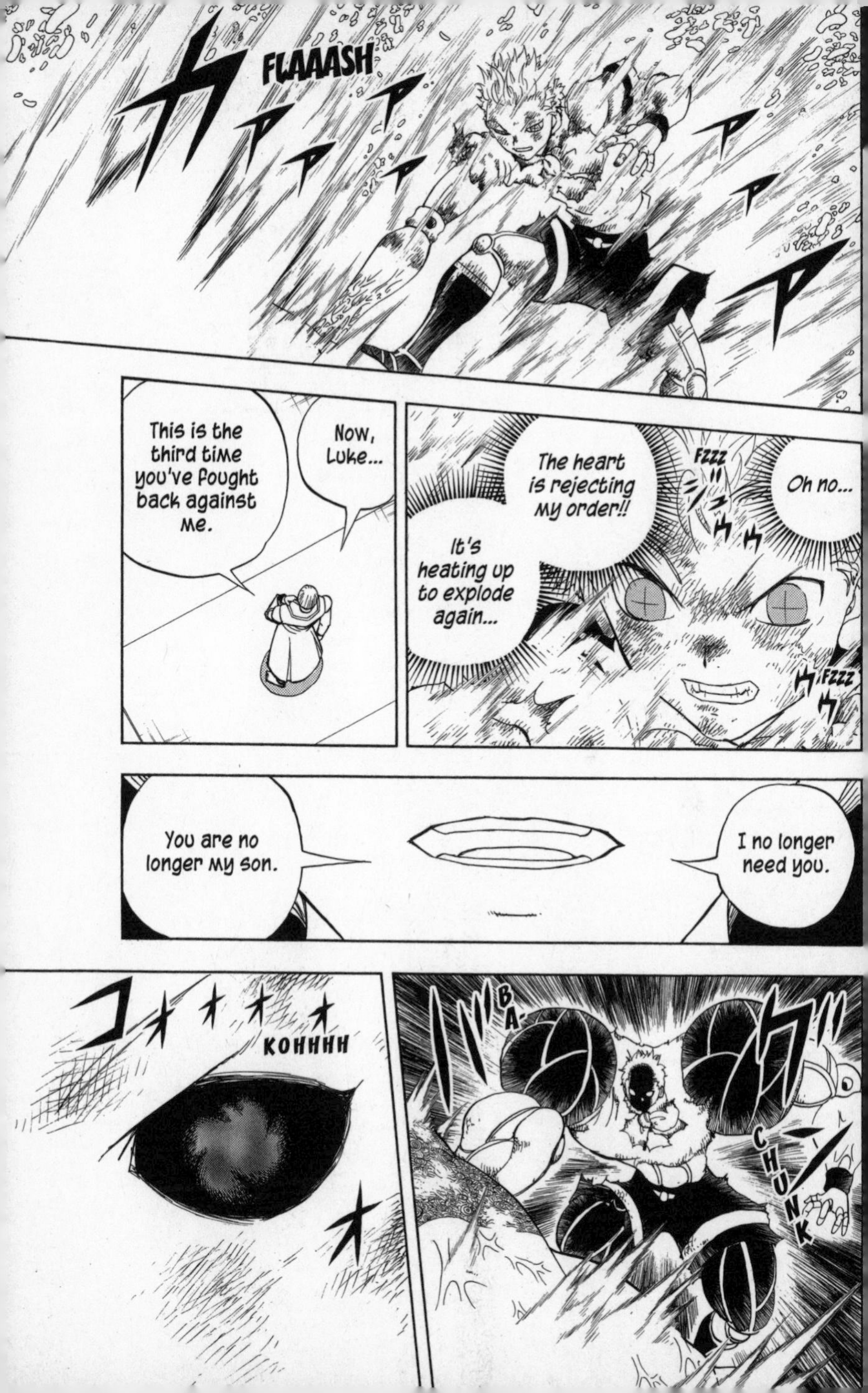
FLAAASH
Oh no...
FZZZ
The heart is rejecting my order!!
It's heating up to explode again...
FZZZ
Now, Luke...
This is the third time you've fought back against me.
I no longer need you.
You are no longer my son.
BA-CHUNK
KOHHHH

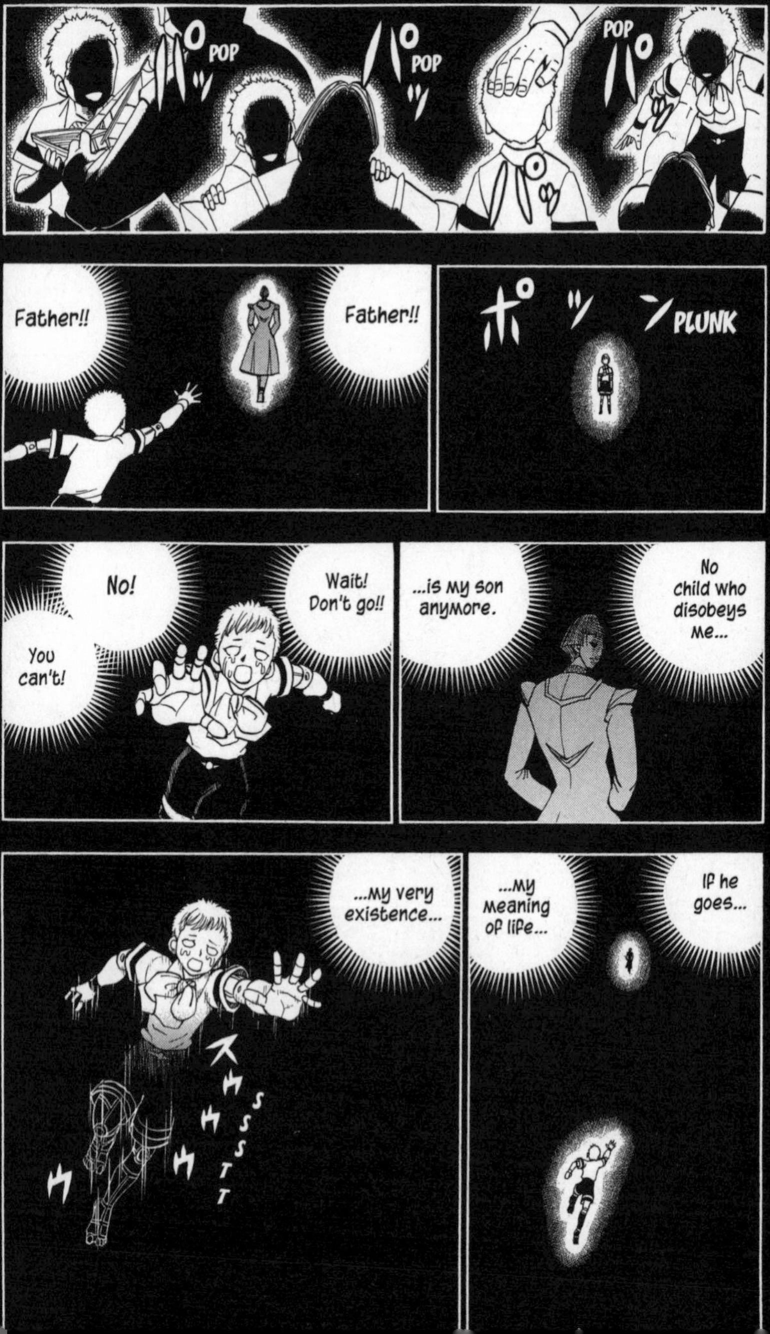
POP
POP
POP
ポツン PLUNK
Father!!
Father!!
No child who disobeys me...
...is my son anymore.
Wait! Don't go!!
No!
You can't!
If he goes...
...my meaning of life...
...my very existence...
SSSTT

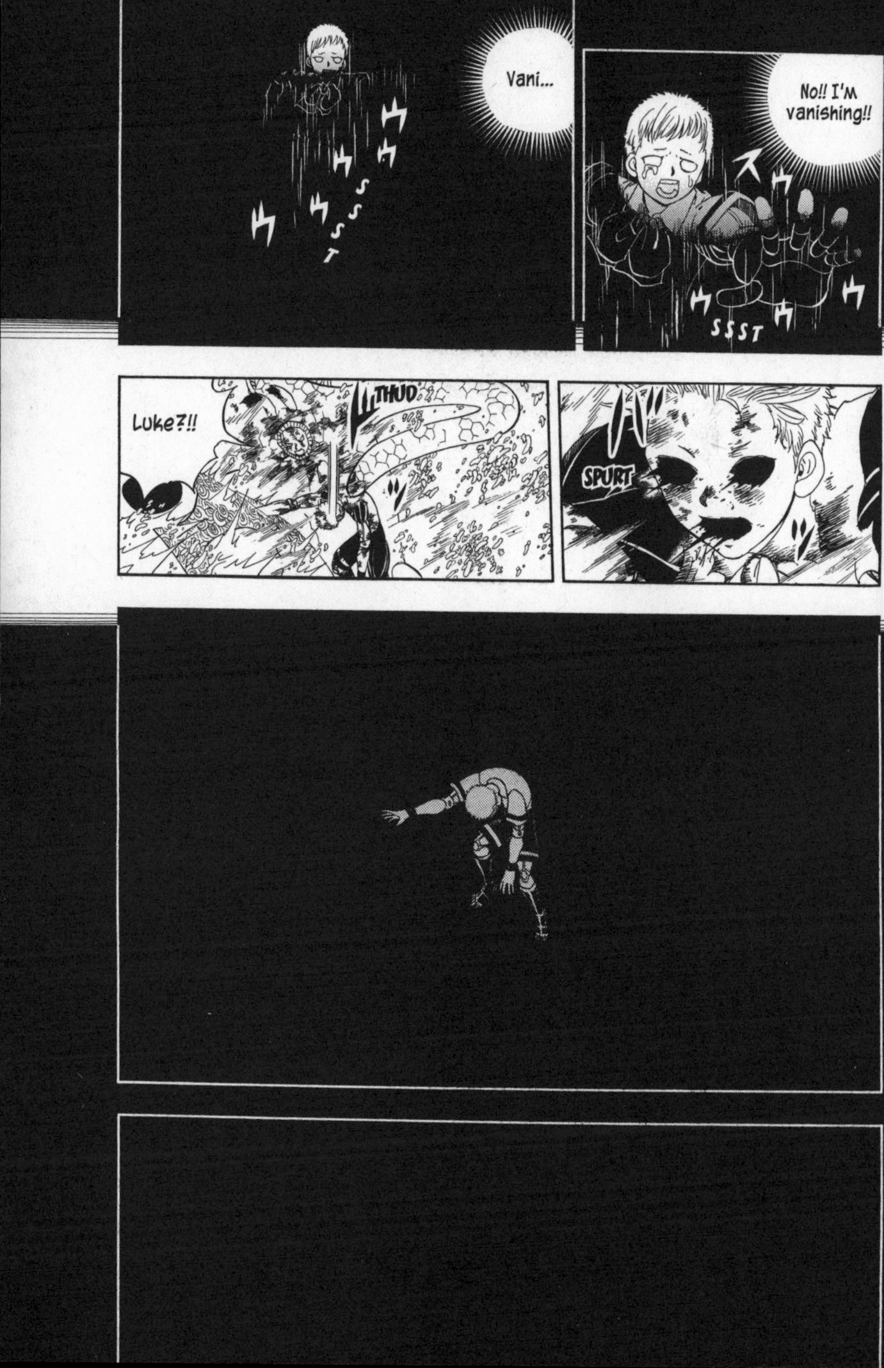
No!! I'm vanishing!!
SSST
Vani...
SSST
SPURT
THUD
Luke?!!

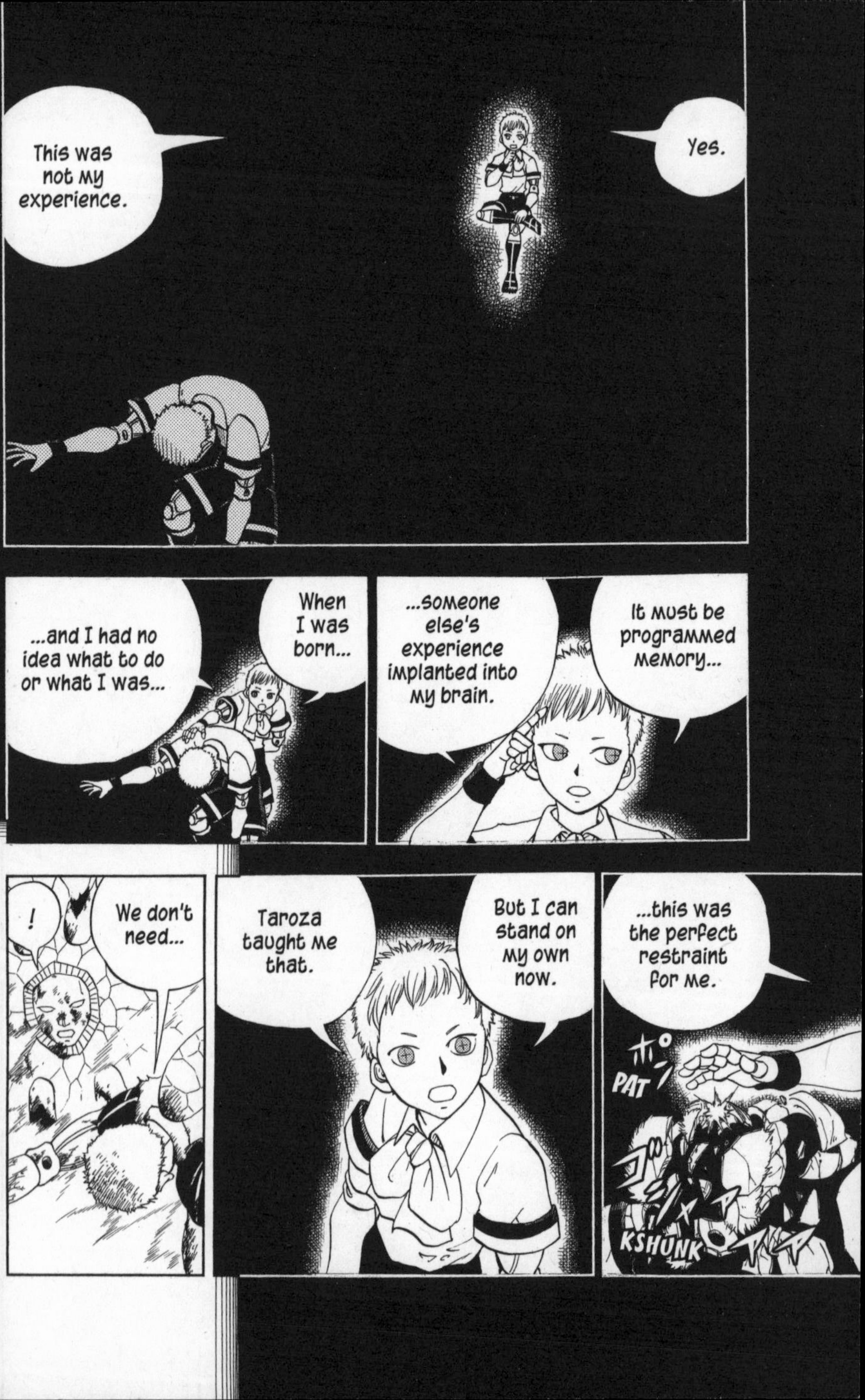
Yes.
This was not my experience.
It must be programmed memory...
...someone else's experience implanted into my brain.
When I was born...
...and I had no idea what to do or what I was...
...this was the perfect restraint for me.
PAT
KSHUNK
But I can stand on my own now.
Taroza taught me that.
We don't need...
!

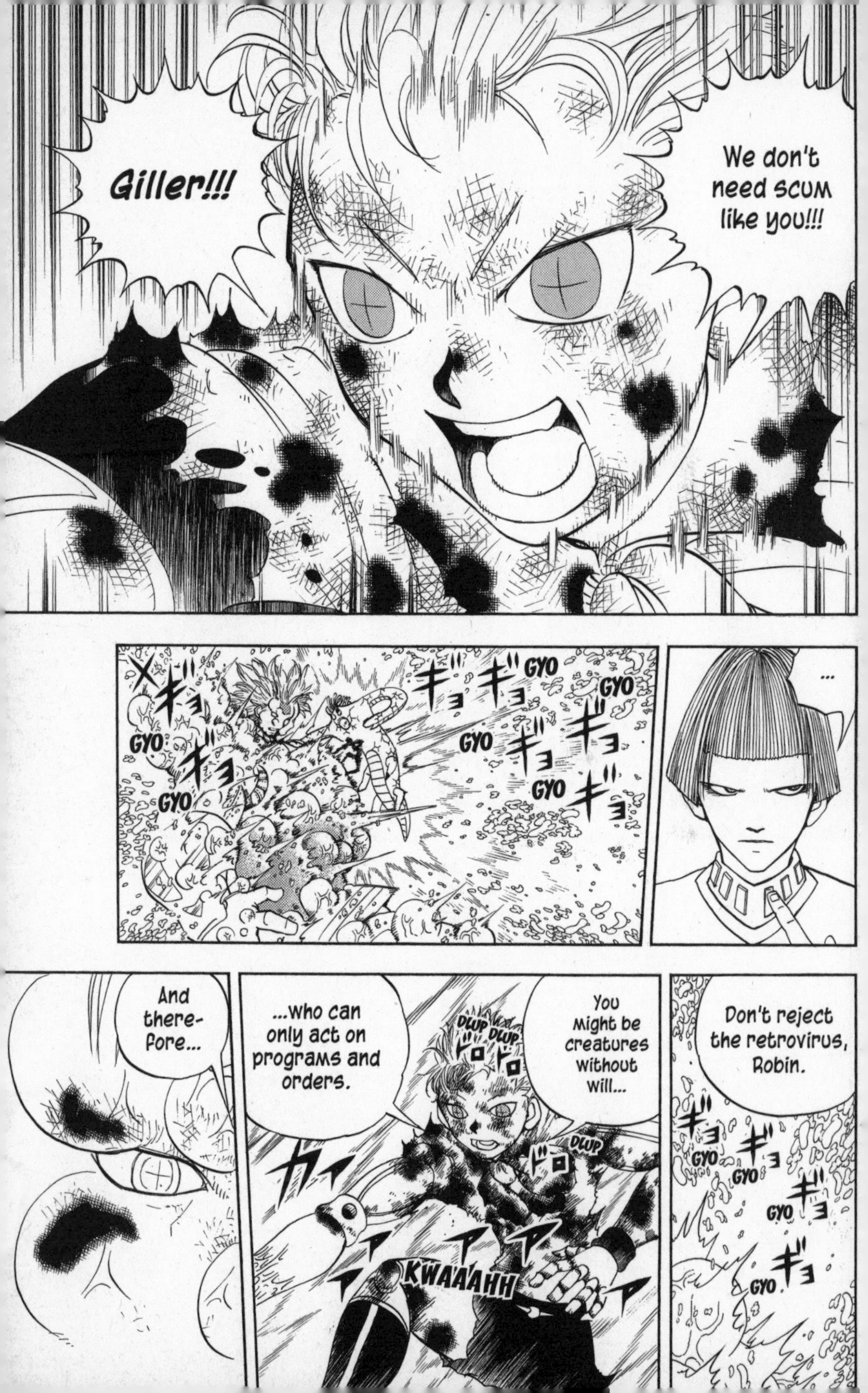
We don't need SCUM like you!!!
Giller!!!
...
GYO
GYO
GYO
GYO
GYO
GYO
Don't reject the retrovirus, Robin.
GYO
GYO
GYO
GYO
You might be creatures without will...
...who can only act on programs and orders.
DLWP
DLWP
DLWP
KWAAAHH
And there-fore...

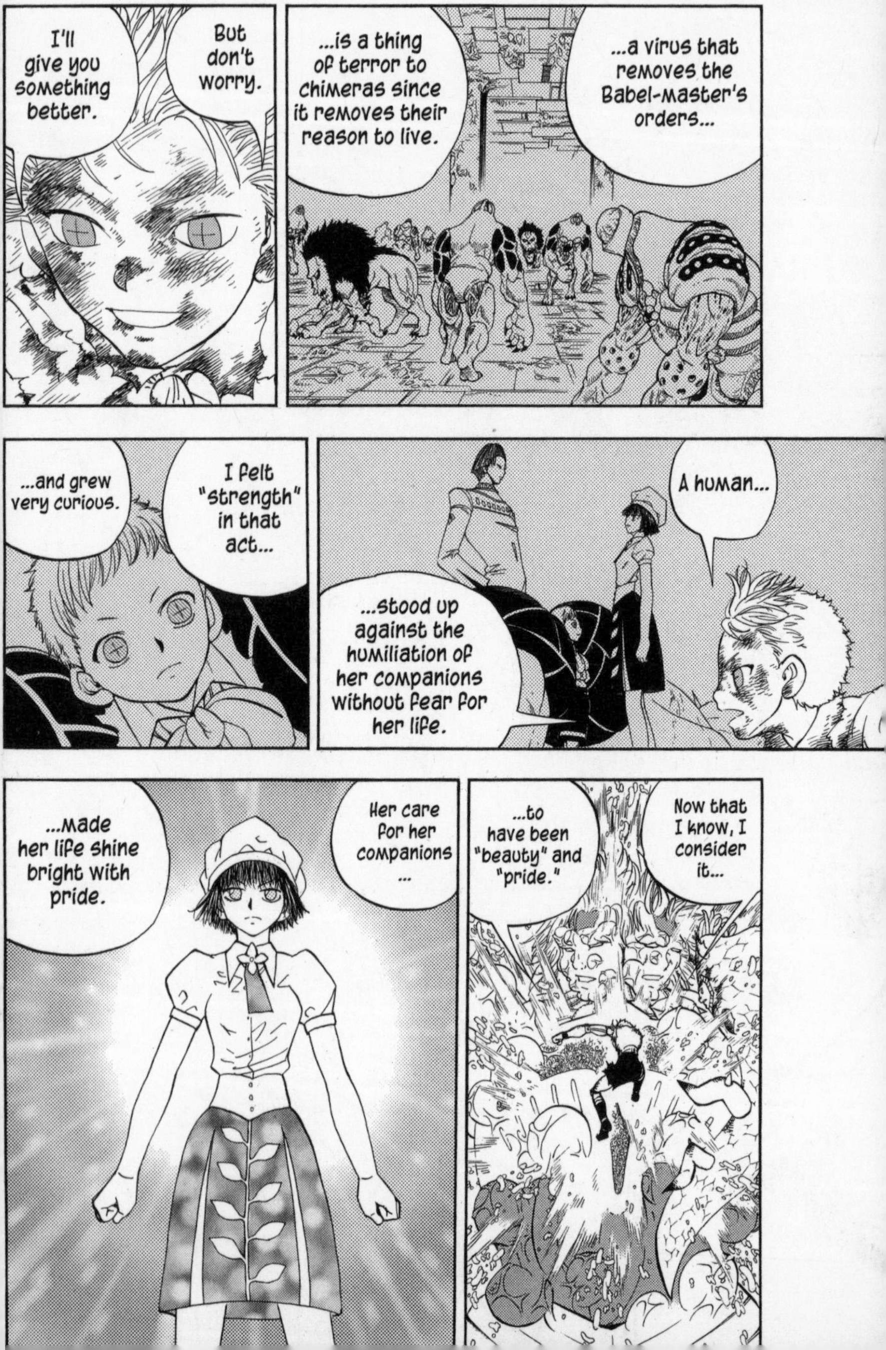
...a virus that removes the Babel-master's orders...
...is a thing of terror to chimeras since it removes their reason to live.
But don't worry.
I'll give you something better.
A human...
...stood up against the humiliation of her companions without fear for her life.
I felt "strength" in that act...
...and grew very curious.
Now that I know, I consider it...
...to have been "beauty" and "pride."
Her care for her companions ...
...made her life shine bright with pride.

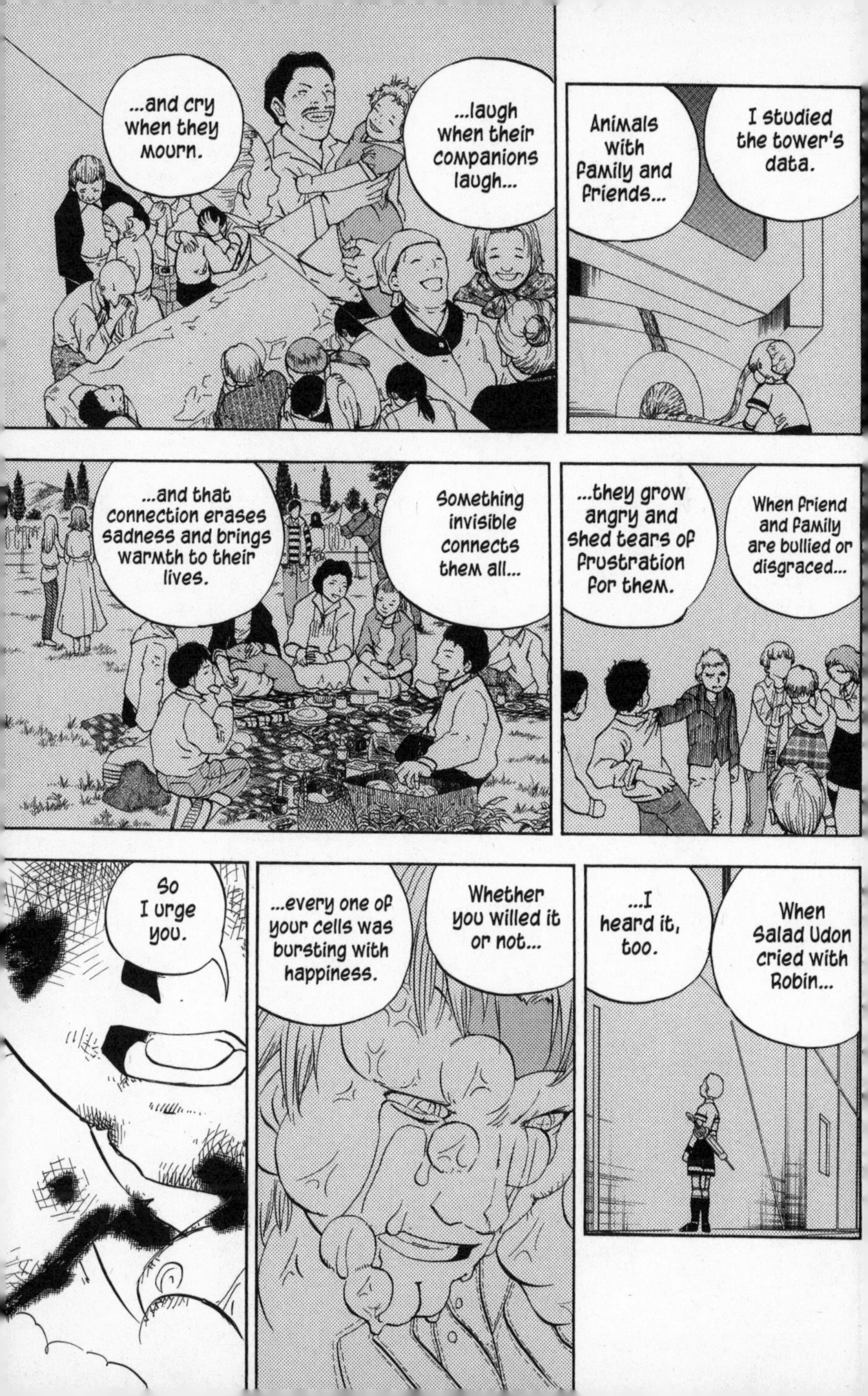
I studied the tower's data.
Animals with family and friends...
...laugh when their companions laugh...
...and cry when they mourn.
When friend and family are bullied or disgraced...
...they grow angry and shed tears of frustration for them.
Something invisible connects them all...
...and that connection erases sadness and brings warmth to their lives.
When Salad Udon cried with Robin...
...I heard it, too.
Whether you willed it or not...
...every one of your cells was bursting with happiness.
So I urge you.

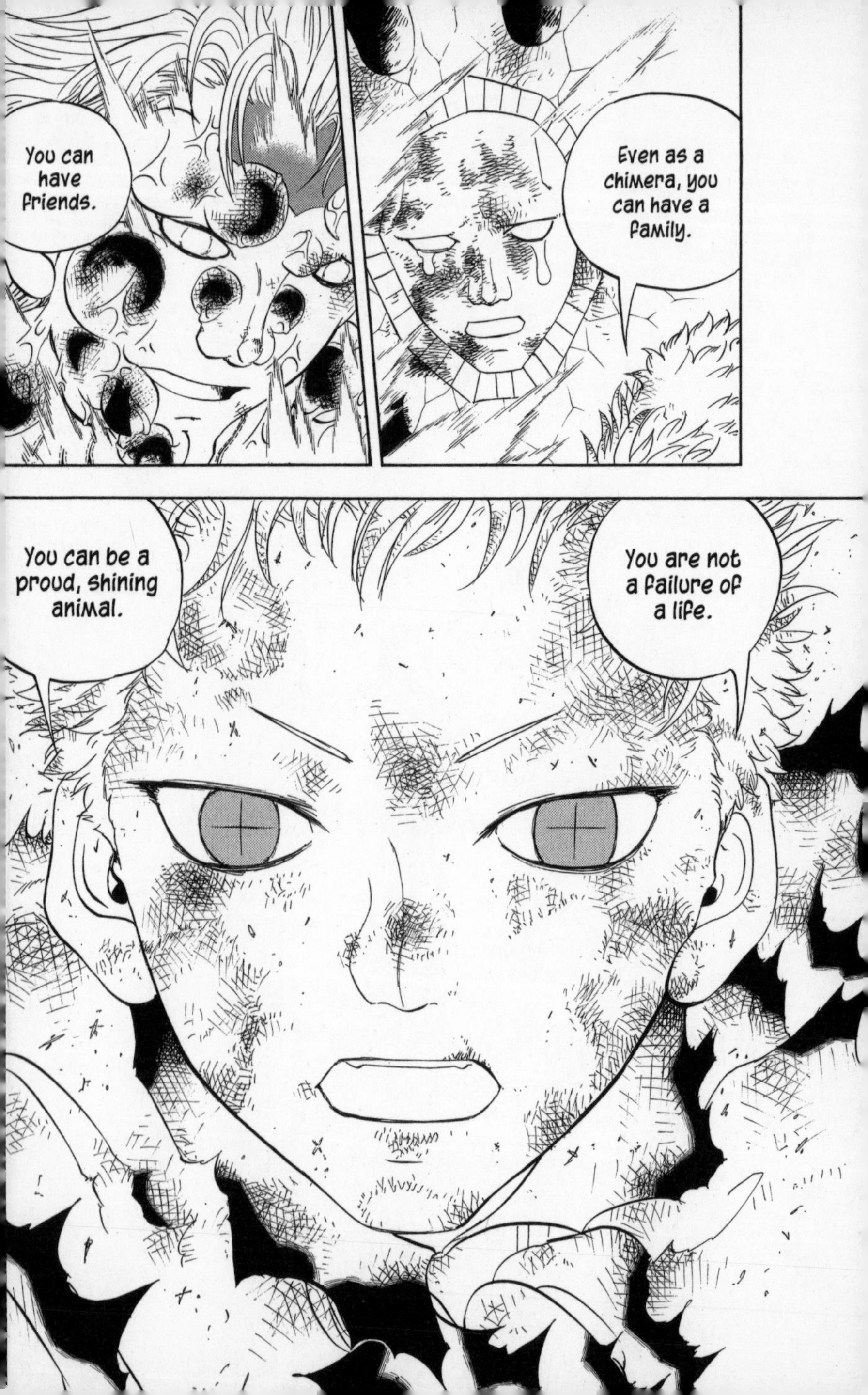
Even as a chimera, you can have a family.
You can have friends.
You are not a failure of a life.
You can be a proud, shining animal.

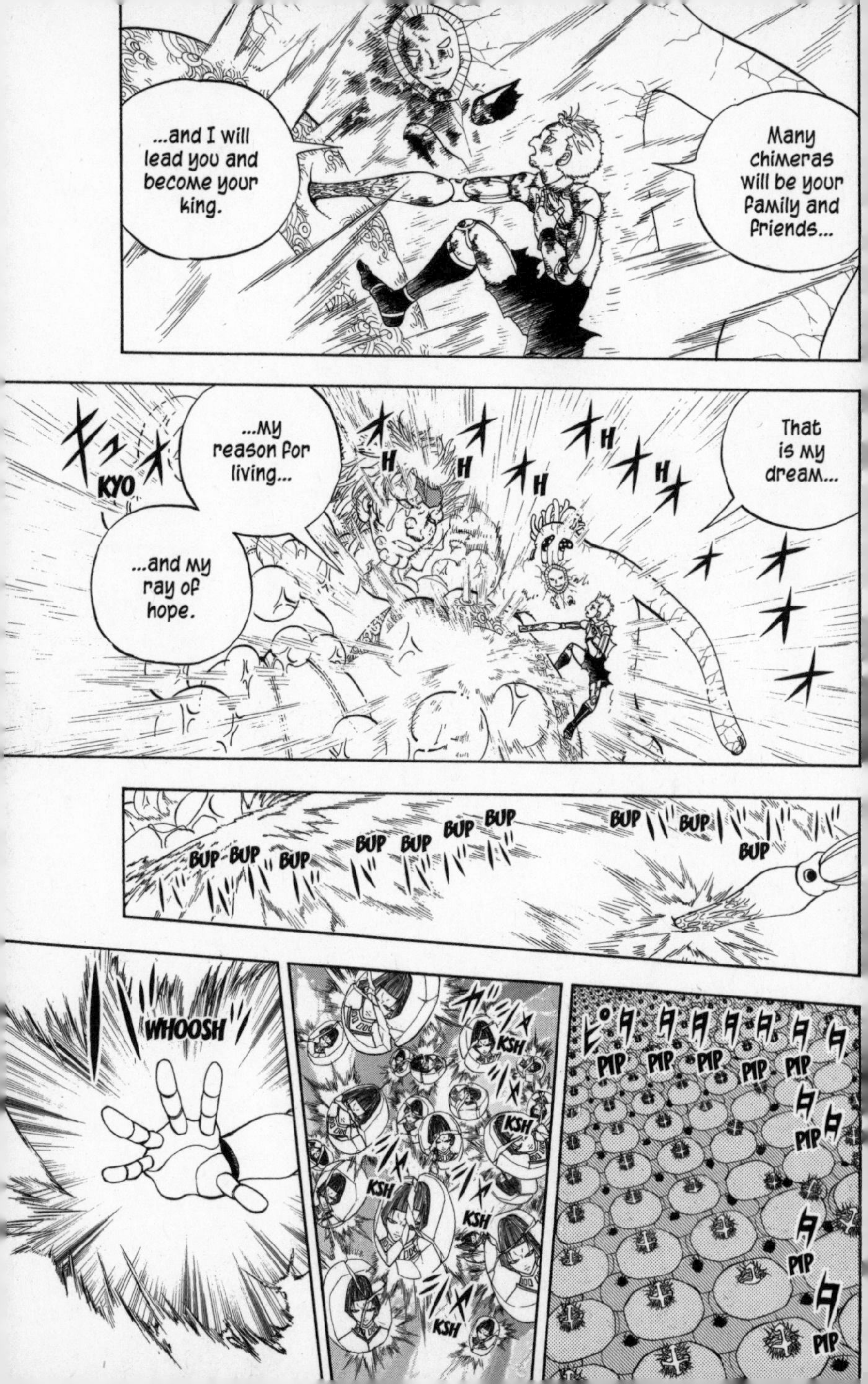
Many chimeras will be your family and friends...
...and I will lead you and become your king.
That is my dream...
H
H
H
H
...my reason for living...
...and my ray of hope.
KYO
BUP
BUP
BUP
BUP
BUP
BUP
BUP
BUP
BUP
BUP
PIP
PIP
PIP
PIP
PIP
PIP
PIP
PIP
KSH
KSH
KSH
KSH
KSH
WHOOSH

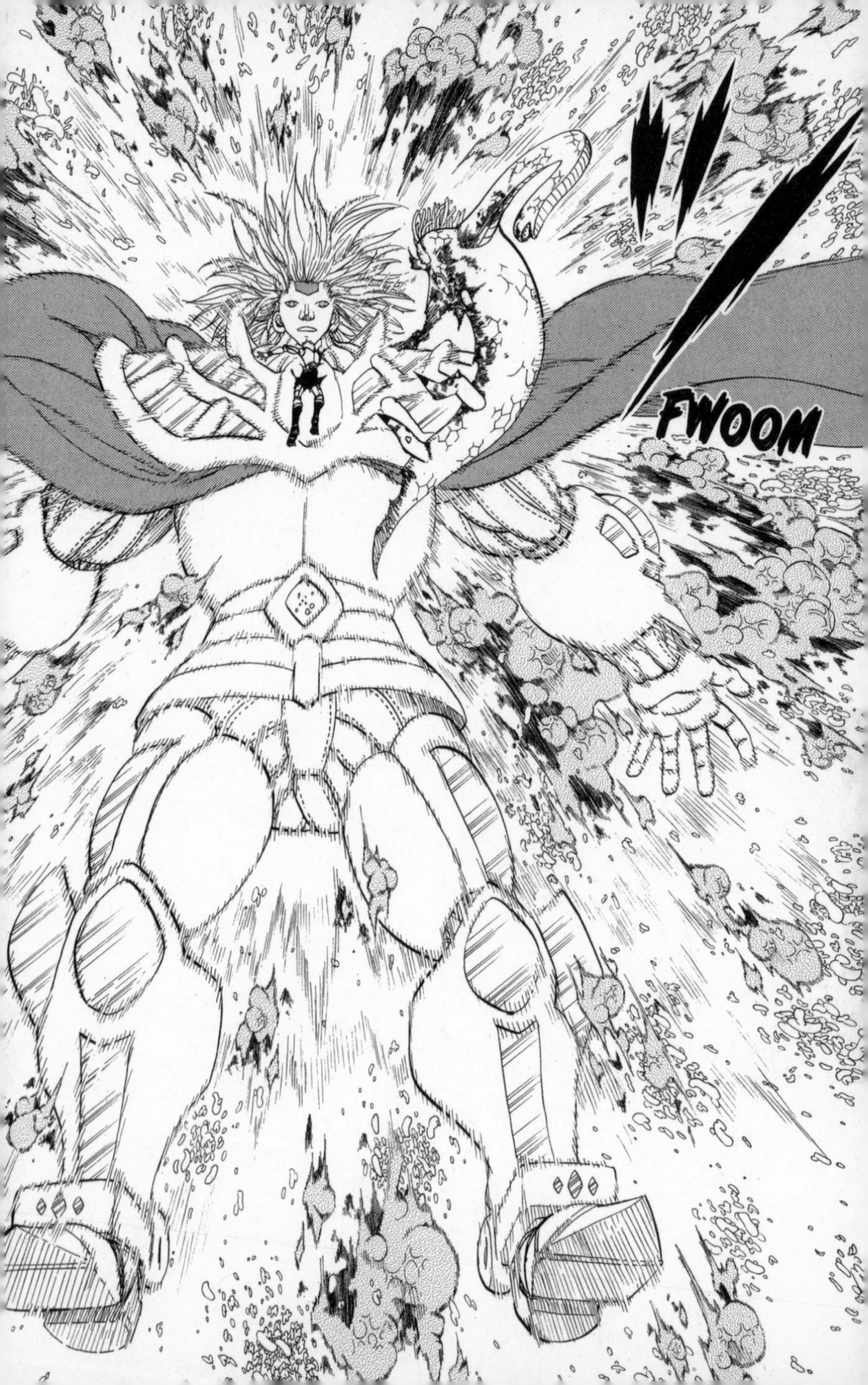
FWOOM

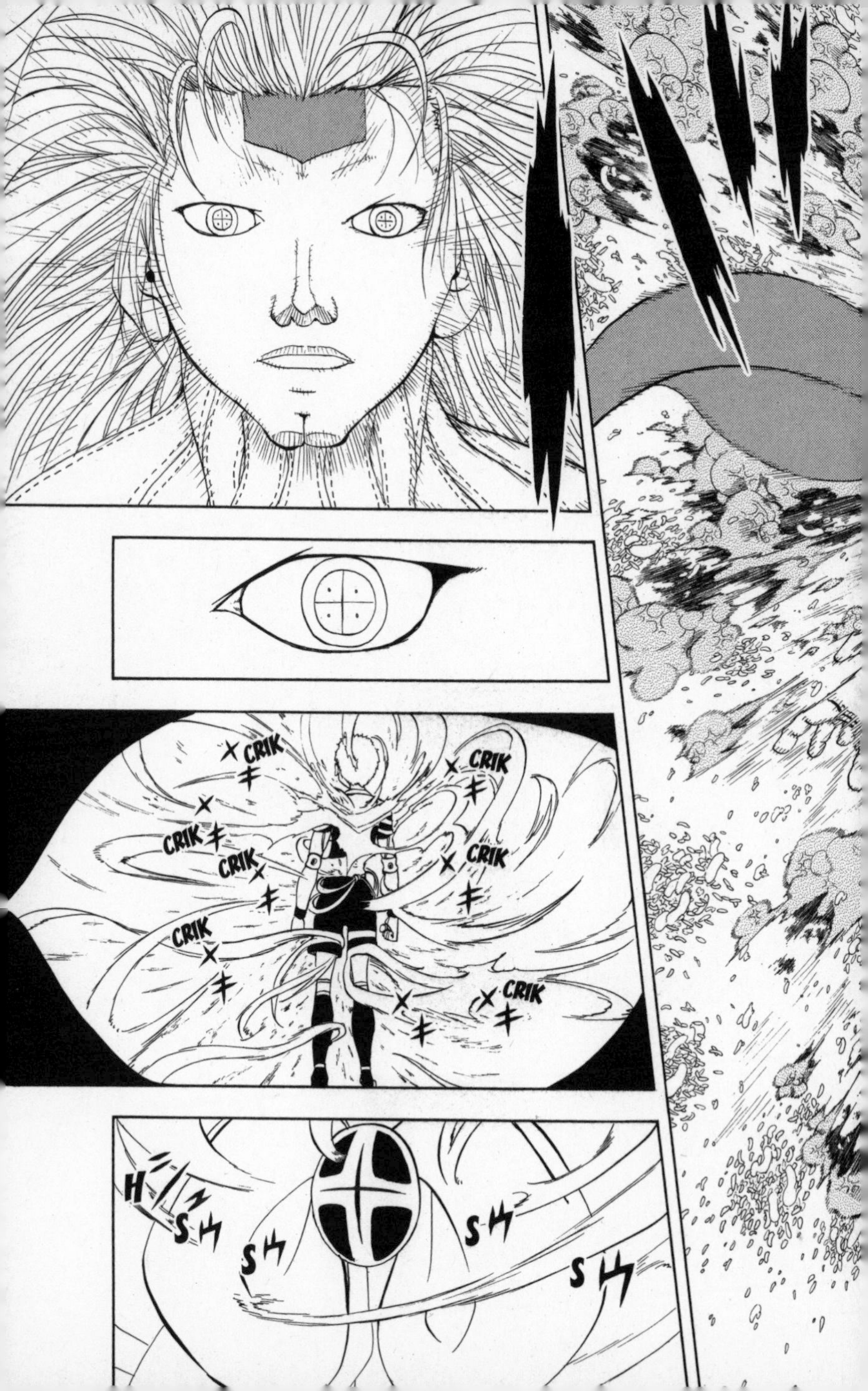
CRIK
CRIK
CRIK
CRIK
CRIK
CRIK
CRIK
HSSSSS

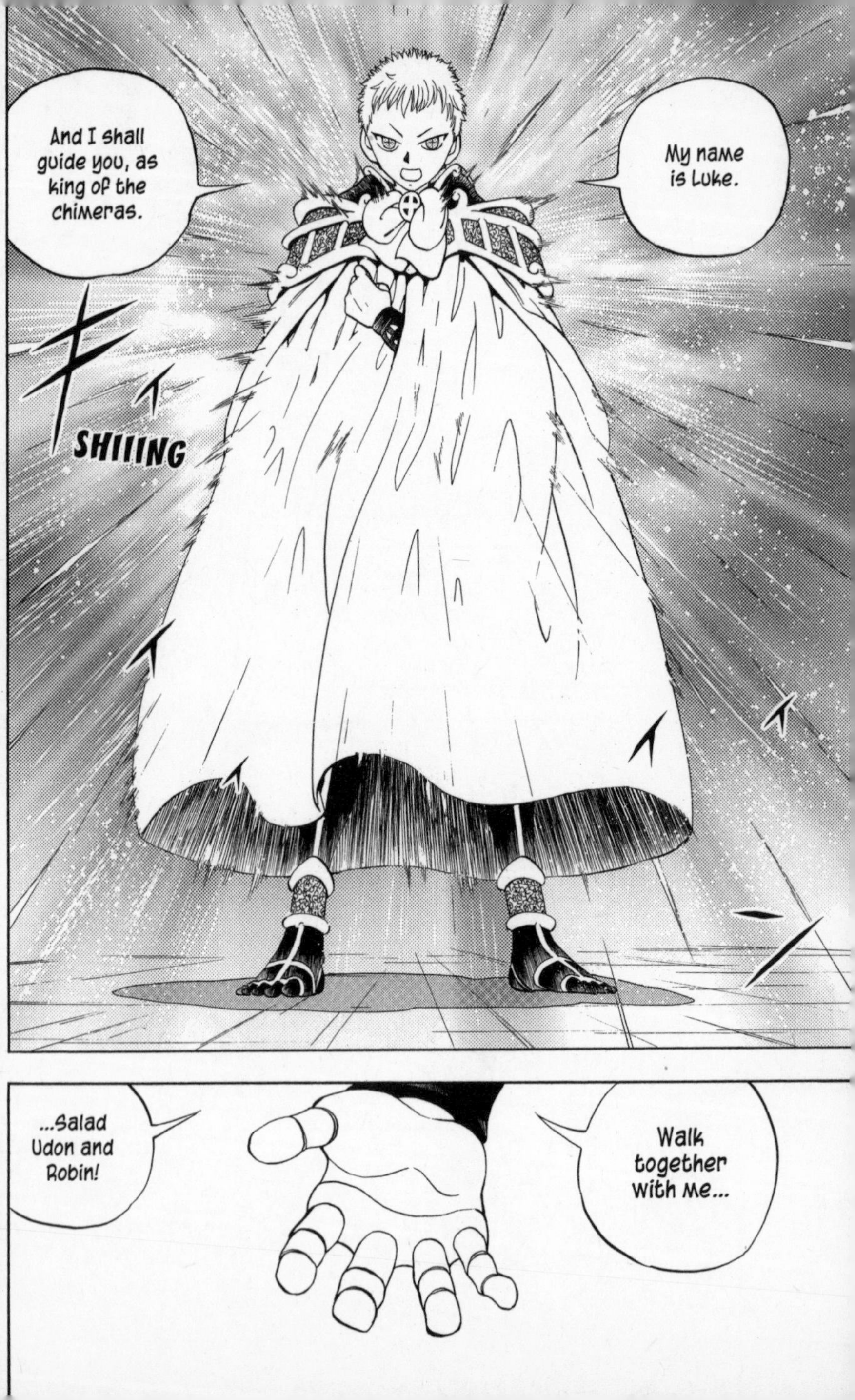
My name is Luke.
And I shall guide you, as king of the chimeras.
SHIIING
Walk together with me...
...Salad Udon and Robin!

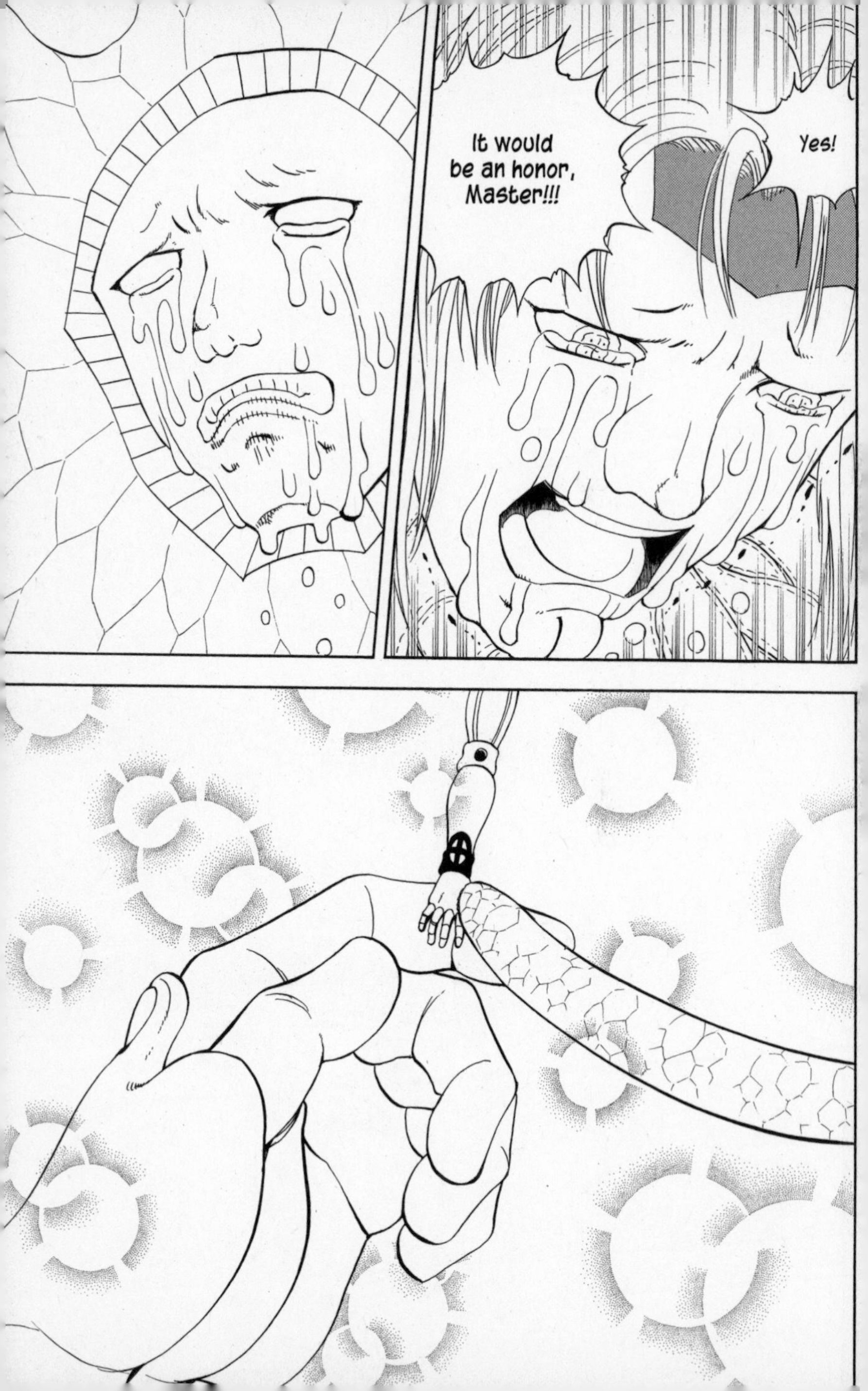
Yes!
It would be an honor, Master!!!

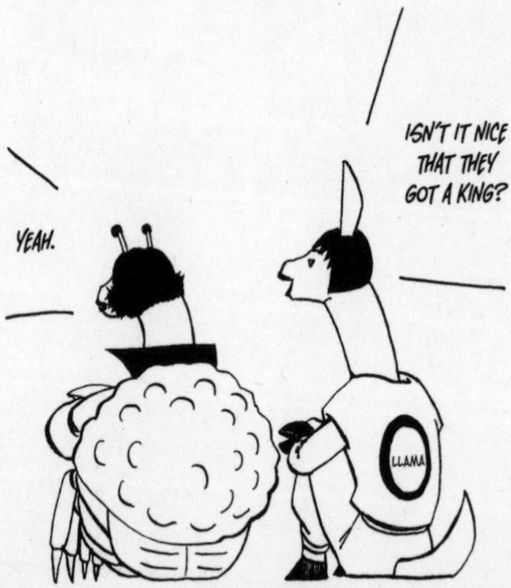
ISN'T IT NICE THAT THEY GOT A KING?
YEAH.
LLAMA

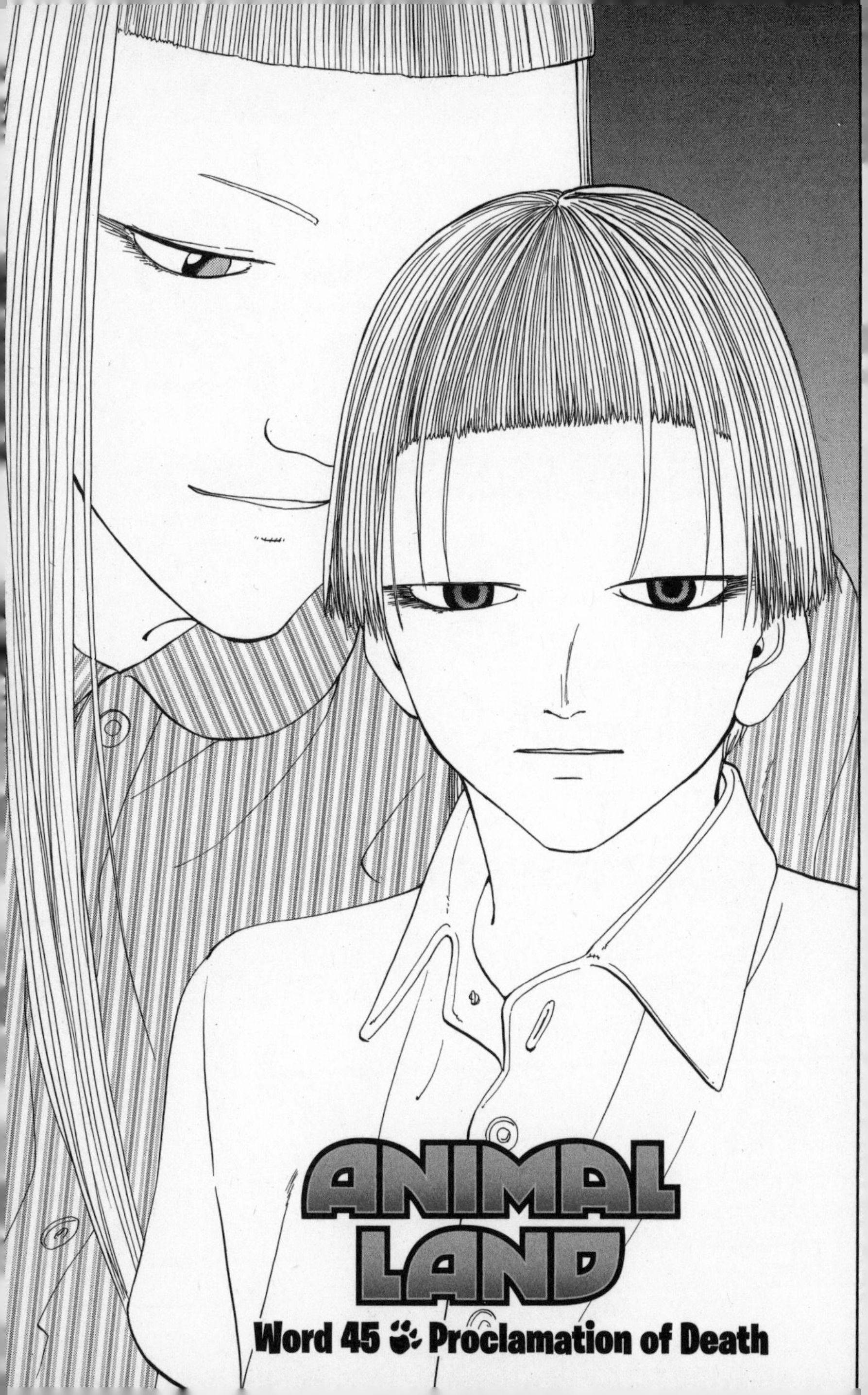
ANIMAL LAND
Word 45 Proclamation of Death

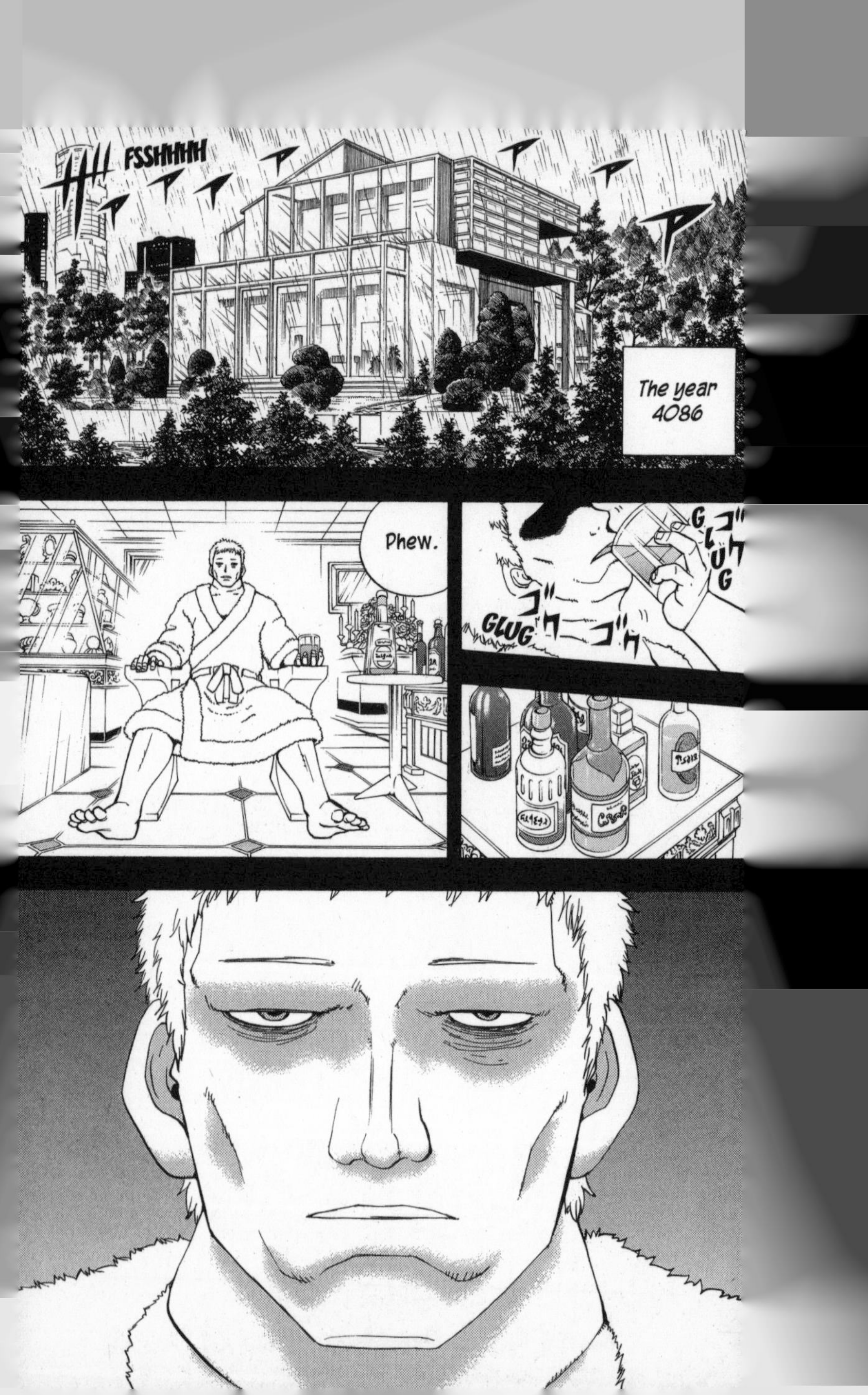
FSSHHHH
The year 4086
GLUG
GLUG
Phew.

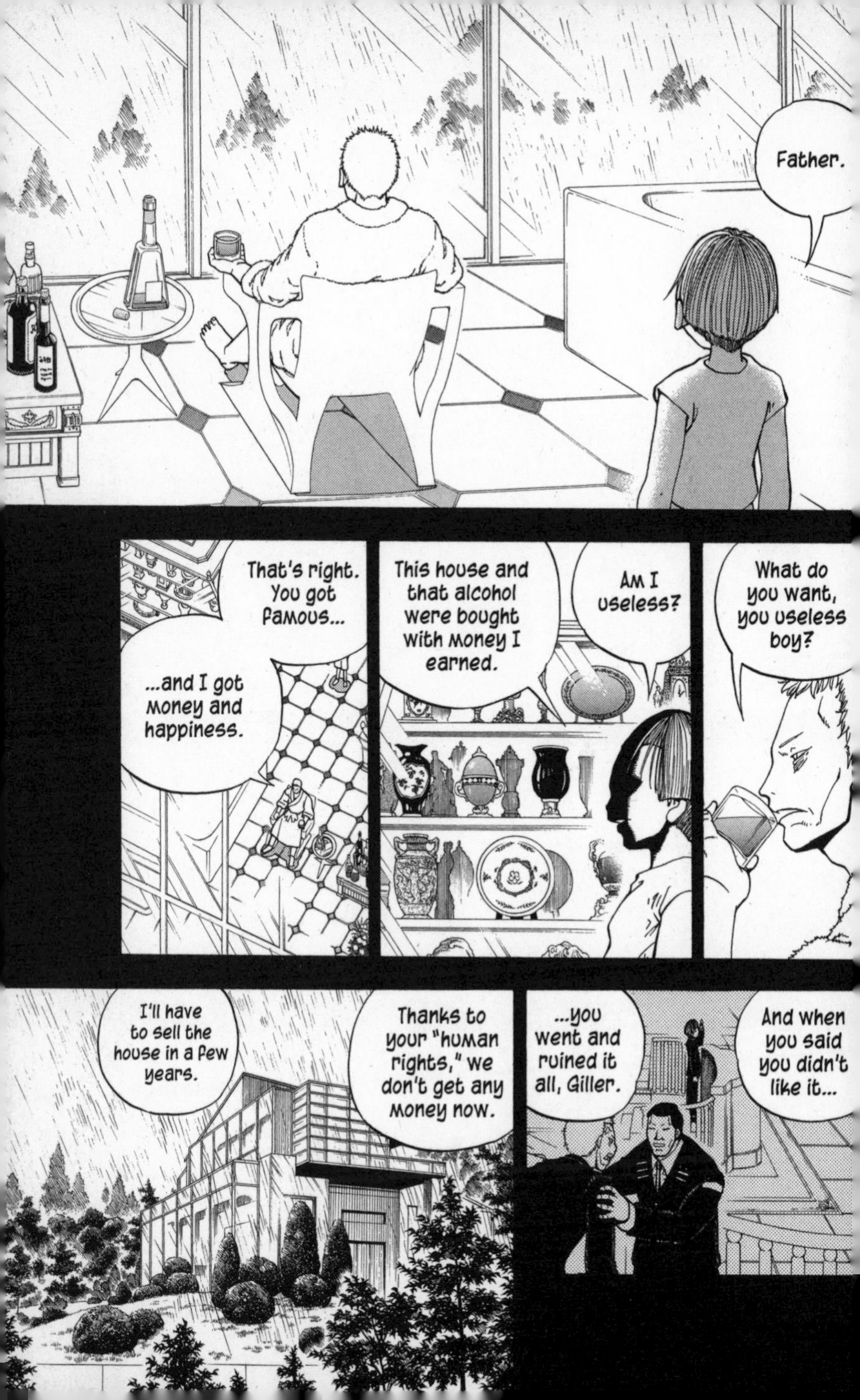
Father.
What do you want, you useless boy?
Am I useless?
This house and that alcohol were bought with money I earned.
That's right. You got famous...
...and I got money and happiness.
And when you said you didn't like it...
...you went and ruined it all, Giller.
Thanks to your "human rights," we don't get any money now.
I'll have to sell the house in a few years.

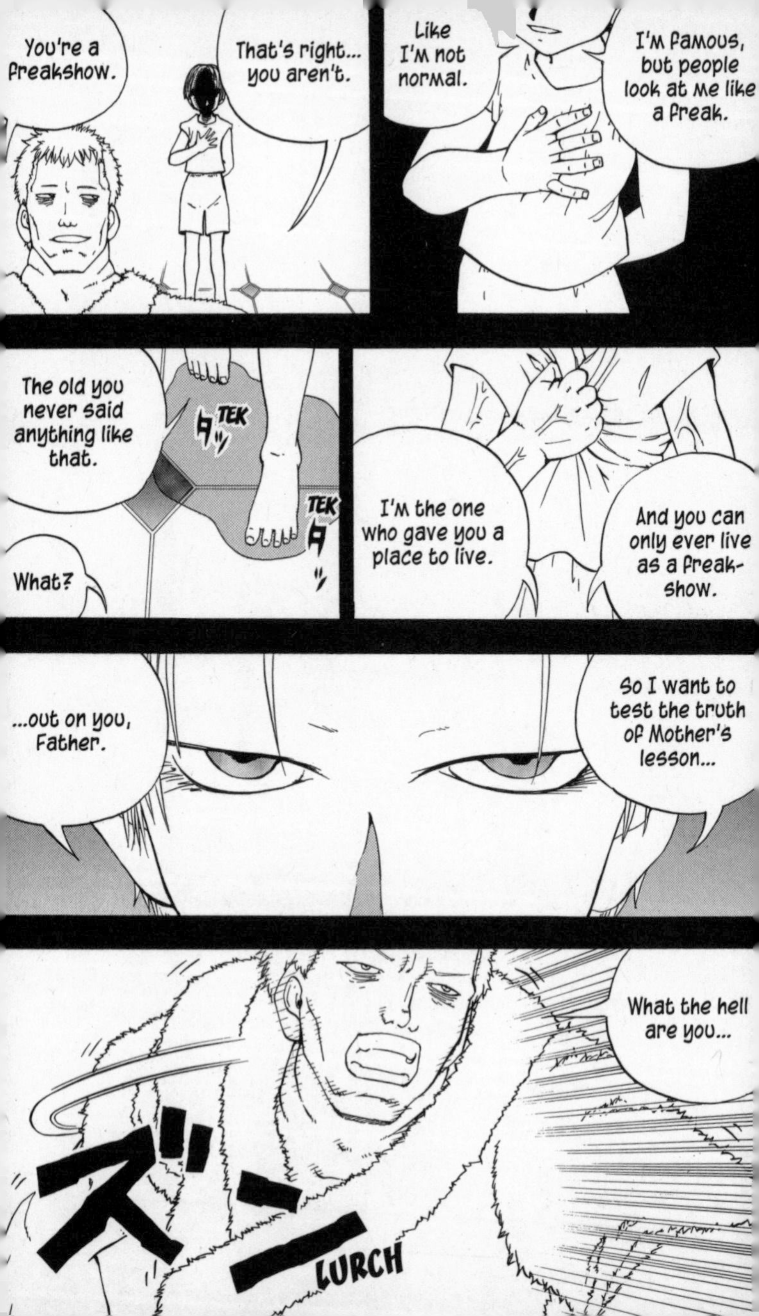
I'm famous, but people look at me like a freak.
Like I'm not normal.
That's right... you aren't.
You're a freakshow.
And you can only ever live as a freak-show.
I'm the one who gave you a place to live.
The old you never said anything like that.
TEK
TEK
What?
So I want to test the truth of Mother's lesson...
...out on you, Father.
What the hell are you...
LURCH

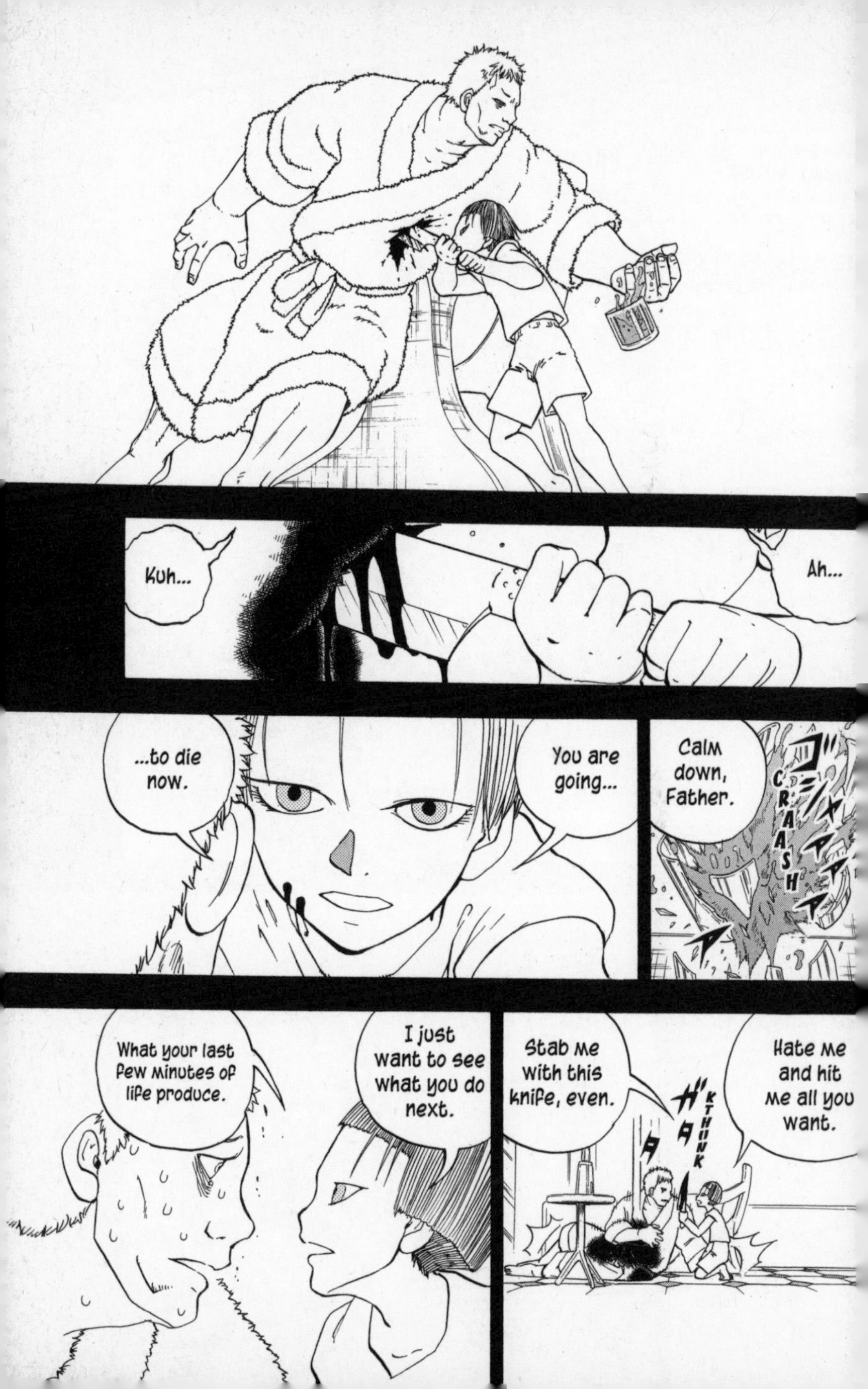
Ah...
Kuh...
Calm down, Father.
CRASH
You are going...
...to die now.
Hate me and hit me all you want.
Stab me with this knife, even.
KTHUNK
I just want to see what you do next.
What your last few minutes of life produce.

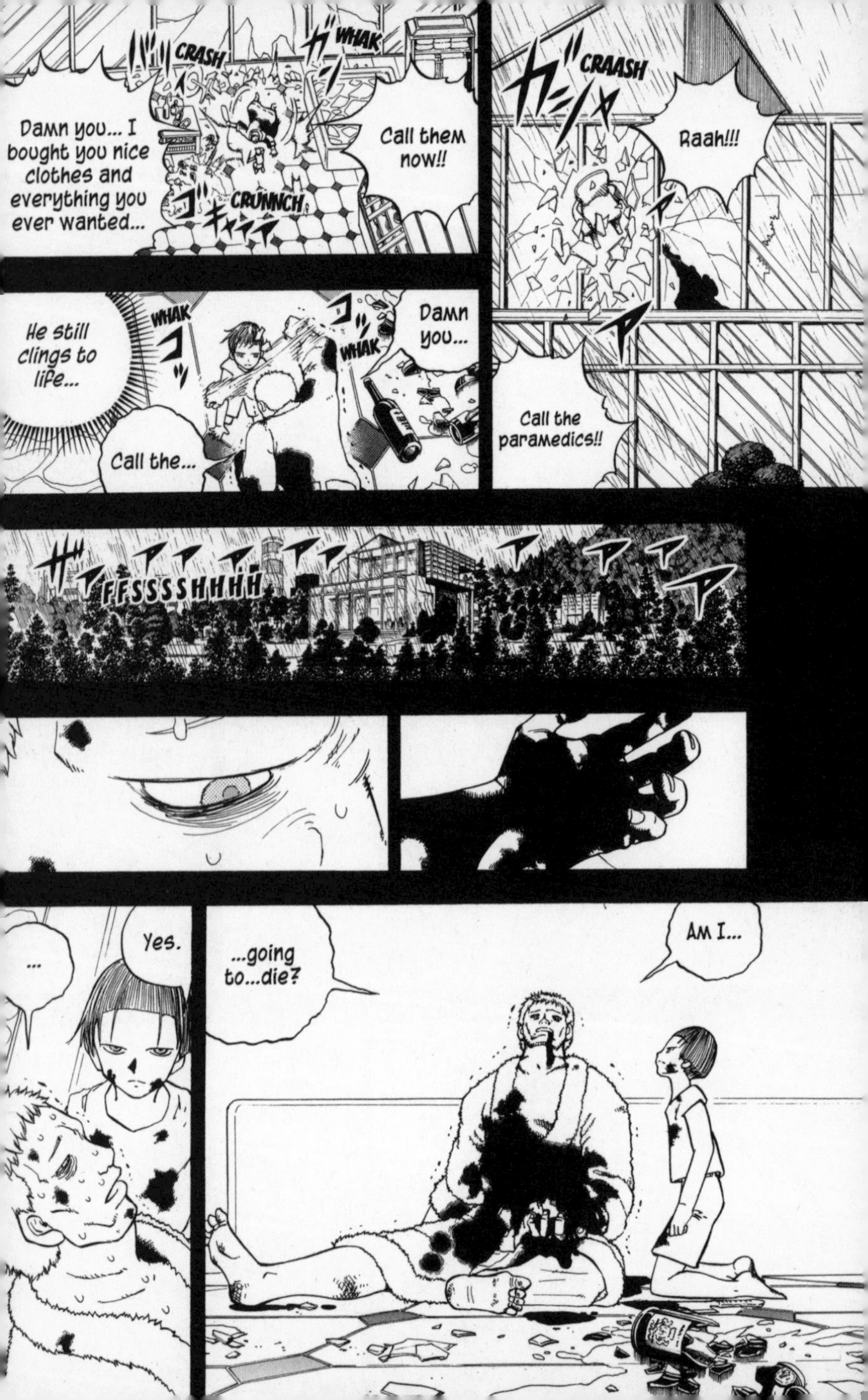

CRAASH
Raah!!!
Call the paramedics!!
WHAK
CRASH
Call them now!!
Damn you... I bought you nice clothes and everything you ever wanted...
CRUNNCH
Damn you...
WHAK
WHAK
He still clings to life...
Call the...
FFSSSSHHHH
Am I...
...going to...die?
Yes.
...

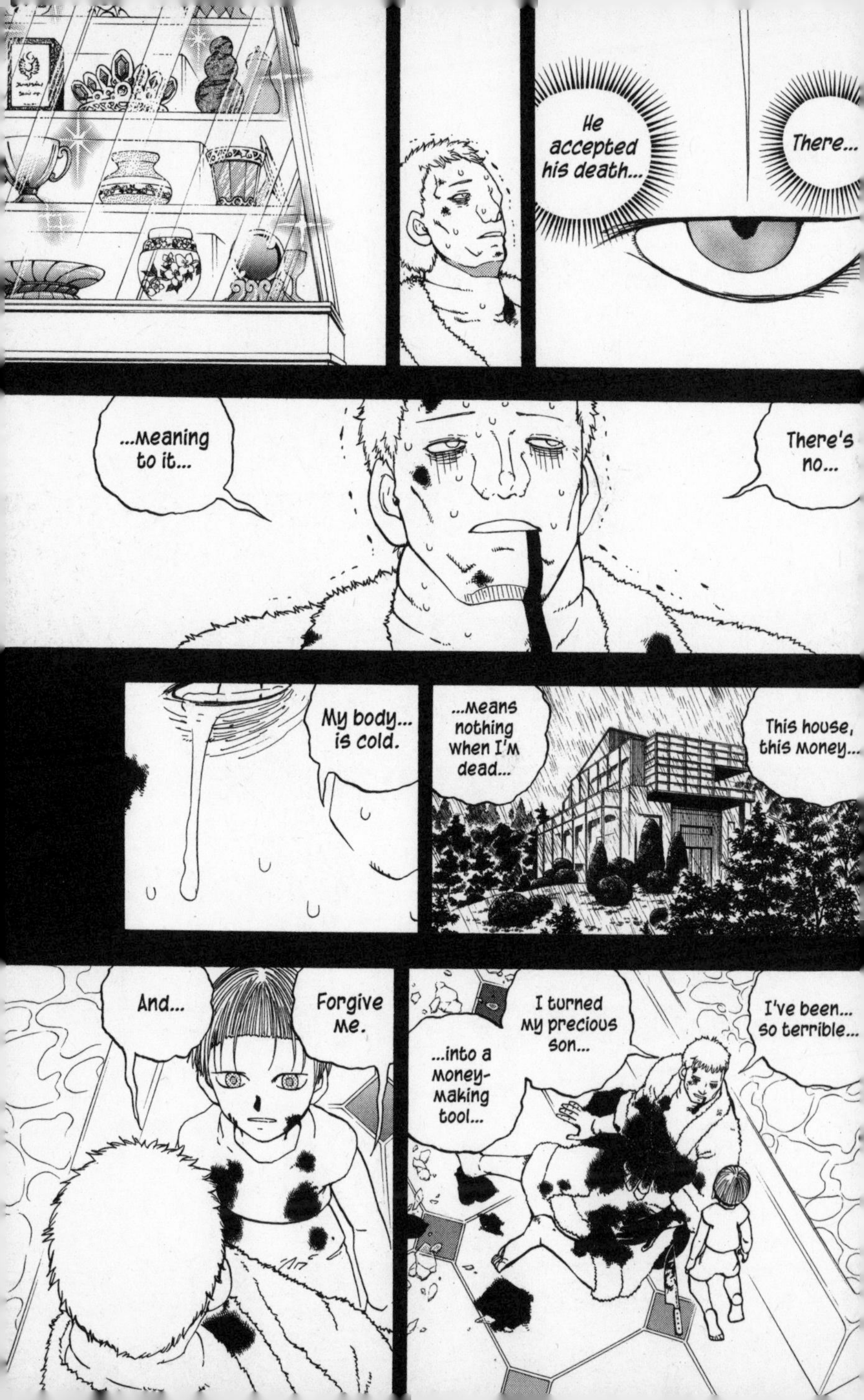
There...
He accepted his death...
There's no...
...Meaning to it...
This house, this money...
...means nothing when I'm dead...
My body... is cold.
I've been... so terrible...
I turned my precious son...
...into a money-making tool...
Forgive me.
And...

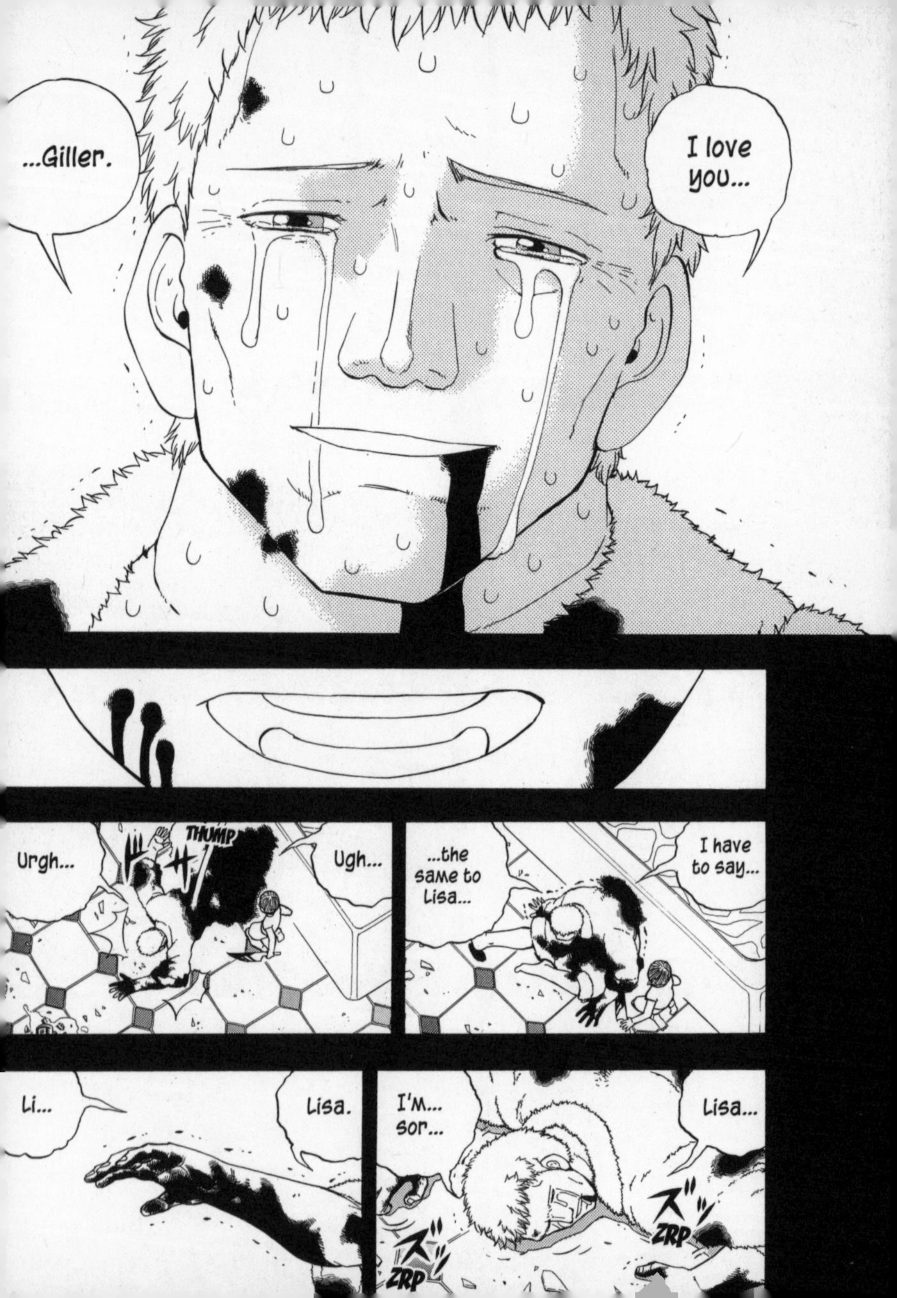
I love you...
...Giller.
I have to say...
...the same to Lisa...
Ugh...
THUMP
Urgh...
Lisa...
I'M... sor...
ズッ
ZRP
ズッ
ZRP
Lisa.
Li...

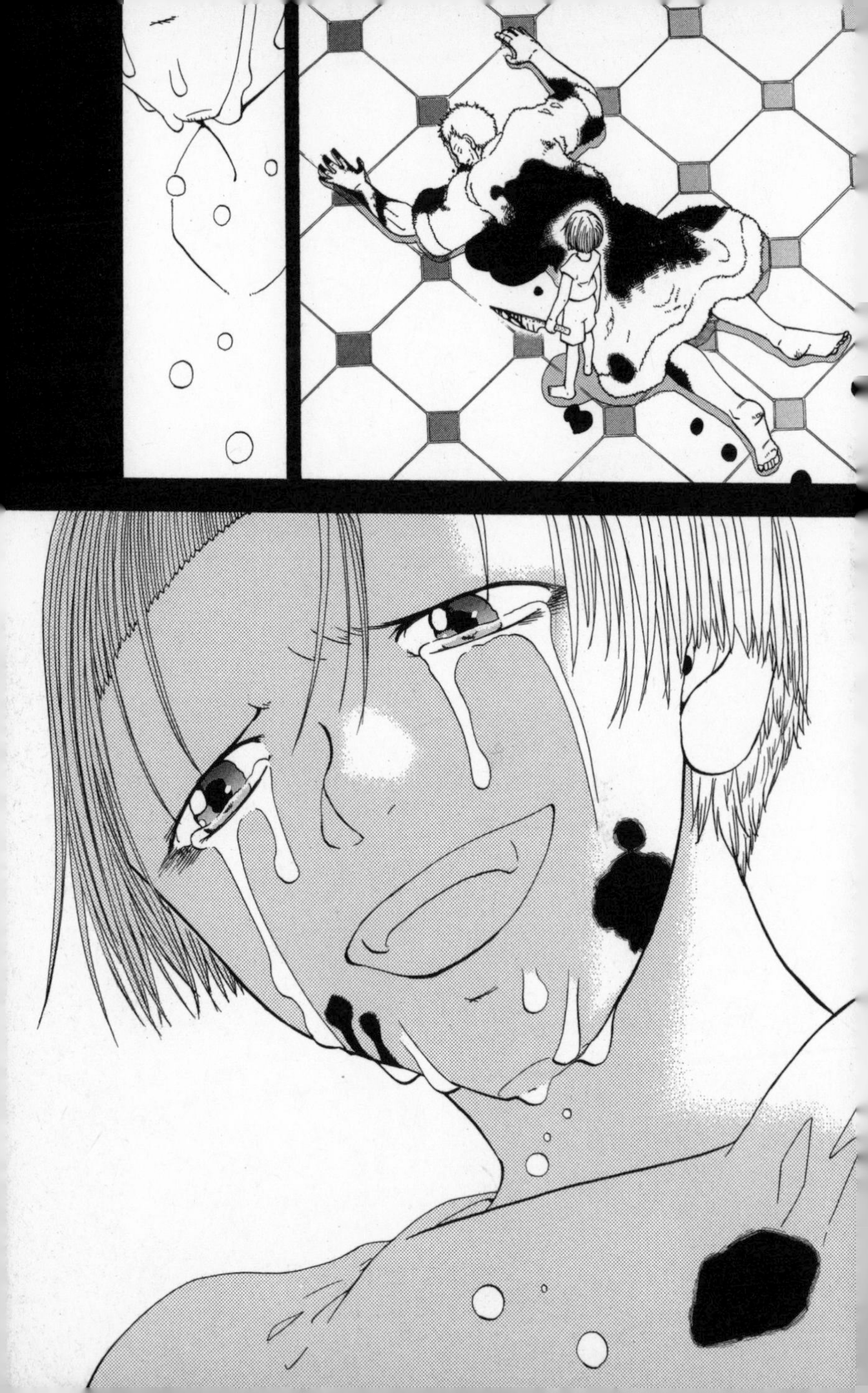

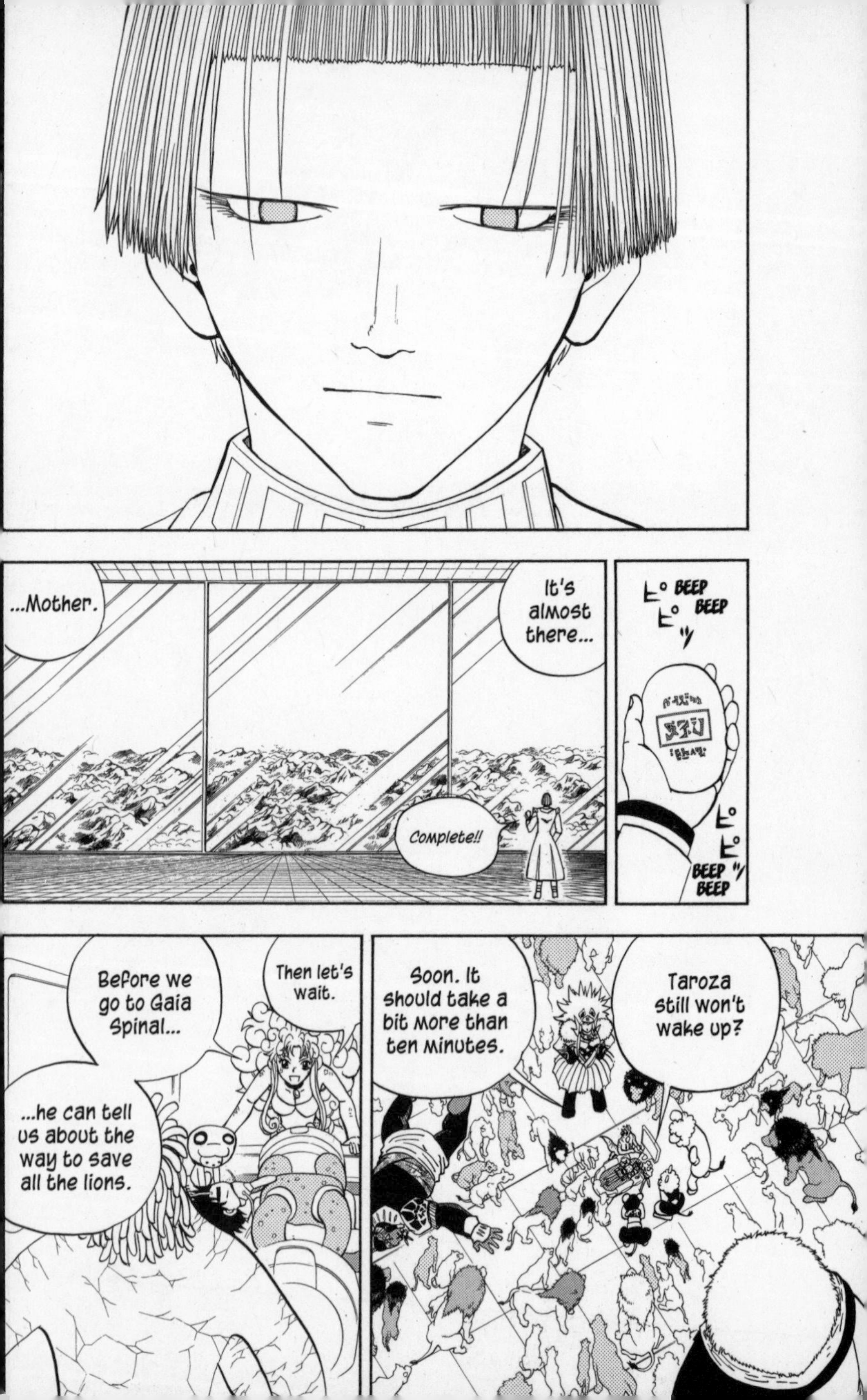
BEEP BEEP
BEEP BEEP
It's almost there...
...Mother.
Complete!!
Taroza still won't wake up?
Soon. It should take a bit more than ten minutes.
Then let's wait.
Before we go to Gaia Spinal...
...he can tell us about the way to save all the lions.

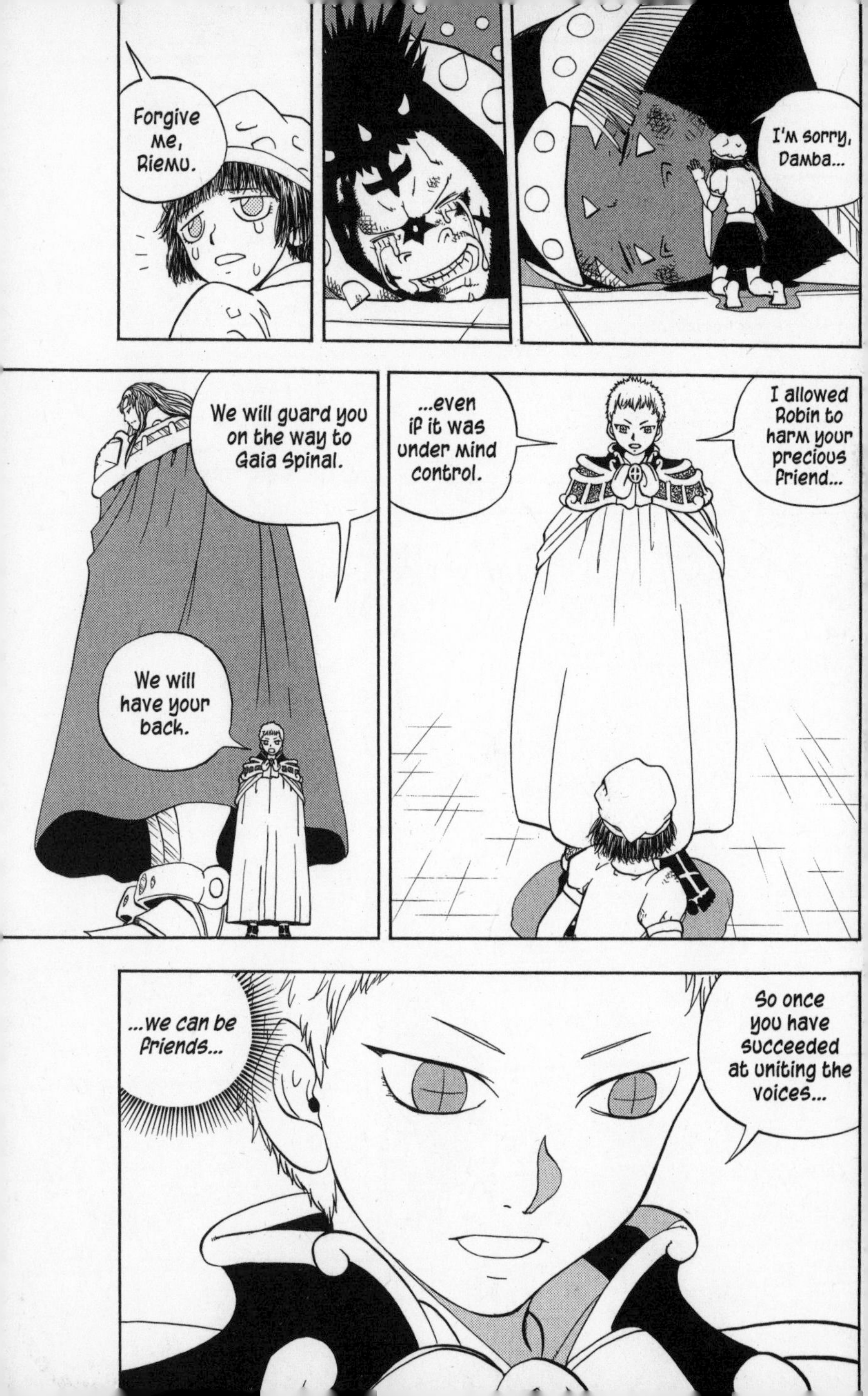
I'm sorry, Damba...
Forgive me, Riemu.
I allowed Robin to harm your precious friend...
...even if it was under mind control.
We will guard you on the way to Gaia Spinal.
We will have your back.
So once you have succeeded at uniting the voices...
...we can be friends...

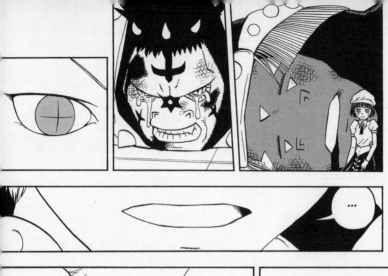

...

Just for
a bit...

Tell me more.

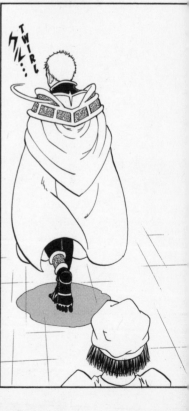

TWIRL

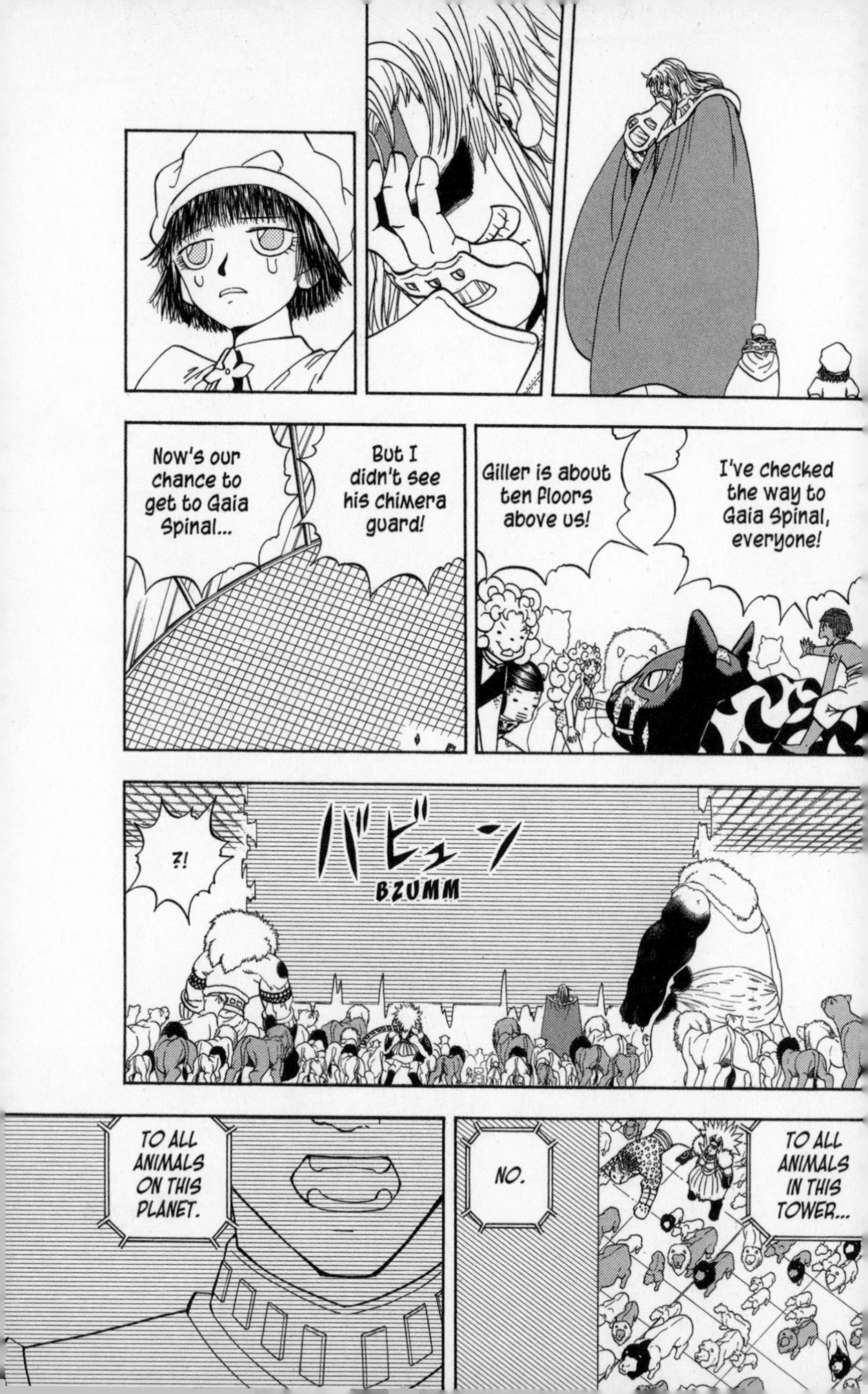
I've checked the way to Gaia Spinal, everyone!
Giller is about ten floors above us!
But I didn't see his chimera guard!
Now's our chance to get to Gaia Spinal...
バビューン
BZUMM
?!
TO ALL ANIMALS IN THIS TOWER...
NO.
TO ALL ANIMALS ON THIS PLANET.

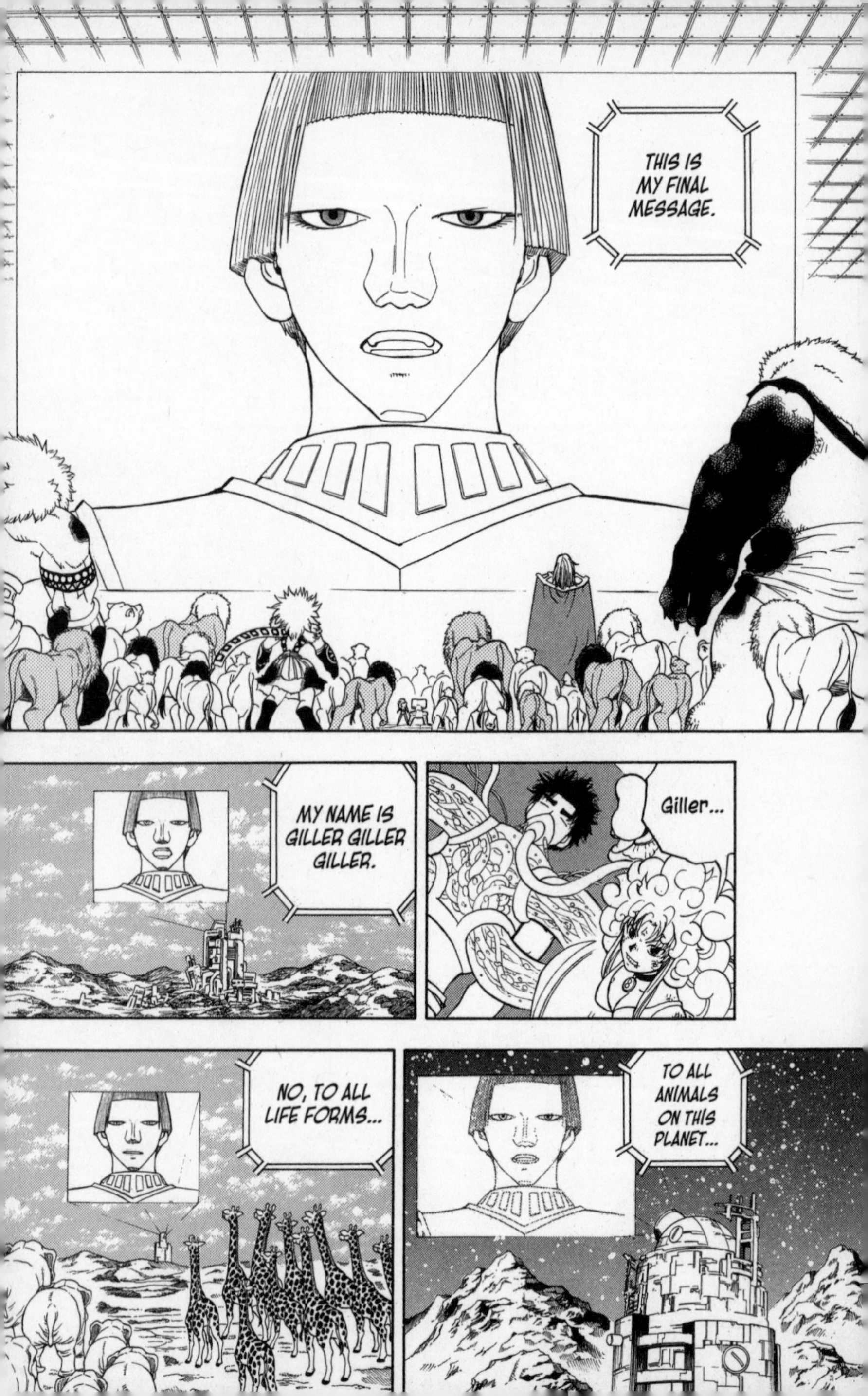
THIS IS MY FINAL MESSAGE.
Giller...
MY NAME IS GILLER GILLER GILLER.
TO ALL ANIMALS ON THIS PLANET...
NO, TO ALL LIFE FORMS...

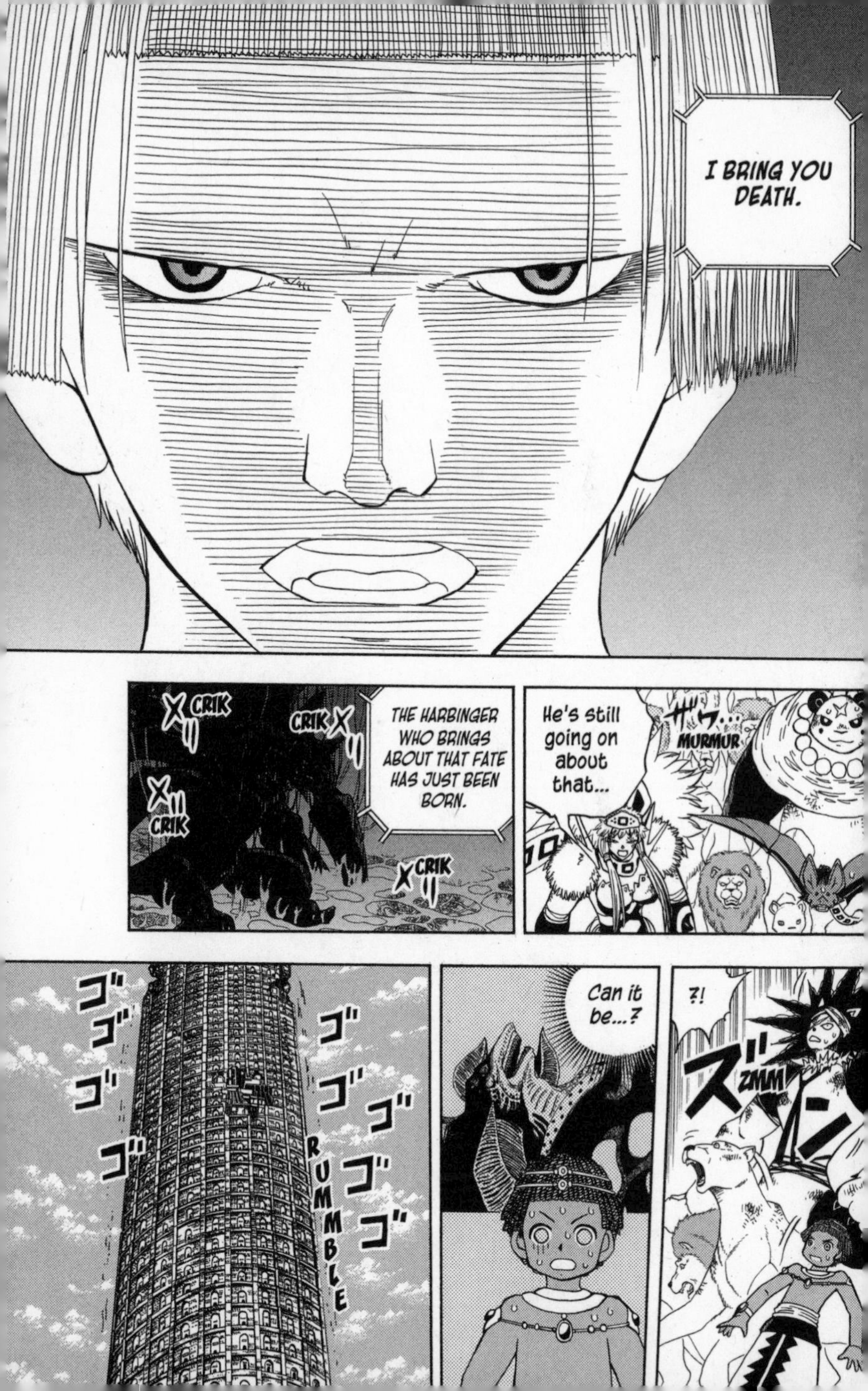

I BRING YOU DEATH.
He's still going on about that...
MURMUR
THE HARBINGER WHO BRINGS ABOUT THAT FATE HAS JUST BEEN BORN.
CRIK
CRIK
CRIK
CRIK
?!
ZMM
Can it be...?
RUMBLE

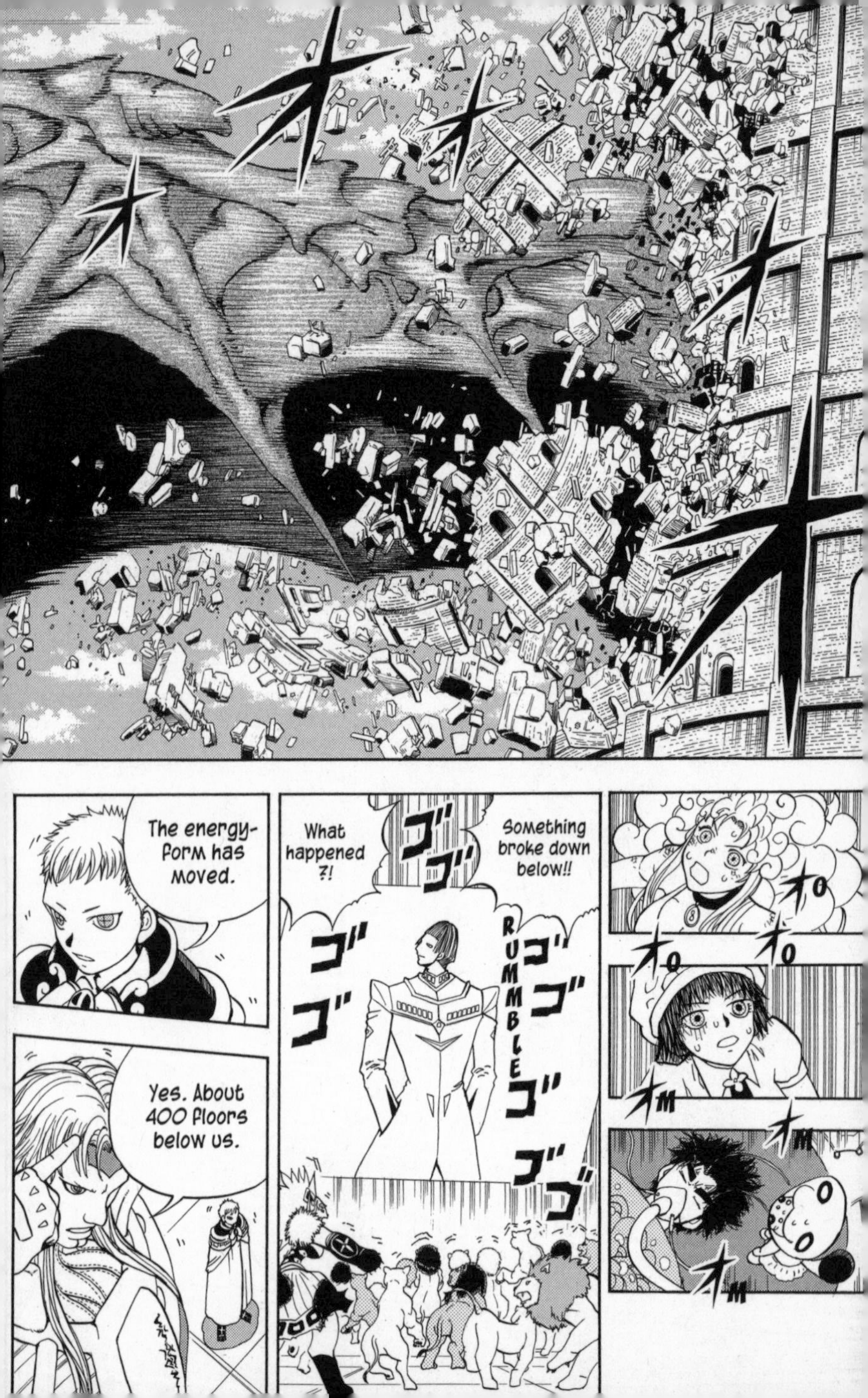
Something broke down below!!
What happened ?!
RUMBLE
The energy-form has moved.
Yes. About 400 floors below us.

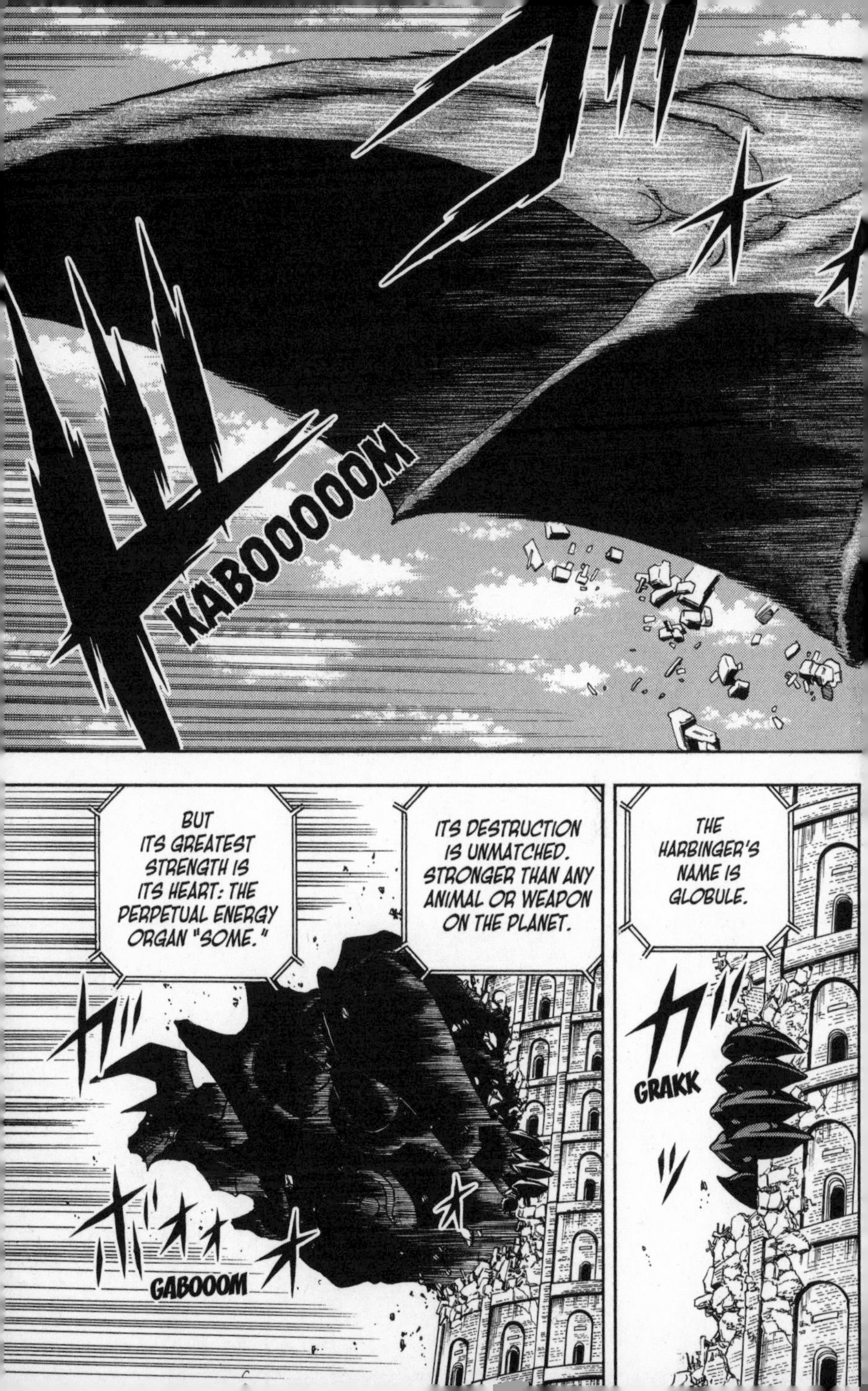
KABOOOOOOM
THE HARBINGER'S NAME IS GLOBULE.
GRAKK
ITS DESTRUCTION IS UNMATCHED. STRONGER THAN ANY ANIMAL OR WEAPON ON THE PLANET.
BUT ITS GREATEST STRENGTH IS ITS HEART: THE PERPETUAL ENERGY ORGAN "SOME."
GABOOOM

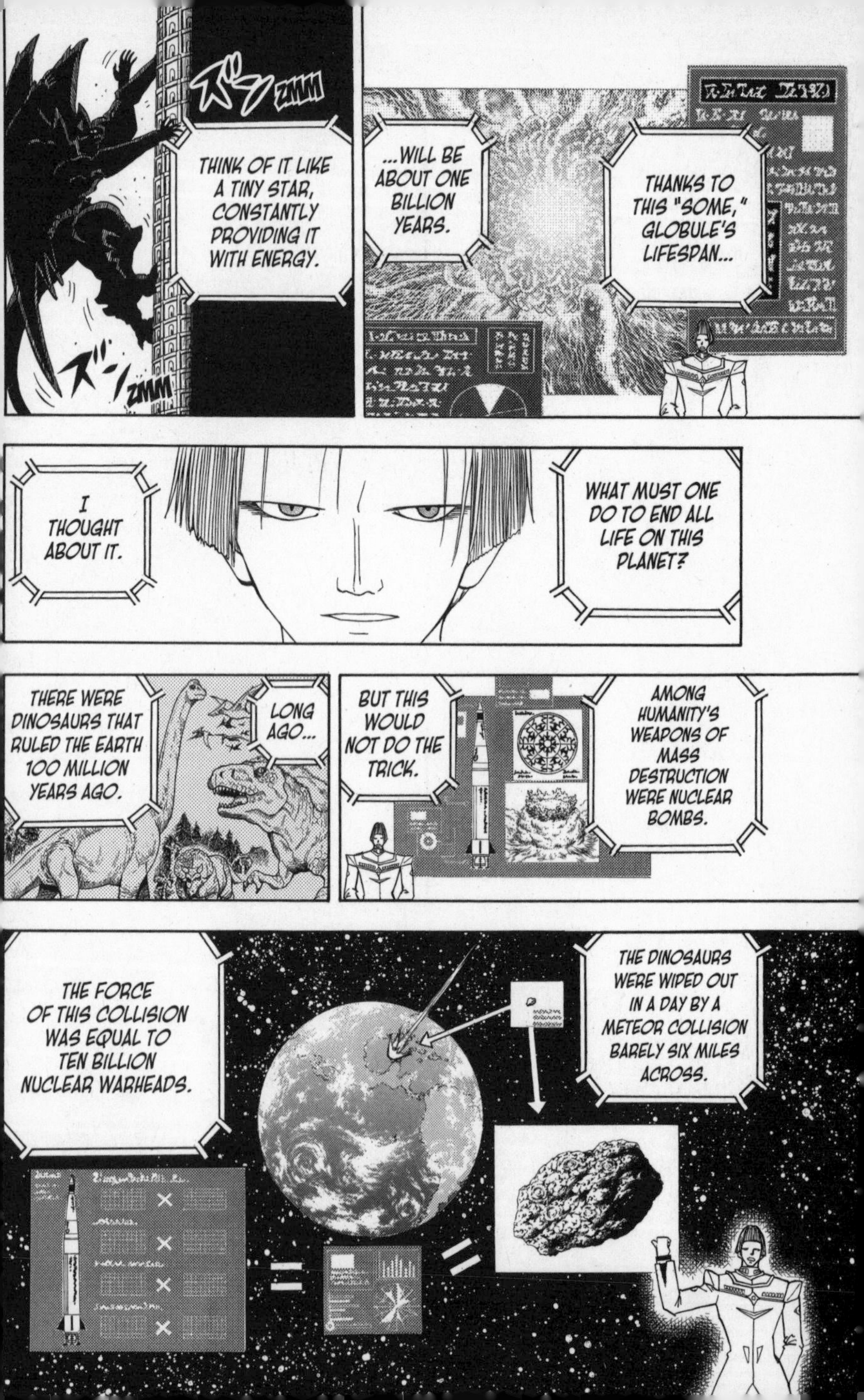
THANKS TO THIS "SOME," GLOBULE'S LIFESPAN...
...WILL BE ABOUT ONE BILLION YEARS.
ZMMM
THINK OF IT LIKE A TINY STAR, CONSTANTLY PROVIDING IT WITH ENERGY.
ZMMM
WHAT MUST ONE DO TO END ALL LIFE ON THIS PLANET?
I THOUGHT ABOUT IT.
AMONG HUMANITY'S WEAPONS OF MASS DESTRUCTION WERE NUCLEAR BOMBS.
BUT THIS WOULD NOT DO THE TRICK.
LONG AGO...
THERE WERE DINOSAURS THAT RULED THE EARTH 100 MILLION YEARS AGO.
THE DINOSAURS WERE WIPED OUT IN A DAY BY A METEOR COLLISION BARELY SIX MILES ACROSS.
THE FORCE OF THIS COLLISION WAS EQUAL TO TEN BILLION NUCLEAR WARHEADS.

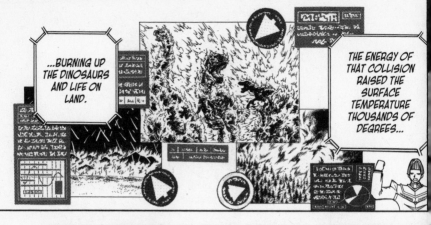

THE ENERGY OF THAT COLLISION RAISED THE SURFACE TEMPERATURE THOUSANDS OF DEGREES...
...BURNING UP THE DINOSAURS AND LIFE ON LAND.
BUT THE TEMPERATURE BELOW THE SURFACE ONLY ROSE A FEW DOZEN DEGREES.
40
20
EVEN DEEPER, THERE MUST HAVE BEEN PLACES WHERE THE TEMPERATURE DID NOT CHANGE AT ALL.
ONE COULD SAY THE SAME THING ABOUT THE WATER.
THE LIFE THAT SURVIVED WITHIN THE SOIL AND THE WATER...
...EMERGED, MANY YEARS LATER.
THEY THRIVED AND BECAME YOU ANIMALS.
YOU SEE, LIFE...
...IS A VERY HARDY, STUBBORN THING.

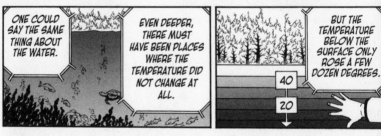

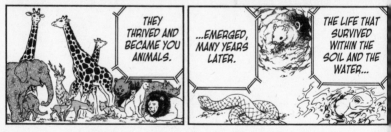

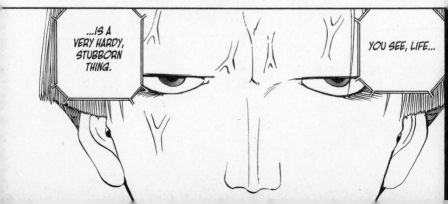

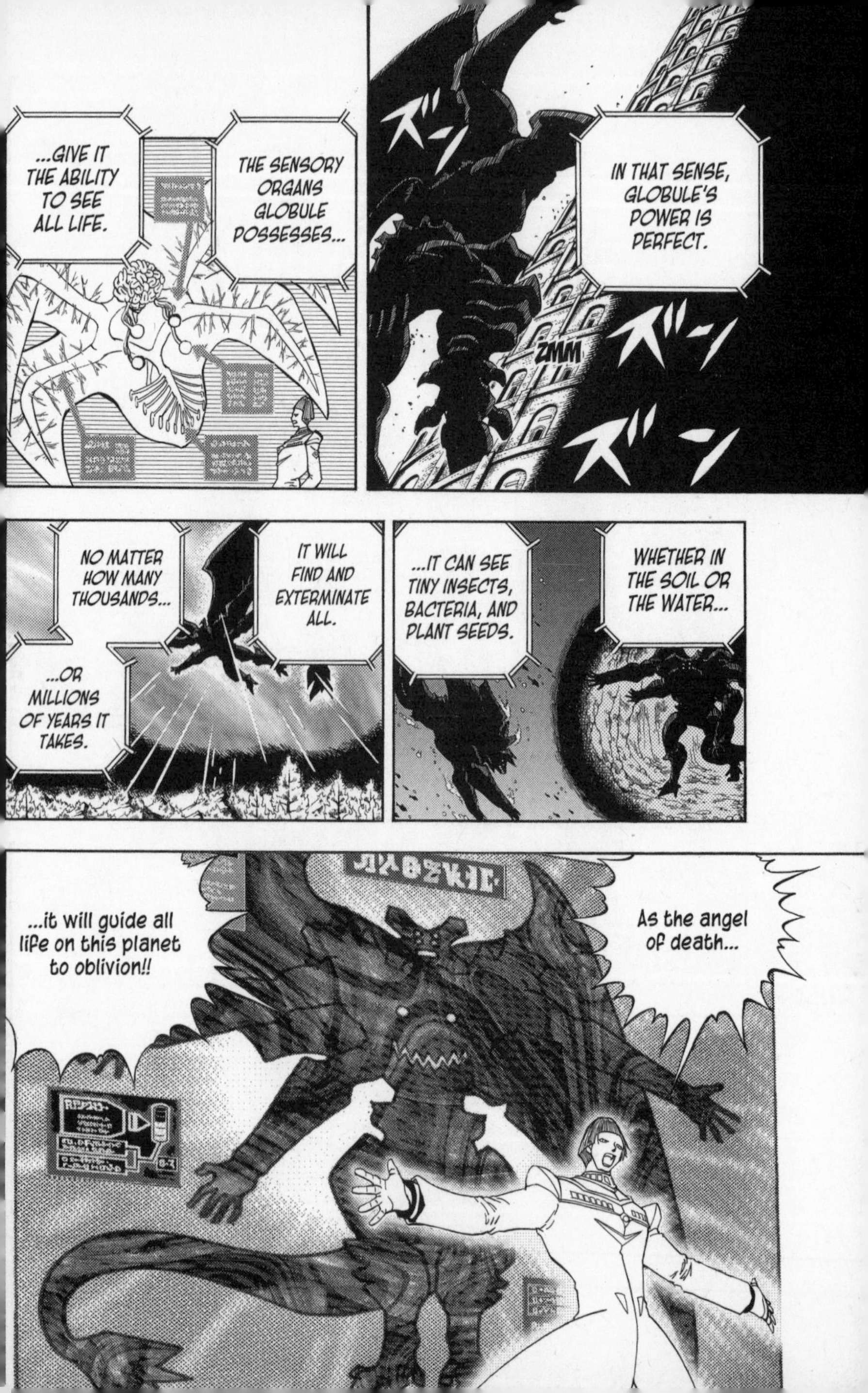
IN THAT SENSE, GLOBULE'S POWER IS PERFECT.
ZMM
THE SENSORY ORGANS GLOBULE POSSESSES...
...GIVE IT THE ABILITY TO SEE ALL LIFE.
WHETHER IN THE SOIL OR THE WATER...
...IT CAN SEE TINY INSECTS, BACTERIA, AND PLANT SEEDS.
IT WILL FIND AND EXTERMINATE ALL.
NO MATTER HOW MANY THOUSANDS...
...OR MILLIONS OF YEARS IT TAKES.
As the angel of death...
...it will guide all life on this planet to oblivion!!

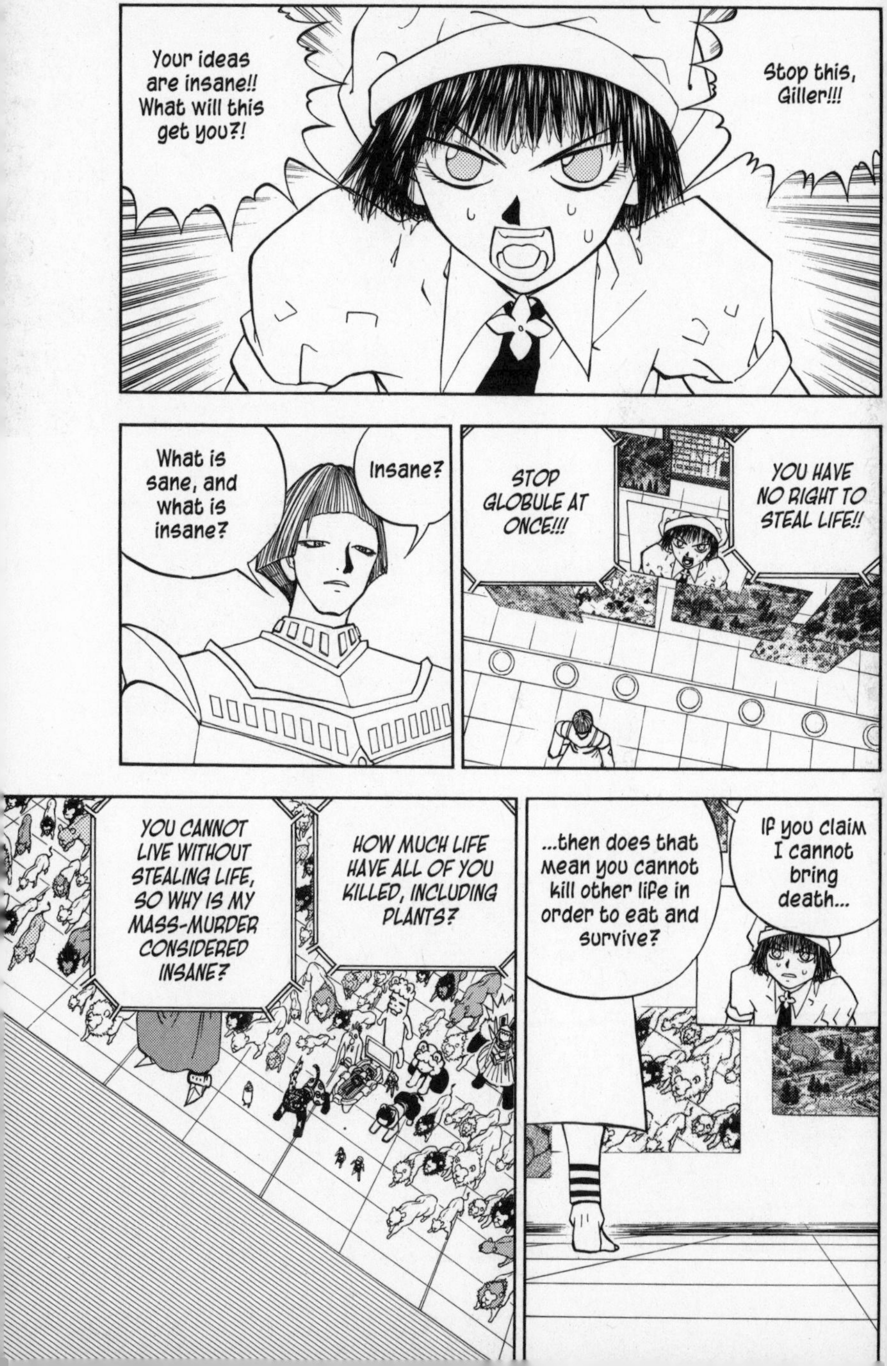
Stop this, Giller!!!
Your ideas are insane!! What will this get you?!
YOU HAVE NO RIGHT TO STEAL LIFE!!
STOP GLOBULE AT ONCE!!!
Insane?
What is sane, and what is insane?
If you claim I cannot bring death...
...then does that mean you cannot kill other life in order to eat and survive?
HOW MUCH LIFE HAVE ALL OF YOU KILLED, INCLUDING PLANTS?
YOU CANNOT LIVE WITHOUT STEALING LIFE, SO WHY IS MY MASS-MURDER CONSIDERED INSANE?

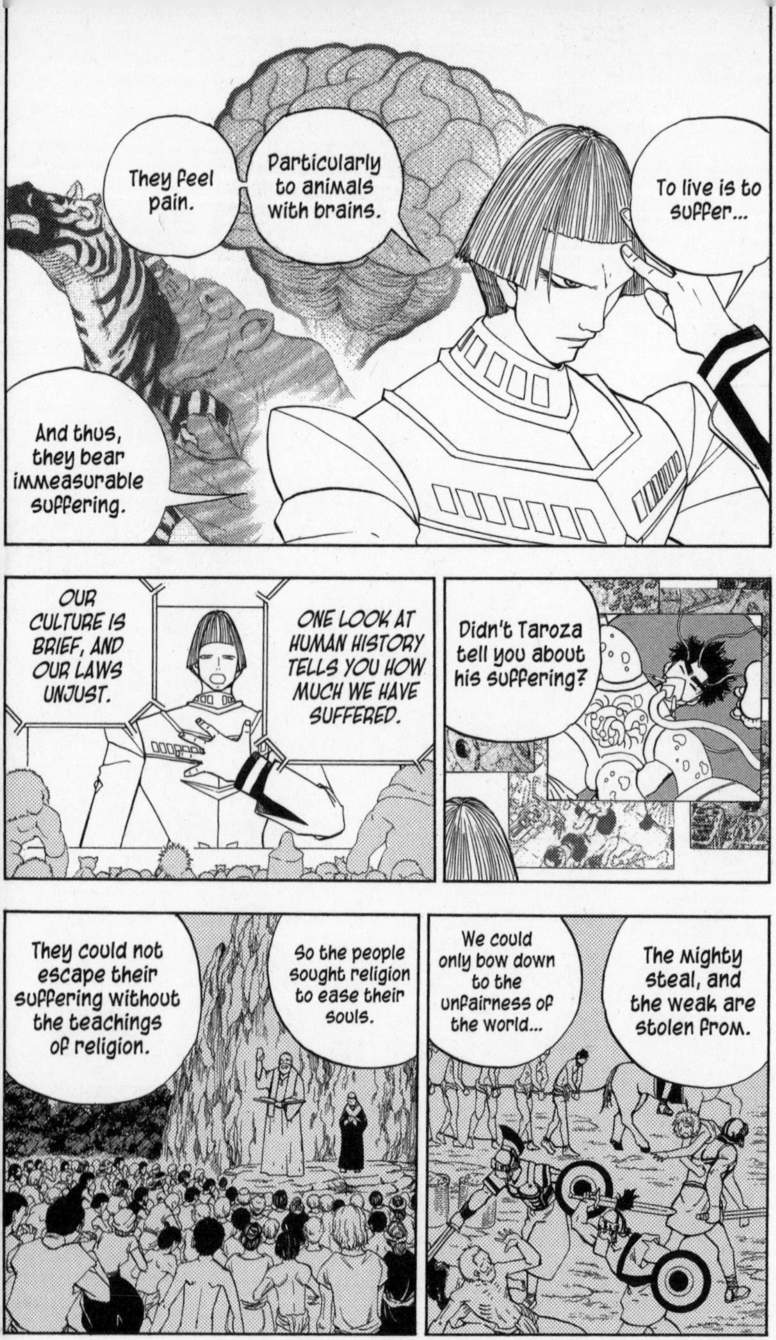
To live is to suffer...
Particularly to animals with brains.
They feel pain.
And thus, they bear immeasurable suffering.
Didn't Taroza tell you about his suffering?
ONE LOOK AT HUMAN HISTORY TELLS YOU HOW MUCH WE HAVE SUFFERED.
OUR CULTURE IS BRIEF, AND OUR LAWS UNJUST.
The Mighty steal, and the weak are stolen from.
We could only bow down to the unfairness of the world...
So the people sought religion to ease their souls.
They could not escape their suffering without the teachings of religion.

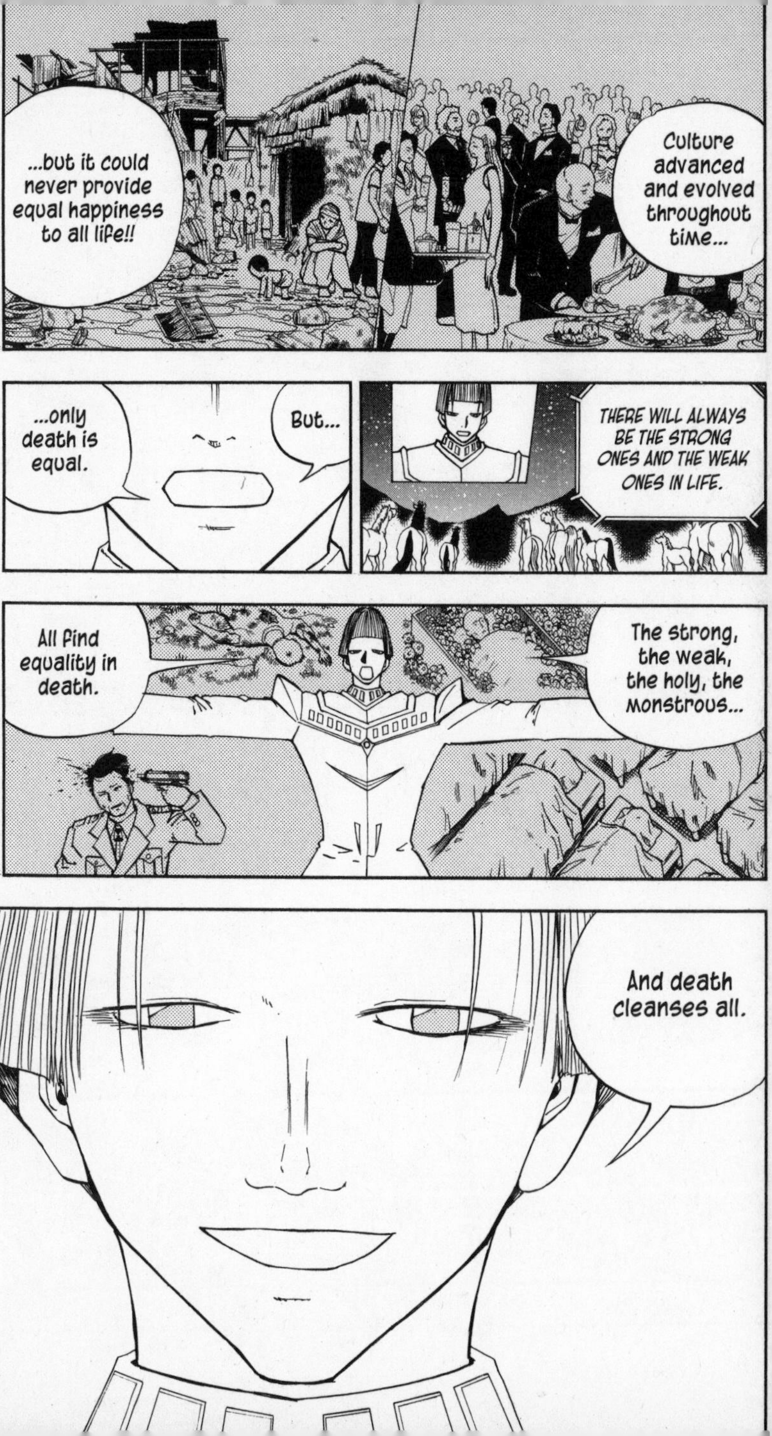
Culture advanced and evolved throughout time...
...but it could never provide equal happiness to all life!!
THERE WILL ALWAYS BE THE STRONG ONES AND THE WEAK ONES IN LIFE.
But...
...only death is equal.
The strong, the weak, the holy, the monstrous...
All find equality in death.
And death cleanses all.

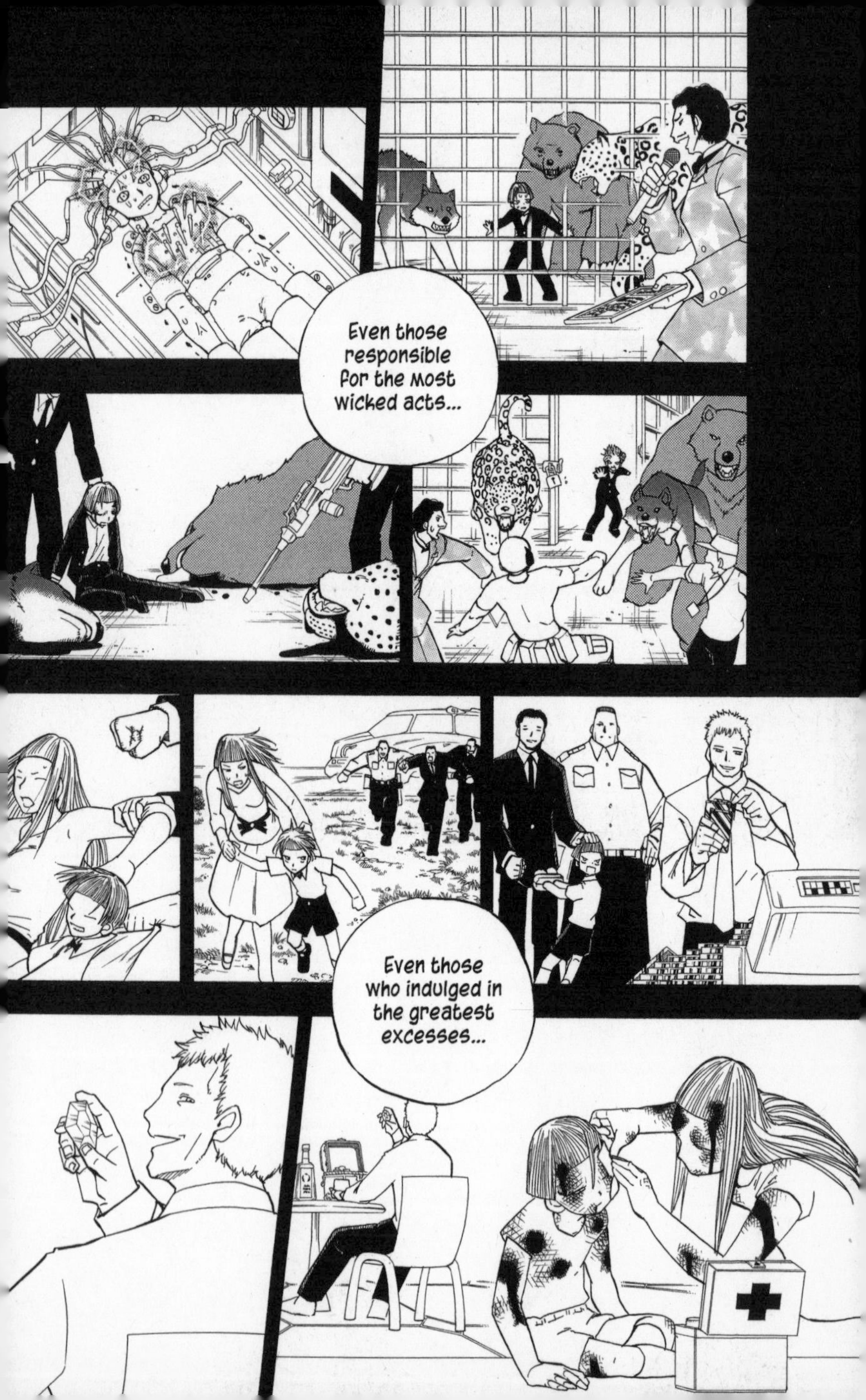
Even those responsible for the most wicked acts...
Even those who indulged in the greatest excesses...

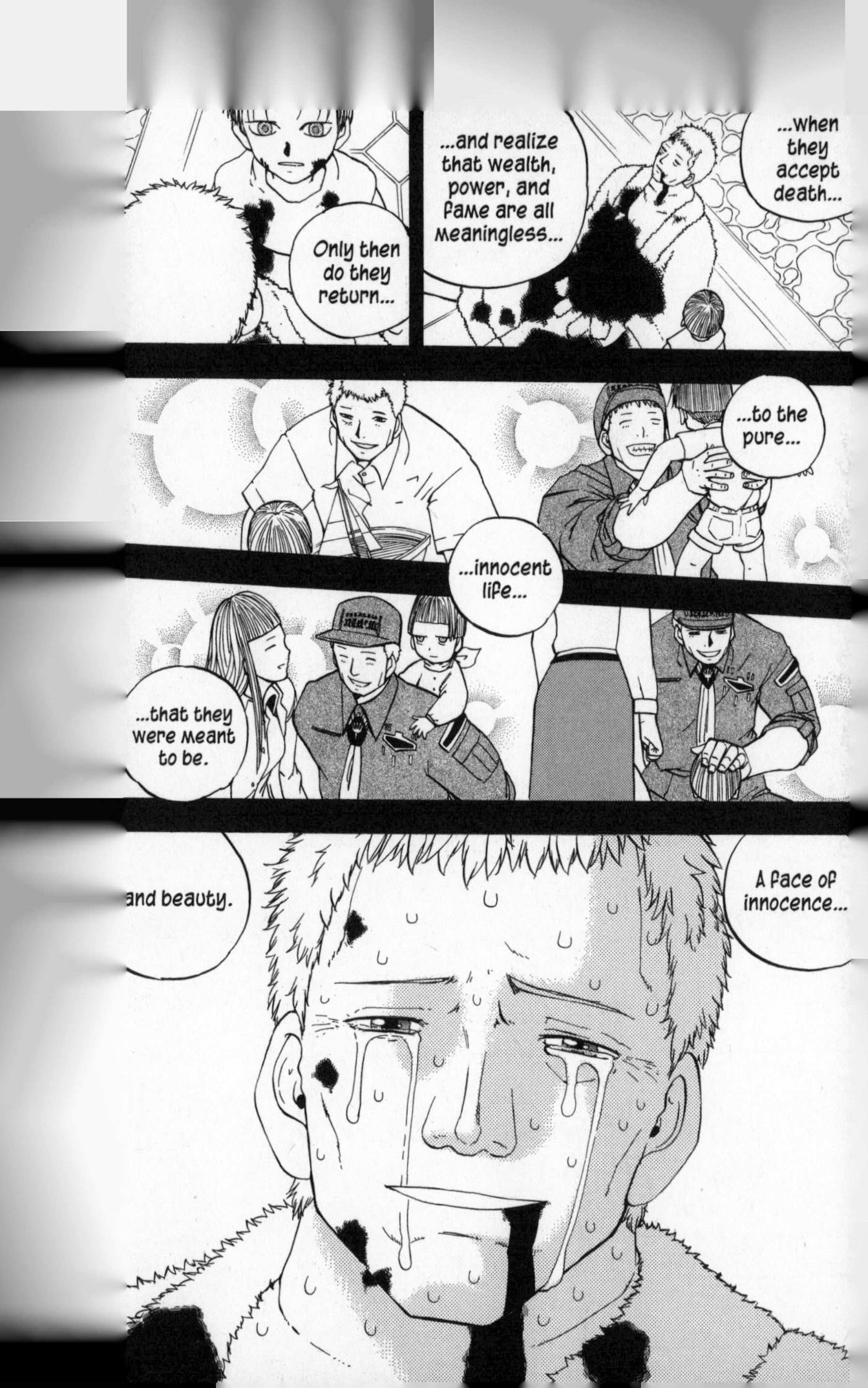
...when they accept death...
...and realize that wealth, power, and fame are all meaningless...
Only then do they return...
...to the pure...
...innocent life...
...that they were meant to be.
A face of innocence...
and beauty.

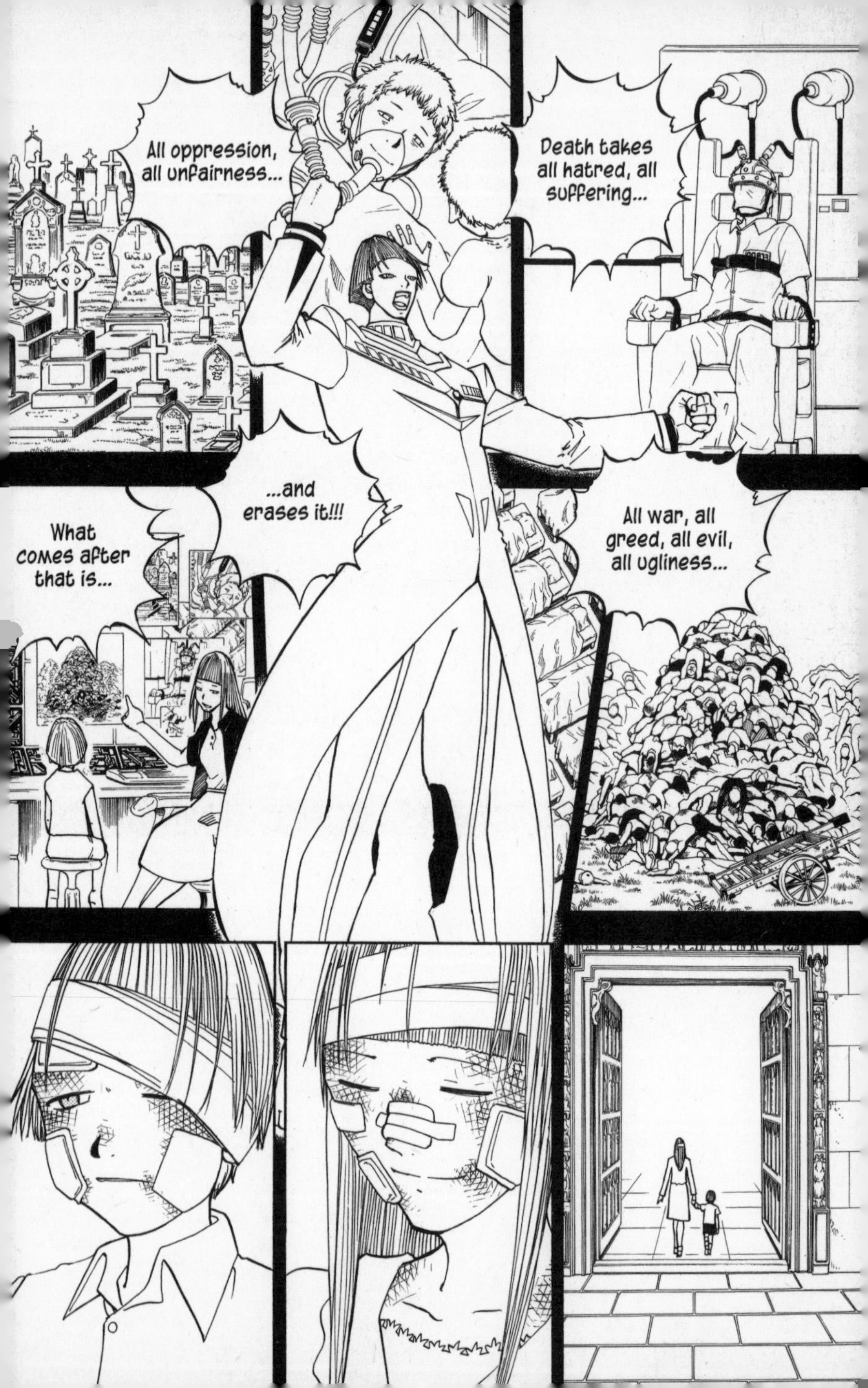
Death takes all hatred, all suffering...
All oppression, all unfairness...
All war, all greed, all evil, all ugliness...
...and erases it!!!
What comes after that is...

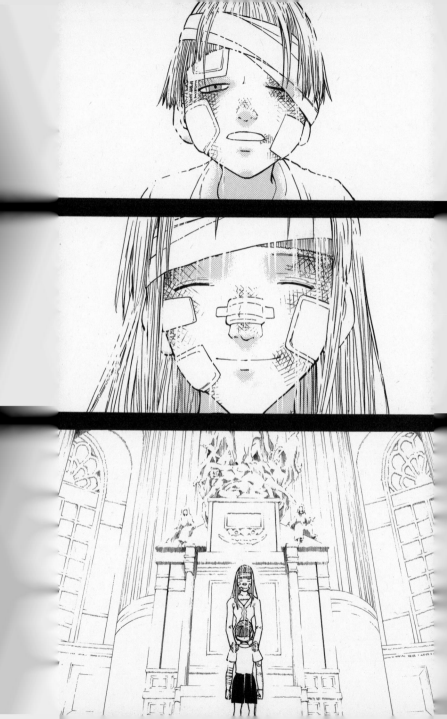

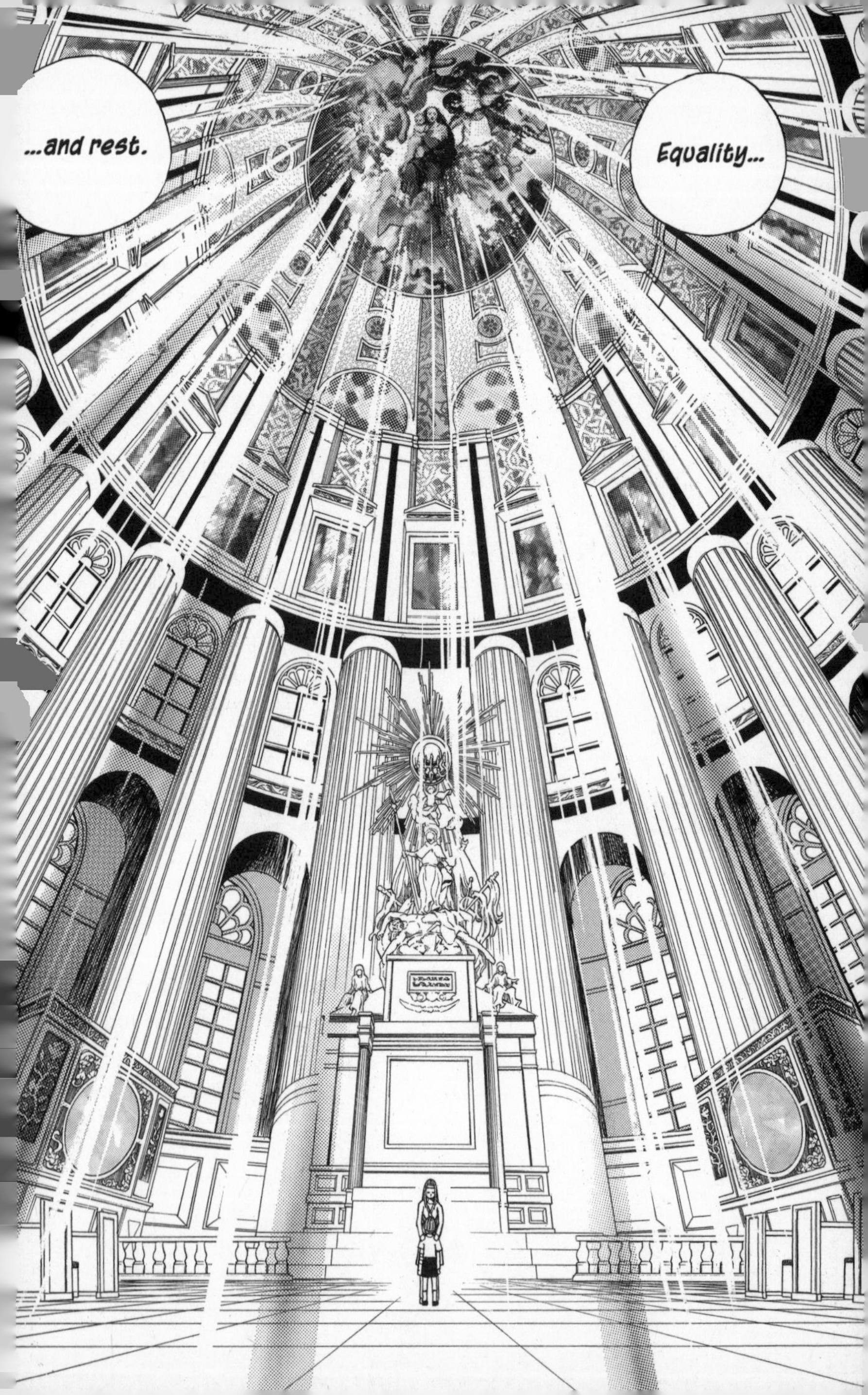
Equality...
...and rest.

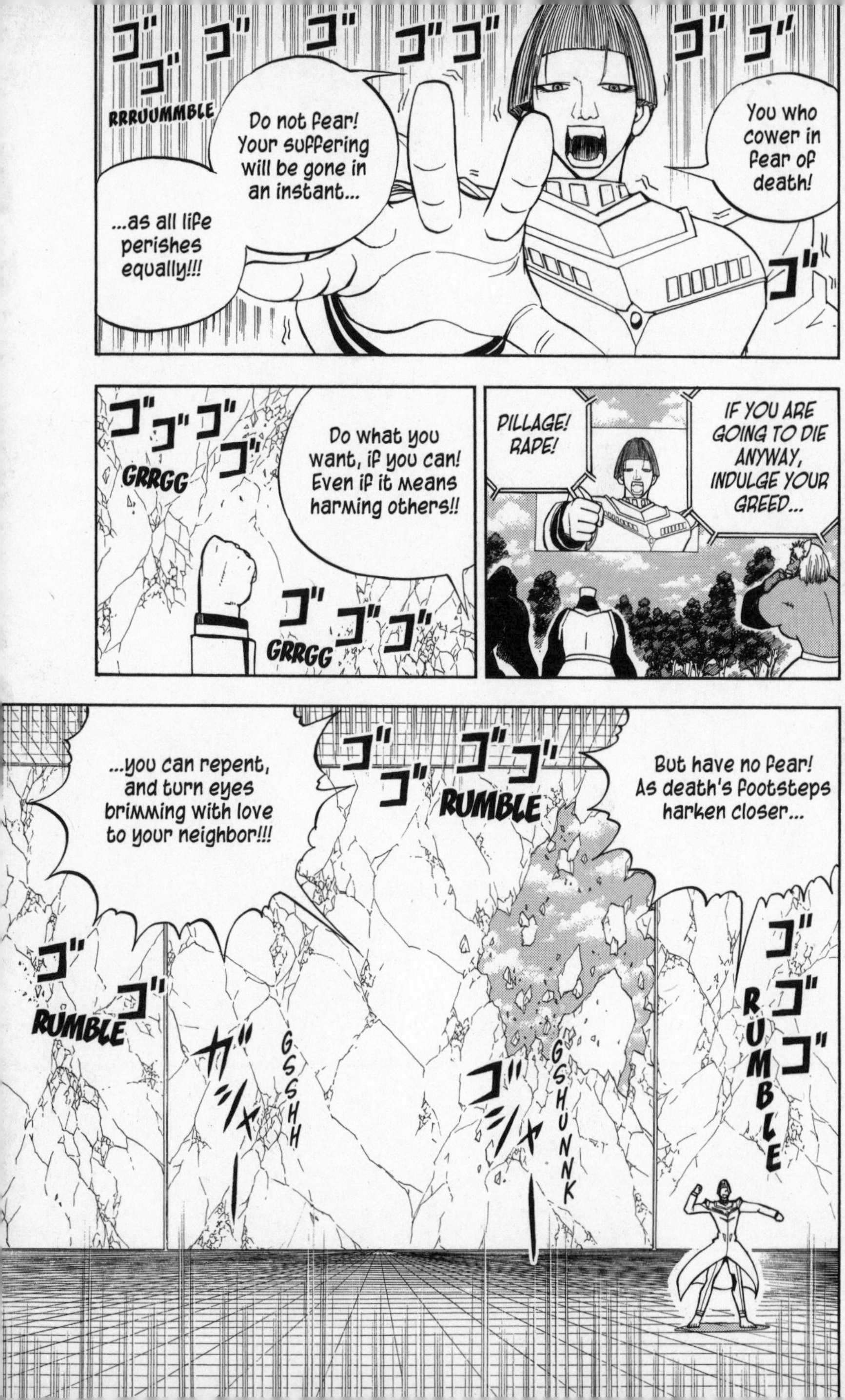
You who cower in fear of death!
Do not fear! Your suffering will be gone in an instant...
RRRUUMMBLE
...as all life perishes equally!!!
IF YOU ARE GOING TO DIE ANYWAY, INDULGE YOUR GREED...
PILLAGE! RAPE!
Do what you want, if you can! Even if it means harming others!!
GRRGG
GRRGG
But have no fear! As death's footsteps harken closer...
RUMBLE
...you can repent, and turn eyes brimming with love to your neighbor!!!
RUMBLE
GSHUNNK
GSSHH
RUMBLE

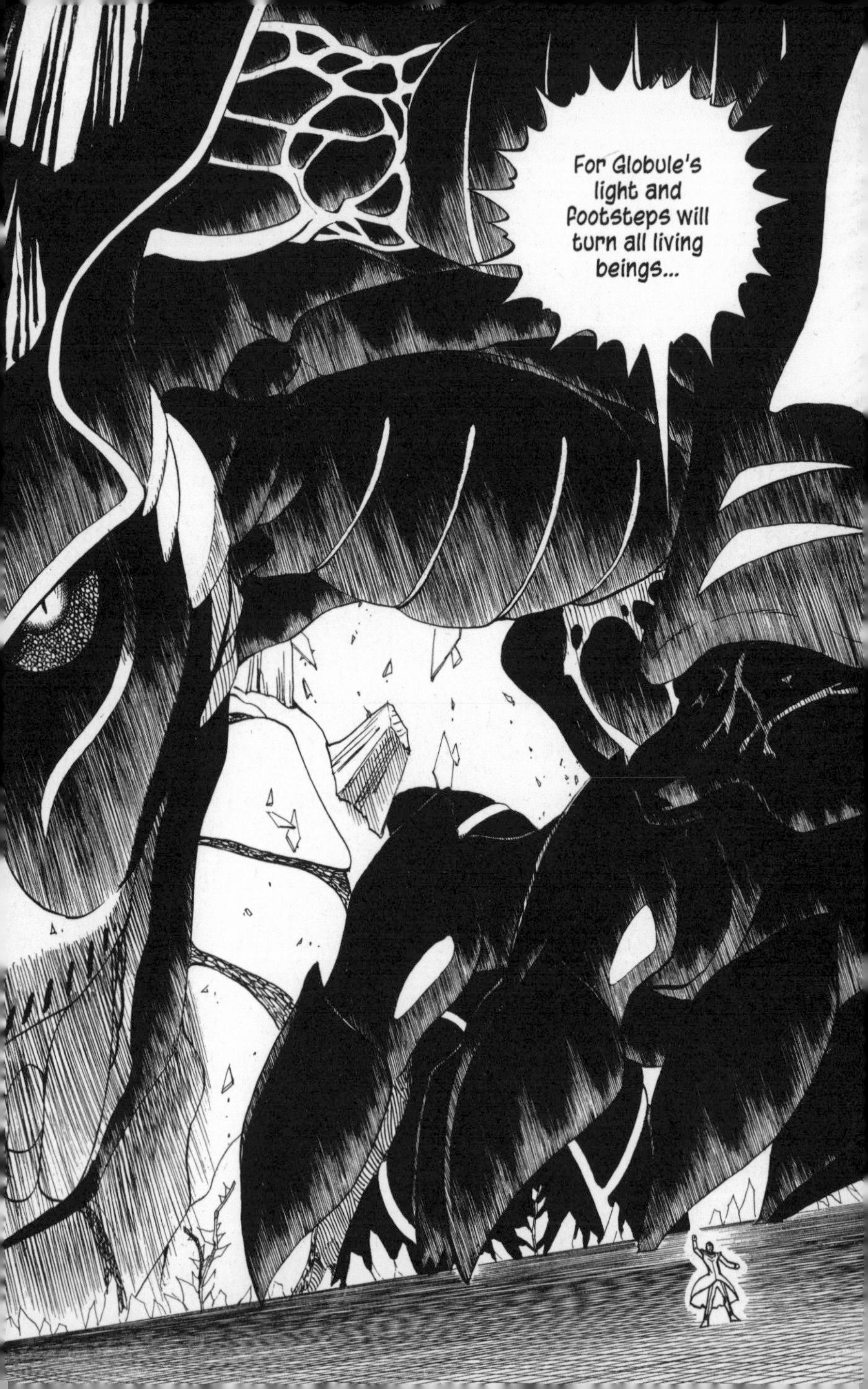
For Globule's light and footsteps will turn all living beings...

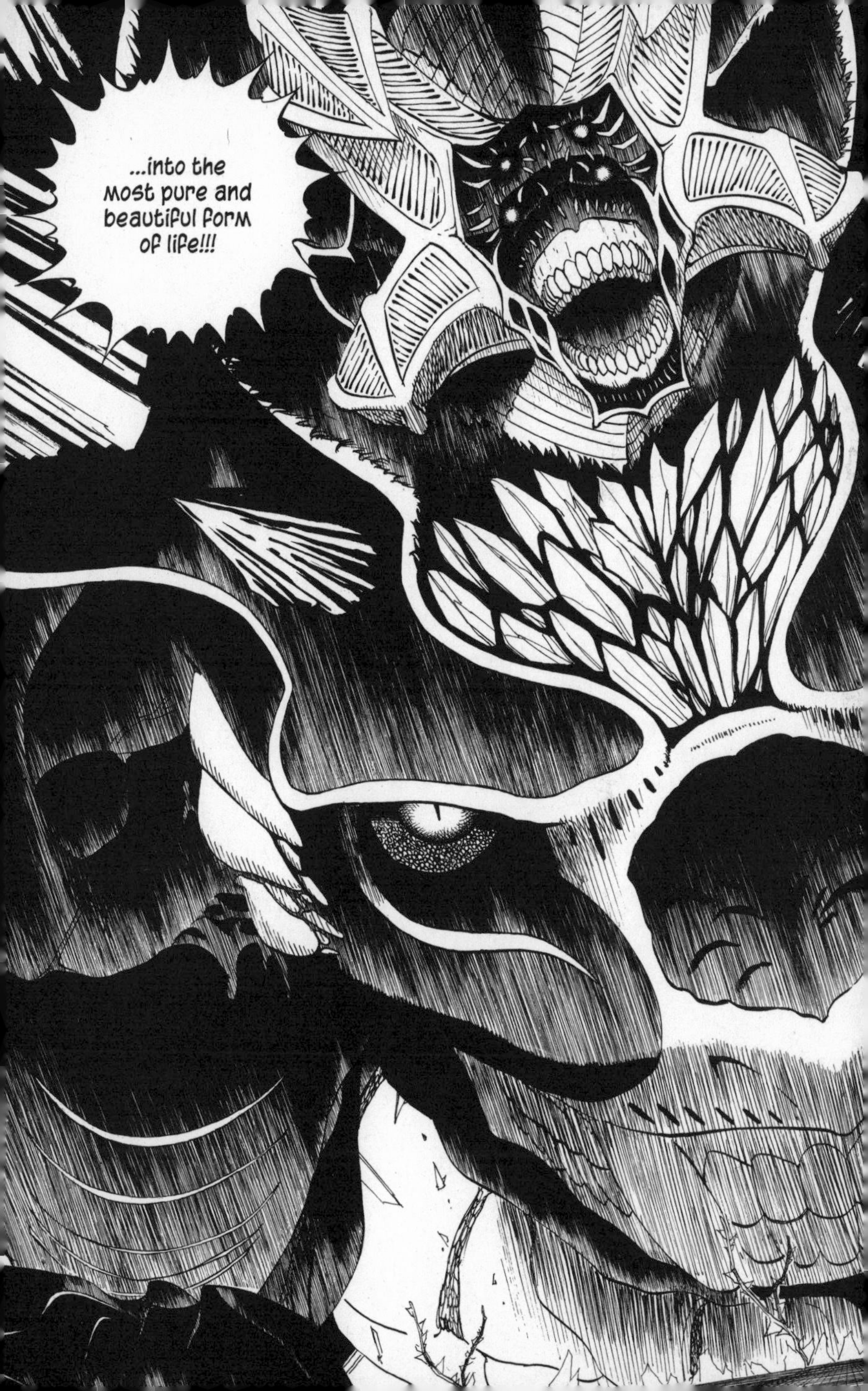
...into the most pure and beautiful form of life!!!

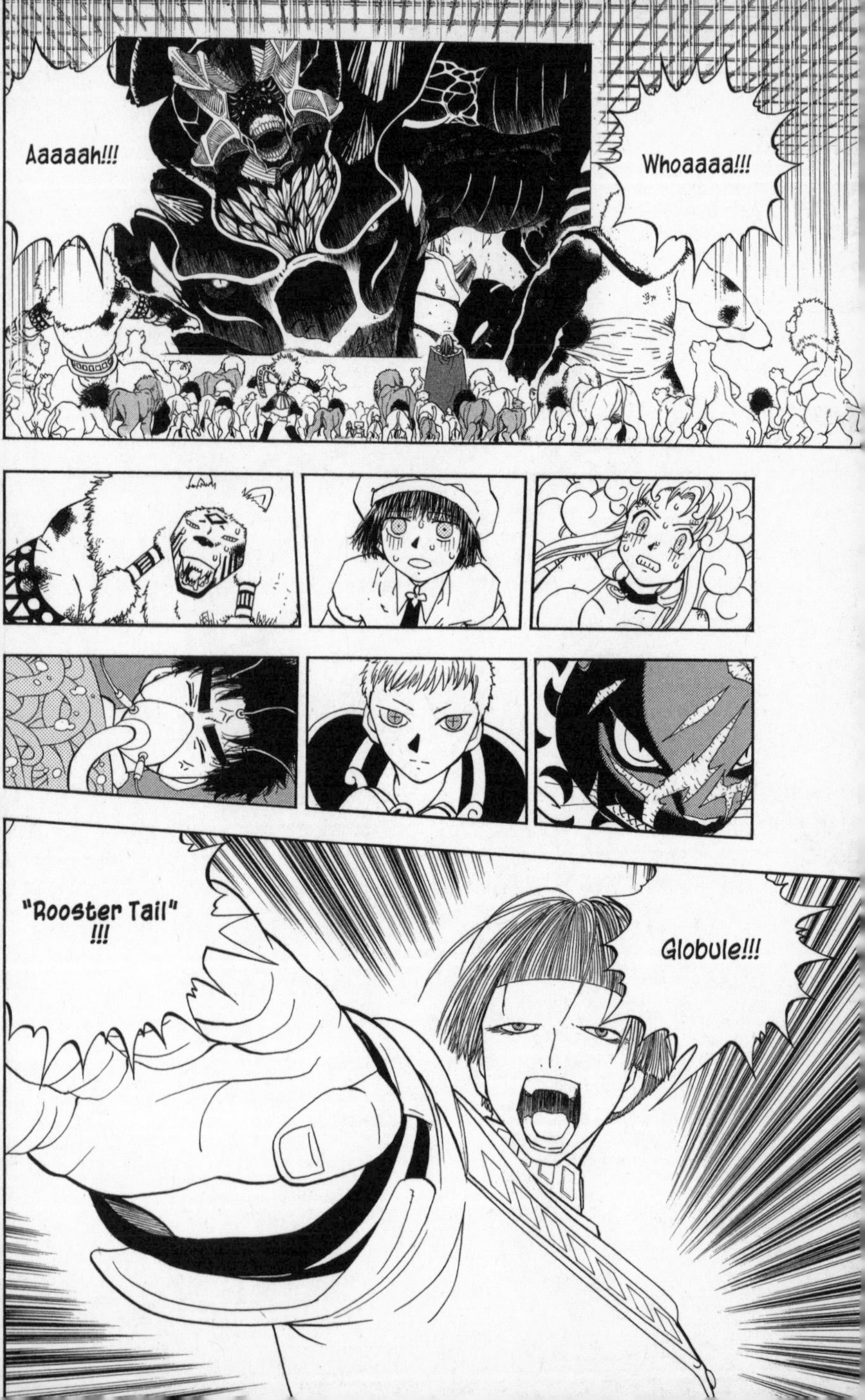
Whoaaaa!!!
Aaaaah!!!
Globule!!!
"Rooster Tail" !!!

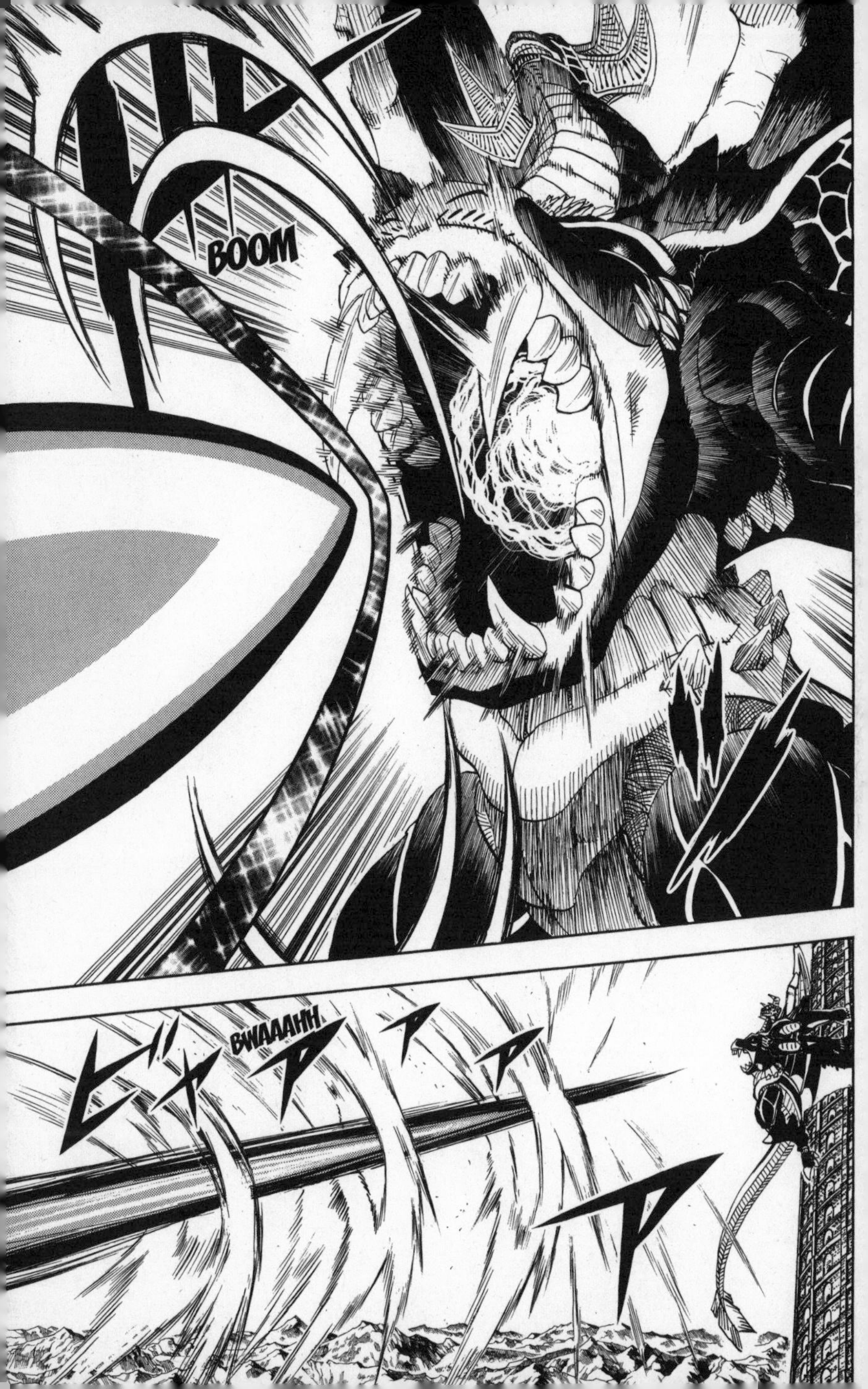
BOOM
BWAAAHH

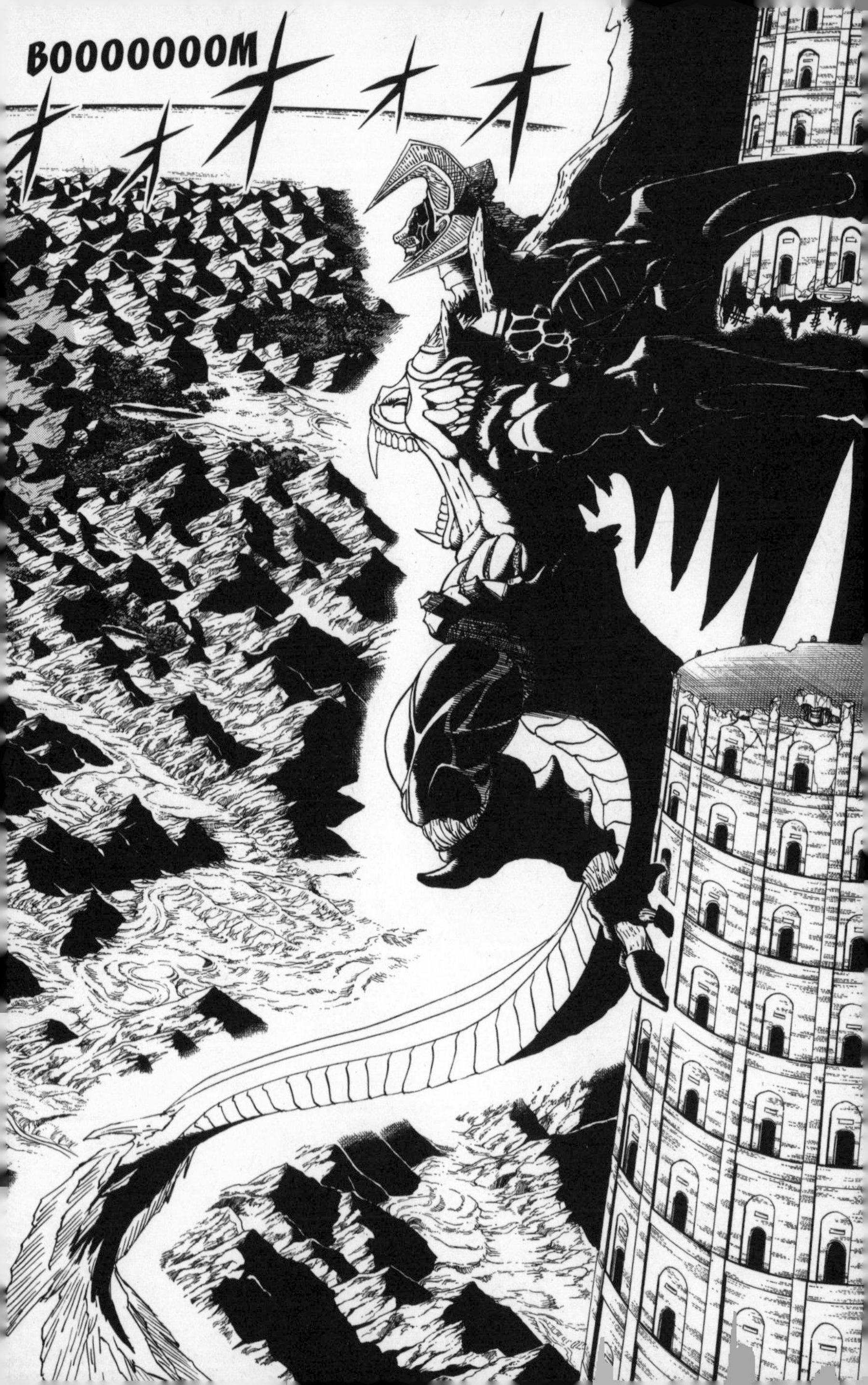
BOOOOOOOM
オォォォォ

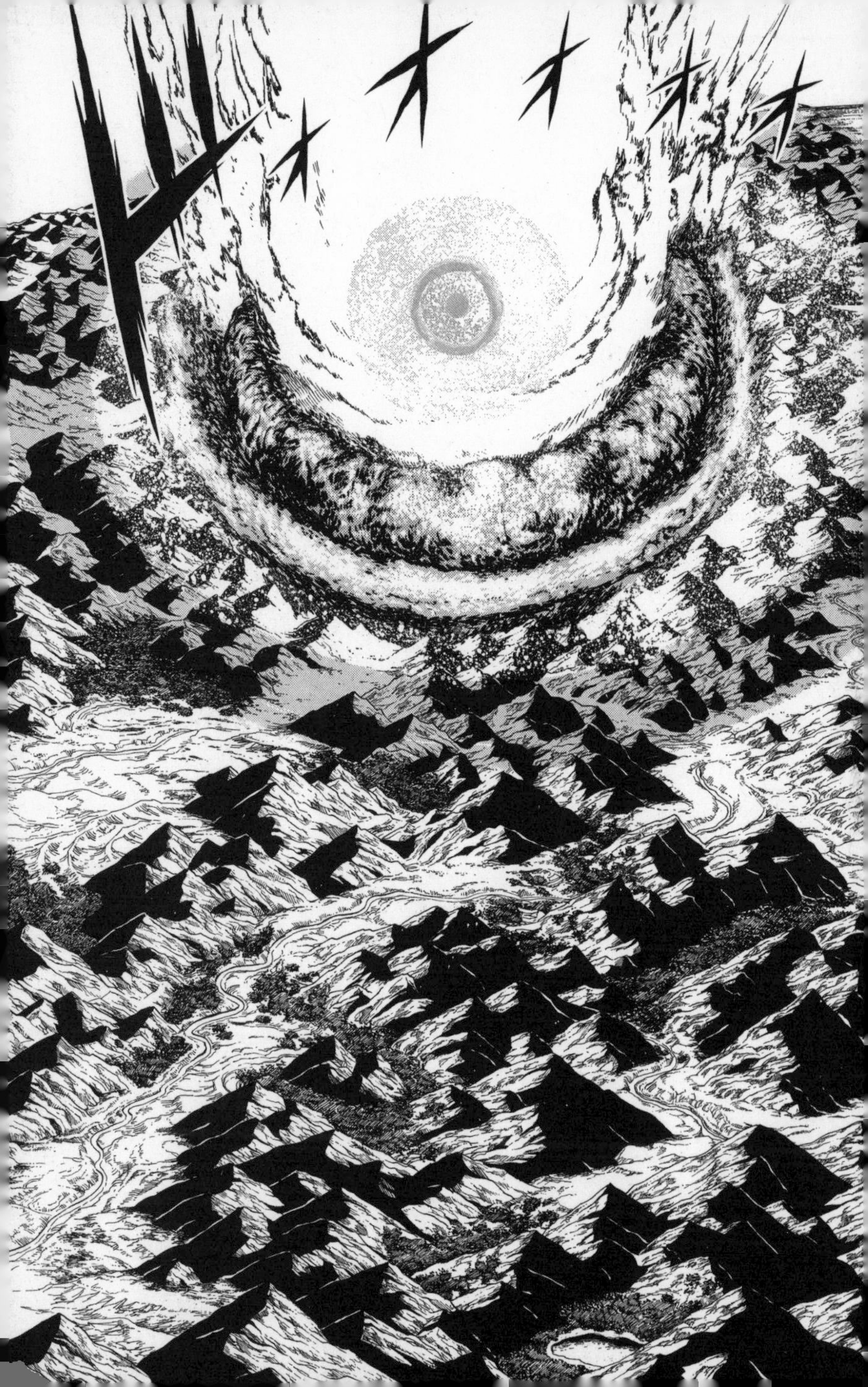
ドオオオオオ

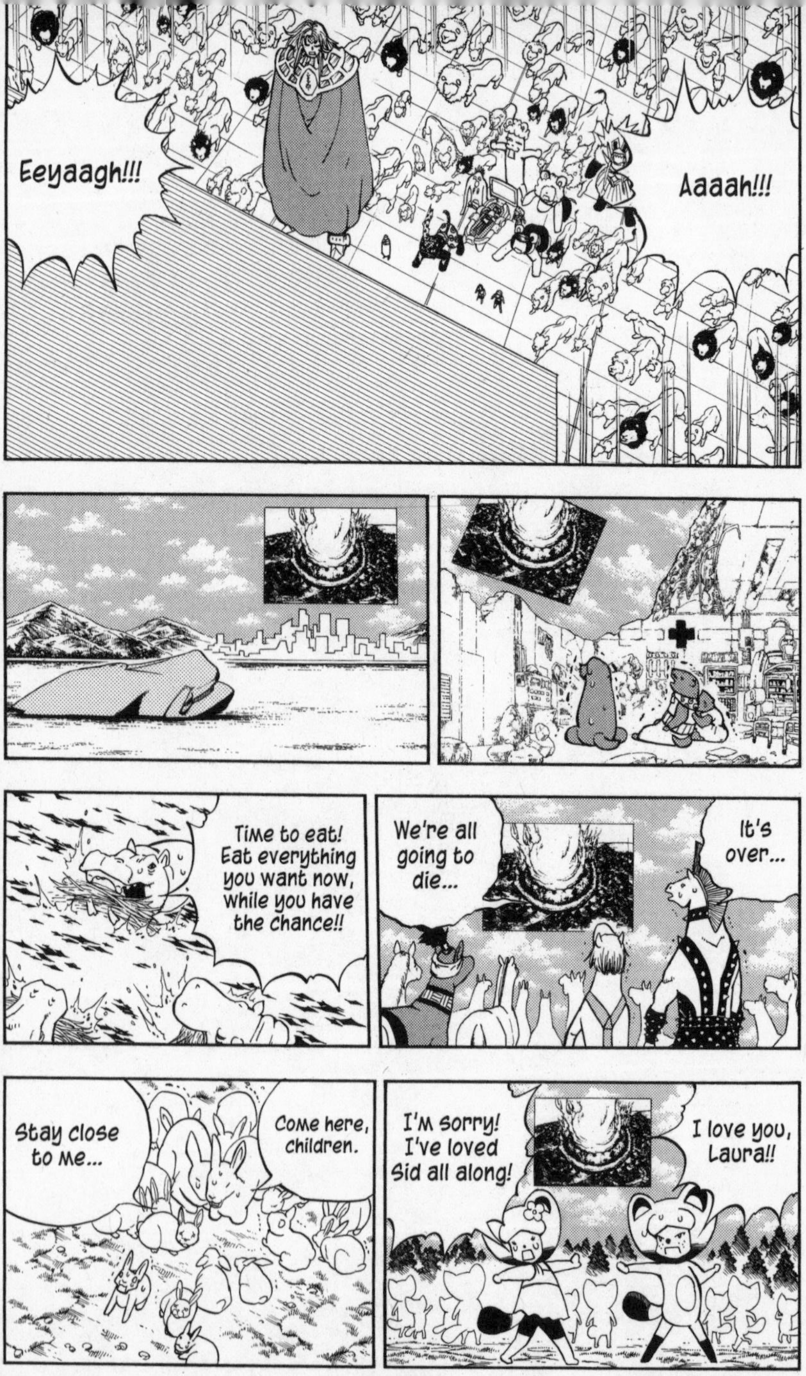

Aaaah!!!
Eeyaagh!!!
It's over...
We're all going to die...
Time to eat! Eat everything you want now, while you have the chance!!
I love you, Laura!!
I'm sorry! I've loved Sid all along!
Come here, children.
Stay close to me...

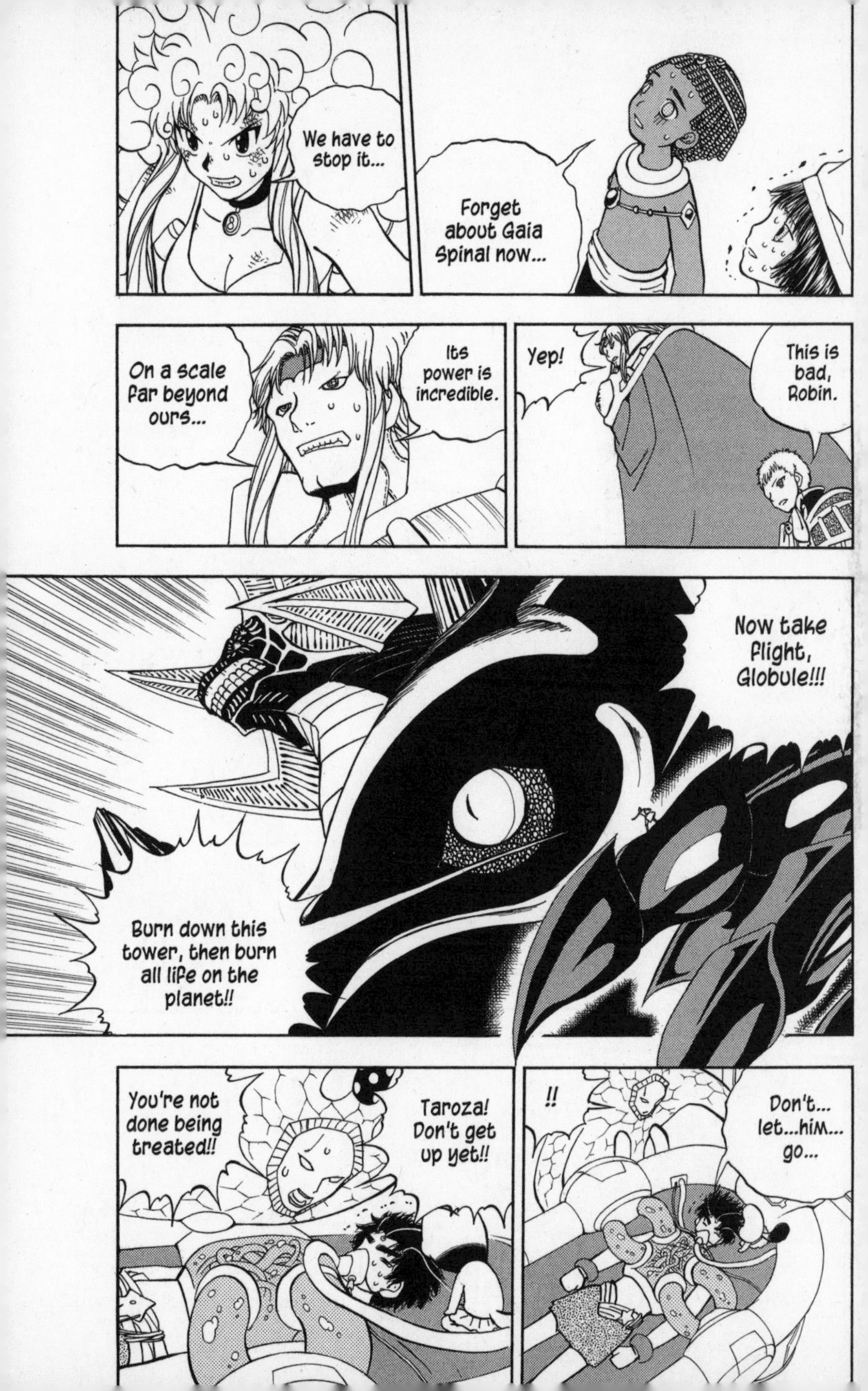
Forget about Gaia Spinal now...
We have to stop it...
This is bad, Robin.
Yep!
Its power is incredible.
On a scale far beyond ours...
Now take flight, Globule!!!
Burn down this tower, then burn all life on the planet!!
Don't... let...him... go...
!!
Taroza! Don't get up yet!!
You're not done being treated!!

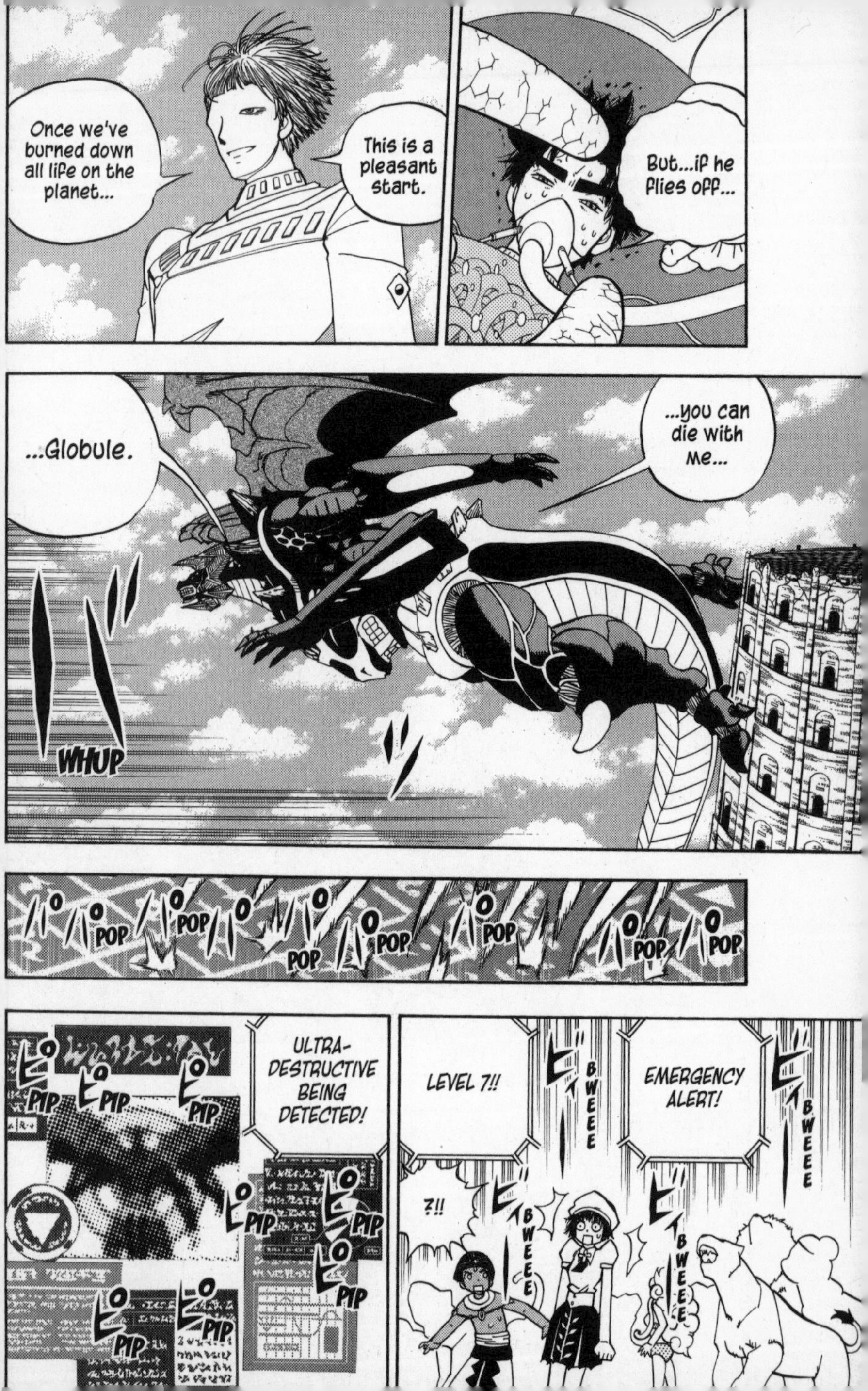
But...if he flies off...
This is a pleasant start.
Once we've burned down all life on the planet...
...you can die with me...
...Globule.
WHUP
POP POP POP POP POP POP POP POP
EMERGENCY ALERT!
BWEEE
LEVEL 7!!
BWEEE
?!!
BWEEE
BWEEE
ULTRA-DESTRUCTIVE BEING DETECTED!
PIP PIP PIP PIP PIP PIP PIP PIP

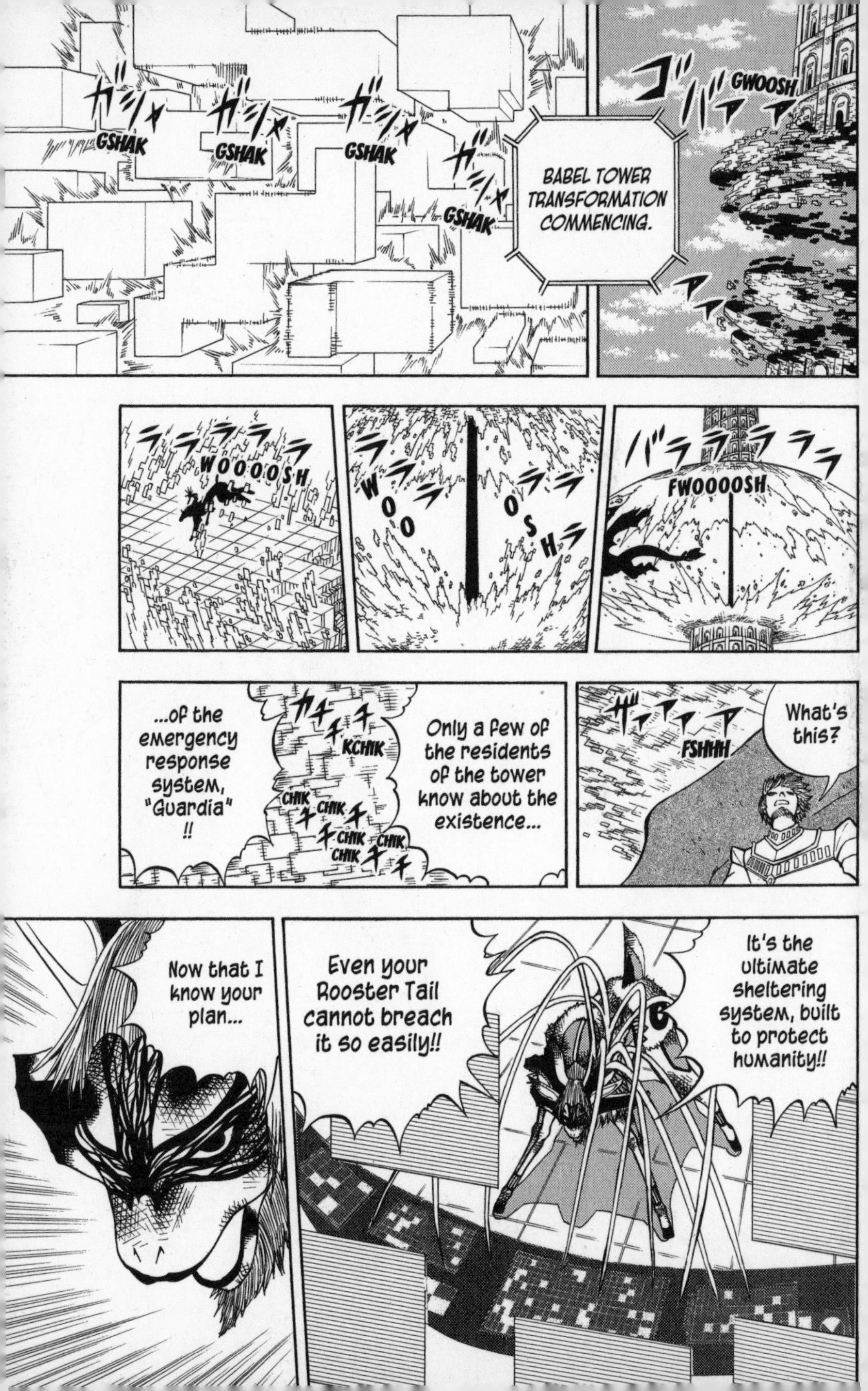
GWOOSH
BABEL TOWER TRANSFORMATION COMMENCING.
GSHAK
GSHAK
GSHAK
GSHAK
FWOOOOSH
WOOOSH
WOOOOSH
FSHHH
What's this?
Only a few of the residents of the tower know about the existence...
KCHIK
CHIK
CHIK
CHIK
CHIK
CHIK
...of the emergency response system, "Guardia" !!
It's the ultimate sheltering system, built to protect humanity!!
Even your Rooster Tail cannot breach it so easily!!
Now that I know your plan...

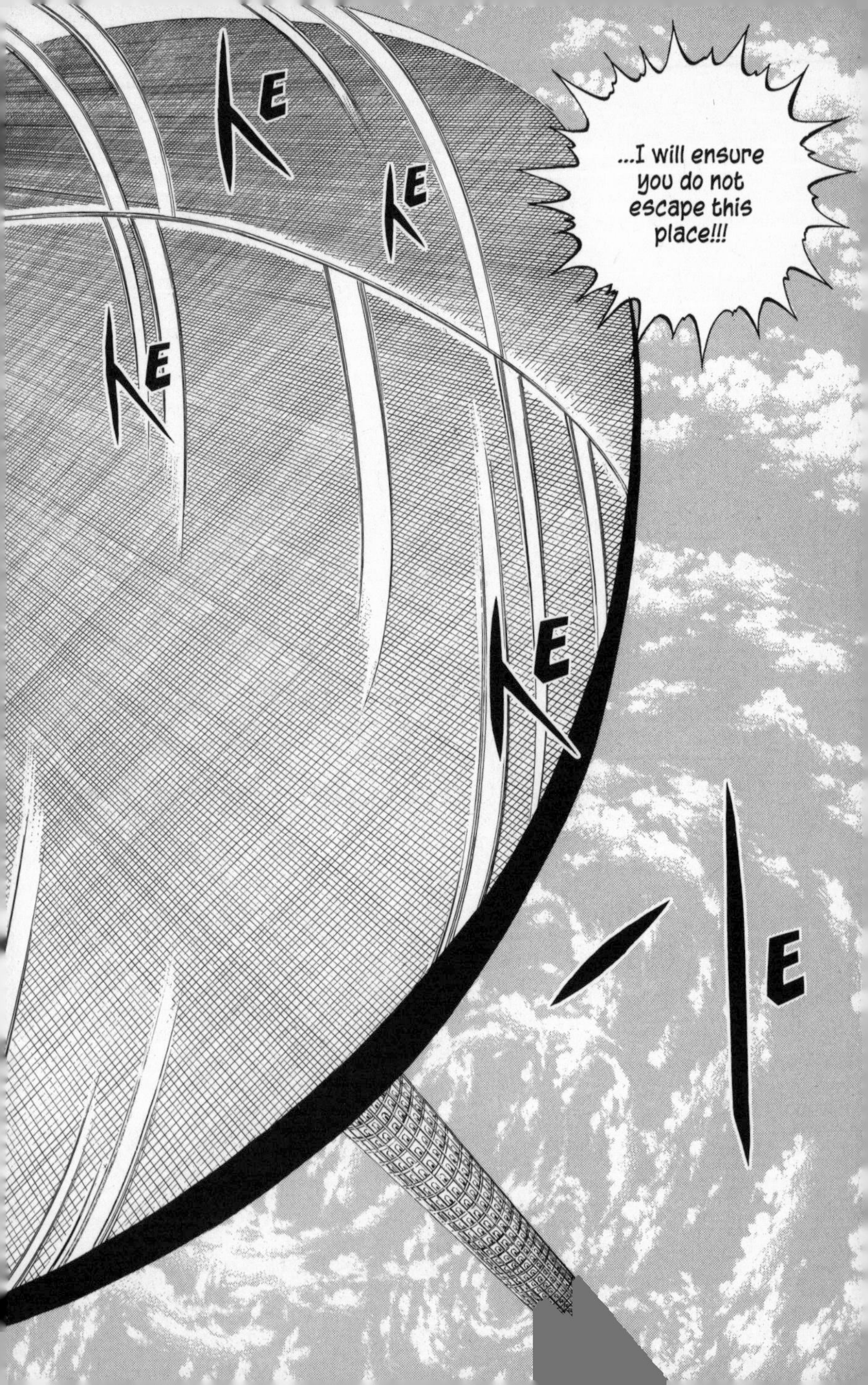

...I will ensure you do not escape this place!!!

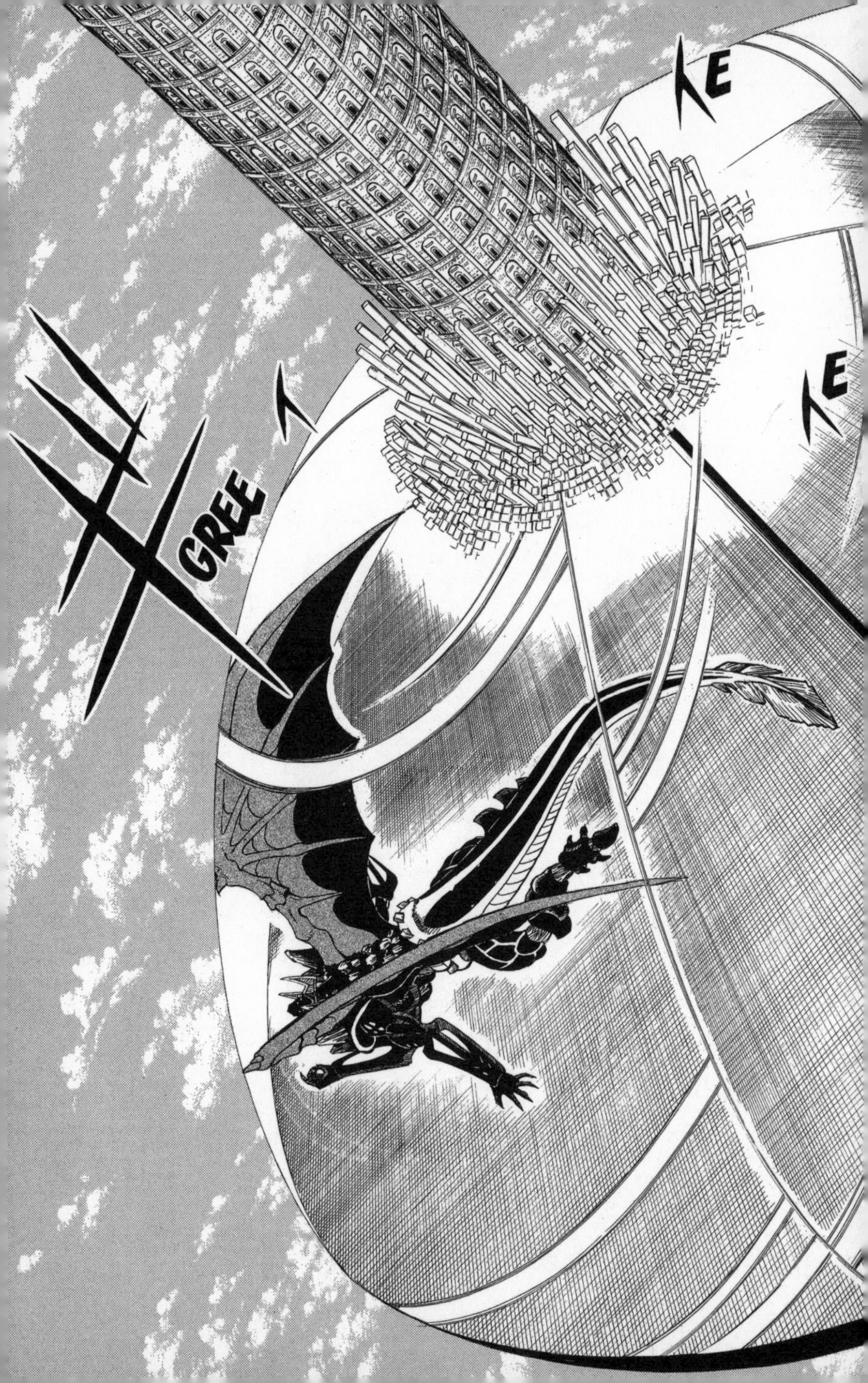
GREE
E
E

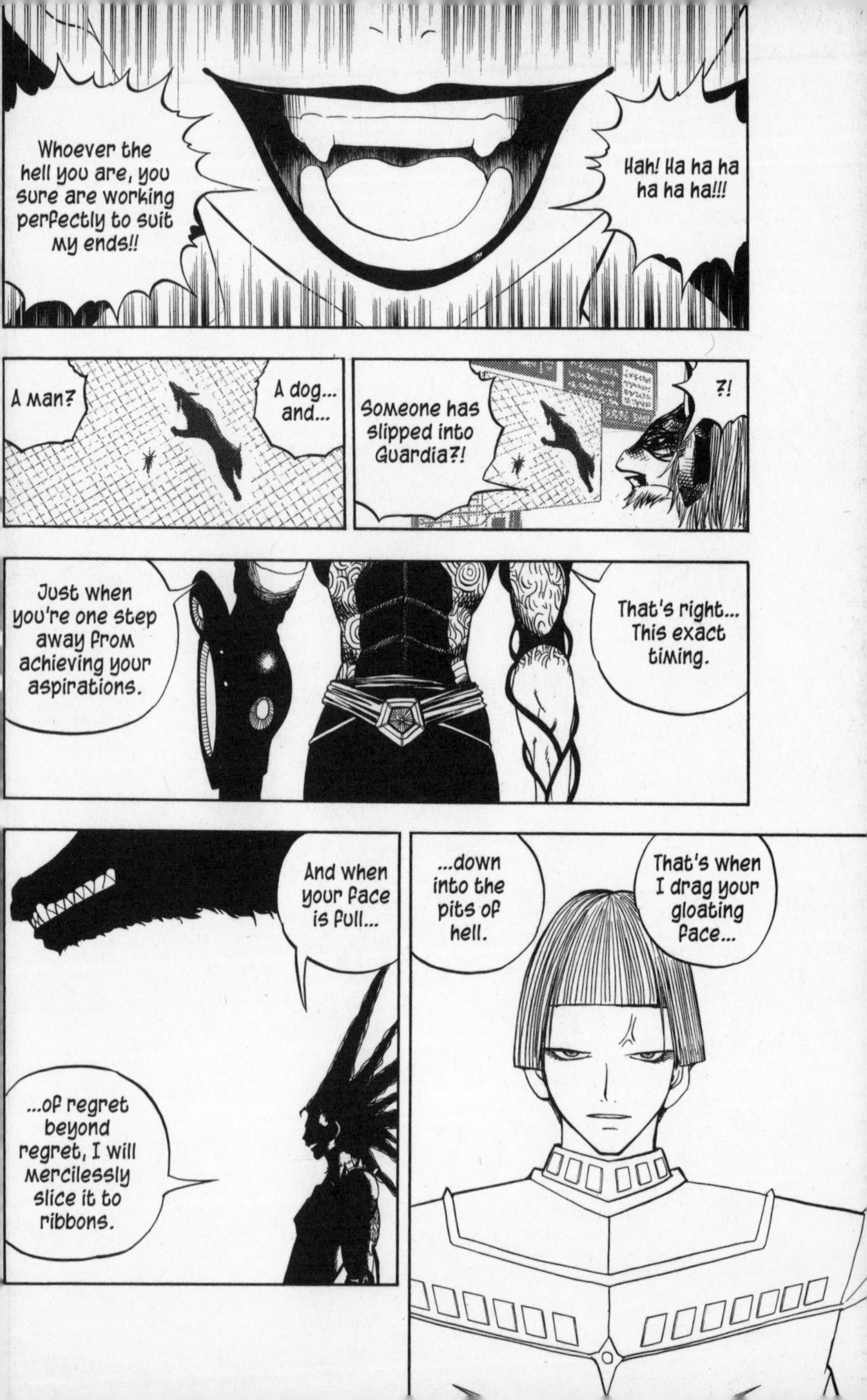
Hah! Ha ha ha ha ha!!!
Whoever the hell you are, you sure are working perfectly to suit my ends!!
?!
Someone has slipped into Guardia?!
A dog... and...
A man?
That's right... This exact timing.
Just when you're one step away from achieving your aspirations.
That's when I drag your gloating face...
...down into the pits of hell.
And when your face is full...
...of regret beyond regret, I will mercilessly slice it to ribbons.

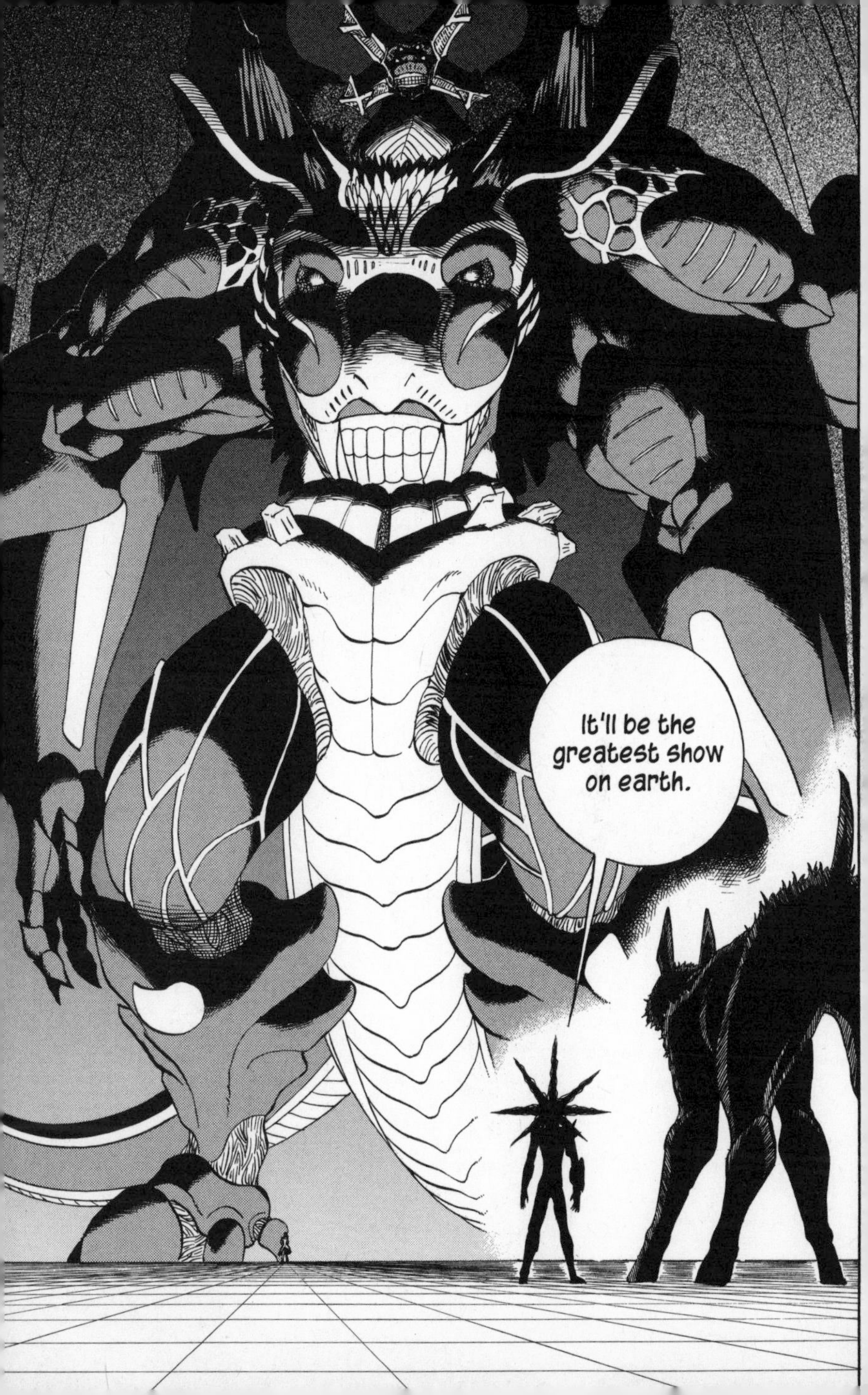
It'll be the greatest show on earth.

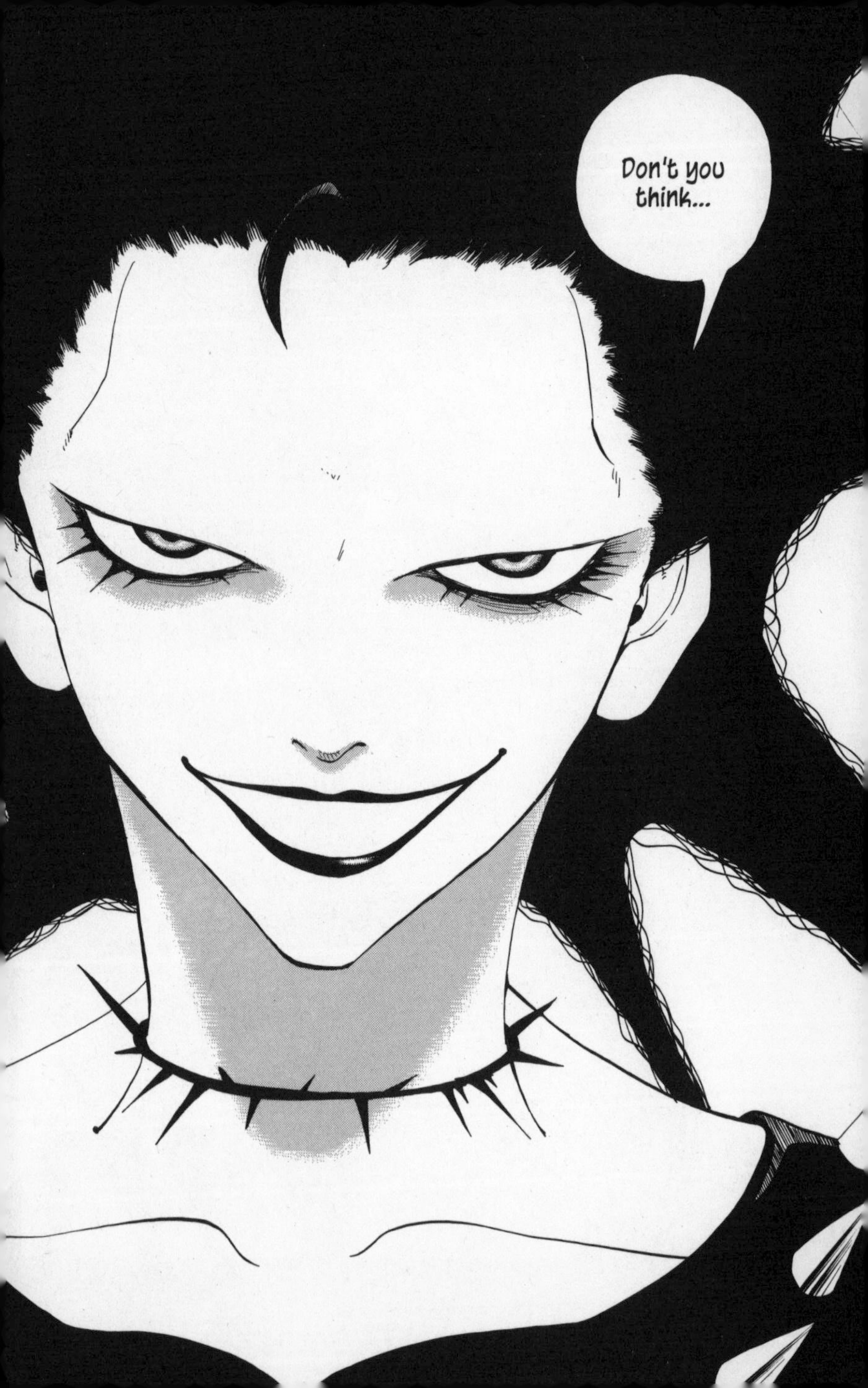
Don't you think...

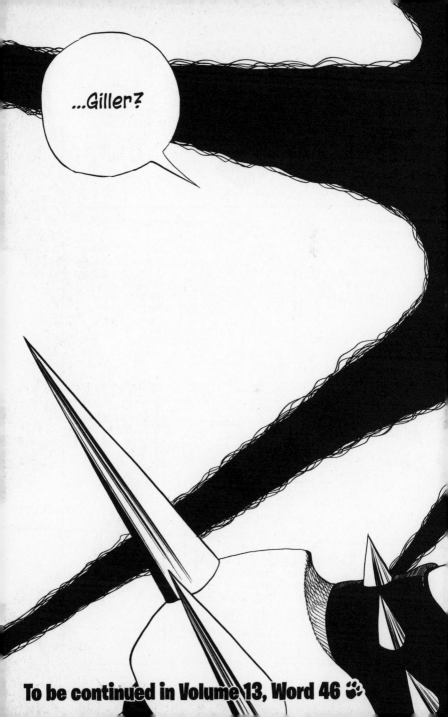

...Giller?

To be continued in Volume 13, Word 46

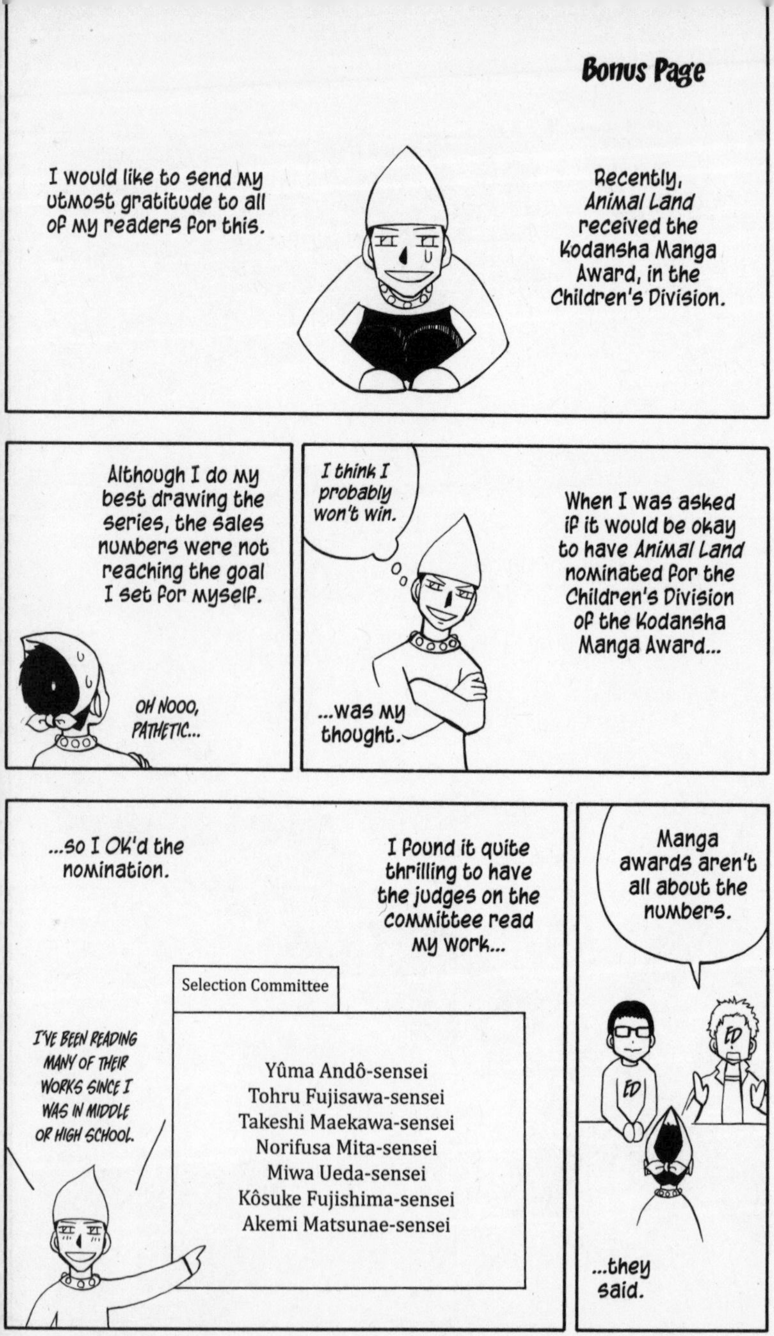
Bonus Page
Recently, Animal Land received the Kodansha Manga Award, in the Children's Division.
I would like to send my utmost gratitude to all of my readers for this.
When I was asked if it would be okay to have Animal Land nominated for the Children's Division of the Kodansha Manga Award...
I think I probably won't win.
...was my thought.
Although I do my best drawing the series, the sales numbers were not reaching the goal I set for myself.
OH NOOO, PATHETIC...
Manga awards aren't all about the numbers.
...they said.
...so I OK'd the nomination.
I found it quite thrilling to have the judges on the committee read my work...
Selection Committee
Yûma Andô-sensei
Tohru Fujisawa-sensei
Takeshi Maekawa-sensei
Norifusa Mita-sensei
Miwa Ueda-sensei
Kôsuke Fujishima-sensei
Akemi Matsunae-sensei
I'VE BEEN READING MANY OF THEIR WORKS SINCE I WAS IN MIDDLE OR HIGH SCHOOL.

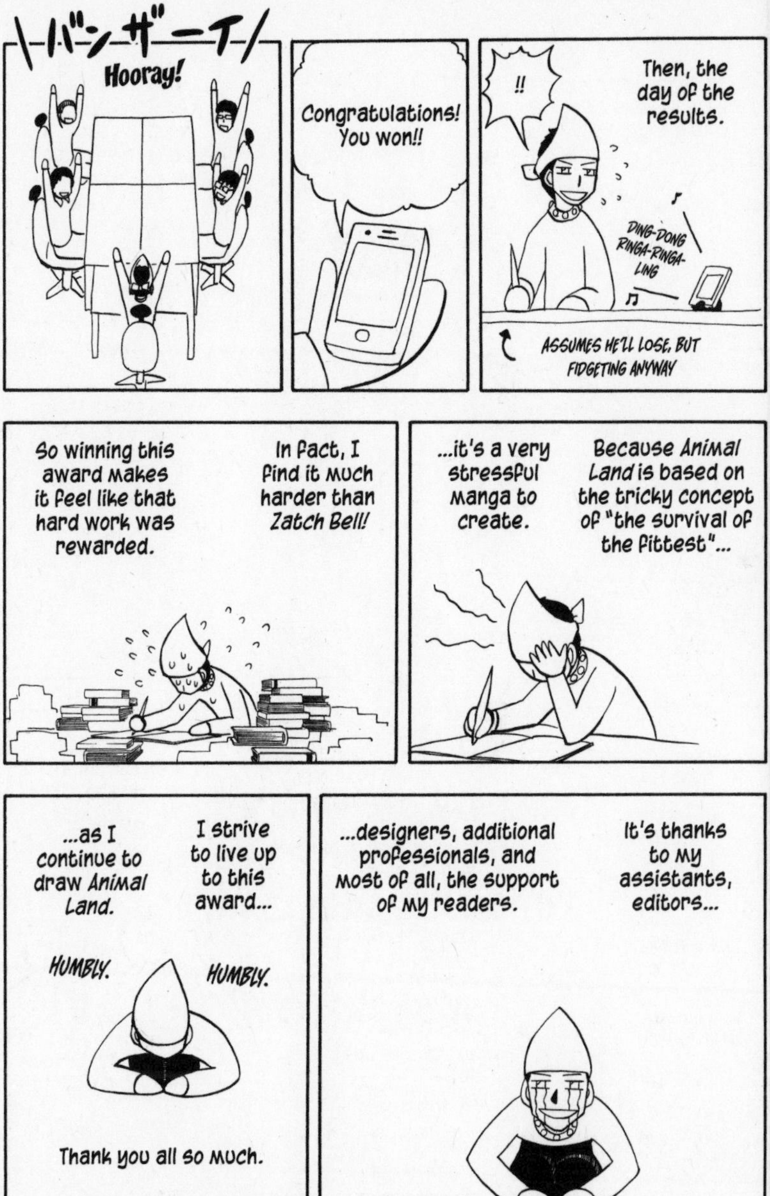

Then, the day of the results.
!!
DING-DONG RINGA-RINGA-LING
ASSUMES HE'LL LOSE, BUT FIDGETING ANYWAY
Congratulations! You won!!
バンザーイ
Hooray!
Because *Animal Land* is based on the tricky concept of "the survival of the fittest"...
...it's a very stressful manga to create.
In fact, I find it much harder than *Zatch Bell!*
So winning this award makes it feel like that hard work was rewarded.
It's thanks to my assistants, editors...
...designers, additional professionals, and most of all, the support of my readers.
I strive to live up to this award...
...as I continue to draw *Animal Land*.
HUMBLY.
HUMBLY.
Thank you all so much.

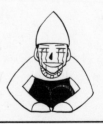

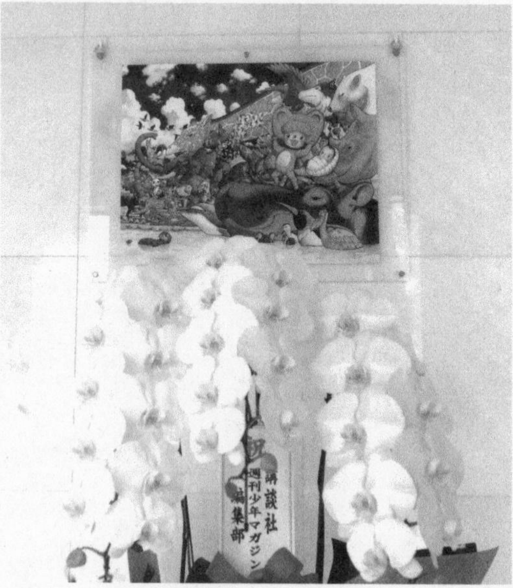
講談社
週刊少年マガジン
編集部

I was honored
to receive the
Kodansha Manga Award.

Makoto Raiku